I Thought
We Were Making Movies,
Not History

WISCONSIN FILM STUDIES

Patrick McGilligan
Series Editor

I Thought
We Were Making Movies,
Not History

Walter Mirisch

THE UNIVERSITY OF WISCONSIN PRESS

The University of Wisconsin Press
1930 Monroe Street, 3rd Floor
Madison, Wisconsin 53711-2059

www.wisc.edu/wisconsinpress/

3 Henrietta Street
London WC2E 8LU, England

1   3   5   4   2

Printed in the United States of America

Library of Congress Cataloging-in-Publication Data
Mirisch, Walter.
I thought we were making movies, not history /
Walter Mirisch.
p.   cm. — (Wisconsin film studies)
Includes index.
ISBN 0-299-22640-9 (cloth: alk. paper)
1. Mirisch, Walter.
2. Motion picture producers and directors — United States — Biography.
I. Title.   II. Series.
PN1998.3.M568A3   2008
791.4302′33092 — dc22
[B]
2007046830

For

PAT,

my wife of fifty-seven years, who shared it all with me.

❧

For

HAROLD and MARVIN,

my brothers, partners, and collaborators, who participated in all
the achievements of the Mirisch companies.

❧

For

MOM, DAD, and IRVING,

my parents and eldest brother, who enriched my life.

❧

For

JESSIE PONITZ,

my assistant for more than thirty years, who made it all easier.

❧

For

ANNE, DREW, and LARRY,

my children, whose love, devotion, and loyalty continue to sustain me.

❧

For

MEGAN,

my granddaughter. This is her legacy.

❧

And for
all of the actors, filmmakers, and craftspeople
who brought these films to life.

Contents

Foreword

SIDNEY POITIER

I admire you, Walter Mirisch, for having so often touched our hearts and left in our possession indelible memories of all that you are: legendary producer, visionary filmmaker, courageous seeker of truth, especially in troubling times. I respect you for your decades-long insistence that integrity maintain a constant presence in the creative output of the American motion picture industry and for continuing to be a tireless advocate for accountability, balance and taste in the art, the history, and the culture of American filmmaking.

Your creative and intellectual gifts have long been in the service of the common good. Your life and values have represented that which is most honorable in all of us. They speak clearly and eloquently in our best interests.

Finally, I am delighted that you have now made it possible for others to share the story of your life and work, in your own words. I am honored to have played a part in your story. The Mirisch brothers, Walter, Harold, and Marvin, have enriched the lives of countless numbers of our fellow human beings the world over, and they have certainly made one hell of a difference in this life of mine.

Foreword

ELMORE LEONARD

When you have produced close to a hundred motion pictures since 1947, you're allowed a series of *Bomba the Jungle Boy* movies during the early years — *Bomba*, in a jungle created on a soundstage, gazing out at African wildlife footage Walter was able to get his hands on. By the time he was twenty-nine, Walter was running production at Monogram-Allied Pictures, coming out with second-bill, low-budget pictures, one after another that could be shot in eight days for less than a hundred thousand.

The story Walter chose as the first one he'd produce himself was a short story by Cornell Woolrich called "Cocaine." Monogram Pictures said, "Are you kidding? *Cocaine?*" The title was the first thing Walter lost to the Breen Office, our morals watchdog at the time. Next came all references to drugs and the impact of the picture was gone. Walter called it *Fall Guy.*

He made *Flight to Mars* and another three dozen pictures for Monogram, *Bomba* showing up now and again — but wait a minute. Walter also produced *Wichita*, a Joel McCrea western that won a Golden Globe in 1955. The next year he supervised production of *Invasion of the Body Snatchers*. Walter was getting ready to make first-run movies with stars.

He had gone to work in Hollywood with degrees in history from the University of Wisconsin and in business from Harvard. The combination couldn't have worked better. History opened Walter's eyes to a wide scope of film possibilities, while the business degree gave him the clout to make solid deals with studios, to produce stories that he liked and bring them to the screen.

I dedicated my Hollywood novel, *Get Shorty*, to Walter with the inscription, "To Walter Mirisch, one of the good guys."

To me, the bad guys in the business were the ones who optioned my books, had the stories rewritten, and allowed actors to roam through the plot making up their own lines. Finally, when I was given the chance to write a script, a studio exec said to me, "All you've done is adapt your book, scene for scene." I said, "Yes?" He said, "You don't have to be a screenwriter to do that."

Well, Walter believed I could write movies.

Among the sixty-seven pictures his company made for United Artists, one is from an original screenplay of mine called *Mr. Majestyk.* Charles Bronson starred as a Colorado melon grower who has a run-in with a vicious gangster played by Al Lettieri. Dick Fleischer directed. The only change in the script has Bronson bringing in a crop of watermelon instead of cantaloupe, since cantaloupe was out of season by the time they started shooting in Colorado. The picture cost $2 million to make, Bronson getting a big chunk of the budget, and grossed $18 million in film rental. Walter gave me a bonus the moment the picture was in the black. Since then, *Mr. Majestyk* has been paying residuals for as long as Walter and I have been friends, going on thirty-three years.

Before I realized writing movies wasn't nearly as much fun as writing books, and quit trying, Walter asked me to do another one for him. Rewrite a script for *Wheels,* Arthur Hailey's novel about the car business. Walter thought I was right for it since I lived in Detroit and had spent several years writing car ads. I remember asking my agent, H. N. Swanson, "Do I have to read the book?" and Swanie saying, "It won't hurt you." I changed the focus of the book from styling to the ten-day sales report, what the car business was all about, selling cars; but I don't recall what Walter thought of it. I think he was busy packing, about to join Universal after seventeen years of producing one hit after another for United Artists.

But what if, in the early years, Walter had gone to work for his brother Harold at RKO theaters instead of going to work for Monogram and learning how to make movies? I wonder who would've made *In The Heat of the Night* and *The Magnificent Seven.*

Or the string of terrific pictures the Mirisch Company, Walter and his brothers, produced for United Artists: *Some Like It Hot, The Great Escape, The Pink Panther, The Fortune Cookie, The Russians Are Coming, The Russians Are Coming, The Thomas Crown Affair, Fiddler on the Roof,* the Mirisch Company winning Best Picture Oscars for *In The Heat of the Night, The Apartment,* and *West Side Story.*

Walter set up *Midway* at Universal. The studio said, "It's going to cost way too much . . . but go ahead." And Walter brought it in as his biggest moneymaker. He's won Oscars and Golden Globes, served as president of the Motion Picture Academy from 1974 to 1978, and has earned every lifetime achievement award offered by the industry.

He's a straight-shooter with an easy sense of humor, a pleasure to have as a friend. He doesn't hold grudges or make unkind remarks about all the egos he's dealt with in the business. You'll read in these pages about his heated arguments with directors, but to my knowledge he's thrown a punch at only one. *Walter?* Yes, Walter. Studio heads who come and go have tried to limit his production, give him fewer movies to make, and he excuses them saying, "The poor guys, they're under a lot of pressure, the company that owns the studio breathing down their necks." Walter's cool. He remains in place because he knows what he's always known: you begin with a good story.

I remind him of endless meetings we had with an actor Walter wanted for *LaBrava,* a book I wrote in 1983.

"Oh, God," Walter said, looking back at that agonizing time. "I spent almost two years of my life on that guy." But then the next moment he's smiling. What he's looking at could be funny, even if it means laughing at himself.

There we were sitting in a hotel suite in New York, a revised treatment of *LaBrava* the movie on the coffee table. We're waiting for the actor to arrive. The actor is bright, intelligent, a little guy with a big nose who does have good ideas, loves the character Joe LaBrava, but can't quite commit yet to play the part. Walter listened, commented, without any indication the actor's indecision was driving him nuts. Two days in a row during the fourth month, the actor cut the meetings short to take care of personal business. The next morning the actor arrived chipper, walked in and said, "Wasn't it great yesterday, the sun out all day? What did you guys do, go to the park?"

Walter might've said yes, he came three thousand miles to visit Central Park and watch the Mets play baseball on television. But he didn't. I didn't mention I could've been home playing tennis. We remained rational. We took the meeting and several more to come until the short actor finally said yes, he'd make the picture. Eventually though, he came up with an excuse to walk out. You'll read what Walter felt about that.

Walter said, "I thought the guy wanted to make *LaBrava*. It turns out all he wanted to do was talk about making the movie. You know what his next picture was?" Walter started to smile. "*Ishtar.*"

Now we were both smiling.

Walter said, "You know why *LaBrava* was never made? We talked it to death. The idea became worn out."

Walter said, "It would work fine today. All those wacky characters with angles. Shoot it in trendy South Beach."

"With the same actor?"

"He's too old."

Walter is older, too, but still knows what he knows, has a table lined with all the awards, and credit for at least a decade of movies that rank high among the best to come out of Hollywood. Any time he wants, Walter can put his feet up and take it easy. But what if there's still another picture he's dying to make?

Wouldn't that be something?

Acknowledgments

John Sturges, my friend and the esteemed director of *The Magnificent Seven* and *The Great Escape,* among many other films, phoned me one day a few years back from his boat moored in a Mexican harbor. He told me that he had been asked to write a magazine piece about *The Great Escape.* There were a number of things that he wanted to refer to, but he wasn't sure that he still remembered correctly. He asked me if by chance I still had a copy of the script, and if I did would I please send it to him. I was amazed. I said to John, *"The Great Escape* is one of the best films you ever directed, how is it possible that you haven't kept a copy of the script?" He replied, "What are you talking about? All of that was nearly a half century ago, and I thought we were making movies, not history." Obviously, his remark resonated with me, so thank you, John.

Thanks to Bruce Davis, executive director of the Academy of Motion Picture Arts and Sciences. Both he and Robert Rehme, its past president, have been constant supporters of this project from its inception.

Thanks to Anthony Slide for his editorial assistance and to Gasper Tringale for his jacket cover photo.

Thanks, too, to Doug Bell of the Academy of Motion Picture Arts and Sciences, who patiently led me through an oral history, which inspired me to embark upon this work and to expand and shape our dialogues. Thanks must also go to MGM, Warner Bros., and the Academy for permission to use photographic material.

Thanks to the University of Wisconsin, which afforded me a superb education and gave me, as an undergraduate history major, a rudimentary grounding in historical research. I am flattered that its press has seen fit to publish this book.

Thanks again to each of the actors, directors, writers, cinematographers, musicians, film editors, production designers, craftspeople, and technicians who contributed to this body of work.

And finally, thanks to my brothers and partners, Harold and Marvin, to whose enormous contributions I have probably not paid full justice and whose families I hope will remember that I have, Rashomon-like, told this story as I remember it.

I Thought
We Were Making Movies,
Not History

Prologue

In March 1989 I was taken completely by surprise when Donna Shalala, then chancellor of the University of Wisconsin at Madison, telephoned with the news that the appropriate faculty group had voted to confer an honorary doctorate on me, in recognition of the accomplishments of my long career. I felt a great deal of pride and excitement to be so recognized by an institution in which I was once just one of a mass of students, and was now being singled out for work that I would have paid for the privilege of doing.

I hadn't given much attention to what had been going on at my alma mater for many years, but I remembered that, at my own graduation, honorary doctorates had been conferred on General Douglas MacArthur (in absentia) and Georgia O'Keeffe, both of whom were Wisconsin natives and whose accomplishments were obviously in a realm far beyond what I had ever aspired to.

I asked Chancellor Shalala what I would be required to do. She told me, "Nothing but appear."

I did just that, and on the occasion of the conferral on May 20, 1989, my wife Pat and I were proud enough to invite our three children, Anne, Drew, and Larry, and our granddaughter, Megan, to accompany us on the trip. It was a great pleasure to return and see the changes in the university since the last time I had been there. It had now grown into an institution of some forty-five thousand students. Although much had changed, more had remained the same. The degree was conferred during the evening hours in the Field House, a basketball arena, at the commencement ceremonies for graduate students.

Upon arriving at the arena, I was gowned and instructed to assume a particular place in a line of academics, shortly after which Chancellor Shalala came up to me and said, "I'm going to ask you to speak after we make the presentation."

I said to her, "Oh no, you don't understand. I asked you that, and you said I wasn't going to be called upon."

She smiled, somewhat archly, and said, "Oh, I always say that. I think it's much better if one speaks extemporaneously."

I began to think hurriedly, "What do I say besides 'thank you'?" The ceremonies began, the medical doctors, lawyers, and Ph.D.'s were given their degrees, and finally they came to the honorary degrees. A very flattering presentation was made to me, including a recitation of whatever facts of my career they thought might be of interest to the attendees, consisting mostly of the parents of the graduates. I was sitting on a platform with various deans, trying to think of something to say that would be short and sweet and that would get me out of there without too much embarrassment. Finally the ideal thing popped into my head. When called upon, I arose, walked to the microphone, and said, "My mother would have surely loved this." It was the solemn truth, and all the mothers and fathers of the graduates responded immediately. They laughed and applauded. I spoke for a while after that, but it didn't make much difference what I said, because they were all on my side after my opening remark.

Here I was at the university where my adult life had started. Did I know then what my future held? Of course not. In the early 1940s, when I had last set foot on the campus, my association with the film industry was nonexistent. Now, I was a producer involved in whole or part in more than one hundred films, the most notable of which include *Friendly Persuasion, Moby Dick, Some Like It Hot, The Apartment, The Magnificent Seven, West Side Story, The Great Escape, The Pink Panther, In the Heat of the Night, The Thomas Crown Affair, Fiddler on the Roof, Same Time Next Year,* and *Midway.*

I have worked with such legendary directors as John Ford, Michael Curtiz, Billy Wilder, Blake Edwards, William Wyler, John Huston, John Sturges, Norman Jewison, Fred Zinnemann, and George Roy

Hill, all icons of their art. The players in our films—Marilyn Monroe, Jack Lemmon, Tony Curtis, Gary Cooper, Audrey Hepburn, Joel McCrea, John Wayne, Errol Flynn, William Holden, Yul Brynner, Shirley MacLaine, Steve McQueen, Natalie Wood, Gregory Peck, James Garner, Robert Mitchum, Kirk Douglas, Rod Steiger, Charlton Heston, Henry Fonda, Peter Sellers, and Sidney Poitier—have ascended to the pantheon of the stars.

I have enjoyed a career that absorbed me and provided some wonderful high points as well as some terrible lows. I have experienced relationships with an incredibly large number of people, some talented to an amazing degree, others reliable and supportive, and still others disappointing and undependable. Many of these relationships deepened into friendships that were exclusively personal with people from many diverse walks of life, which have given me opportunities to participate in how the "other half" lives. Doctors, lawyers, educators, and business people, all of whom I've enjoyed and whom I hope I've been able to "give to" as well as "take from."

I have been lucky enough to have had relative financial security most of my adult life, which has allowed me to concentrate my efforts on my careers—personal, commercial, communal, and familial. I've enjoyed honors and high points, far beyond what I could ever have hoped for. The low points, well, they've been tolerable. To sum it all up, I consider myself among the most fortunate of men. My long journey, which still seems short to me, has been a wonderfully rewarding trip.

My honorary degree was some confirmation not only of my successful career as a movie producer but also that my work has extended beyond Hollywood and affected individuals in all walks of life. I could never be more proud than I was on that day in May 1989.

1

My Family

My mother, Josephine Frances Urbach, and my father, Max Mirisch, were married in New York City on March 4, 1917. He was the proprietor of a custom tailoring business that made men's clothes to order for a largely upper-middle-class clientele, a business that he had been in for about twenty years.

Max Mirisch had come alone to America in 1891 at the age of seventeen as an immigrant from the city of Krakow, which was then a part of the Austro-Hungarian Empire but incorporated into Poland after World War I. He was born there to Sarah Freundlich and Moses Mirisch in the *Juden Gasse* (Jew Street), where his father had been a dealer in old clothes. At the age of ten my father had been apprenticed to a tailor, and that trade became his lifelong work.

Feeling the sting of anti-Semitism and the utter lack of opportunity in the ghetto in which he lived, Max determined to come to America at the first opportunity, and so when he was hardly more than a boy, he marshaled the incredible courage necessary to embark from Hamburg on his great adventure. He traveled in steerage aboard a German ship with only a few pennies in his pocket.

After arriving in New York, he first stayed with relatives, mainly an older sister, Anna, who had preceded him to America and had financed his passage. He struggled to find work, earn a living, and learn the English language. When he was in his early twenties he set up his own establishment as a custom tailor in the Harlem area of New York City.

My mother was born in Keyport, New Jersey, in 1891, the daughter of immigrants. Her father, David Urbach, who had also been born in Krakow, was a watchmaker by trade and had come to America with his Hungarian-born wife, Sidonia. Their two children, my mother and her younger brother, Louis, were both born in Keyport, where my grandfather had set up a jewelry and watch-making store.

After settling in New York, my father never saw his parents again, a not uncommon experience for an immigrant child. Both died in 1911. He loved them deeply, wrote and sent them money, but they were very poor, and the journey across the Atlantic was both expensive and formidable. His parents had agreed to Max's immigrating to America because of the virulent anti-Semitism in Krakow. Probably like many others at that time, they wanted their children to have an opportunity to escape the bleak poverty and persecution of their own lives, and so they were willing to endure the sacrifice it cost them.

Somehow or other Max's elder sister, Anna, had managed to immigrate to America. How she had financed it, I don't know, but she sent him money for his passage. As a young immigrant she had worked in a clothing sweatshop. Later on, she and my father sent money home, and a younger sister, Lena, who also had the courage to uproot herself, came to join them. There were originally seven children in their family. All those who remained behind, along with their families, perished in the Holocaust.

When my father arrived in New York in 1891, there was a great depression in progress resulting from the stock market panic of that year. He said that although he thought economic conditions were terrible in Krakow when he left home, they were just as bad in New York. He struggled to earn a living until conditions began to improve, and when finally they did, he showed his entrepreneurial spirit and started his own business as a custom tailor.

He was a genial man and made friends easily. He liked people, and they liked him. He was warm and sensitive, and though he was a fine craftsman, his business was largely based on his personality.

His customers mainly consisted of people who had come out of the same background as he had. They were older immigrants and their sons, who had by then become affluent. Many were manufacturers in the textile or fur industries, while others were professional people, doctors and lawyers, to whom he had been recommended. He ultimately developed a large and affluent clientele at his shop, which was originally located on 118th Street and Madison Avenue, where it remained for many years. In 1926, as the Harlem area deteriorated and more and more of his customers relocated to midtown Manhattan, my father moved and opened another showroom and small shop in an office building at 31st Street and Fifth Avenue. He continued to work out of that location for as long as he remained in the clothing business in New York.

My father was originally married to another daughter of immigrants, Flora Glasshut, by whom he had two sons. The elder, Irving, was born on March 17, 1903, and the younger, Harold Joseph, was born on May 4, 1907. Tragically, Flora Mirisch developed cancer and died when she was about forty years old. My father was left a widower with two sons, Irving, fourteen, and Harold, ten.

Through a mutual friend, he was introduced to my mother. He was forty-four years old at the time, and my mother was twenty-five. She was an attractive, intelligent, and exceedingly articulate woman who exuded an air of confidence. After their marriage they lived in an apartment above my father's store at 1806 Madison Avenue in Harlem, where my elder full brother, Marvin Elliot, was born on March 19, 1918. I was born there on November 8, 1921. As was the custom at the time, we were both born at home.

When my father moved his business to 303 Fifth Avenue, he and my mother decided to relocate our family to the then-developing West Bronx, where we moved into a lovely new six-room apartment at 2065 Morris Avenue. At the age of five, I began school in the Bronx and enrolled in Public School Number 79. I started in kindergarten and continued there through junior high school.

Our apartment had three bedrooms; my parents occupied one, Harold and Irving shared another, and Marvin and I shared the third. The early relationship between the two sets of brothers was affectionate but remote, since Irving and Harold were so much older than Marvin and I, and we had little in common. They had also, by then, begun to move into their own worlds.

Harold had left high school and, eager to go to work, had found a position at age fourteen as an office boy in the home offices of Warner Bros. This constituted the first exposure of our family to the motion-picture industry. Harold remained with Warners in various capacities for fourteen years, working there in the formative years of that company before the introduction of sound, when it was very insecure and unstable. He experienced much of the early growth of Warner Bros.

Irving had also left high school before graduation and had gravitated into the clothing business, where he worked as a salesperson at the College Shop, a haberdashery located close to the Columbia University campus. So, when they were still in their teens, both of my older half-brothers had left school and found jobs, though they both continued to live at home. Harold had met a young lady, Lottie Mandell, for whom he found a secretarial position at Warners. In 1928 they decided to marry; he was twenty-one and she was eighteen years of age.

At about the same time, an executive at Warner Bros., who had taken an interest in Harold, advised him to get into the theater-management side of the business. He arranged for Harold to go to Memphis, where he would learn to manage a movie theater. He and Lottie left immediately after their wedding, and he started to work at the Warner Theater where, according to plan, he became the manager within a year.

One year prior to Harold's marriage, Irving was married to a young lady, Frances Lewis, who had previously been married and divorced, and who had the custody of her young daughter, Florence, later called Nan. Before their marriage, Irving and Frances decided, most unpredictably, to pool their savings and buy a farm. They found a place they liked near Lake George, in upstate New York, and they set out to become farmers in 1929. I suppose it seemed very romantic, but all of this coincided with the stock market crash and the onset of the Great Depression. What Irving and Frances were trying to do on their farm would have been difficult for neophytes in the best of times. During the Depression, it was probably impossible. Irving lost all of the money that he had invested along with what our father had been able to lend him and whatever else he had been able to borrow from friends.

I was nine years old when Irving, Frances, and young Nan, having lost their farm, came to our apartment in the Bronx, absolutely broke. They had debts and nowhere to go. They called Harold and he came to their rescue. He said that if Irving could get himself down to Memphis he would employ him to be the assistant manager of the Warner

Theater, and he could also learn to manage theaters. I had a little money saved up—maybe fifteen or eighteen dollars—and I gave it to them. They pulled themselves together, and the three of them set off in their little car and drove to Memphis. During those years, Marvin and I were still going to grade school.

The 1920s had been a prosperous decade for my father. The country was booming, and his business was very good. However, in the 1930s, after the stock market crash, his business deteriorated into a struggle for survival. The majority of his customers were terribly hurt by the Depression, and few could still afford his relatively expensive clothes. Unfortunately, his business never recovered from the effects of the Great Depression, and we soon moved to a smaller, less expensive apartment at 2085 Walton Avenue in the Bronx, where we remained for as long as we continued to live in New York. It was a great struggle for my father to support his little family. These were difficult times for us, just as they were horrendous times for our whole country. The unemployed were selling apples on street corners, war veterans held bonus demonstrations, and bank closings occurred frequently. The early days of the Roosevelt administration saw real panic in the country. It's still hard to believe that those things happened in our great, rich nation.

After the stock market crash, my father would come home and tell my mother that this friend or that customer had committed suicide. Those people, heavily margined in stocks, had lost everything they owned and couldn't face their futures.

When President Roosevelt declared a bank holiday in 1933, my parents were panicked. Although my father never had much money in the bank, now all he had was what was in his pocket. That's all there was to buy food. Fortunately, his bank didn't remain closed for long, but the struggle continued.

In order to operate his business, my father had required occasional bank loans that were in relatively small amounts. He had friends among the bankers whom he could always count on for a couple of thousand dollars to keep his business going. But now these channels dried up on him. It was very frightening. He had people working for him and payrolls to meet, people who were not just nameless but who were his friends. He suffered if they didn't have money to take home to feed their families.

When I was thirteen, I started to work as an unpaid delivery boy for my father. Occasionally the customers would give me tips. Marvin, by now, attended Evander Childs High School, and I soon attended De-Witt Clinton High School. After graduation, Marvin entered the City College of New York (CCNY), a free-tuition municipal institution of high academic repute. My mother, who had gone to a teachers college herself for a year, which was really quite extraordinary for a girl of her family's means at that time, was absolutely determined that Marvin and I should go to college. She did whatever she could to make that happen.

Marvin had worked in theaters as an usher while he was going to high school and after he entered college. After he had finished two years at CCNY, with Harold's help, he found a summer job with an independent production and distributing company called Grand National Pictures that made B films, second features on double bills. His position was that of assistant booker in the company's New York exchange, the office from which salesmen leased the films to theaters. Our family's financial needs then dictated that, after attending CCNY for those two years, he transfer to the college's evening sessions while continuing to work at Grand National during the day.

By this time, Harold had twice been relocated by Warner Bros. and had managed theaters for them in St. Louis and Chicago. Irving had been sent to Oklahoma City, where he managed the Liberty Theater. Eventually, by the early 1930s, Harold had been reassigned to Milwaukee, where he was made the assistant general manager, and later the general manager, of the Warner Bros. Wisconsin circuit of theaters.

Irving had been in Oklahoma City for a while when he was transferred to St. Louis and later to Philadelphia. After that he was given a theater to manage in Gettysburg, Pennsylvania. Gettysburg was then a small town of 2,500 people. I sometimes went there to visit him, and I was always fascinated to visit the battlefield. It was a good time for Irving, living in a lovely town, earning a modest salary, while his family was growing. By then, he and Frances had a son, David, as well as Nan.

Harold and Lottie lived in Milwaukee, and by now had two children, Maxine and Robert. When I was sixteen and a half years old, I graduated from DeWitt Clinton High School and was accepted as a freshman at CCNY.

The summer of 1938, before I started college, Harold helped me find a job ushering at the State Theater in Jersey City, New Jersey. I commuted every day by subway to this theater from our home in the Bronx. It took me about an hour and a half each way. I worked in the theater seven days a week, and I was paid the then-minimum wage of 25 cents per hour for a sixty-hour week, earning a grand total of $12.50. The State was a first-run theater. The ushers wore wing collars, white gloves, and starched dickeys, and we marched on and off duty. I had enjoyed going to movies since I was very young and found them a wonderful escape from the realities of life. My job now gave me a complete immersion in the world of theater.

Later during that same summer, I got a job as a checker at a theater. This involved checking the tickets sold at the box office against the actual receipts. I held a counter in my hand, and I would count everybody who went into the theater to make sure that the numbers on the tickets that were issued conformed to the number of customers I had clocked going in. Some dishonest theaters would sell tickets that didn't have numbers on them, so that when they accounted to the distributor they could cheat on the amount of the gross receipts.

The State Theater was part of the Skouras chain, operated by George Skouras, a brother of Spyros and Charles Skouras, who managed the Fox theater chains. Through Harold's recommendation, George Skouras had become a customer of my father, and during the time my father made clothes for him, he sent our family an annual pass for his theaters. We were all grateful to George Skouras. I went to the movies as often as possible and they extended my horizons far beyond my narrow life.

I started to attend CCNY in the fall of 1938, while our family was still living in our four-room apartment at 2085 Walton Avenue. We had a bedroom for my parents, a living room, and a kitchen; Marvin and I shared a daybed in the dining room. While going to college, I continued to work on Saturdays and Sundays and two evenings a week as an usher at the Park Plaza Theater, also part of the Skouras chain, located a few miles from our home.

Harold had by then become a respected and skilled buyer and booker of films. He had an excellent mathematical mind and had become a talented negotiator, gifts that stood him in great stead in his later career.

I loved the movies, from the late silents I saw as a child to the early talking pictures, and I went to as many as I could. Clearly they also provided an escape from my difficult everyday life experiences. I was fascinated by the idea of making movies, which was, of course, a long reach from my theater-ushering experience. The idea of ever actually producing movies still seemed too distant and remote even to contemplate.

By 1939, my father's business had reached its absolute low point. He was sixty-five years old and worn down by ten terrible years of the Depression. He could no longer cope with all his financial problems and experienced an emotional breakdown. He became depressed, and it was a most difficult time for our family.

Harold had left Warner Bros. a few years earlier in order to accept an opportunity to operate two deluxe, subsequent-run theaters in Milwaukee, the Oriental and the Tower, which were owned by Moses Annenberg, the father of the later ambassador Walter Annenberg. Harold saw this as a good opportunity, since he would be able to participate in the profits of the theaters as well as receiving the same salary he had been earning while working for Warner Bros. At the same time, Harold started a concession business, the Theaters Candy Company, supplying candy and popcorn to independent theaters.

About a year after Harold started the Theaters Candy Company, he asked Irving to leave his theater-managing job in Gettysburg to join him in Milwaukee and operate the vending operation. Irving, who had been living in Gettysburg for many years by then, decided that he would like to be closer to his family. He took advantage of the opportunity offered to him and moved to Milwaukee.

At CCNY, I had decided to major in history, and my first year at college was difficult for me. Either because I was younger than my classmates, or because I was working at the theater while trying to keep up with my schoolwork while having financial and emotional problems at home, I didn't do well at college my first year—passable, but not as well as I had been accustomed to doing. I had gotten excellent grades in high school while skipping one whole year, but I found college studies much more demanding. I had started serious dating by that time and somehow managed to develop some real relationships.

The year 1939 was a terrible time. In September, Germany invaded Poland and World War II began. My father's business now deteriorated rapidly. He was compelled to call upon Harold to send him whatever money he could afford to help keep us afloat. Marvin had been working full-time at Grand National while continuing to attend CCNY classes in the evening session. By early 1939, the final blow came when Grand National Pictures went bankrupt, thereby cutting off the income that Marvin had been able to contribute to the family.

My father was emotionally ill and wasn't able to cope with his problems any longer. My mother discussed all of this with Harold and Irving on the telephone, and they decided that we should join them in Milwaukee. Harold said that he could arrange a job for Marvin with National Screen Service, a supplier of theater trailers and other publicity materials, and it would be better if we were all there together where they could help look after my father.

Having hit bottom, I rather welcomed the move. I had, on a couple of occasions, visited Harold in Milwaukee. I liked it there. My mother helped my father close up his business and settle his debts. The people he had dealt with for so long were very understanding. Woolen companies from which he had bought for many years and which were now his creditors were compassionate and understanding. They said he had been a wonderful customer and a dear friend, and that he should forget the debts he owed them. They would just write them off. He was deeply moved by their generous gestures.

So our family moved. I remained in New York to finish the second semester of my sophomore year at CCNY. I lived at the apartment of a friend's family for about two and a half months until the college semester came to an end. Harold and Irving, together with their wives, Lottie and Frances, helped my father, mother, and Marvin find an apartment in Milwaukee.

All the changes were clearly a relief to my dad, and he began to feel better. Along with recuperation, his entrepreneurial spirit picked up. He was now sixty-six years old, but he found a custom tailor in Milwaukee and arranged to occupy some of this man's space. He went out and called on some potential customers, mainly friends of Harold and Irving, and he began to sell clothes again. It kept him occupied and contributing, and yet it was in a very unpressured situation. He began to resume his usual good nature and gradually pulled himself out of his depression.

2

The University of Wisconsin

As soon as I arrived in Milwaukee, in May 1940, I began to work at the Oriental Theater, one of the two that Harold managed. Our family was settled in a nice apartment in a good neighborhood. Marvin was earning more money at National Screen Service than he had earned in New York. I wanted to continue my education and started to look around at the local Milwaukee colleges. Fortunately, by the time we left New York, Marvin had completed all his requirements for graduation from CCNY, and he had succeeded in earning his B.A. degree while attending night school.

I visited Marquette University, in downtown Milwaukee, and considered enrolling there. But at this juncture, a young man, also an usher at the Oriental, asked me to drive with him to Madison, where the University of Wisconsin is located. There I saw an entirely different kind of college life. Madison, at that time, was a city of about a hundred thousand people. About nine or ten thousand of them were students in the university. It was what I had always thought of as a typical college town, only prettier than most.

There were only two principal industries in Madison, the state government and the university. Most of the population was involved with either one or the other. There are two big hills in Madison that dominate the city. On the top of one stands the state capitol, which is a replica of the capitol in Washington, D.C., and on top of the other, about a mile away, sits the main building of the university, Bascom Hall. You look across from one to the other. And then, as you turn your head around that perimeter, you see a lake on either side of you. Madison is about seventy-five miles from Milwaukee, and I began to think about going to school there.

I discovered that the tuition for out-of-state students was $250 a semester. For in-state students, it was $32. I'd been going to CCNY, where not only did they not charge tuition but they sometimes gave you your books. The Madison tuition presented a serious problem. I inquired about the availability of some kind of scholarship, and I was told that if an out-of-state student was designated by a legislator for a nonresident scholarship, that person could be admitted at the in-state tuition fee. I started to haunt the offices of state senators and representatives in Milwaukee. I went armed with my high school and college grades, so that I might persuade them that I was a worthy recipient of their designation. I was finally able to convince a state senator, and he agreed to select me, so that I could attend the university at the in-state tuition rate of $32 a semester.

The candy company in Milwaukee supplied candy and popcorn to the Capitol Theater in Madison. I arranged that I would check this theater, which meant that I would inventory what was sold at the candy counter and the number of popcorn boxes that had been used. In that way, I would determine what had been sold and what supplies were needed, such as how many boxes of Mars Bars or how many Oh Henrys should be sent. Then the warehouse in Milwaukee would ship in what was ordered. I hoped to earn enough money doing that to take care of my living expenses. I had already saved enough money out of my salary during the summer to pay my $32 tuition.

Before school started, and while I was still working at the Oriental Theater, a young man, Edward Freschl, came to the theater and asked for me. He told me that he was the president of a Jewish fraternity in Madison, Zeta Beta Tau, and that he had seen my name on a list of incoming students and wanted to talk to me about their fraternity. I said, "Thank you, that's great, but I'm sure I can't afford fraternity life. I'm just planning to try and find the cheapest housing available." He replied, "Why don't you drive up with me anyway. You can stay at our fraternity house until you find a place to live." I accepted his offer and saw him socially a few times after our introduction. He was a nice young man, just starting his senior year, while I was now a junior.

While staying at the Zeta Beta Tau house, I looked around Madison for an inexpensive place to live. After a few days of searching, my fraternity friend said that he and some of the other fellows in the house liked me and wanted me to stay on with them. They understood that I was having financial problems, but they would work it out so that I could join the fraternity and pay a rent that was cheaper than anything I could find elsewhere in the city. Of course, I leaped at the offer. I joined the Zeta Beta Tau fraternity at a ridiculously low cost for my dues and my room and board, and I was now able to give my full attention to my schoolwork. I enjoyed a wonderfully productive year.

I was told there was an arrangement at the university whereby if you'd finished all of the requirements for an undergraduate degree in your junior year, you could enter a professional school in your senior year. I was able to take an additional course over the Easter vacation and finish all of my required subjects for graduation. I completed thirty-six academic units in that one year and received A's in all of my courses. And so, in my senior year, thinking I might want to become a lawyer, I enrolled in the law school and was also elected president of our fraternity.

That summer, after the completion of my junior year at Madison, my family was getting along better. My dad was feeling healthier and was doing a little business. He wasn't making very much money, but he kept occupied. Marvin had a good job, and my mother was becoming adjusted to a new environment and making a few friends. For the summer of 1941 I went back to Milwaukee to work again in the Oriental as a doorman, earning money for the following year.

In the fall, I was a student in the law school, when on December 7, 1941, the Japanese attacked Pearl Harbor, changing everybody's lives forever as America went to war. I wasn't enthusiastic about my law school experience. I liked studying history better, so I decided I wanted to take another history course, working under the supervision of a particular professor, Chester Easum, who was a favorite of mine. I wrote a thesis on the history of the Rome-Berlin Axis, a study of the origins of the relationship between Nazi Germany and Fascist Italy and what underlay the final coming together of these two countries. I enjoyed the project immensely. It was a good piece of work that covered 155 pages. After I presented it, I was told by the appropriate committee that if I went on and took a master's degree, my study would qualify as my master's thesis.

At my graduation in June 1942, I was designated as the university scholar in European history and an honors graduate. It was very flattering and pleased my proud mother and father greatly when they attended my graduation.

I now considered whether to enlist in one of the armed forces or wait to be drafted. Recruiters came to Madison from various universities and colleges, and I attended an orientation talk by a representative from the Harvard Business School, who explained what it offered, both in its regular curriculum and in terms of preparation for war service. It trained officers for the Naval Supply Corps and for the Air Force statistical unit. It seemed fascinating to me, these people who, among other things, computed the probabilities of hitting targets and the amount of tonnage required to fall on a given target to yield a statistical probability of destroying it. I thought it was most interesting, and so I requested an application to the Harvard Business School.

At this juncture, I was awarded a scholarship in history at the University of Wisconsin. I puzzled over my options, deciding that I'd just keep going to school until I was drafted.

I was called in for a meeting by the chairman of the history department at the university around graduation time. He asked me if I was planning to accept the scholarship and the teaching assistantship that had been offered to me. He told me that he would like to know as soon as possible because if I didn't accept the scholarship, the department wanted to offer it to someone else. I told him I hadn't yet made up my mind. Very archly he said to me that I should give it a great deal of thought, because I needed to understand that there really wasn't much opportunity for a man like myself in the academic world, and that aside from a few universities in New York, most colleges and universities around the country would not provide a ready opportunity for me to find employment as an academic.

I had never been so boldly faced with anti-Semitism before, and to this very day I regret that I didn't stand up to him and label him the bigot that he was. But I didn't. I said nothing. I just steamed inside. He was a man for whom I had a lot of respect. He was a highly esteemed, well-respected scholar, and I was outraged. I am sure he would say that he was just giving me good practical advice, but it was advice that served his purpose, namely to give my position to someone else. I no longer wanted a position in a department he chaired, and so I sent my application to the Harvard University Graduate School of Business Administration.

I thought if I could borrow the money to pay the tuition at Harvard that I could earn enough working in theaters to cover my living expenses. Ten years earlier, my maternal grandmother had left me an inheritance of $250 that now amounted to about $1,000. I was to receive the inheritance when I was twenty-one years old. My uncle, her son, who was a lawyer living in New York at the time, was the executor of her estate. By then he and my mother had quarreled and hadn't spoken to one another in years. I was twenty years old, so I decided to get in touch with him and ask him to give me my inheritance a year early. I contacted him, and fortunately he agreed. My tuition at Harvard was $1,200 for the year. And then, as usual, I sought a job in a theater.

My brother Harold had been managing the two Annenberg theaters in Milwaukee when Edward Alperson, a good friend of his, secured a position as general manager of the RKO theater chain. He asked Harold to come to New York and become the chief film buyer for the RKO circuit. Harold accepted the job, moved to New York, and went to work for RKO, buying and booking films for its theater circuit.

RKO then owned about a hundred theaters from coast to coast, with at least one major outlet in almost every large American city. They were almost all first-runs, except in New York, where RKO operated a chain of deluxe neighborhood theaters. The RKO theater circuit was made up largely of what had been the old Keith-Albee-Orpheum vaudeville group. In New York City, Loew's also had a big circuit, and these two chains dominated the New York exhibition business.

When Harold moved to New York, Irving remained in Milwaukee, managing the candy concession company, where Marvin joined him. Harold's move into this particular position, at that time, was very important to everything that subsequently developed for our family. Later, when I wanted to go to California and find a place in film production, Harold by then knew people in the production end of the business to whom he could refer me.

My first year at the Harvard Business School was difficult. I attended school throughout the summer, with no time off. The work was unfamiliar, and the unique teaching system required a considerable adjustment for me. The Harvard campus, however, was a revelation. It seemed extraordinarily filled with history and tradition, and you were quickly made to feel a part of it. It was very exciting, and I considered it an incredible opportunity. I lived in a dormitory where a roommate and I were lodged in a bedroom–living room arrangement in Apley Court, a building that was probably over a hundred years old. All the courses were skewed to preparing you for war service. My accounting instructor was Robert McNamara, who later became secretary of defense in President John F. Kennedy's cabinet. There was a lot of military on the campus; men already in the Naval Supply Corps were training there, and a number of them were in our classes. The school piled an immense amount of work on us, and the assignments were never-ending. Going to school and subsisting on an income of next to nothing was most stressful. I had to budget down to a gnat's eye to get along. I wanted to do well in school and to prepare myself as best as I could for the time when my war service would begin. I wasn't able to help myself financially because I simply could not squeeze in an after-school job.

I didn't experience any anti-Semitism at Harvard, and although there was a certain amount of segregation, I'm not really sure whether it was imposed or not. Probably there was a quota for Jewish students at that time. I don't know if it was coincidental, but my roommate, Robert Mack, was also Jewish in a class with very few Jewish men. One felt rather segregated, since there was not a great deal of intermingling. However, I did try to squeeze some social life into my schedule, too, and there were lots of girls to meet at Radcliffe, Wellesley, Smith, and all the other women's colleges in the Boston area.

By June 1943, I had finished three semesters of what had been a four-semester program. The military then took over the Harvard Business School completely, and I now planned to apply for a commission in the Naval Supply Corps. As my classmates and I had completed only three of the four semesters required for an MBA, my class was awarded a wartime degree of I.A., Industrial Administrator, and admonished to come back when the war was over and finish our fourth semester, after which we would be granted our MBA degrees.

I returned to Milwaukee and applied to the naval recruiting office for a commission. To my surprise, I was diagnosed with a heart murmur and also a hernia. I had not been accustomed to much medical attention up to then and was completely unprepared for this news. I had hoped as a graduate of the Harvard Business School that I would be readily accepted in the Naval Supply Corps. When I wasn't, my hopes were shattered. I had grown up in a difficult environment. I had long been oversensitive and had experienced much insecurity and neuroses that I had tried to overcome, with only marginal success. When I later presented myself to the draft board and went through the evaluation process I was rejected for psychological reasons.

I still wanted to serve the war effort, and I contacted the Harvard Business School. It put me in touch with a recruiter for the Lockheed Aircraft Corporation, who seemed impressed with my qualifications and offered to pay for my transportation if I would agree to work in its plant in Burbank, California. It was building medium bombers, Vega Ventura search planes for the Navy and P-38s, fighter planes for the Army Air Force. The company operated in immense plants, and I was put through its personnel procedures, where I was classified as a manufacturing engineer and assigned to a project involving the simplification of assembly-line procedures.

I had previously received a certain amount of training in this kind of work in industrial engineering courses at the Harvard Business School. Although I wasn't at all involved in designing the components of the airplane, I was involved in designing the processes by which they were produced. The airplanes were constantly being modified; consequently there were ongoing problems of efficiently integrating the modifications into the already existing assembly lines. Then there were also new planes that came on line as the old ones were phased out. One plane that I was assigned to for a while had originated as a passenger plane but now had been converted into a troop transport, designated the C-69. As a passenger plane, it was later called the Constellation. Our group worked in setting up those assembly lines.

3

Los Angeles and Monogram

I t was the summer of 1943 when I first arrived in Los Angeles. Harold had suggested I call a friend of his, Rodney Pantages, who operated the Pantages Theater in Hollywood and might be able to help me get settled. The Pantages was an affiliate of RKO's. I called Rodney, who was very hospitable, and at his invitation I spent my first night in Los Angeles at his lovely home in the Los Feliz area of the city. He suggested that I stay at the Hollywood Athletic Club until I could find more permanent housing, and he made the arrangements for me. On the following day I moved in. I couldn't afford to stay there long, but it was a good halfway house for me.

Already germinating in my mind was the idea that having now arrived in Los Angeles, I could perhaps, after peace came again to our country, find a position in the movie industry. Shortly after I started work at Lockheed, I met a design engineer there who told me that he had a furnished duplex apartment in the Wilshire district that he was sharing with two other young men. He asked if I would like to move in with them and pay one quarter of the rent. I accepted, and the four of us roomed in this two-bedroom apartment. It had twin beds in each of the bedrooms and was very inexpensive. I couldn't afford a car, but Lockheed ran its own buses, which took me to work every morning and also brought me home, or at least within a few blocks of home, every night.

I contacted a friend of mine, a young man whom I'd known at Madison, who was an aeronautical engineer working for North American

Aircraft in Inglewood. This classmate was married and had a young daughter. We became good friends again and spent a great deal of our leisure time together.

These were busy times, and although I was working very hard, six days a week, I thought I could make available to other companies some of the methods and practices that we had developed at Lockheed. I began to write articles, which had to be cleared for publication by Lockheed, for various industrial magazines. I wrote a number of them for *Factory,* one of which, called "Drafting Controls," was quite detailed. It was an intricate system that we had devised and put in place at Lockheed. I collaborated on that article with another engineer, and we were pleased later on when we learned that other companies had picked it up and were using it. In all, I wrote a half dozen pieces that were published in various magazines during that period. I took a great deal of pride in the contribution they may have made to help the war effort. Most of the people I worked with, at all levels, were serious about trying to do their best, as quickly and as efficiently as they could, in order to keep airplanes coming out of the hangar doors.

I continued to work at Lockheed until the war ended dramatically with the dropping of the nuclear bombs on Hiroshima and Nagasaki. At that point, I decided I could now pursue the real ambition of my life, and I started to look around for a position in the movie business. My brother Harold had remained in New York during the war, working as chief film buyer for the RKO theaters. Later on he became general manager of the entire circuit. He spoke to a friend of his, Leon Goldberg, the general manager of the RKO Studio in Hollywood, on my behalf. Leon had also graduated from the Harvard Business School. He was very friendly, but no job offer was forthcoming. Harold next suggested I see a man named Steve Broidy, then the general manager of Monogram Pictures Corporation.

Monogram was a movie company that produced so-called B pictures, or second features, during the era when most theaters played double features. I would much rather have worked at RKO if I could have found a position there, but I didn't. Monogram owned a little studio, located on Sunset Drive, near Sunset Boulevard and Virgil Avenue, which had three small soundstages and a not-very-convincing New York Street. It was able to shoot only one film at a time, since generally all three stages would be required to accommodate one picture. It also had an arrangement with a Western location in Newhall, California, then called the Monogram Ranch, which it utilized for its Western pictures.

Monogram's program consisted of a large number of so-called series pictures; it produced three Charlie Chan films a year, four Bowery Boys, two "Bringing Up Fathers," and two Joe Palookas. That type of product was the backbone of its program.

Its pictures were distributed domestically by franchise holders, individuals who owned the film exchange or sales office in a particular city or in a particular group of cities. These franchise holders were responsible for paying the expenses of their exchanges, and they had exclusive rights to distribute the films made by the production company. Most film companies had started that way because it was a less expensive method by which to operate. The production company was able to avoid most of the expenses of distribution, while still controlling its sales policy. The franchise holders generally did not make any contribution to the costs of production, although occasionally they might be called upon for loans or advances. Monogram retained ownership of its key exchanges such as New York, Chicago, and Dallas.

Republic Pictures Corporation also operated through franchise holders for a long time, but Republic was a much bigger company. It owned a bigger studio, as well as its own laboratory, Consolidated Film Industries. But the practice with those companies was to keep acquiring the franchises, so that the production company had more control and ultimately more of the earnings.

Monogram's pictures were sold abroad through sales agents by territories or countries. Some of their arrangements ran for a period of years, and in some areas they were sold by groups of pictures. In the United Kingdom, a franchise holder, Associated British Pathé, a subsidiary of the Associated British Theater Circuit, the second-biggest theater chain in Britain at the time, distributed its pictures. Largely owned by Warner Bros., Associated British was a good distributor for Monogram because it had access to its own theater circuit. Associated British also owned a production company and a studio at Elstree, just outside of London.

When I joined the company, Monogram's stock was listed on the American Stock Exchange. The president of the company was W. Ray Johnston, and the head of production was Trem Carr. Steve Broidy was the general manager and also supervised the sales of its pictures. He was a great salesman, who once said jokingly that it took great salesmen to sell Monogram's product.

Steve hired me and started out by giving me assignments to "Help him do this," or "Follow up on that," or "Check these figures." And then he progressed to, "How do we make this place work better? Do we have too many guards at the gate? Can we operate the editorial department differently? Should we move it off the lot?"

There were trade-offs. For example, the studio didn't have a sound department on the premises. All the sound work was done at an outside company, Sound Services. It would do the scoring and dubbing in its facilities and rented its equipment for production and post-production. Monogram had its own editorial rooms and did all the editing on the studio lot. The studio didn't have a camera department, and rented all its cameras, although later on it did buy its own cameras.

We were constantly attempting to determine whether we were operating in the most cost-effective way possible. The studies of operations that I did provided me with a marvelous opportunity to see how the whole motion-picture production process worked. I spent time on the soundstages and watched the pictures being shot. I observed the editorial, scoring, and dubbing phases of post-production. If I had gotten a job at RKO, I doubt that it would have given me the opportunities that I was getting in this small studio.

The men responsible for producing the Monogram pictures at that time were Sam Katzman, who was doing a series of inexpensive musicals called "The High School Kids"; Sam Burkett, who was producing three Charlie Chan pictures per year; and Hal Chester, who was producing two Joe Palookas. Jan Grippo was producing four Bowery Boy pictures. The Bowery Boys were what was left of the original Dead End Kids, in the persons of Leo Gorcey and Huntz Hall, supplemented by Billy Benedict and Gabriel Dell. Jeffrey Bernerd produced exploitation pictures such as *Black Market Babies*, *Allotment Wives*, *Divorce*, and *Where Are Your Children?* during that period and also produced a Cinecolor picture with Anthony Quinn titled *Black Gold*. He also made a few pictures with Kay Francis near the end of her career.

Most of the Monogram pictures were shot in eight days. The budgets of the Charlie Chan, Bowery Boys, and Joe Palooka features were

$80,000 to $100,000 each. Personalities in Monogram pictures at that time were Duncan Renaldo, who played the Cisco Kid, and Sidney Toler, who played Charlie Chan. Monogram also made some films with ice skater Belita. Elyse Knox was an attractive young woman who played ingénue leads in a number of its pictures and finally in one of mine. She later married Tom Harmon, the football player and sports announcer. Gale Storm was another attractive young woman who played ingénue leads. Finally, though, it was film noir that was a favorite genre for Monogram's program of inexpensive pictures.

In 1946, after I'd been with the company for about a year, there was a shakeup in the executive suite of Monogram, to which I was not privy, and Steve Broidy emerged as president of the company. Soon after I started working for Steve, I began to nag him to give me an opportunity to produce a film. My argument was simply that I could do it better than the people who were then doing it. He counseled me to be patient. But after he became president and, I suppose, became weary of my badgering him, he said that I could proceed to find a property. If I found something that he approved, I could produce it.

The first project I brought to him was Ring Lardner's short story "Champion." Wildly enthusiastic, I called the deceased author's son, Ring Lardner Jr., also a writer, and asked him about its availability. He said, "You know, nobody's talked about making a picture out of that for years. I'll ask my mother about it." He later called back to tell me his mother approved, and he would have his agent negotiate a deal with me.

I dealt with an agent at William Morris, and I finally had worked out an arrangement under which I could buy an option on "Champion" for $500. Steve Broidy and Trem Carr, who was still in charge of production, both told me, "You can't make this picture. The leading character is too unsympathetic." I could not change their minds, but I thought that if I had $500 I could have bought the option personally. I tried to borrow the money from a friend and was turned down. Not too long after that, the William Morris agent with whom I had dealt sold the story to Stanley Kramer, who made it into a very successful film starring Kirk Douglas.

Next I came upon a short story by Cornell Woolrich titled "Cocaine." This also had problems. First, of course, we would have to change the title. The Production Code specifically prohibited making a film having to do with drugs. "Cocaine" is the story of a young man who's out on the town when somebody gets him to sample cocaine. He passes out and has no memory of what subsequently happens to him. I thought the story had exploitable angles to it, but ultimately they were, step by step, completely removed to satisfy the Production Code Administration, as one can see from this extract from a letter from Joseph Breen, the code administrator:

> It would be acceptable as a springboard for your story for you to suggest that your young man lead had been given some sort of "knock-out" drops, without further identifying them, which causes his mental confusion, this would give you substantially your present premise. There are several ways in which the objectionable angle of the "dope ring" could be overcome, in that they might be suggested as racketeers whom the murdered man, Doyle, threatened to expose to the police. Or you might even use some sort of diamond-smuggling angle which this group of crooks were engaged in.

Clearly the whole thrust of the story was finally eviscerated, and it turned out quite badly.

I had also been led by the studio executives into choosing a certain director, Sidney Salkow. But I got into a serious quarrel with him about two weeks before we started to shoot. I insisted on replacing him, and the studio had to pay him some money to buy off his contract. He was replaced by a director named Reginald LeBorg. The screenplay was by writer Jerry Warner. The leading role was played by Robert Armstrong, who was best known for having played the lead in *King Kong* a number of years earlier. Leo Penn (called Clifford in the credits), a young actor of the John Garfield type, played the victim. The rest of the cast consisted of Teala Loring, Elisha Cook Jr., and Christian Rub. I retitled the picture *Fall Guy*.

After I had pressured Steve into letting me produce the picture, he told me that I would be taken off salary, since I would be getting a fee for producing the picture. I had been earning $75 a week as an employee of the studio. My fee for producing *Fall Guy* was $2,500. I soon realized that I could quickly starve to death while waiting for subsequent films to be approved. Now I understood the value of the series pictures to their producers. They provided a minimum subsistence income to producers who were trying to survive in a most unstable profession. Realizing that

I needed to earn a regular livelihood, I started to look for a subject that could become a series and that would provide a minimum income for me while I was searching for better films to do.

Fall Guy was released in March 1947. Despite all of my attempts to give it some guts, I failed. Reginald LeBorg had done numerous other so-called poverty-row pictures, so named for the skimpiness of their budgets. He was a suave, charming Austrian gentleman, whose real name was Grobel, LeBorg spelled backward. I always thought that was a rather amusing touch. Surprisingly, the *Hollywood Reporter* (February 27, 1947) described the direction of *Fall Guy* "by far the best ever delivered by Reginald LeBorg."

🦅

However, something more important than *Fall Guy* happened in 1947, the culmination of a meeting that took place in the summer of 1944, about a year after I arrived in Los Angeles and while I was still working at Lockheed. A mutual friend had arranged a blind date for me with a distant cousin of his, who was visiting in Los Angeles from her home in Kansas City. Arriving at her hotel room, I was met by two attractive young ladies, one of whom was my friend's cousin, and the other was her friend, Pat Kahan, also a visitor from Kansas City, in whom I was more interested.

Pat was twenty years old, about five foot four, weighing one hundred pounds, give or take a few, with blue eyes, brown hair, slightly blonde-streaked, with a great figure. She was very animated, and fun seemed to radiate from her. She was bright, intelligent, and loved movies. I was immediately taken with her.

Pat had been born and brought up in Kansas City, Missouri, where her father, Will, was a manufacturer of boys' clothing. He had come to the United States from Russia with his parents when he was an infant, and he had been raised in Brooklyn, New York. After serving as a second lieutenant in World War I, he had moved to Kansas City, where he found employment in a retail store. He soon met Pat's mother, Gertrude Feld, who had been born and grew up there in an Hungarian-Jewish immigrant family. They married and had two children, Pat and her younger brother, Don. Will soon found his way into the manufacturing business and, with a partner, developed a very successful company.

At the time we met, Pat was a sophomore at Skidmore College, located in Saratoga Springs, New York, where she was majoring in sociology. We were attracted to one another at once, and we dated regularly during her Los Angeles visit. Later we continued to correspond when she returned home and resumed her college studies.

Over a Christmas vacation period, while I was making a trip to Milwaukee to visit my parents, I stopped in Kansas City to spend a few days with Pat, and I met the rest of her extensive family. Our relationship deepened and, the following year, she came to Milwaukee, where she met my family. Our relationship was growing deeper all the time. With the end of the war, Pat graduated from Skidmore, lived for a while in New York, and then returned to Kansas City, where she found employment with the Department of Social Services.

Having finally arrived at a point where I thought I could support a wife, I asked her to marry me. She accepted, and we were married on October 10, 1947, in a ceremony at the Muehlbach Hotel in Kansas City, with most of her family and my family present. We drove from Kansas City to Los Angeles on our honeymoon, stopping en route at all the recommended points of interest, such as Santa Fe, Taos, the Grand Canyon, and Las Vegas. We then found a pleasant furnished apartment on Canon Drive, in Beverly Hills, where we embarked on our married life.

🐟

Although released in 1947, *Fall Guy* had been produced in 1946, when I was twenty-five years old. Despite the fact that it wasn't a very good picture, it was a great learning experience for me. *Fall Guy* cost $83,000 to produce, and while it wasn't a world-beater, it grossed about as much as similar pictures did for Monogram.

I next found another story of Cornell Woolrich's, "I Wouldn't Be in Your Shoes," again with a plot in the film noir genre. I employed Steve Fisher, a novelist, generally of pulp material, to write the screenplay. Steve had worked at the major studios, and as a writer was a step up from Jerry Warner. He wrote quite a good script for the film and I cast it with two young actors named Don Castle and Elyse Knox playing victimized lovers; a detective was played by Regis Toomey, a reasonably well-known character actor.

I Wouldn't Be in Your Shoes is the story of Tom and his wife Ann, an out-of-work team of dancers. Tom is convicted of the murder of a local miser on circumstantial evidence. Ann, helped by one of the detectives in charge of the case, makes hopeless efforts to save Tom when, in the last minutes before Tom's execution, Ann accidentally discovers that the detective himself had committed the murder in the hope that Ann would later marry him. The *Hollywood Reporter* described it as a "suspense picture adroitly produced" with "imaginative production by Walter Mirisch, directed with an eye for solid dramatic effect by William Nigh."

Bill Nigh, whose career dated back to the silent era, was quite an elderly man at that time. He would tell marvelous stories about the silent days and all the craziness of making pictures in that period. He had directed many films for MGM but had fallen to directing short-scheduled, inexpensive supporting features. I appealed to him, saying things like, "You've got to give it your very best, you've got to be inventive. Be as creative as you can, and work with the actors." I believe he did try to get the most he could out of the time, the material, and the people he had to work with.

At about this time, Trem Carr, who was in charge of production at Monogram, died. He was replaced by Scott Dunlap, a big, bluff producer, whose career also went back to silent films, and whose experience was also confined to inexpensive B pictures. He was a friend of Steve Broidy's and now succeeded to the position as head of the studio. He didn't involve himself much in supervising what I was doing. By now my relationship was with Steve Broidy, and I would talk to him about the things that I wanted to do, while keeping Scott Dunlap informed.

Even before *Fall Guy* had started production, I had realized that among the most successful of all the series pictures were the Tarzan films still being produced by RKO, which train of thought led me to remember an old series of teenage boys' books titled "Bomba, the Jungle Boy." Simplistically, I put the two ideas together and, with Monogram's money, I acquired the rights to do a possible series of "Bomba" pictures. This development led me to check the availability of Johnny Sheffield, who had played Johnny Weismuller's son in the Tarzan pictures made first at MGM and later at RKO. Johnny agreed to play Bomba.

The problem of doing a jungle series—with animals and action, all in exterior African locales, on the limited budgets and short shooting schedules allowed me—was daunting. I had committed myself to Monogram's spending no more on the first "Bomba" than I had spent on *Fall Guy* and *I Wouldn't Be in Your Shoes*. I researched the stock footage libraries and viewed many miles of jungle films. I finally found an old documentary, *Africa Speaks*. The film was grainy and of poor quality, but there were some good sequences in it, and I made a deal with the owner of the film that gave me the right to select as much film as I wanted, for which I would pay him a certain number of dollars per foot.

I looked around for someone to write the script. The story, of course, was dictated by the genre. Bomba is a teenage boy living alone in the jungle. His parents have died on safari. He is brought up by a naturalist who lived in the jungle and who has also died at a point where the boy is able to fend for himself. The plot we imposed on this springboard concerned a group of cameramen who have come to the jungle to shoot a documentary. The film they were shooting gave us the ability to intercut our stock film. So, as they are photographing leaping impalas or herds of elephant or whatever else we chose out of *Africa Speaks*, we were able to create an ambiance of jungle life.

I selected Ford Beebe, who had been recommended to me, for the assignment as writer-director. I was in my middle twenties, and Ford Beebe was in his late sixties. He was a wonderful man, soft-spoken, mild, always wearing a big Western hat, and he had been working in films since the silent era, when he had begun as a writer of titles. In his most active years in the film business, Ford made both B pictures and serials. He wrote and directed many serials for both Republic and Universal and was very much at home in the cliffhanger medium, as well as accustomed to the constraints of low-budget production. Ford considered himself retired at the time I met him. He lived on a ranch in Elsinore, near San Diego. I liked him in a grandfatherly way, and I flatter myself to think he liked me and enjoyed working with me. I gave him a first-draft script that had been written for me by Jack DeWitt, and Ford went back to his ranch and rewrote it, after which I fiddled with it. Soon we had a shooting script.

Johnny Sheffield, who had already agreed to play Bomba, was about seventeen or eighteen years old at the time. He came from a family of English actors; his father was a frequently employed actor and in most pictures with an English background you'd find Reginald Sheffield as a

Everyone has to start somewhere, so herewith is the poster for *Bomba, the Jungle Boy* in 1949. Reproduced courtesy of Warner Bros.

member of the cast. The family lived in Santa Monica. Johnny had a sister, Mary Alice, called Missy, who was married to Sidney Franklin Jr., whose father was a prominent director and producer at MGM. Johnny was a good looking young man, well built, athletic, and an ideal choice for Bomba.

Monogram financed *Bomba, the Jungle Boy,* paid the interest, prints, and advertising costs, and charged distribution fees of 35 percent of the domestic gross and 40 percent of the foreign. It also had the right to charge overhead and various other kinds of expenses to the film, after which I had a 50 percent participation in what was then called the profits. Clearly, then and now, profits are very difficult to attain for participants, mainly because of the effect of the continuing distribution fees and the imposition of interest charges. I was, however, paid an up-front salary of $2,500 for all my services, charged to the budget of the film.

For the ingénue lead, I chose Peggy Ann Garner, who had enjoyed a great success in *A Tree Grows in Brooklyn* and some other pictures at Fox a few years earlier. She was now about the same age as Johnny, and we made an offer for her services that her agent accepted. Onslow Stevens played Peggy Ann's father, and Charles Irwin played a game warden. Peggy Ann's character was named Pat, in honor of my recently married wife.

Concerned about controlling costs, I decided to try to shoot the entire film on a soundstage and not be subject to inclement weather conditions. It wasn't the best way to shoot the picture, but I didn't want it to go over budget, since so much of my future would be riding on it. I found a well-known, ingenious art director, Gordon Wiles, who had done some important films but had now fallen on hard times. He felt confident he could create the jungle sets on soundstages using greenery in combination with backings and cutouts. He created a veldt by having wooden stands with vegetation nailed to the top of each. It was all quite ingenious. Ford Beebe adapted to the sets and was able to maintain the illusion of a jungle.

Bill Sickner, our cameraman, was a regular Monogram cameraman, long experienced in short schedules and the lightning speed required to meet them. We shot *Bomba, the Jungle Boy* in eight days. Given our problem with the stock film and our synthetic jungle, I decided to release the picture in sepia tone, which involved putting our answer print through a sepia bath, hopefully to smooth out the differences in quality between the stock film and the production film and also to achieve a kind of glow in the ersatz jungle that had been created for the film.

After viewing the picture, Steve Broidy agreed to a release policy under which it would play as a first feature in its initial openings in the so-called action theaters in each of the principal cities. The challenge was that Monogram had to be willing to spend the money on advertising that was required for a picture playing as a first feature. The distributor, then and now, pays the advertising costs and has to be willing to invest the amount of money required to publicize the booking.

Besides advertising, we supported *Bomba, the Jungle Boy* with exploitation stunts. In the Chicago zoo was a famous gorilla named Bushman. A publicity man came up with the idea that we get a 16mm projector and project our film in front of Bushman's cage. We invited all the newspapers to be present for the screening, watching the reaction of

Bushman to our film! The newspaper photographers kept observing him, looking for some kind of amusing response, and they'd find him either yawning, at which point they felt he was bored with a particular sequence, or jumping up and down, when they decided that it was exciting to him. In any event, we got a great deal of free publicity out of the stunt. In many of the other principal cities we collected about a dozen or so monkeys, with trainers, and put them in a projection room on folding chairs. We supplied them with peanuts and ran the picture for them. We invited the press to come and see this preview of the picture for the monkeys. They would photograph the monkeys' reactions, and we would make the newspapers again. It didn't cost very much for this kind of promotion, and we got a great deal of space with it. The newspapers were great and went along with the gag, and reporters competed in making witty remarks about the monkeys' reactions. It was all in good fun, and I think it helped the film.

Amazingly, the reviews of the picture were excellent. *Film Daily* wrote, "The film is, in kind, and in the scope of its appeal, an exemplification of Monogram president Steve Broidy's recent declaration of intent to swing studio production policy away from the lurid type of melodrama which community and club groups have been protesting about, and toward adventures in which a wide variety of excellently photographed jungle animals figure." The film was also successful abroad, again following the pattern of the Tarzan pictures. *Bomba, the Jungle Boy* cost about $85,000 and netted about $500,000 for Monogram. I even earned some money from my participation in the profits of the film.

It was a successful launch for the series, and Steve Broidy decided we should make two "Bomba" pictures a year. They became the base for my income, because I now knew that I was going to earn at least $5,000 a year. I could then try to develop other films that hopefully would be more challenging, so that my fees would amount to a livable income.

My relationship with Ford Beebe was excellent. I wanted him to continue to work on the "Bombas," and he was agreeable. We would frequently just decide on a title and then create a story to fit. We would work out the story together, and Ford would then go back to his ranch and do a first draft of a script. We would continue to work together until we had a final script. While he was writing, I was screening stock film, generally from the libraries of other studios. For *Bomba on Panther Island,* for example, I brought in all the film relating to panthers. Then we would determine what we wanted to use and write sequences around the stock material.

We also now felt enough confidence to shoot exteriors, and we began to film at the arboretum in Arcadia, California, "Lucky" Baldwin's former home, which is located near the Santa Anita racetrack in Baldwin Park. It had been used as a jungle film location for years and had a little lake in it and a lot of jungle vegetation, with a house at one end. Baldwin Park became a key set for our future pictures. We also went to other locations, such as Jungleland, where we would devise sequences that could be shot with real animals. We went to where the animals were located, so that we didn't have to transport them. We would do a fight with a lion and would create all the material surrounding it. After the lion leaped, which often was a stock leap, we would use a real lion, and we would now have the trainer doubling for Johnny, playing with the lion while pretending to be fighting it. We would then personalize our fight by making cuts of Johnny scuffling with a stuffed lion. In this way, we opened the pictures up somewhat and still shot them on pretty much the same schedules as before, but by now we were being more ingenious and were no longer hemmed in by a soundstage. As the years went by, inflation inevitably increased our budgets. The actors received more money, and the behind-the-camera people also got raises.

4

Allied Artists

After I had completed production of my first three pictures for Monogram—*Fall Guy, I Wouldn't Be in Your Shoes,* and *Bomba, the Jungle Boy*—my brother Harold, who by then was the general manager of the RKO theater circuit based in New York, told me that he had gotten into a serious quarrel with the people for whom he was working and had either quit or was fired from his position. He told me he hoped something interesting might now turn up for him. I immediately thought, "Wouldn't it be great if he could come to Los Angeles and join me at Monogram?" I suggested it to him. He had helped me get started by making the connection with Steve Broidy, so that I could get my job at Monogram, but now asking for a position for himself was rather more difficult or embarrassing for him. In any event, I decided to broach the idea to Steve.

I found an opportunity to comment to him that Harold had resigned his job, and since there were increasing numbers of Allied Artists films, the higher-priced line of pictures that were being produced by Monogram, Harold, with his excellent contacts among the exhibitors, would be a wonderful choice to supervise the sales of those pictures. In 1947 there were three Allied Artists pictures that were released by Monogram, *It Happened on Fifth Avenue, Black Gold,* and *The Gangster.* The Allied Artists, or higher-cost, group of pictures that they represented were Monogram's reaction to the fact that the B-picture market was drying up. Harold had no background in picturemaking. All of his experience had been in theater operation and dealing with distributors, but it clearly wouldn't be a big leap for him to become a distributor. The naming of a separate sales chief would help differentiate the Allied Artists pictures from the Monogram product, and Steve liked the idea. He was fond of Harold and respected him, and I think Steve was sorry he hadn't thought of it himself. He made Harold an offer to come to Hollywood and become vice president in charge of distribution for Allied Artists.

Harold's job was to see that those pictures were given special treatment, and that they were all handled as first features. Persuading exhibitors to give Allied Artists valued playing time and percentage terms was often a matter of personal relationships with the exhibitors, and Harold had numerous such connections throughout the country.

Steve had created the Allied Artists label by making a deal with director Roy Del Ruth, who had worked most of his career at Warner Bros. and MGM and had made many successful and important films for those companies. Steve brought him to Allied Artists, made him a producer-director, and announced a program of pictures that would be expensive, top-of-the-bill films. The first film under that arrangement was *It Happened on Fifth Avenue,* made at a cost of about $1 million, a great deal more than Monogram had ever spent on a film before. It was shot like a major picture, although it was made physically at the Monogram studio. Harold joined Allied Artists in 1947, at just about the time that *It Happened on Fifth Avenue* was going into release.

Del Ruth's *It Happened on Fifth Avenue* is the story of a rather elegant hobo, played by Victor Moore, who follows a family that in the wintertime lives in Palm Beach and in the spring and fall lives in a mansion on Fifth Avenue. When the hobo sees they have made their move to Palm Beach, he breaks into the house and spends the winter on Fifth Avenue. Then he reverses course in the summertime, when he goes to Palm Beach. The second film that Del Ruth made for Allied was *The Babe Ruth Story,* and the third film was a melodrama, *Red Light,* which starred George Raft. None of the films were successful, but they did help to open some single-feature markets to Allied Artists.

Harold was paid $400 a week, but he more than repaid the company's investment in him shortly after he started work. He received a phone call from a friend in New York, Josef Auerbach, a Czech refugee who had come to New York in the late 1930s after Hitler's invasion of Czechoslovakia. He had worked in the film industry there, most notably as producer, or presenter, of the film *Ecstasy,* which introduced Hedy Lamarr. He immigrated to New York and became a trader and a deal-maker in films, working with remakes, foreign rights, and financing. Auerbach told Harold that he could make a deal to acquire the reissue rights, for a limited period of time, to the "Our Gang" comedies.

These were a rather well-known series of one-reel shorts that had been produced by Hal Roach and distributed by Metro-Goldwyn-Mayer. The casts were made up of a group of young, mischievous kids. Hal Roach had originally financed these films for distribution by Metro-Goldwyn-Mayer. At some point in their arrangement, Metro-Goldwyn-Mayer had taken over the financing of the films, but the ownership of the earlier negatives, some of which were silents, remained with Hal Roach. He was now interested in leasing the reissue rights to the one-reelers for a cash advance. It was Joe Auerbach's idea for Monogram to distribute these old "Our Gang" comedies theatrically. Harold was enthusiastic about the proposal, and he and Steve thought they could do a good job of reissuing the films. In the discussions that followed, they expanded the rights they would acquire to include television.

The big problem was that MGM was still distributing new films under the title "Our Gang," so Monogram had to retitle the pictures. We thought that would be a handicap because of the lack of audience familiarity with a new title, but Steve finally suggested the title "The Little Rascals." Monogram secured a seven-year license on the pictures, which was later extended. Following that extension, they reverted back to Hal Roach. The name "Our Gang" is probably of little value now, and these films are now mainly identified in the public's mind as "The Little Rascals."

There was another serious problem to face when Monogram took over the films. The negatives were sent to the laboratory that did its release printing; it inspected them and reported that the negatives were so shrunken that they couldn't make new prints. The negatives were then sent to a number of other laboratories, all of which agreed they were too deteriorated to yield good prints. Finally Joe Auerbach found a small laboratory in New York where they said they could do the printing. And so, with tender loving care, they made new prints. Amazingly enough, all these many years afterward, "The Little Rascals" are still with us, and I'm sure they're still making prints off those negatives. Theatrically the shorts grossed well over $1 million. The advance wasn't significant, and finally the television distribution also became tremendously profitable. "The Little Rascals" became a hugely successful acquisition for Monogram.

Harold then busied himself with the release plans for the next three Allied Artists pictures, *Black Gold, The Gangster,* and *The Babe Ruth Story.* Unfortunately, like *It Happened on Fifth Avenue,* all of these pictures suffered from a lack of star power. The big stars and their agents still resisted the stigma of being in a picture for Monogram, even though the name of the company had been changed to Allied Artists. They feared that after a personality of some importance had been in a picture for "that company," the majors might no longer want them or would sharply cut their salaries, so they resisted appearing in Allied Artists pictures. A concerted effort was made to secure Jack Carson to play the lead in *The Babe Ruth Story,* but Warner Bros., to whom he was under contract, wouldn't loan his services to Allied Artists. Finally the company settled on Bill Bendix, who was not as big a star or as well suited to the role as Carson would have been.

This was also the period of the blacklist, and Monogram had the same policy as the majors, namely that all actors, writers, and directors had to be cleared before they could be approved to work in a film. It was terrible, but all the studios were doing it, and Monogram went along with what was happening elsewhere in the industry. During this awful time, I never did learn exactly who did the clearing. The American Legion was active in the blacklist crusade, and I assumed that it had a group that was checking names against a list of people who had either joined or contributed to so-called liberal causes. The horrors of all this have been written about at great length, and it is to my everlasting regret that I just went along with the company's policy. It is to the shame of the whole industry that it disregarded the basic freedoms of Americans, whose right to work and earn a living and support their families was denied to them and whose hard-won reputations were destroyed.

People began to read meanings into pictures that were never intended. *The Invasion of the Body Snatchers* is an example of that. I remember reading a magazine article arguing that the picture was intended as an allegory about the Communist infiltration of America. From personal knowledge, neither Walter Wanger nor Don Siegel, who directed it, nor Dan Mainwaring, who wrote the script, nor the original author, Jack Finney, nor myself saw it as anything other than a thriller, pure and simple.

When I produced *Hiawatha,* there was even an article published in the *New York Times* commenting on the fact that it had communistic overtones. The *Hiawatha* story was about an attempt to work out a peaceful settlement among various warring Indian tribes, which led to the Confederation of the Five Nations. Somewhere or other this fueled a suspicion that the story was a dovish Communist allegory. It would have been amusing, had it not been so pitiful. Certainly Henry Wadsworth Longfellow, who was responsible for most of our story, would have been appalled.

I continued to produce the "Bomba" pictures, which Monogram was still selling to its exhibitor customers on a two-per-year basis. I needed the $2,500 fees I was paid for producing each film, and they still served as a base for my relationship with the company. Although I was still doing the "Bomba" films, I was relying more and more on Ford Beebe to help me produce them.

I liked working in color and wanted to upgrade the types of films I was doing. I looked for different subject matter that would have wider canvases and some kind of presold titles that could be booked as first features. *County Fair* presented such an opportunity. It wasn't a series picture and had to stand on its own. *County Fair* was to be a romantic comedy about sulky racing, and it had been started by another producer at Monogram, Jeffrey Bernerd. He was an elderly man, and while preparing *County Fair* he suffered a serious heart attack. I told Steve Broidy that I would take over the picture and forego receiving a fee for producing it, so that Jeffrey could be paid his full salary. A writer, Charles Marion, had already been selected, and I worked with him on the script, as I did with director Bill Beaudine, with whom I had never worked before but who had been directing pictures at Monogram for many years.

Beaudine had done most of the Bowery Boys pictures, as well as many others at the studio. He was sixtyish, a very tall, thin man with a waxed mustache who always worked wearing a topless visor with a green plastic screen, intended, I suppose, to protect his eyes from the lights. Bill had come out of silent pictures and had earlier spent a considerable period of time in England making quota pictures for Warner Bros., but he was a regular at Monogram by the time I arrived there.

County Fair was the first film that I produced in the Cinecolor process, a two-color printing process at a time when Technicolor had already progressed to its three-color system. Cinecolor tended to be either bilious or garish. We worked hard to try and mute it and get the best results we could, always fighting against its inherent limitations. It also tended to be unstable. We would send takes back to the lab for reprints frequently. We struggled with the process, but it was reasonably inexpensive. In lower-budget films such as *County Fair*, it wasn't just the cost of raw stock and production processing that concerned us; it was the print cost. The cost of color prints was much greater than that of black-and-white prints, but Technicolor prints were a great deal more expensive than Cinecolor prints. This was a halfway measure to allow us to add the dimension of color into films that would benefit from it.

We sent a small photographic unit to the Pomona County Fair and photographed the sulky races, which were featured in their regular program, in 16mm Kodachrome that was later transferred to Cinecolor. So we created our own library of film, which would provide the action sequences of *County Fair*. Later on we went back to the same track, when it was not being used, with our first unit, and we made close shots with our actors in sulkies and used a camera car, which effectively put our people into the long shots that had been previously photographed. It worked fine.

The lightweight story revolved about a boy-girl misunderstanding told against the background of a county fair. It is clearly derived from *State Fair*, the Rodgers and Hammerstein Twentieth Century-Fox musical. Rory Calhoun, an attractive young man who played juvenile leads, largely in Fox pictures, took on the male lead. He was the best-known actor with whom I had worked up to this time. Jane Nigh, a vivacious, young light comedienne, played the female lead, and Florence Bates, a character actress, was also very good in the film. *County Fair* influenced a whole group of pictures that I later produced, the next of which was *Cavalry Scout*, directed by Lesley Selander.

Lesley was also a veteran director of the period and had mainly done Westerns, including many in the Hopalong Cassidy series. Les had grown up in the business and was very experienced. He was thin, tall, gray-haired, and good-looking—a man's man. I had been talking with Dan Ullman, a writer friend, and I told him I wanted to do a Western. We discussed many possibilities and finally came up with the springboard for the story of *Cavalry Scout,* which revolved around the robbery of a shipment of Gatling guns from the army and their sale to a group of hostile Indians.

Cavalry Scout starred Rod Cameron, James Arness, and Audrey Long, and it marked the beginning of my relationship with Cameron, who had previously done one or two pictures for Monogram. Rod evoked the traditional Western hero—tall, broad-shouldered, strong-jawed, and very masculine. He had the physical characteristics, but not the acting ability or charisma, of John Wayne and Gary Cooper.

The film was also my first production shot at a distant location. The exteriors were photographed in Cinecolor at Idyllwild, California, and its pictorial values certainly contributed greatly to the film. It was well reviewed and gave a good account of itself at the box office. It wasn't expensive, costing about $125,000, but it was very profitable.

Monogram had traditionally made a large number of inexpensive and low-profit program Westerns that were mainly produced to be exhibited at Saturday matinee performances throughout the South and Southwest, where Westerns were a lot more popular than anywhere else. Monogram's salespeople in the southern territory had to provide these pictures to accommodate their customers. They cost about $35,000 each, were shot in black-and-white, and ran sixty-five to seventy minutes in length. Johnny Mack Brown, Jimmy Wakely, and Whip Wilson were the stars. Monogram produced eighteen of them a year, and financing them caused the company a cash drain. Harold succeeded in interesting Ralph Branton, a friend of his who had been managing a large circuit of theaters in Iowa and Nebraska and who wanted to move to Los Angeles, in financing this group of pictures. Branton's investment in the pictures was guaranteed by Monogram, and he was to be paid on delivery of the films.

Branton also wanted to create an opportunity for his son-in-law, Vincent Fennelly, to learn the movie-production business. So Harold and Steve Broidy worked out a deal with Branton for him to finance this group of pictures. These new films were budgeted to cost between $35,000 and $40,000 apiece; six of the films were to star Johnny Mack Brown, six to star Whip Wilson, and the last six Wild Bill Elliott. These eighteen pictures were to be shot on schedules of five days each. I agreed to supervise the operation, which I named Trans-Western Pictures. Vincent Fennelly came to Los Angeles from Des Moines, and he became the producer of the films. Ralph financed the pictures, in part, with the remaining funds being supplied by a bank, and Monogram gave him a guaranteed pickup after they were delivered.

There wasn't much money to be made in the production of those films. Generally there was only an override and the supervision fees that were paid to the producer. But having access to part of those fees for my services allowed Harold and me to provide enough income to enable us to offer a decent salary to my brother, Marvin, so that he could move his family to Los Angeles and I could teach him the production business at the same time we were mentoring Vince Fennelly. The eighteen-picture Western program continued for a few years, after which Monogram finally stopped making them, because television ultimately dried up the market for those films, even in the Deep South. Vince Fennelly then became a producer at Monogram.

In July 1951, Steve asked me to replace Scott Dunlap and take charge of the entire production program of Monogram and Allied Artists. I was now in charge of developing and producing the company's entire program, including approving casting, scripts, budgeting, editing, and post-production. I was twenty-nine years old, and I was given the title of executive producer in charge of production and moved my office to the one formerly occupied by Trem Carr and Scott Dunlap. My salary was increased to $1,000 per week, and I began to build a staff. I selected Dick Heermance, who had become the editor of all of my films, as my assistant, mainly in charge of supervising the editing of our entire program.

Monogram was a publicly traded company, listed on the American Stock Exchange. Much of the stock had originally been held by earlier management, namely W. Ray Johnston, who had been the president of the company, and production chief Trem Carr. Sometime after Harold and I had become active in the company, these founders of Monogram, or their estates, wanted to dispose of their stock holdings. They offered them to Steve Broidy. He, in turn, invited Harold and Ralph Branton, who by then was also working for the company setting up a television subsidiary, to join him in the purchase. An arrangement was completed to acquire the stock so that it wouldn't be thrown on the open market. Steve Broidy acquired most of it, and Harold and I agreed to acquire some, as did Ralph Branton. Harold and I borrowed the money that was required of us and collateralized the loan with the stock itself. The total purchase price of this block of stock, principally acquired by Steve, was about $400,000.

5

The 1950s

Steve Broidy rightly felt that it was necessary for film companies to get into the business of making films for television. He also felt that, because of the low cost of its operations, Monogram was particularly well suited for television production. He asked me to be the head of a television subsidiary, Interstate Television, which he formed. Unfortunately, Monogram never was able to provide sufficient funding to do very much with this venture. As a consequence, nothing much came of Steve's well-intentioned initiative.

Some time later, Steve asked Ralph Branton to involve himself in television, and Ralph managed to put together a few programs. One involved Joan Bennett as the master of ceremonies in an anthology show. Jennings Lang, who was later involved in a scandal with Joan, was the agent for the show.

I continued to develop features that would build on the success of the *Cavalry Scout* and *County Fair* formula, namely inexpensive family or action films made in Cinecolor. I tried to create backgrounds of size and a certain amount of spectacle. For *Rodeo*, I dispatched a crew to photograph rodeos, which became the action basis for the film, released in February 1952.

Another of this type was *Roar of the Crowd*, about the Indianapolis 500, for which we photographed the actual race. Howard Duff starred in this film. Then there was *The Rose Bowl Story*, also using the same formula. We photographed the Rose Parade and football game and developed a romantic comedy around it, starring Marshall Thompson, Vera Miles, Natalie Wood, and Jim Backus. These films all cost about $125,000 apiece and served to upgrade the quality of our second features or co-features program.

Still another in this vein was *Flight to Mars,* an original science-fiction idea that I developed. In this film, a group of people are selected to be astronauts and are sent on the first space flight. They arrive on Mars, find an underground city, and become involved in the problems of that culture. The Martians looked just the way we do, although their clothes were considerably different. Cameron Mitchell played the lead, with Marguerite Chapman, Virginia Houston, and Arthur Franz. We used models for the spaceship and its launch. It was really comic-strip space travel, but it did anticipate what was to become reality twenty years later.

The most important effort I made using this formula was 1952's *Flat Top,* the script I developed with Steve Fisher, the writer of *I Wouldn't Be in Your Shoes. Flat Top* was the story of an aircraft carrier during the Korean War. We received permission from the Navy Department to put a camera crew aboard an aircraft carrier and shot a lot of material in 16mm Kodachrome that we blew up to 35mm Cinecolor.

Originally I had cast Richard Carlson and Bruce Bennett, but about two weeks prior to production I discovered, while talking with his agent, that I could secure the services of Sterling Hayden to play the lead. It was a difficult decision, and expensive. But I was convinced it was in the best interests of the picture, so I paid off Bruce Bennett with his full salary and employed Sterling Hayden to play the leading role, a tough, hard-bitten naval officer. Lesley Selander directed the film in expeditious fashion.

We decided to stage a big publicity premiere to launch *Flat Top.* We brought a portable projector aboard the USS *Princeton,* the aircraft carrier on which we had shot some scenes and which was stationed in San Diego harbor. We brought all of the press from Los Angeles down to San Diego. They, along with all of the officers and crew of the aircraft carrier, were given folding chairs on the flight deck, and we used a portable projector to run the film for them. The stunt generated a great deal of publicity.

Flat Top received excellent reviews and I was thrilled when it was nominated for an Academy Award for Best Film Editing. It was the first film that I had produced to gross over $1 million domestically. Having been made at a cost of about $250,000, it was a very successful film. The Academy nomination was the cherry on the cake.

The "Bomba" pictures continued to be made at the rate of two a year, and I relied more and more on Ford Beebe to carry the burden. The grosses on the pictures were declining, and after six years and twelve films, we finally discontinued the series.

By 1950 it had become overwhelmingly clear that Monogram–Allied Artists had to break out of its niche and get into the first-feature business. The number of theatergoers had dropped from ninety million a week to forty million as a result of the overwhelming impact of television. Competing with television, the accustomed Monogram second features weren't much better, or even as good, as what you might be able to find on your television set at home, for free. As a result, most theaters changed their exhibition practice to single-feature programs. Our company's first reaction to this was to develop as many exploitation pictures as we could. Exploitation pictures were modestly budgeted films that lent themselves to strong advertising campaigns. In a sense, that's what *Flat Top* was, and that's what *Hiawatha* was. They had presold titles that could be marketed to specific audiences.

Two of our most outstanding exploitation pictures, released much later in the decade, were *Riot in Cell Block 11* and *Invasion of the Body Snatchers,* both of which were produced by Walter Wanger. Wanger had produced many outstanding films for decades, including *Queen Christina* with Greta Garbo, *Stagecoach, The Long Voyage Home, Algiers,* and *Canyon Passage.* After a disastrous failure with his *Joan of Arc,* starring Ingrid Bergman, Wanger reached a low point in his career in the early 1950s. He had made a film for television, *Aladdin and His Lamp,* shot in 16mm Kodachrome, but it failed to generate a television sale. An attorney in New York called my brother Harold to ask if we would be interested in shooting some additional film and expanding *Aladdin* into a feature. That seemed reasonable to us. We looked at the film and saw that it was a conventional retelling of the Aladdin story, with the leading roles played by John Sands and Patricia Medina. We met with Walter

Wanger and worked out an arrangement under which we would invest some additional money to shoot the added footage to bring *Aladdin* to feature length. This added another film to our color-picture program at a reasonably small cost.

Walter Wanger was in his late fifties at that time and, after a distinguished career, had fallen on hard times. He needed to work and needed to make some money. The *Aladdin* arrangement led to a personal relationship between Walter Wanger, Harold, and myself. After bringing Steve Broidy into the negotiation, we made an arrangement for Walter under which he would produce four pictures for Allied Artists. We agreed to provide him with an office and secretary, and he would receive fees and profit participations if and when films were made. Despite his financial problems, Walter hoped to resuscitate his career, which he miraculously did. He was still very energetic and full of ideas, and his name was well known in the industry. He was a former president of the Academy of Motion Picture Arts and Sciences and an industry leader. We also thought that being able to present to our customers a program of Walter Wanger pictures would be prestigious. And we hoped that he would be able to attract stars to his films.

Walter was married to the actress Joan Bennett, and they had two children. They'd been married for quite a long time, and Walter had made a number of pictures with Joan in an effort to bolster one another's career. Joan was in her forties and still a beautiful woman, but at an awkward age insofar as her career was concerned. She had started to do some work in television, and she was having an affair with her agent, Jennings Lang. Walter, depressed and infuriated by all these developments, accosted Joan and Jennings Lang in a parking lot adjacent to the MCA agency office where Lang was employed. In a fit of temper, he fired a gun and shot Lang in the groin. Walter was arrested, and Lang was taken to a hospital. A huge scandal erupted. Fortunately, Lang subsequently recovered. Walter was arraigned and finally sentenced to four months in prison.

After the shooting occurred, Harold had gone to the police station and arranged bail for Walter. On the following day I was in my office when Walter walked in. "What are you doing here?" I asked.

He replied, "What else am I going to do?"

I invited him to come home to dinner with me, despite the fact that Pat was completely unprepared for any company, particularly a gentleman whose name was on the front page of every newspaper in America. He was marvelous at dinner that night, charming as always. Of course, none of us referred to the elephant in the room.

While Walter was in jail, I showed him some scripts that I had been preparing. I told him that if he was agreeable, I would put his name on the films as producer, pay him the producer's fees on the pictures while he was in prison, and would undertake the producing chores. It was a terrible time for him. He had to meet his home expenses and keep his children in school while paying his legal bills.

One of the pictures we made for him was *Kansas Pacific,* a Western starring Sterling Hayden. Walter's name appeared on the picture as producer, and he got the producing fee and profit participation. The other picture was *Battle Zone,* the story of a war correspondent played by John Hodiak. Walter was grateful for my help, and I was glad to be able to assist him. When he emerged from four months in prison, he was so appalled at the conditions he saw there that he immediately wanted to do a picture that would call attention to the need for prison reform. It was out of this experience that he developed the original script for *Riot in Cell Block 11.* It was directed by Don Siegel and cost about $225,000. Richard Collins wrote the screenplay, and it was shot on location at Folsom Prison, where we were provided with an unoccupied cellblock area as well as its prison yard. Neville Brand played the lead in *Riot,* and the picture garnered a great deal of publicity. Released at the end of February 1954, it was very well reviewed and successful, earning Walter additional income from his profit participation.

Riot in Cell Block 11 was also interesting for another reason. Don Siegel, its director, told me that a young man had come to see him about getting a job on the picture. He was impressed with him and wanted to employ him as a dialogue director. His name was Sam Peckinpah. We were all soon taken with him. He returned to Hollywood with us after *Riot* was completed and worked as dialogue director on numerous other pictures that we produced at the studio.

One day he said to me, "Walter, I've been offered a job writing, over at a television company, Four Star, and I'd like to take the job."

I said, "That's great, I wish you luck." Sam went there and began writing television shows, and the rest is history.

About this time Walter Wanger came to me and said he had found a story he liked in *Redbook* magazine. He asked me to read it quickly, because he thought that there was going to be a lot of bidding for it. I read it that very evening, and I was fascinated. It was "The Invasion of the Body Snatchers." We bought the rights the next day and took it off the market. Daniel Mainwaring wrote the script, Don Siegel directed, and Kevin McCarthy and Dana Wynter starred.

Invasion of the Body Snatchers is a picture of which I'm very proud. It is a seminal film in the science-fiction field. The central idea, of aliens taking over the bodies of its victims, has been copied repeatedly.

A short time after I had been put in charge of production for Monogram, I was visited one day by a literary agent, Alvin Manuel, who presented some available projects and writers to me. As we talked, he came to a project that was apparently giving him a considerable problem. He told me that a writer client of his, Pierre La Mure, had written a book titled *Moulin Rouge.* He was trying to get this picture put together, and he was having great difficulty with it.

I said, "Well, tell me about it."

He replied, "The story is a biography of Toulouse-Lautrec. John Huston has indicated that he would like to direct it, and Jose Ferrer has said that he would be interested in playing Lautrec."

I said, "What's the problem?"

He replied, "The project has been turned down by every studio in the city, since nobody wants to finance a picture about a dwarf, despite the fact that it doesn't require a great deal of money." My ears perked up. "The picture will be made in London and in Paris, and we have a deal with James and John Woolf, well-known English producers. They are agreeable to putting up the below-the-line cost of the picture. However, all the above-the-line elements have to be paid in dollars."

As this was six years after the end of World War II, funds were still not transferable between England and the United States. The Woolf brothers simply couldn't provide the dollars to pay to the above-the-line talents, namely Huston, Ferrer, and La Mure.

I asked, "How much will be required?"

He replied, "About $250,000." To obtain this money, the Woolf brothers were willing to give up the distribution of the picture in the United States and Canada, although they wanted a participation in the profits of the picture in those territories. They would distribute the picture in the rest of the world. I could scarcely believe that he had not been able to procure this minor investment from a major company. Jose Ferrer had won the Academy Award for Best Actor the previous year for *Cyrano de Bergerac,* and although he was not a big box-office star, he was certainly an actor of great prestige.

I said, "Let us talk about it, and I'll get back to you tomorrow." I discussed the project with Harold and Steve, and they agreed this was a good investment for our company. It could be a leader for the program we were putting together, and it would show our customers we were seriously getting into the A film business. We decided that we would make the deal. The next day I called Al Manuel and told him our decision.

He said, "That's marvelous. Let me inform all of the parties." After a short period of time, he called me to say, "We can't go forward with you, because Jose Ferrer's agent will not agree to his being in a film to be distributed by Monogram or Allied Artists. He thinks it would be disastrous to his career."

Harold, Steve Broidy, Ralph Branton, and I discussed this new development and finally decided we would invest the money personally and agree that a major company would distribute the film. We relied on Harold, who thought he could promote the money in New York. He called David and Louis Stillman, entertainment-attorney friends of his, who responded enthusiastically. "We can put a group together here. Between our group and yours we'll be able to secure a bank loan."

Steve said that there was to be a meeting of the board of directors of Monogram shortly. He would inform the board of the circumstances of the deal and that we wanted to make personal investments in the picture. Furthermore, he said he would tell them that if we could change Ferrer's mind, we would deliver the picture to Monogram–Allied Artists to distribute. If not, it would only be an outside investment for us, and we would arrange to deliver the film to another company. We hoped we could eventually change Jose Ferrer's mind, but we needed to know that ultimately there would be a distributor.

The attorneys in New York arranged a bank commitment, and the final group was made up of Harold, Steve, Ralph, Marvin, Irving, and me on the West Coast and, in New York, Eliot Hyman, the Stillmans, and some others. All became stockholders of a company we named Moulin Productions. The group agreed to borrow the money, with each of us individually responsible for his own share.

We had now succeeded in cutting down considerably the amount for which each of us would be individually responsible. We didn't plan to borrow the money until the picture actually began production. We met with Jose Ferrer's agent, Kurt Frings, and with Ferrer himself, to try to convince them to let Allied Artists distribute the picture. But we could not move them.

At just about this time, Arthur Krim and Bob Benjamin had taken over control of United Artists from Mary Pickford and Charlie Chaplin but had little or no product to distribute. United Artists was in dreadful shape. It was demoralized, and Krim and Benjamin had to arrange financing so they could cover the overhead of their company. We decided that product-short United Artists would be the most receptive customer for our package. On a Sunday morning, Harold and I went to meet Arthur Krim in Beverly Hills, and we presented our arrangement on *Moulin Rouge* to him.

Arthur and Bob Blumofe, his West Coast production chief, evinced great interest in doing a deal with us, under which United Artists would distribute *Moulin Rouge*. The arrangement we made with them called for United Artists to take over the bank loan that had been arranged in New York by the Stillmans. We agreed to give UA a distribution fee of 30 percent, as well as 15 percent of our 35 percent of the profits. Moulin Productions now had no money invested in the movie and owned 20 percent of its possible profits.

Moulin Rouge went into production in Paris in the summer of 1951. It coincided with the production of a film Allied Artists had co-financed with Associated British entitled *24 Hours in the Life of a Woman*, later retitled *Affair in Monte Carlo*, which starred Merle Oberon, Leo Genn, and Richard Todd. I went to London with Pat to see the first cut of the film and to discuss the production with Victor Saville, the film's producer-director.

Pat and I then joined Harold, Steve Broidy, Eliot Hyman, and

On the set of *Moulin Rouge* is Jose Ferrer as Toulouse-Lautrec in 1952. © 1953 Metro-Goldwyn-Mayer Studios Inc. All rights reserved.

David Stillman, who had come to Paris to visit the set of *Moulin Rouge.* We had a marvelous time there, watching John Huston filming in the streets, with Jose Ferrer walking with his legs bound up behind his knees, getting a sense of the size and the sensitivity of the film. While in Paris we also cemented a great friendship with John Huston before I returned to London.

Moulin Rouge was completed in the fall of 1951. We saw the finished picture and were very impressed. United Artists was also pleased with it, and plans were made for its premiere showings when the next brouhaha erupted.

Jose Ferrer and John Huston had allowed their names to be attached to certain groups or committees that the American Legion, which was deeply involved in the anti-Communist campaign, considered un-American, and consequently it picketed the opening of the film. Despite that, *Moulin Rouge* was exceedingly well received. It is a very unusual film. Its color treatment was extraordinary. Commercially it was very successful, generating a great deal of profit, and spawning a whole series of developments that became tremendously important in my future career.

🐟

Hiawatha, which I produced in 1952, was inspired by the classic Longfellow poem that most of us have read in school. The idea of doing a film entirely about Indians appealed to me. The poem was in the public domain, and I interested a writer, Arthur Strawn, in the project. Later Dan Ullman polished the script. We shot the film at Bass Lake, California, near Yosemite National Park.

I chose Kurt Neumann, a talented German refugee, to direct. Since he had lost a leg, Kurt used an artificial limb. He had done some interesting low-budget films, and I thought he would bring a refreshing sensitivity to the story. We chose Vince Edwards, an attractive young man, rather reminiscent of a young Burt Lancaster, to play Hiawatha. Since this was a story of America before the coming of the white man, the cast, in the custom of the time, were all Indians portrayed by Caucasian actors.

I hoped the story would appeal to young people. We used some of Longfellow's poetry, contrived a romantic Romeo and Juliet story, and photographed it amid beautiful scenery in Cinecolor. Unfortunately, since we lacked an adequate budget, everything in the film cried out to be bigger and better. The villages, the numbers of canoes, the numbers of extras, the battles, all should have been more lavish. It wasn't a particularly successful film, although I'm glad that I made it, since it did seek to explore some interesting new ideas. I'm proud of the *Hollywood Reporter* (December 8, 1952) review: "Although grownups may find the film somewhat slow-moving and talky, the kids will love it, judging by the enthusiastic reaction from the many youngsters among the preview audience at the Academy Award Theater last Thursday night. Walter Mirisch's production is necessarily a simple one, avoiding any unrealistic settings for the sake of display, counting on the excellent photography, tinted in Cinecolor, and on Marlin Skiles' fine music for handsomeness and mood."

By 1953 the CinemaScope process had burst upon the movie world. Twentieth Century-Fox had decided to make *The Robe* in this widescreen process, which changed for all time the ratio of motion-picture theater screens. Whereas, traditionally, the theater screen had been in a ratio of 4 to 3, the CinemaScope lenses were about 2.5 to 1. Twentieth Century-Fox, having made a big investment in *The Robe*, then embarked on the difficult problem of getting theaters to junk their old screens, install screens in the new, wider proportions, and acquire new projection lenses. It took a tremendous campaign on the part of Spyros Skouras, the president of Fox, and Darryl Zanuck, who had produced *The Robe*, to get the theaters to convert. They had to promise the theater owners that they would make a large number of films every year in CinemaScope. They were also anxious to encourage other companies to make films in that proportion so that they would fulfill their promise to the exhibitors.

As part of Fox's commitment to the exhibitors, we at Allied Artists were able to conclude a deal with Twentieth Century-Fox in 1953 for three films, all in CinemaScope, in which Fox would invest 50 percent of the cost of the pictures. For its investment, Fox would get the foreign distribution and Allied the domestic. It was an arrangement that served the purposes of Twentieth Century-Fox and Allied Artists. By this time, too, Technicolor was more readily available, and we were able to get commitments from that company. These new films would all be shot in Technicolor, and *The Adventures of Haji Baba*, an Arabian Nights project of Walter Wanger's, was the first of the CinemaScope pictures that Allied Artists released. Fox also agreed to co-finance a film that I had developed with Dan Ullman entitled *The Black Prince*, which was later retitled *The Warriors*. This was a story about the medieval Black Prince of England, a name given to Prince Edward of Woodstock, an historical character. With Fox co-financing, we were successful in securing the services of Errol Flynn, in the twilight of his great career as a star of swashbuckling films, to play the title role.

Part of the financing for *The Black Prince* also came from Associated British Pathé, which was Allied Artists' distributor in the United Kingdom, where we utilized its studios in Elstree for the production. Henry Levin, who had made a number of swashbuckling pictures in Hollywood for Twentieth Century-Fox and Columbia, was chosen to direct.

Fortunately we were to start shooting not long after MGM had made *Ivanhoe* at its London studios. The exterior castle set, built by MGM for that film, was still standing on the back lot, and we were able to arrange to rent that set, allowing us to make a great savings in the cost of production. Joanne Dru played the female lead, and I was also fortunate enough to have chosen a rising young English actor, Peter Finch, to play the villain.

Walter Wanger produced *The Adventures of Haji Baba*, the first of the Fox co-productions, in 1953, and we began the second, *The Black Prince*, in 1954. At my first opportunity, shortly after the start of production, I went to London where I saw a moustache-less Errol Flynn. Fearing that he might be unrecognizable without his nearly trademark lip adornment, I asked for an explanation. He told me that he thought he would look younger without it. I said I didn't agree and worked out a plan where we showed him shaving off his moustache for a plot point and after a passage of time we saw him with his then regrown moustache.

Errol Flynn was a larger-than-life personality, a wonderful raconteur with great charm, but very alcoholic at this point in his career. We had a great deal of difficulty shooting around his drinking. One day, for example, when we were doing a scene in the great hall of the castle, the actors were all sitting at a dining table talking with big goblets in front of them. It was getting late in the day. British crews didn't have to work overtime without their consent, and we were trying desperately to finish shooting on that set that day, so we could strike it that night and go outside the following day while the weather was good and do some shooting at the exterior of the castle. I suggested to Henry Levin, the director, that we talk to the shop steward and ask him to extend the time we could work, so that we could finish the great hall set that night. To return to it for an hour or two on the next day, and then have to make a long move out to the MGM Studio, would have wasted hours.

In the meantime, the prop man continued to refill Errol's goblet. Knowing his answer in advance, I nevertheless asked the prop man why he kept refilling the mug.

He replied, "It's vodka. He wants me to keep it full."

We then received word that the crew had consented to keep working until we had finished on that set. I took Errol aside, and I said, "Will you do me a big favor, and work until we finish this sequence tonight so we can make our move overnight?"

He said, "Of course, I'll do whatever's good for the picture. You want me to do it, I'll stay for as long as it takes." He then took another drink out of his goblet. Thirty minutes later we had to stop shooting. We simply couldn't go on any longer, since his speech was nearly unintelligible. Consequently we had to return to that set the next day to finish the sequence. I believe he had every intention of finishing, but it was just not possible.

Unfortunately, he also did not look well in the picture. His face was puffy and he was clearly too old for the role, but I hoped careful photography might help offset that. It didn't. Before we started to shoot, I asked him to diet and hopefully lose some weight, which he didn't do. There were only traces left of the face, physique, and charisma that he had brought to *The Adventures of Robin Hood, Captain Blood, The Sea Hawk,* and all those other great adventure films of his youth.

![symbol]

My promotion to executive producer at Monogram-Allied Artists had occurred in July 1951, five years after I had produced my first film, four years after I had married Pat, and in the same year that my eldest child, Anne, was born. Two years later our second child and first son, Andrew, was born.

Meanwhile at Allied Artists, we continued to produce the bread-and-butter pictures, as we used to call them, to pick up whatever business was left for second features. The Bowery Boys continued under the helm of Ben Schwalb. Dick Heermance, who had been my preferred editor, was now my assistant, and I created an effective and efficient organization in the studio. David Milton, who had been at Monogram for a long time, headed up the art department. Barney Shapiro, who had also been there for many years, was in charge of business and legal affairs. Al Wood managed our physical production department. Les Sansom, who had been our film librarian, now supervised our editorial department. We also kept increasing our program of color films and exploitation films that could be played as first features, or as equal-feature bookings, in many theaters.

Among the films were those with backgrounds that allowed us to present a certain amount of spectacle. *The Rose Bowl Story, The Roar of the Crowd, Rodeo,* and *Pride of the Bluegrass* were all in this category. Then there were color Westerns, including the earlier ones with Rod

Cameron, such as *Cavalry Scout, Fort Osage,* and *Wagons West.* We later produced others, mainly starring Sterling Hayden, such as *Kansas Pacific, Arrow in the Dust,* and *Shotgun. Flight to Mars* was a science-fiction color film, and then came the war film *Flat Top,* which became the most successful of them all.

Another interesting film of the period was *The Maze.* Following the introduction of CinemaScope, people looked for other gimmicks to entice audiences back into the theaters and away from their television screens. One of these was a 3-D picture, *Bwana Devil.* The 3-D effect had been used before, but not in color. The effect is achieved by a double-image on the screen that is clarified for the viewer by wearing colored glasses. *Bwana Devil* was very successful, and other companies soon jumped on the bandwagon. The major companies began making pictures in 3-D, and I felt we should also make one.

In the inventory of unmade properties that Monogram owned was a book titled *The Maze,* by French author Maurice Sandoz. The most interesting thing about the book was that it had been illustrated by Salvador Dali. The artwork was fascinating. I thought the title was provocative and would lend itself to a good suspense film. We rushed to prepare a script and make it a 3-D picture.

I attempted to negotiate an arrangement with Natural Vision, which had developed the 3-D cameras with which *Bwana Devil* had been made. It was now leasing its cameras to the major companies. It asked for a percentage of the gross of the picture, and I thought that was outrageous. I was on a set at the studio one day, talking to our camera crew about 3-D, and our camera assistant, Maurice "Bud" Davidson, said to me, "I don't know what all the fuss is about. If you want one of those cameras, I'll put it together for you in a couple of weeks."

I said, "You're on! Let's see you do it." And, of course, he did. He joined two cameras alongside one another, shooting in synchronization. To direct, I chose William Cameron Menzies, a well-known production designer and director. Menzies was an interesting man, about sixty or so at this time, who had enjoyed a varied career. He'd reached the height of his production-design career with *Gone with the Wind.* Earlier, in England, he had directed *Things to Come,* based on H. G. Wells's novel, with which I had been very much impressed. But Menzies's career at this time was not at a high point, and he had already directed a few inexpensive pictures. I thought he would be a good choice. The background of the picture was a Scottish castle, and Bill had lived a long time in England and had a good feel for that milieu.

I cast Richard Carlson and a young English actress, Veronica Hurst, who was under contract to Associated British, as the leads. Harry Neumann, aided and abetted by Maurice "Bud" Davidson, was our cinematographer. Unfortunately, by the time we finished the movie, the 3-D craze had just about petered out, and the picture was not successful, either artistically or commercially. But we did show that we were able to keep up with the major film companies. *Variety* (July 3, 1953) wrote, "Logical use is made of the depth medium to narrate a mystery, and though it's slow in getting underway it builds to a terrific climax in which 3-D plays a vital part. . . . William Cameron Menzies, who also handled above-average production design, is responsible for good direction which keeps the story moving."

Vincent Fennelly continued to produce pictures for Monogram, one of which was another Dan Ullman Western, *At Gunpoint*. Fred MacMurray played the lead in it, and Walter Brennan and Dorothy Malone were also in the cast.

Fennelly also produced another picture that Dan Ullman wrote for us, *Seven Angry Men,* in which Raymond Massey played John Brown, the Civil War abolitionist. I had always thought the John Brown story an exciting historical event that had a great deal of importance in American history and deserved to be told. It was touched upon as a subplot in a Warner Bros. film, *Santa Fe Trail,* in which Raymond Massey had played Brown. But *Seven Angry Men* was exclusively the story of John Brown and his sons, told from his point of view. Charles Marquis Warren had been a well-known novelist before he began to write and direct films, and I thought that he could help us with both the script and in his direction of the picture. Considered as a group, these pictures were a big step forward from the kind of product that was being made at Monogram when I first arrived there.

Hayes Goetz also produced pictures at Monogram at this time. His father, Ben Goetz, was an important executive at MGM, and his uncle was William Goetz, the founder of International Pictures who was later in charge of production for Universal-International. Hayes had produced a few films at MGM, and his father, who was a cousin of my brother Harold, had indicated that he would be willing to co-finance some pictures that Hayes would produce. Securing partial financing was very attractive to perpetually underfinanced Monogram. The first of the pictures that Hayes produced was a horseracing picture, *Pride of the Bluegrass,* shot in Cinecolor. Bill Beaudine directed, and it gave a good account of itself at the box office.

About this same time, Harold and I were both anxious to bring the rest of our family out to Los Angeles. Pat and I had been blessed with our first son, Andrew, called Drew, in 1953, but my parents were living in Florida and Harold and I both felt that we would like to be with them in their declining years. My father, in 1954, was eighty years old, and my mother was sixty-three, so we arranged for them to move to Los Angeles. Our wives found an apartment for them and helped to get them organized so that, as they continued to age and needed more care, we and our wives would be available to provide it.

Marvin had remained in Milwaukee, working with Irving for the candy company, and Harold and I thought it might also be an opportune time for Marvin to move to Los Angeles. The theater-concession business in Milwaukee was running into serious difficulties, as the larger theaters and the theater chains moved to own their own candy and popcorn operations. The drop in theater attendance also hurt them, and the business they were able to keep was retained largely by giving monetary advances to the theaters, which called for considerable and expensive financing. Harold and Irving now began to consider the possibility of selling their concession business. Harold and I also saw an opportunity for Marvin to learn the movie production business as an associate with Hayes Goetz, since his independent deal with Monogram had by then been set up. He also was able to draw some income from the Trans-Western Pictures Co. This occurred in 1953, when Marvin was thirty-six years old.

The films that resulted from that deal were *Arrow in the Dust* with Sterling Hayden, *Pride of the Bluegrass* with Lloyd Bridges and Vera Miles, and *The Human Jungle* with Gary Merrill and Jan Sterling. After working on these films, and because his own interest lay in the administrative side of the business, Marvin became assistant to George Burrows, the vice president and treasurer of Monogram and Allied Artists.

6

The Screen Producers Guild

Shortly after I became head of production at Monogram in 1951, I received a telephone call from Arthur Hornblow Jr., a well-known producer at Paramount and at Metro-Goldwyn-Mayer. He introduced himself and told me that he and a group of other producers had been talking about organizing a Screen Producers Guild, along the lines of the writers and directors guilds, in order to enhance the recognition that they felt producers lacked and that they felt was not achievable without an organization. He invited me to lunch, and I very much enjoyed meeting him. I was then working on the proverbial other side of the railroad tracks, and he in the fabled halls of MGM at its zenith. I was very flattered. On his part, he seemed interested in how low-budget production functioned. We had a pleasant lunch, and he invited me to attend the organizing meeting of the Screen Producers Guild, to be held in a private dining room at Chasen's restaurant. I am sure Arthur and the other organizers each had assignments to call a certain number of people and inquire whether they would be interested in joining.

The organizers were principally interested in lobbying the Academy of Motion Picture Arts and Sciences to present the Academy Award for the Best Picture to the producer of that picture, not to a studio head, which had been the practice up until then. The organizers of the guild were the most prominent producers of the time—Arthur Freed, William Perlberg, Sol Siegel, Lawrence Weingarten, Pandro Berman, and others—the people producing the films that won those awards, and it didn't sit too well with them that they weren't the recipients.

There were other, serious injustices about which producers complained. At certain studios, principally Republic, producers were still not given credit on their pictures as producers. They were called supervisors. Some studios called all producers associate producers, with the studio head considered the producer of all the studio's films. There were other injustices, such as lack of pensions and health and welfare plans. The producers felt that if they had an organization of their own they could afford publicity representatives who would undertake campaigns to make the press and the public aware of what the role of the creative producer was in the making of motion pictures. Those were the major reasons for the creation of the Screen Producers Guild, later renamed the Producers Guild of America.

The Screen Producers Guild constituted my first real involvement in industry affairs, and I found it most stimulating. It was a wonderful opportunity for me to make the acquaintance of most of the other producers in the industry, and it was also useful in other ways. People in the industry were always calling one another to inquire, "What do you know about that writer? What was your experience with that director?" Now they knew one another. So the whole fraternal aspect of the guild also became of use to its members, because they came to know people from all segments of the industry. It was useful to producers in the big studios who had all of the facilities of those behemoths available to them. It was even more useful to me, in that little studio off of Sunset Drive, down near Vermont Avenue, to be able to call the producers at MGM or Paramount or Fox and have a discourse on a serious matter of business. William Perlberg was elected the first president of the Producers Guild, and Sol Siegel was the second.

For tactical reasons, the guild avoided taking a strong position against the blacklist, although most everybody on the creative side opposed it. It generally depended on how far out in front of the issue any individual wanted to be, or could afford to be. The guild charged its members dues and hired an executive secretary, Bess Bearman, who had formerly been Darryl F. Zanuck's secretary. She had excellent connections in the industry and was effective in her job. The guild undertook publicity campaigns and began a tradition of annual dinners, which became important social affairs as well as publicity vehicles for the producers. It chose the most important people in the industry as the recipients of its annual presentation, the Milestone Award, to honor an individual whose work had represented a milestone in the industry or had made a historic contribution to the entertainment field. The first honoree was Jesse Lasky, who was considered the first producer, credited with *The Squaw Man,* which was generally acknowledged as the first feature-length movie made in Hollywood. Lasky was also a member of the guild. A number of our members later became studio heads themselves, such as Sol C. Siegel, who became studio head at MGM, and Buddy Adler, who succeeded Zanuck at Fox. David O. Selznick, Samuel Goldwyn, and many others became members. Later on, television producers were admitted to membership.

The guild has accomplished a great deal for its members. The fact that my name is now on an Academy Award for Best Picture I owe to the fact that, many years ago, the Producers Guild put on a concerted campaign that was finally able to persuade the Board of Governors of the Academy to pass a rule that the Academy Award for the Best Picture was to be presented to the producer of that film. That rule alone has given the producer a great deal of prestige, making the title "producer" something to be jealously defended.

The guild also started a publication, the *Journal of the Producers Guild,* edited by John Houseman, who was also one of our members. It carried varied articles of interest to producers. The journal was also sent to people of influence in the industry and press and became a valuable contributor to the guild's educational campaign.

Unfortunately, a great deal of what was achieved by the Producers Guild in those early days has been lost, either by default or from pressure by the Directors Guild, which clearly had a great deal more power with the studios. If directors go on strike, they can stop production. If producers go on strike, substitutes, at least on a temporary basis, are readily available. Without success, the Producers Guild has attempted to acquire the rights of a bargaining agent many times over the years, particularly when directors and writers were given residuals in pictures that producers were certainly also entitled to receive. Many pictures that I produced were based on my own ideas. I originated them and, with writers and directors, I developed them. Everyone else had residuals in their future showings, but I had none. However, the National Labor Relations Board has ruled that producers are a part of management and would not recognize the guild's right to act as a bargaining agent.

After I took over the management of the production program for Allied Artists–Monogram in 1951, I exercised both the individual producer and studio executive functions. Besides supervising the studio program, I continued to personally produce a few pictures every year. That was not unusual at that time. Darryl Zanuck, who was in charge of production for Fox, personally produced a certain number of pictures every year, as did Dore Schary at MGM. I also continued to function in that way during the entire seventeen-year span of the Mirisch Company–United Artists affiliation.

After having completed a few films at Monogram in the late 1940s, I felt that I might be qualified to join the Academy of Motion Picture Arts and Sciences, which itself was still in its early years, having been organized in the late 1920s. Scott Dunlap, who was in charge of production at Monogram, was an early member of the Academy, and he offered to sponsor my membership. My membership proposal was signed by Dunlap and by I. E. Chadwick, who at that time was president of the Independent Producers Association, a negotiating body for the independent studios. My membership application to the Academy was filed and accepted by the board in December 1947.

My association with the Screen Producers Guild has continued without interruption since I became a founding member. I attended meetings regularly, enjoyed friendships with other guild members, served on various committees, and was elected to a number of offices until I was voted into the presidency in 1959. My dedication to promoting the guild's aims and objectives became stronger than ever.

During the first year of my presidency, 1960, the guild voted Jack Warner, the president and head of production of Warner Bros, to be the recipient of its prestigious Milestone Award. Jack Benny, the master of ceremonies at the dinner, commented, "Tonight we are honoring the Mark Twain of Burbank. He would rather be an actor than a producer, and he even envies Don Rickles. He's always wanted to be a comedian, and doesn't realize that he is one."

Also making a presentation was Eva Marie Saint, who was to present an award for a collegiate student film. Introducing Eva Marie

Saint, Jack Benny made some overblown comments about her youth, beauty, and charm, all intentionally overstated. Eva Marie came to the microphone and said, "Oh, shit." She succeeded in bringing the house down, and although it seems rather tame now, it created quite a fuss at the time. In good humor, it got a tremendous amount of publicity for the dinner. Gary Cooper made the presentation to Jack Warner, and a great time was had by all.

In 1961, the second year of my presidency of the Screen Producers Guild, the board voted to present its Milestone Award to Adolph Zukor, the founder of Paramount Pictures and one of the few surviving pioneers of the industry. This banquet also provided a nostalgic evening. The ninety-year-old Zukor walked into the room on the arm of Mary Pickford, his first great star. The evening again gave the guild an opportunity to say thank you to one of the founders of the industry.

The third Milestone Award that was voted during my presidency was presented in 1962 to Bob Hope, at one of the really great Producers Guild dinners. Hope was a tremendously popular figure, and the dinner emphasized his contributions to the entertainment of service people. Behind the dais was a huge map of the world, outlined in small lights. After the dinner and the humorous part of the evening, it had been arranged through the U.S. Armed Forces Radio Service that there would be incoming telephone calls to Bob Hope at the dinner table, from various parts of the world. Bulbs lit up on the map, showing where the calls emanated. First there was a call to Bob from a SAC airplane, in flight somewhere over Eastern Europe, with the captain and the crew of the airplane speaking to him. The voices of the callers, as well as Bob's answers, were put through loudspeakers so everyone in the room could hear them. Then Bob spoke to men in submarines and to soldiers, airmen, and sailors all over the world. It was a most exciting evening, topped off by the Marine Band. It was a great tribute to Bob Hope and another important public-relations event that redounded to the benefit of the Screen Producers Guild and the entire motion-picture industry.

In 1962 I completed my third term as president of the Screen Producers Guild and was succeeded as president by Lawrence Weingarten. After my term as president, I was elected president of the Motion Picture Permanent Charities. This was an organization that served as the fund-raising arm for the industry, to raise money for various charitable causes, either by payroll deductions or donations, and to allocate gifts to various deserving charities within the community. I found this an interesting and fulfilling position and was glad to be able to serve its cause.

Following my service as president, which concluded in 1962, I became less active in the guild. In 1964, I was elected to the board of the Academy of Motion Picture Arts and Sciences and then became more interested in the affairs of the Academy.

7

Back at Allied Artists

In 1954, I was finally able to get the Technicolor Corporation to agree to process a film for Allied Artists. I considered this a great coup and another step forward for the Allied Artists product. I looked carefully for a subject that would justify the additional expense, since both the processing and the print costs of Technicolor were much greater than either black-and-white or Cinecolor. I finally decided on a film to be titled *An Annapolis Story*, with a screenplay by Geoffrey Homes and Dan Ullman. My idea was to do a story that would allow us to photograph the colorful background of Annapolis, with rousing patriotic military formations and music, and weave it into a story of young people, combining football, sibling rivalry, and the Korean War. The plot revolved around two brothers, both midshipmen at Annapolis and in love with the same girl.

I had been impressed with the great job that Don Siegel had done on *Riot in Cell Block 11*, and I was delighted when Don agreed to direct *An Annapolis Story*. He made a number of good story suggestions and asked that we bring in a fresh writer, Daniel Mainwaring. For his own reasons, Mainwaring chose to use his nom de plume, Geoffrey Homes, on the film. With the cooperation of the Navy Department, we did some second-unit shooting at Annapolis. The navy also allowed us to do second-unit work aboard an aircraft carrier.

The film cost about $450,000. It starred Kevin McCarthy, who also appeared in *The Invasion of the Body Snatchers*, John Derek and

Diana Lynn, a very capable young actress whose work, up until that point, had been mainly at Paramount, where she had appeared as an ingénue in a large number of pictures. *An Annapolis Story* pleased audiences and marked another film where our product could be equated with that being made by major studios.

In 1955 the last of the "Bomba" productions, *Lord of the Jungle*, again directed by Ford Beebe, was released.

I next began to think about another subject for CinemaScope and Technicolor filming, and this time I chose a Western locale. I had long wanted to do a Wyatt Earp story, and Dan Ullman and I had talked about it frequently, over a period of years. Most of the Wyatt Earp stories are told about his adventures in Tombstone. Many years earlier, John Ford had directed *My Darling Clementine*, with Henry Fonda playing Wyatt Earp, and that too was a Tombstone story, concluding with the gunfight at the O.K. Corral. However, after seeing a period photograph in a book entitled *Trail Driving Days* that showed a Western street with a banner draped across it shouting "Everything Goes in Wichita," I decided to focus the picture on the period when Earp was marshal of Wichita.

Dan wrote an excellent script, one of the best that he had ever done for me, and I was exceedingly enthused about its possibilities. I was determined to get a major star. I had a long meeting with Kirk Douglas, trying to convince him to do *Wichita*, but he chose to decline. I also made an effort to borrow the services of Robert Ryan from RKO, but that didn't succeed either. As chance would have it, I attended a luncheon of the Permanent Charities Committee, at which well-known movie star Joel McCrea spoke. I decided to beard the lion.

I had never met Joel before, but I had seen him in many films during his long career. Joel had begun working in films in the early days of sound and had started as just a young, good looking leading man, but he soon progressed to a very successful career in light comedy. His great films were Preston Sturges's *Sullivan's Travels* and *The Palm Beach Story*. He had also appeared in William Wyler's *These Three*, George Stevens's *The More the Merrier*, Alfred Hitchcock's *Foreign Correspondent*, and Cecil B. De Mille's Western epic *Union Pacific*. At this time, Joel was in his late forties, certainly not at the height of his career, and largely working in Western films for the major companies. I told Mr. McCrea, as I called him that day, about my *Wichita* script and said I would like to send it to him for his reading. He encouraged me to do so.

Joel, who had grown up in Hollywood, had gravitated toward the Western life early on. As soon as he was able, he had acquired a ranch in the San Fernando Valley, on which he ran cattle, and he loved the life of the rancher. He and his wife, Frances Dee, who had also been a most successful ingénue in films, lived with their children in a beautiful ranch house on their 2,700-acre property.

I was pleased to get a phone call from Joel in which he told me that he liked the script and would ask his agent, Bert Allenberg of the William Morris Agency, to call me. Instead of waiting for Allenberg to call me, I called him, saying, "I'd like to try to work out a deal for Joel to do this film."

He replied, "Joel is enthusiastic about this project, and he says he's got a lot of faith in you, but I told him that I don't think making a film for Allied Artists is a good career move for him at this time, and I don't think he should do the film. However, Joel said to me, 'I like this script, and I like that kid. I want to do the picture, Bertie, so go work it out.'" And so he did.

The supporting cast in *Wichita* was excellent, consisting of Wallace Ford, a marvelous character actor, Edgar Buchanan, who also lent great flavor, Lloyd Bridges, Peter Graves, and female lead Vera Miles. Vera had earlier played the lead for me in *The Rose Bowl Story*. When it was announced that we were going to make *Wichita*, she came to see me, and said, "You know, I have to play the lead in this picture, because I come from Wichita. My whole family's going to see it, and I've just got to be in it."

Joel and I talked a great deal about who should direct. Finally he suggested Jacques Tourneur, who had directed him at MGM in *Stars in My Crown*. Jacques "Jack" Tourneur had made some outstanding pictures by then, such as *Out of the Past* and the horror picture *Cat People* at RKO. I liked him very much and found him good to work with.

On the first day of production, we were shooting out on a Western street in Newhall, where Monogram shot most of its Westerns in those years. I was on the set, bright and early, when I saw a big, beautiful white Cadillac come through the gate. Joel was driving it. When he saw me he said, "Well, I'm here, just as I said I would be. Where do you want me to go?" I shook his hand, wished him well, and I recall him saying to me, "This is a new car. I only picked it up this week, so is there someone who can see to it that it gets under some covers, so that it isn't filled with dust by the time I drive it out of here tonight?" We took care of his car, got him into his wardrobe, and shooting began on the picture.

Production went exceedingly well. It was produced at a cost of about $400,000. Harold Lipstein was the cinematographer, and Hans Salter composed the score. I was now trying to employ a different level of directors and had gotten away from the old-line Monogram Pictures standbys. I tried hard to branch out and bring in new talent from the major studios.

Wichita was very well received, with excellent reviews, and became the highest-grossing picture I'd produced up to that time.

I had by then also decided on another vehicle that I wanted to do with Joel. We had enjoyed a happy and successful experience together, so I had approached him with my idea of doing a film based on the life of Sam Houston. I was in the process of preparing that film, which we called *The First Texan,* when the telephone rang in my office one day. The man at the other end of the phone identified himself as the Cadillac dealer in Oxnard, California, and he said to me, "What color car would you like, Mr. Mirisch?"

I said, "No, you don't understand, I haven't ordered a car."

He replied, "I know that. Mr. Joel McCrea ordered one for you. I need to know what color and style you would like."

Well, after figuratively picking myself up off the floor, I chose white. I called Joel and said, "You know, this is a most extraordinary gift, and your gesture is really overwhelming."

He said, "No, I'm very proud of what we did, despite Bertie's advice not to do it. I've probably had participations in the profits of twenty or twenty-five pictures by now, and I've never earned a nickel out of any of them. But I've been getting generous checks from this picture, and I think you should share in it."

I was working for a not-great salary at the time, and I was thrilled to get this beautiful gift from Joel. I subsequently made a total of six films and TV series with him, and we remained friends up until the end of his life.

The second film with Joel, *The First Texan,* directed by Byron Haskin, is a romanticized telling of the saga of Texas independence. It was an exceedingly successful picture for Allied Artists, and Joel was very happy with it. Allied Artists was now eager to make a deal for additional pictures with him. However, very flattering to me, he insisted on a key-man clause in his contract that provided that I had to produce his pictures.

The third picture I made with Joel was *The Oklahoman,* also based on a script by Dan Ullman, in which Joel played a frontier doctor. It was directed by Francis D. "Pete" Lyon, who had been an editor and had done some quite good work as a director. I was disappointed with the picture, and that was the only time I worked with Pete.

The Tall Stranger was the fourth film that I produced with Joel at Allied Artists. It was based on a Louis L'Amour novel and was scripted by Christopher Knopf. Virginia Mayo was Joel's co-star, and Thomas Carr directed. *The Oklahoman* and *The Tall Stranger* were both shot in CinemaScope and Technicolor. Neither of these two films had the size or the scope of the Wyatt Earp or Sam Houston pictures, but they were good vehicles for Joel and gave good accounts of themselves.

8

Moulin Productions, Inc.

M^{*oulin Rouge*} had been released by United Artists in 1952 and had received marvelous reviews. It was also nominated for an Academy Award for Best Picture of that year. Jose Ferrer, John Huston, and Colette Marchand were all nominated in their respective categories, and it received seven nominations in all.

It was also most successful financially, and our investment group, under the umbrella of Moulin Productions, Inc., received its share of the profits from United Artists. John Huston now offered his next production, a new version of Herman Melville's *Moby Dick,* to Moulin. John had originally told us about it when we all first met in Paris, while he was shooting *Moulin Rouge.* He had great plans for *Moby Dick,* which he originally wanted to do with his father, Walter Huston, playing Captain Ahab. It sounded fantastic to us, but unfortunately Walter Huston died in 1950, so John decided to film *Moby Dick* with Gregory Peck. We agreed we would do this deal with John, but he felt that he had to offer the picture for distribution to Warner Bros.

John had a long career as a writer at Warner Bros. before he began to direct. At various times in his career he had made stabs at writing a script for *Moby Dick,* so the studio owned a lot of his *Moby Dick* written material, and he didn't want any litigation over it. Warner Bros. also had priority on the title, having produced previous versions, and retained it on its permanently protected list of titles.

The Allied Artists–Moulin group was anxious to encourage John to make films for Allied Artists and had been discussing such an arrangement with him for some time, but we understood that *Moby Dick* couldn't be offered to Allied because of the problems with Warner Bros. Although John wanted to make a deal with Allied Artists, he didn't want it to appear to the industry as a step down in his career. I remember him saying to us, "You know, I'm ready to do this deal, but I don't want to do it alone. I've talked to some friends about it, and suggested to them the advantages of working in a company where we would have independence, where there isn't going to be a great deal of overhead charged to our pictures, and where we can have a more meaningful participation in profits."

We asked, "Who have you talked to?"

He replied, "Billy Wilder and Willy Wyler." He continued, "You should talk with those fellows, because I think they're interested."

This was very exciting news. Wilder and Wyler were two of the most sought-after directors in the world. They were both represented by MCA, so Lew Wasserman, reputed to be the toughest agent in the industry, would now be on the other side of the negotiating table from us. We discussed various formulas to try and make this deal attractive, particularly to MCA, an agency that, on its own, would not look favorably on the affiliation of these top talents with a marginal studio. John Huston, on the other hand, was represented by an independent agent, Paul Kohner, who was helpful in trying to progress the proposal.

The credit for evolving the ultimate proposal belongs to my brother Harold. It was quite simple. When they made a picture for Allied Artists, they would receive the same remuneration as they received from other companies. However, they would also receive options on 25,000 shares of stock, valued as of the time they signed their contracts. If they produced successful films for Allied Artists, that would be reflected in the value of the stock. Our argument was that one successful picture could easily double the value of the stock of this small company. One successful film from one of these men could double or triple the overall gross of the company. We were dealing now with the possibility of eventually getting nine films from the three of them. Potentially, the value of the stock could appreciate immensely.

All of this was in the context of the fact that in the highest bracket, income tax was 70 percent at the time. High earners were trying to avoid these mammoth taxes. Therefore, the possibility of earning capital gains, which could be realized by the sale of stock and were taxed at only 25 percent, was a big incentive. We believed that these directors would make fine, successful films and would transform Allied Artists into a major company, immeasurably enhancing the value of its stock.

They all agreed to it for their own reasons. It came at an opportune time in Billy Wilder's career. Billy had been making pictures at Paramount for many years. But at that time he was in the midst of a big argument with the studio over his picture *Stalag 17,* in which Paramount wanted to make editorial changes so that it could be distributed in Germany. Billy, who had lost his mother in the Holocaust, refused to make any changes and said he didn't care if his picture was ever distributed in Germany. Paramount insisted and made the changes without his approval. He was furious and ready to move elsewhere.

Willy Wyler had been a partner in Liberty Films, a corporation owned by Wyler, Frank Capra, and George Stevens. Liberty Films had been sold to Paramount, resulting in a big capital gain for him. He saw the Allied Artists plan as another Liberty deal, except that now he would be associated with men who were closer friends. So he, too, found merit in this proposal.

John Huston was an Irish resident who paid no taxes, but the plan greatly enhanced his earning potential. The deal clearly had benefits for all of the directors. The announcement of the signing of the agreements constituted a new era in the history of Allied Artists.

In the meantime, Harold had negotiated a deal with Warner Bros., under which Moulin would produce *Moby Dick.* We had estimated that the film would cost approximately $2 million. Warner Bros. agreed to provide an advance of $1 million, in return for which it would get worldwide distribution rights to the film for a period of seven years. The negative would be owned by Moulin Productions, which also agreed to provide any over-the-budget costs of the film out of its own funds, which consisted of its profits from the distribution of the film *Moulin Rouge* and its other investments.

John Huston told me that he had decided he would like to write the screenplay in collaboration with Ray Bradbury, the well-known science-fiction writer, who had not yet done a screenplay. John felt that Ray was a most imaginative person and wanted to work with him. I met Ray Bradbury, and we discussed the project. I told him John wanted him to come to London, where they could collaborate on a script. Bradbury was most enthused about the venture and agreed to go abroad.

The Moulin investors had earlier agreed that instead of dividing up the profits of *Moulin Rouge,* they would continue to operate the company, attempting to parlay its profits by investing them in other ventures. Moulin employed Alfred Crown to become its president and act on its behalf in its ongoing ventures. Crown had been primarily a distribution executive at various film companies, and had been in charge of distribution for Samuel Goldwyn's pictures for a time. He was a well-respected figure in the industry.

The first venture that came along was a proposition brought to Moulin by Aubrey Schenck and Howard W. Koch, who wanted financing for a war film, *Beach Head,* for distribution by United Artists. They had arranged for the services of Tony Curtis to play the lead in the film, and it was to be directed by Stuart Heisler. Their production was to cost approximately $450,000, with a bank loan already arranged. The cash investment required of Moulin was about $200,000. The film was shot in Hawaii, was reasonably successful, and earned profits for Moulin as well as the producers of the picture.

Moulin was also offered the purchase of a group of nine films that had been made many years before by International Pictures, which later merged with Universal. The films were owned by the founders of that company, Leo Spitz and William Goetz, had all been released theatrically, and already had a considerable amount of television exposure. However, we believed there was still a great deal of television life left in this package, which included two Orson Welles films, *Tomorrow Is Forever* and *The Stranger;* two Gary Cooper pictures, *Along Came Jones* and *Casanova Brown;* a film with Olivia de Havilland, *The Dark Mirror;* and a few others. Moulin acquired this package and arranged to put the films back into television distribution and foreign sales under Al Crown's supervision. They remained quite valuable and are still playing to this very day.

We also were presented with another project by independent producer Marcel Hellman, titled *Duel in the Jungle.* This film was to star

Dana Andrews and Jeanne Crain and be directed by George Marshall. Warner Bros. had agreed to distribute it, and we decided to make this investment as well. The film was shot in Africa and London and did reasonably well.

As there was now a stream of revenue coming into Moulin, we felt confident that Moulin Productions could finance its share of the projected cost of *Moby Dick*.

John Huston wanted to shoot in Wales, and we chose an American production manager, Lee Katz, to work with him. We sent Katz to London to meet with John and discuss the plans for the physical production of the picture, while John and Ray Bradbury were finishing the writing of the script. A sailing ship was located and converted into the *Peqoud*. Alan Villiers, a sailing master, took command of it and sailed it to the Welsh city of Fishguard, where the shooting was planned.

There was much discussion about models, and how that was going to be done. At one point, John made an extraordinary suggestion about avoiding models and having a shark, which would be encased in a whale suit, put into the water, and somehow or other controlled on some kind of wires. In that way we might avoid having a phony-looking whale. We finally were able to convince him that wasn't going to be feasible.

We arranged to do the interiors of the film at the Elstree Studios of Associated British Pathé. John chose Richard Basehart to play Ishmael and Friedrich Ledebur to play Queequeg, the much-tattooed Polynesian harpooner. Peck, Basehart, Ledebur, and Orson Welles were the only non-British members of the cast since the Eady Plan required mainly British actors.

Production was started in Fishguard. The weather was the most abysmal in its history. The seas were very angry. When the ship was put out to sea, cast, crew, everybody, became ill. The ship became unmanageable. There was a great deal of damage done at various times, and it needed to be repaired. We were able to maintain little or no schedule. John Huston, in his autobiography, wrote that *Moby Dick* was the most difficult film to shoot of his entire career. It seemed as if everything that could go wrong did.

The costs mounted quickly and finally depleted the funds that Moulin had available. The financing of *Moby Dick* soon resembled the climax of Jules Verne's *Around the World in Eighty Days*, when Phileas

Fogg's ship exhausts its fuel supply and finally has to burn almost the entire ship in its boiler so that it has enough steam to finish its journey. That's pretty much what happened with *Moby Dick*. After we had exhausted all of the funds of Moulin, we began to sell its assets. First we sold the International Pictures negatives. Later, we sold our interest in *Beach Head* and *Duel in the Jungle*. Finally the costs rose to about $4.4 million, and Moulin sold its interests in both *Moulin Rouge* and *Moby Dick* to United Artists, on the basis that when the Warner Bros. distribution license on *Moby Dick* expired after seven years, United Artists would take over the distribution rights and would own the film in perpetuity. It was quite sad that all of the fruits of *Moulin Rouge* were finally consumed, and all of the equity we owned in Moulin Productions was now completely gone.

Moby Dick opened in New York to incredible reviews. The *New York Times* (July 5, 1956) wrote that it was "herewith devoutly recommended as one of the great motion pictures of our times. . . . This is the third time Melville's story has been put upon the screen. There is no need for another, because it cannot be done better, more beautifully or excitingly, again." Unfortunately, the film did not do well commercially. It may have been too poetic, too grim, or perceived as an "art film." Forty-five years have passed, and the investment has still not been recouped, but the film continues to be shown and has attained a cult status that keeps it evergreen.

9

William Wyler and
Friendly Persuasion
and Billy Wilder and
Love in the Afternoon

Willy Wyler was the first director we had signed who became available to Allied Artists, and as his first project he proposed *Friendly Persuasion*, a script that had been written by Michael Wilson, based upon a book by Jessamyn West. The script was owned by Paramount but probably had been considered too gentle and bucolic for production. Willy had great enthusiasm for it. From the beginning, he saw doing it with Gary Cooper, and Cooper immediately agreed to it. We then began the preparation of *Friendly Persuasion*.

Billy Wilder was busily involved in *The Spirit of St. Louis*, a picture he was directing for Warner Bros., and we had to wait for him to become available. John Huston was still involved with *Moby Dick*, and so Allied Artists also faced further delay waiting for him.

During the preparation of *Friendly Persuasion*, a great deal of rewriting was done on Michael Wilson's script by both Robert Wyler, Willy Wyler's brother, and Jessamyn West. Willy Wyler felt strongly that they should all have the screenplay credit for the picture. Ultimately this issue was argued with the Writers Guild, but the guild wouldn't agree with him. Finally he decided that we should exercise the right the guild extended to have no screenplay credit on the picture, rather than giving it to Michael Wilson, a writer who had been an unfriendly witness before the House Un-American Activities Committee.

I worked intimately with Willy Wyler in the making of *Friendly Persuasion,* first because of its importance to Allied Artists, and second because of the opportunity it afforded me to learn picturemaking from a master. I was also enthusiastic about the script. I was very fond of Willy Wyler. He was warm and witty, generous with his time and his knowledge, and, in my opinion, one of the best directors of the twentieth century. I don't think there is anybody who staged scenes better than William Wyler. His composition is extraordinary. There are elements registering with the viewer in the foreground, in the center of his picture, and in the background of his frames. He is a brilliant composer of scenes. The classic ones are Fredric March coming home in *The Best Years of Our Lives,* one of the most moving pieces of film ever shot, and the brilliant scene in *The Little Foxes* with Bette Davis's head on the left-hand side of the frame and behind her, on a sofa, her dying husband, Herbert Marshall, saying, "Regina, give me my pills! Give me my pills!" We remain on her face, as she does nothing to help him. As we continue to see her face in the foreground, we see Herbert Marshall get off of the sofa and drag himself across the floor, struggling to climb up a flight of steps to reach his pills. She is immobile as he finally collapses dead on the steps.

Willy Wyler is also a director of impeccable taste. There's a story Charlton Heston once told me about him. When Heston was doing *Ben-Hur,* there was one scene in the picture that had bothered him ever since he'd read it. He told Willy he wanted to discuss the scene with him, since he wasn't comfortable with it. Willy kept postponing the subject, saying, "We'll talk about it later."

Finally, a few days before they were going to shoot the scene, Heston said to Willy, "I want to discuss that scene we're going to shoot next week!"

Willy said, "Okay, I'll see you over by my chair, and we'll go over it."

Heston walked over to Willy's director's chair, and on it he found the script of the picture, enclosed in a beat-up old leather binder that Wyler had apparently been using for many years. Engraved on the binder, rather faded, was a list of Wyler's pictures. He ran his eyes down the list and saw the titles *Wuthering Heights, Dead End, The Little Foxes, Roman Holiday, The Best Years of Our Lives*—all of them extraordinary films. When Willy came over to him, Heston simply said, "Forget it."

Laurence Olivier once told me he thought Wyler was the best director with whom he had ever worked. Wyler not only had exquisite taste but patience beyond belief. He wouldn't quit on a scene until he felt that it was the best he could possibly get. I saw him make up to fifty and sixty takes of a scene. I saw him reduce actors to tears. I saw actors come up to him and say, "I don't know what to try anymore. What do you want me to do?"

Wyler invariably would say, "When I see it, I'll know it." Nothing could hurry him.

We had a serious problem casting the leading lady in *Friendly Persuasion*. From the very beginning, Willy wanted Katharine Hepburn, and for whatever reason, she declined the role. We discussed every conceivable actress. We talked early on about Dorothy McGuire, but Willy always felt that we could cast someone more interesting. I think he felt that way because nothing ever seemed to him as good as he thought Katharine Hepburn would be. Or he simply held out the hope that she would eventually change her mind. Every so often we would go back and try to get her interested, but to no avail. Finally, we could delay no longer, and we cast Dorothy in the role.

On the first day of shooting, Willy was working on a farm we had constructed on a ranch site in the San Fernando Valley. He phoned me and said, "I think you have to come out here."

I said, "Oh? I'll be out there within the hour."

When I arrived, he said to me, "Walter, we made a terrible mistake. I just don't think Dorothy is going to work out." He was really desolate.

I watched him shoot a scene with her, and I thought it was just fine. I said to him, "The only thing wrong with her is that she's not Katharine Hepburn!"

He said, "No, no, no! I'm past that." He kept suffering with that problem for a while, until finally it just cooled off.

I believe that he made an absolutely marvelous film. However, the amount of *Friendly Persuasion*'s cost overrun presented a huge problem to Allied Artists, which was compelled, during production, to sell

MGM the foreign distribution rights to the picture, in return for which MGM paid a large advance, enabling Allied to keep shooting. So, from the very beginning, financial problems began to erode some of the purposes of the three-director deal. The cost overage on *Friendly Persuasion* also caused a problem in the financing of *Love in the Afternoon,* which became the first of the Billy Wilder pictures.

Friendly Persuasion opened at the Radio City Music Hall, the most prestigious theater in America. Allied Artists hired William Rodgers, who had just left his position as vice president and sales manager of MGM, to supervise the distribution of the picture. Unfortunately, it simply was not as commercially successful as it needed to be, though it got marvelous reviews. It was chosen as one of the five Best Picture nominees of 1956 by the Academy of Motion Picture Arts and Sciences. It won the Palme d'Or at Cannes. But it was a financial disaster for Allied Artists. *Friendly Persuasion* was budgeted at about $2 million, and it had cost over $4 million to produce.

Love in the Afternoon was the first Billy Wilder picture for Allied Artists. Billy had decided that he wanted to adapt a book, *Ariane,* written by Claude Anet, as the basis of a film to star Audrey Hepburn, who had previously starred in his very successful *Sabrina.* Billy next chose Maurice Chevalier to play her father, which was inspired casting, with the great, confident charmer revealing himself as just another vulnerable father.

While we were preparing the picture, Billy Wilder was doing postproduction work on *The Spirit of St. Louis* at the Warner Studio, and I generally went there to lunch with him about once a week.

He was working at Warner Bros. with Iz Diamond, with whom he had chosen to collaborate on the screenplay of *Love in the Afternoon.* Billy had told me that he wanted to work with Diamond and asked me to work out a deal for his services. That marked the beginning of a career-long writing partnership.

One day, after lunch, Billy said to me, "Come back to the office, I want you to listen to a record. It's very old and scratchy, but I think it would be wonderful for the gypsies." He put a record on a portable phonograph, and this was the first time that I heard "Fascination." It was incredible. The song was used in the film and is now always identified with it.

There were great difficulties about casting the leading man in *Love in the Afternoon*. Originally Billy Wilder wanted Cary Grant to play the part, but he declined it. For a while, Billy became interested in the possibility of Yul Brynner playing the male lead. It was his intention, if it turned out to be Brynner, that the role would be modeled on Aly Khan, who at the time was having a romance with Rita Hayworth. In that context, the character would have become a dashing, romantic prince. But that didn't happen. One day Billy said to me, "Gary Cooper."

I inquired, "Gary Cooper?"

"Yes," he said, "It's not Aly Khan, it's Howard Hughes, and Gary Cooper is this American multi-millionaire, Frank Flanagan, who is a heartbreaker and has had affairs with innumerable beautiful women." So it became Gary Cooper. The story is set in Paris, and Billy wanted to shoot it on actual locations.

Because of the financial problems created by *Friendly Persuasion*, Allied Artists had to sell off the foreign distribution rights not only to that film but to *Love in the Afternoon* as well. This deal was made with United Artists, which gave Allied Artists a guarantee against the foreign distribution rights, excluding the United Kingdom, because Associated British already held those rights. This arrangement helped materially in financing the film, and fortunately *Love in the Afternoon* did not go far over its budget of about $2 million.

As fate would have it, *Love in the Afternoon* was a great disappointment in its domestic release. It did much better in foreign release than it did domestically. The general press reaction to *Love in the Afternoon*, however, was very good, although there was exception taken to Cooper as being too old to play opposite the very young Audrey Hepburn. However, the film does have that memorable scene at the railroad station, when the train pulls out and Cooper swoops up Audrey Hepburn in his arms in a marvelous romantic conclusion to the picture. I've often thought the film would have done better had it been in color. But Billy Wilder insisted on using black-and-white in his films, probably longer than audiences liked.

John Huston, by then, had decided on a subject for his next project, and we acquired for him the rights to a short story by Rudyard Kipling, "The Man Who Would Be King." He chose Aeneas MacKenzie, who had worked with him years earlier at Warners, as his writer. It was John's intention to cast the film with Clark Gable and Humphrey Bogart.

MacKenzie wrote a script, but John wasn't pleased with it. I told him I thought he should write it himself. He said he would, but he simply didn't have the time. Besides, he had by then changed his mind and decided that he wanted to do another of Herman Melville's books, *Typee*, and he would do "The Man Who Would Be King" later. We employed Nigel Balchin to write the screenplay of *Typee*, while John was off shooting *Heaven Knows, Mr. Allison* in Mexico.

By this time, we had done a location reconnaissance for *Typee* in the South Pacific. John Huston now took key crew, as well as a production manager, to have a look for himself. The budget, prepared after the location trip, was very high. With all the financial difficulties at Allied Artists as a result of the disappointing grosses on *Friendly Persuasion* and *Love in the Afternoon*, there was very little chance that Allied would proceed with *Typee*.

10

On Our Own

My brother Harold and I now had to accept the fact that our attempt to develop a major film company at Allied Artists wasn't going to succeed. It simply was too underfinanced. We began to look for alternatives. Steve Broidy, a perpetual optimist, felt that the company could return to exploitation pictures for a while and, after it had recovered some financial strength, could try again at a later date to attempt to achieve major studio status. I felt that the company would never again have the opportunity that it had with those three great directors. And so, unfortunately, Allied Artists soon arranged for the termination of the directors' contracts, and the noble experiment came to an end.

All of this posed a serious problem for my brothers and me. Harold and I were both eager to continue to produce A-quality pictures, and Allied Artists was obviously now going in the opposite direction. We therefore had to look elsewhere. We began to talk among ourselves about what other options were open to us.

Among the last Allied Artists films I was involved with were Walter Wanger and Don Siegel's *Invasion of the Body Snatchers*, *Crime in the Streets* with John Cassavetes, which Don also directed, and *Dino*, which, like *Crime in the Streets*, had been a television show, and which we produced starring Brian Keith and Sal Mineo, who had also been in the original television production. More commercially successful than any of those films was *The Phenix City Story*, which Phil Karlson directed.

John McIntire and Richard Kiley starred in the film, and Karlson shot the picture entirely on location as an exposé of an actual sin city in Alabama. He made an excellent movie that was also very successful.

Harold and I had carried the major part of the burden of producing the Wyler and Wilder films, on both the business and creative sides. We didn't want to return to producing small pictures again. Besides, we didn't have a great deal of confidence that there was still much of a market for those pictures. I was then thirty-six years old, married, with two children, Anne and Andrew, and Pat was pregnant with our third child, Lawrence, whom we call Larry. I felt that I could not afford to delay any longer. Harold, now fifty years old, had also expanded his horizons and, like me, had made a great many friends and valuable connections in the Hollywood community. He too wanted to take advantage of those new connections and move forward.

Although it was heart-wrenching, since I had been with Allied Artists for twelve years, starting in a very minor position and rising to be in charge of production, I didn't believe that there was a place any longer for the Allied Artists product of ten years before. And so Harold, Marvin, and I decided that we would take advantage of the many friends and successes we had by now enjoyed and investigate doing a deal with a major company that would permit us to produce a program of films of consequence, allowing us to move into the new era that we were sure the motion-picture industry was now entering.

The "studio system" implied the production of a large program of films every year for theaters that were owned by the production companies, employing contract producers, writers, and directors. Those pictures were cast with contract stars, featured players, and young aspirants who were being brought along by the studios, hopefully to be developed, like baseball players, into the stars of the future. That system, which had worked so well for so long, was coming to an end. With the tremendous competition from television, and after the divestiture of their theater chains, the major studios, in an effort to cut their overheads, gave up their contract players and their commitments to producers, directors, and writers. They became primarily financiers of films rather than producers.

The leader in the transformation of the industry was the new management of United Artists. This company had been formed in 1919 by a partnership of Mary Pickford, Douglas Fairbanks, Charles Chaplin, and D. W. Griffith. It was organized to be a distributor of motion pictures, primarily to be financed and produced by the owner-partners. They also hoped to include other financier-producers, and between the 1920s and the 1940s, they succeeded in attracting a large number of important independent producers, such as Samuel Goldwyn, Alexander Korda, Walter Wanger, and David O. Selznick, among others. Some of these producers, as part of their deals, also became partners for a time in the parent company. United Artists served as a distribution channel and made a gross percentage charge for its services. The rest of the proceeds of the film flowed to the producer-financier, and ultimately the negative returned to him.

However, as time went on, it became increasingly difficult for United Artists to acquire distribution rights to pictures that had been financed by individuals. The company was losing a lot of money, and Mary Pickford and Charles Chaplin were finally the sole remaining owner-partners. By then they were making practically no pictures of their own, and United Artists was completely dependent on outside sources of product. The partners were generally at swords' points with one another, and operation of the company was in the hands of professional managers, which also exacerbated the dissension between the two owners.

And so, Pickford and Chaplin, having very little product to distribute and a very considerable overhead in the operation of a worldwide distribution company, welcomed the proposal of Arthur Krim, Bob Benjamin, Arnold Picker, Bill Heineman, and Max Youngstein to take over the management and financing of the company.

Arthur Krim and Bob Benjamin were attorneys who had become friends when they both joined the New York entertainment law firm of Phillips and Nizer, headed by the much-esteemed Louis Phillips and Louis Nizer. Later the firm name was changed to Phillips, Nizer, Benjamin, Krim & Ballon. However, both Arthur Krim and Bob Benjamin soon decided that they wanted to move from practicing law to operating a film company.

They had made their first foray into motion-picture production some years earlier. Bob Benjamin had represented the British entertainment company J. Arthur Rank Organisation in America, and he had also represented Chesapeake Industries, which owned Hollywood's Pathé Laboratory, which in turn controlled a small B-picture distributing company, rather similar to Monogram, called Producers Releasing Corporation, generally shortened to PRC. PRC produced second features and owned a small studio in Hollywood. Krim and Benjamin evolved a scheme to take these assets and form a new company, to be called Eagle Lion, the Eagle for the American interests and the Lion for the British. Rank agreed to invest in the company, so that he could assure himself American distribution for all the British films that he wanted to export to America. Rank's company often could not secure distribution in America for some of his productions, and now he would have a confirmed channel of his own, over which he would have a large measure of control.

A wealthy financier of the time, Robert R. Young, who controlled the Chesapeake and Ohio Railroad as well as Pathé Industries, also made an investment in the new company. PRC's studio was on Santa Monica Boulevard, not too far from the Samuel Goldwyn Studio, and it too was now renamed Eagle Lion. A longtime producer at Warner Bros., Bryan Foy, was put in charge of production for Eagle Lion, which soon embarked on a program to upgrade the product, much as we were trying to do with Allied Artists and for the same reasons. This entire operation was under the management of Arthur Krim and Bob Benjamin.

After four or five years of operation, its program was not successful and Eagle Lion was dissolved. Arthur Krim and Bob Benjamin returned to their law firm in New York, but they hadn't given up their dreams. Their next attempt to get back into the production business came in 1951, when they made their offer to Chaplin and Pickford to acquire an interest, with them, in United Artists, which at the time was losing about $100,000 per week. The attorneys agreed to underwrite the overhead of United Artists, to take over its management, and to provide a flow of product to the company, in return for an understanding that if they had a profitable year within the first three years of their operation, Chaplin and Pickford would, at no cost, give 50 percent ownership of the company to Krim, Benjamin, and their group.

The latter, in the meantime, arranged a line of credit for United Artists with a Chicago finance company, Walter Heller and Company. The Heller company loaned UA $3 million, which was the main source of funding for United Artists in the early days of Krim and Benjamin's management of the company. They then sought bank financing to go behind the line of credit that they had arranged with Heller. The management group, all of whom had been involved in Eagle Lion, now assumed similar positions at United Artists. Bill Heineman was in charge of domestic sales, Arnold Picker controlled foreign sales, Max Youngstein supervised production and publicity, and Arthur and Bob were the joint chief executives of the company.

Their initial problem was to secure product for their new company, whose distribution pipeline was all but empty. They arranged financing for a number of producers shortly after they took over management. One of the first of their projects was *High Noon*, from Stanley Kramer, which was followed by Sam Spiegel and John Huston's *The African Queen*. Shortly after they took over the company, Harold and I offered them *Moulin Rouge*. With the limited amount of investment that film required, and their great need for product for their pipeline, it's easy to see why they were so eager to make a deal with us. It was good for them, and even better for us. With fresh money, they began to stimulate production, and they made a large number of co-production deals, where they would put up limited amounts of cash and secure Western Hemisphere distribution for the pictures. They obtained *The African Queen* on that basis. And they made a reverse deal with Allied Artists on *Love in the Afternoon*, where they put up a guaranteed advance and secured the foreign distribution rights.

At the end of the first year of their management, UA earned a profit of $313,000, thereby meeting the conditions of their arrangement with Chaplin and Pickford, and they secured 50 percent ownership of the company. In 1955 they acquired Charlie Chaplin's remaining 25 percent of the company for $1.1 million. In 1956 Mary Pickford sold her remaining shares to them for $3.3 million. In 1957 the company offered $17 million in stocks and debentures for sale to the public.

Early in 1957, Harold and I went to see Arthur Krim again and discussed with him and Bob Blumofe, who was in charge of production for UA on the West Coast, the idea of our making an independent deal to supply them with a program of pictures, which they would finance. We asked them to guarantee a certain amount of salary for Harold, Marvin, and myself for our services. They would also have to agree to underwrite our overhead, and we established a target of producing four films per year for them. The films would be subject to their approval of story, leading actors, directors, and budgets. The term of the original deal was for three years.

The decision to leave Monogram and Allied Artists, and more particularly Steve Broidy, after twelve years and innumerable shared experiences, was very difficult. Harold and I explained at great length to Steve the reasons for our action. Steve had given me great opportunities, and it was like cutting an umbilical cord. He acknowledged all our concerns. We asked him to join us, but he owned a great deal of stock in Allied Artists, which constituted the major portion of his estate, and he felt he had to remain with the company until he could get it back on its feet and his stock recovered its value. By this time, Harold and I also owned some Allied Artists stock, as well as holding ten thousand stock options each, which we never exercised because the price of the stock had never gone up sufficiently to justify our exercising them. In any event, our stakes in the company did not represent substantial investments.

For the headquarters of our new company, we decided to lease space at the Samuel Goldwyn Studio, located at Santa Monica Boulevard and Formosa Avenue in West Hollywood. It was, at that time, utilized by Goldwyn for his own productions, and he leased space to other producers. We decided to name our enterprise The Mirisch Company, with the three of us each owning 25 percent of the company's stock. We agreed to give the remaining 25 percent of the stock to our eldest brother, Irving, who was still living in Milwaukee and running the Theaters Candy Company. Harold, Marvin, and I agreed to draw equal salaries in order to reduce the possibilities of friction among us. Joining us in our new company were our trusted Monogram–Allied Artists associates Al Wood, production manager; Ray Krutzman of legal and business affairs; Dick Heermance; Harold' assistant Sylvia Kantor; and my indispensable assistant, Jessie Ponitz, who had joined me from the Screen Prouducers Guild and remained with me for the next thirty-two years.

As quickly as we could, we tried to take advantage of our relationships in creating the elements of a production program for our new company. My first call was to my friend Joel McCrea. When I told him what we were going to do, he was instantly supportive and said, "What do you want me to do?"

"Make a picture for us," I replied. Very fittingly, the first film that we produced for United Artists starred Joel.

Simultaneously, Harold and I contacted Billy Wilder, with whom we also had a good relationship. This extraordinarily talented man was at the height of his career, but when we told our plans to him, he said he would like to join us and would do a film for us as soon as he was available. He was then directing *Witness for the Prosecution*, but we soon began discussing possible vehicles with him.

We had a similar conversation with Willy Wyler, but he was then directing *The Big Country* and had agreed to do *Ben-Hur* after that. These films tied him up for a number of years. Eventually he produced and directed only one picture for The Mirisch Company, *The Children's Hour*, in 1960, although we developed two other properties with him. Willy Wyler was notorious for that. He prepared many pictures and then decided at the last moment that he didn't want to do them. Among such films were *How Green Was My Valley*, *Patton*, and *The Sound of Music*.

We also tried to get a commitment from John Huston, but we weren't able to break into his long commitment schedule. Unfortunately it took ten years, until 1967, before we finally did make a picture, *Sinful Davy*, with John.

On the other hand, starting with *Some Like It Hot*, Billy Wilder remained with us and made films for no other company for seventeen years. During that time, he made eight consecutive films for the Mirisch companies.

Producing films is a chancy business. To produce a really fine film requires the confluence of a large number of elements, all combined in the exactly correct proportions. It's very difficult, and that's why it happens so infrequently. It takes great attention to detail, the right instincts, the right combination of talents, and the heavens deciding to smile down on the enterprise. Timing is often critical. Where is the country's or the world's interest at a particular time? What is the audience looking for? Asking them won't help, because they themselves will tell you they don't know what they're looking for. They don't know what it is until they've seen it. All the elements must come together at exactly the right time.

So, to say one embarks with great certainty on such an endeavor is an exaggeration. We did have confidence in ourselves. We felt that given our experience, taste, and expertise, we could come up with a good program of films, movies that we could be proud of. But you can't tell if the success is going to be the first film, the second, the third, or the fifth. Of course, that's really what misfired at Allied Artists. The hit didn't turn up early enough. It's intriguing to contemplate what the effect of *Some Like It Hot* would have been on Allied Artists, if Billy had made that, instead of *Love in the Afternoon*.

The first two films we produced for United Artists, *Fort Massacre* and *Man of the West,* were both Westerns. Due to the oversaturation of television Westerns in the 1950s and 1960s, I felt strongly that we had to do more adult subjects for the genre. *Fort Massacre,* written by Martin Goldsmith, was such a Western.

For the first time in his career, Joel McCrea played a largely unsympathetic character. He was challenged by the role, but casting against type may have hurt the picture. Or perhaps I was just wrong, and we never had a chance to attract that more adult audience that I was looking for, while simply antagonizing the normal clientele of action Westerns. *Fort Massacre* wasn't an expensive film, costing about $400,000, nor was it terribly successful. But it accomplished something for us that we were anxious to do at the time, which was to put our credit, "The Mirisch Company Presents," on the screen as soon as possible. Joe Newman, who had directed some very good pictures for me at Allied Artists, directed. The response from the trade papers was most gratifying. *The Hollywood Reporter* (April 25, 1958) wrote, "In making *Fort Massacre,* Walter Mirisch brings a mature and accurately researched Western to the screen. For once the Apaches are dressed like Apaches, and the soldiers seem well grounded in cavalry regulations. Martin Goldsmith's script, while having a satisfactory amount of action, takes time to establish personal motives for its characters and to reveal them as complex human beings."

Variety (April 25, 1958) called *Fort Massacre* "an offbeat Western that follows its unusual and honest story to a relentless conclusion." I was pleased, because this was just what I had set out to do.

The Gunfight at Dodge City was the last feature film that I produced with Joel McCrea. By the late 1950s, Joel was approaching sixty years of age, and it was becoming more difficult to find suitable material for him. We talked about developing a subject that might be more commercial than our attempt to break his mold and do a psychological Western, as we had done in *Fort Massacre*. I chose to try to recapture the glory and the success of *Wichita* by suggesting that we do a story based on Bat Masterson, a well-known historical character and famous Western marshal. The picture was originally called *The Bat Masterson Story*, and Martin Goldsmith wrote the original script, although Dan Ullman came in later and also worked on it.

We surrounded Joel with a very good cast, including Julie Adams, John McIntire, and Nancy Gates. To direct, I again selected Joe Newman, for whom I had a great deal of respect, and I hoped that with a more commercially popular subject Joel could make a film that would be successful for us and also career enhancing for him. In an attempt to recapture the magic of *Gunfight at the O.K. Corral*, we retitled the picture *The Gunfight at Dodge City*.

Unfortunately, it did not become another *Wichita*. It wasn't as good a picture, but it did reasonably good business as a supporting feature, and as a first feature in the action markets. It also signified the end of the B Western pictures for me.

After completing *The Gunfight at Dodge City*, I felt that perhaps Joel McCrea, who was now coming to the end of his career as a leading man in theatrical Western films, might refresh his career with a television series. I talked with him about the possibility of our doing a half-hour Western television show, to star himself and his son, Jody. Because of the success of our earlier film, *Wichita*, I suggested a show revolving around a marshal in the city of Wichita and his deputy, rather in the same vein as *Gunsmoke*. Joel said the show sounded like a lot of work to him, and he wasn't too enthusiastic about the idea. But he did want to help Jody get a start in his acting career, and he agreed that *Wichita Town* could offer him an excellent opportunity. Jody was a young man, in his early twenties at that time, tall, handsome, and well built, and it certainly seemed possible that he could have a promising career. We agreed that Jody, acting in the role of his deputy, would be the principal lead in a reasonable number of the shows, although Joel would appear in all of them.

Joel was still represented by the William Morris Agency, and it assumed the sales representation of the show. I told Joel that I thought we should make an attempt to sell our show to a network just on the strength of his name and our concept, without making a pilot film, which is generally done, to serve as a sample of what subsequent shows will be like. William Morris determined that NBC was the best potential customer for *Wichita Town,* and I met the head of its sales department, Wally Jordan, in a bungalow of the Beverly Hills Hotel with Robert Kintner, then the president of NBC. I explained our concept and managed to sell him a program of twenty-six half-hour shows.

Being heavily involved in preparing features, I planned to create an organization that would absorb as much of the onus of putting the television show on the air as I could. To undertake the physical production, William Morris proposed that we make an arrangement with a company, Four Star, which it also represented, and which owned its own studio and had an organization geared to the making of television shows. I quickly embraced the idea of doing such a deal.

However, I did create an organization that would be in charge of the creative side of our television production, since I wanted to find new opportunities and a home for the people who had worked with me for a long time, and on whom I knew I could rely. Dick Heermance assumed charge of the whole operation. Dan Ullman wrote some scripts, with Richard Alan Simmons as story editor. They were based on the Four Star lot, which was formerly the Republic Studio and is now the CBS Studio in Studio City.

Our *Wichita Town* shows were budgeted at $35,000 to $40,000 apiece, and they were photographed in black-and-white. I read all the material, gave notes, ran dailies and first cuts, but principally left production to our creative team. I felt that we were very seriously hurt by the Thursday night, 10:30 p.m. time period that had been assigned us by NBC. I considered that was too late at night to attract the young audiences who would enjoy our show.

I thought it could be very valuable for The Mirisch Company to create a successful television arm. The television production industry was growing and becoming increasingly important. *Wichita Town* had a single sponsor for its broadcasts, Proctor and Gamble. Under the then-prevalent single-sponsor system, the representative of the sponsor felt that he had a right to impose his ideas on the show, and the producer received notes from the sponsor's representative and the sponsor's advertising agency. Today, when sponsors only buy spots on a show, they don't have input into its subject matter, although the networks do.

Unfortunately, *Wichita Town* was not successful in terms of ratings, despite the fact that we made some very good shows. The first segment was an episode titled "The Night the Cowboys Roared," in which James Coburn played the heavy. This was the first time I'd met Jim, and he was so good in the show that I remembered him later when we were casting *The Magnificent Seven*. We delivered the twenty-six half-hour shows, but we didn't receive a pickup for the following season. Joel was not too unhappy about that, because I think he really wanted to retire and continue on in the ranching business. He was disappointed that Jody's career wasn't advanced by the show, but Jody simply hadn't caught the interest of our audience, and subsequently he too left the movie business.

In an effort to continue our television operation, I came up with an idea for another show, which would be a sitcom. Peter Lind Hayes and Mary Healy were attractive specialty entertainers, and I proposed the idea of casting the two of them as a married couple who had been successful in show business and had determined that, to bring up their family, they needed to get away from the bright lights of Broadway and move to the country. We called the show *Peter Loves Mary*. This was also done as a co-production with Four Star and sold to NBC, but that show also ran for only one year, since it didn't generate adequate ratings for renewal.

I had still another idea for a show called *The Iron Horsemen*, about a railroad detective. Again looking for a partner who could service the production side of the project, I discussed doing it with a well-known theatrical producer and later television producer, Louis Edelman. At that time, Lou was producing *The Adventures of Jim Bowie*, a successful television. NBC agreed to finance a pilot for *The Iron Horsemen*, which was written by Leslie Stevens and starred Guy Williams. It was a good pilot, but it was not ordered by the network.

After *Wichita Town* and *Peter Loves Mary* faltered, and *The Iron Horsemen* failed to be ordered for a series, I stopped making efforts in television for a few years and concentrated on the demands of fulfilling our contracts with United Artists.

I continued to pursue our relationship with Gary Cooper, hoping to do a Western with him. Clearly he was one of the great Western stars of all time, and I believed there was a large audience who would appreciate seeing him in that genre again. I submitted a book to him, *The Border Jumpers* by Will C. Brown, which was a mature subject about an ex-outlaw who has been trying to live a decent life until he is finally thrust back into his criminal past.

I secured the services of someone who would seem to be a most unlikely writer to do the screenplay of *The Border Jumpers,* the title of which was later changed to *Man of the West.* Reginald Rose had written many distinguished television shows during the *Playhouse 90* television era, including *Twelve Angry Men* for both television and the big screen. I had made a film at Allied Artists based on one of his television shows, *Crime in the Streets,* which Don Siegel had directed. Reggie agreed to do *The Border Jumpers,* and he gave us a challenging script about a complex ex-outlaw thrown back into the world he had fought so hard to escape.

Decades later, the same premise was used by Clint Eastwood in *Unforgiven,* which won the Best Picture Academy Award in 1995. In talking with Clint Eastwood in 1998, I remarked that his film reminded me of *Man of the West.* He told me that he himself had been a great fan of Gary Cooper's and had narrated a documentary about him. He added that he had seen and admired *Man of the West.* I derived a great deal of pleasure out of that, forty years after the release of our film.

Anthony Mann, an outstanding director of Western films, agreed to direct *Man of the West,* and it became our second UA release. As with *Fort Massacre, Man of the West* was an attempt to create a so-called adult Western. Many of us who had made large numbers of Westerns had realized that the old story plots and devices had all been used and reused in as many ways as possible. I felt that it was important to try and do an honest, realistic treatment of a Western story, which would be distinct from the old-fashioned white-hat, black-hat Western and the run-of-the-mill fare that was shown on television.

Man of the West has been called too violent and sadistic, but there is, I believe, a real honesty in it. Anthony Mann felt as I did about it. When I gave him the script, he was enthusiastic about doing it, particularly since he had never worked with Gary Cooper before. He really pushed the realistic and psychological elements as far as he could. Perhaps too far. Perhaps our attempt to do "a different Western" either shocked, or failed to interest, the wider audience we were looking for. At the same time, we may have antagonized the more simplistic Western fan who wanted to see more action and less complexity of character. *Fort Massacre* and *Man of the West* were attempts on my part—because I developed both these films apart from directors, and the scripts were given to the directors before hiring them—to create more three-dimensional people, to see the warts on the character of the hero, and to make more sophisticated films. Neither picture succeeded commercially, although I think they are both good and interesting films. *Man of the West,* particularly, has been appreciated by cultists who continue to see and discuss it.

Viewing the film recently brought back many memories of its production. I recalled one scene we were shooting on a Western street in Mojave, the site of the deserted town where Cooper comes to reconnoiter a proposed bank robbery. Coop and Royal Dano ride down the street of what is obviously a ghost town, which the mad Lee J. Cobb had supposed would provide a huge cache of money for the bank robbers to steal, and they see not a soul there. That particular day, I saw Coop was very upset. When I asked him what the trouble was, he told me his back pain was just excruciating. Many years earlier, he had been in an automobile accident and broken his hip, and it began to trouble him seriously again in his later years. He told me that the pain of riding his horse down that street was almost unendurable. I could see it in his face. I suggested to him that he let his double, Slim Talbot, who had been with him for thirty years and was an excellent double for him, do the ride in a long shot. But he wouldn't hear of it. He said, "No, I have to do it. You have to be close on me." And he did do the ride down that street himself.

I had forgotten about it until I saw the film recently and saw the pain on his face again, every time the horse posted. I thought he was marvelously brave about it and wonderfully professional about accepting what had to be done. It's just a ride down a Western street, but he endured great pain and suffering to get the shot right. I have the utmost of respect for him.

While we were shooting another scene in *Man of the West*, I told Coop that Joel McCrea's ranch was not terribly far from where we were shooting and Joel had invited me to lunch. I asked Coop if he wanted to come along, and he said yes. He and I went to lunch with Joel McCrea and Frances Dee at their ranch house. I had an absolutely marvelous time, and they all did too, talking about their early days at Paramount. Joel made his usual observation that his whole career had been based on playing the roles that Coop had turned down. Coop, of course, generously said that really wasn't so. But it was good-natured, and both of these great film figures—who had started in silent pictures and were now in the twilight of their careers—enjoyed reminiscing. It was a wonderful lunch, and I shall always remember it.

🐟

Audie Murphy had made a long series of successful Western pictures for Universal-International, and *Cast a Long Shadow* was made to fit into the mold of those films. It was intended to be a program picture, not terribly expensive, and was shot in black-and-white. The female lead was played by Terry Moore. It was directed by Tom Carr, who had worked with me at Allied Artists and had directed *The Tall Stranger* with Joel McCrea. The screenplay was by Martin Goldsmith, who had written *Fort Massacre*, and John McGreevey did a rewrite on Goldsmith's original script.

We had serious budget constraints on the picture, and I arranged to shoot the interiors at the Allied Artists Studio, where I was able to make a less expensive rental deal than the one we worked under at the Goldwyn Studio. Richard Heermance edited *Cast a Long Shadow*, as he had *Man of the West*. He had moved with us from Allied Artists when we set up offices at the Goldwyn Studio for The Mirisch Company.

My brother Harold had acquired a house in Palm Springs by this time and discovered his next-door neighbor was Alan Ladd. Pat and I and Harold and Lottie spent as much time as we could down at this weekend house in the desert, and we came to know Alan and Sue Ladd quite well. First jokingly, and later seriously, we began to talk about doing a film together. I finally suggested a book in which I was interested to Alan and Sue, who was very influential in choosing the films in which Alan would appear. The book was *The Man in the Net* by Patrick Quentin, the story of a man who becomes implicated in a murder plot and is forced to flee in order to try and prove his innocence. He falls in with a group of children, all of whom become helpful in hiding him and ultimately in helping him to exonerate himself.

I gave the novel to Reginald Rose, and he wrote the script. Carolyn Jones was selected to play the leading lady. Alan and Sue Ladd suggested their friend Michael Curtiz direct. Curtiz had enjoyed a long and successful career at Warner Bros. He had been brought to America from Hungary, back in the silent era, by Warners and remained with the studio for over thirty years, directing Westerns, comedies, gangster pictures, and musicals and became the studio's director of choice. Along the way, he had made some of the most popular Warner Bros. pictures of that period, including Errol Flynn's *The Adventures of Robin Hood, Yankee Doodle Dandy, Mildred Pierce,* and *Casablanca.* Curtiz was a colorful man. He had a continental accent, strong features, and an imperious manner; he spoke fractured English and could have passed for a middle-European nobleman. He never attained the star status of some of the other great directors of that period, such as De Mille, Hitchcock, Ford, Huston, Wyler, Wilder, and Lean. When he directed *Man in the Net,* he was hardly at the height of his career and, frankly, was not very inspired.

Nor was this a good time in Alan Ladd's life. Alan, who drank a great deal, drank even more while we were shooting the picture. It certainly affected his performance. I would importune Mike Curtiz, "You've just got to invigorate Alan, you must get him to show some energy." But Alan Ladd was not the most emotional of actors, even under the best of circumstances, and being under the influence of alcohol certainly didn't help.

It was a very plodding, difficult shoot, on location near Worcester, Massachusetts. I developed hepatitis while on location and became very ill. We were also beset by other problems; on a Saturday night, one of the members of our crew got drunk in a bar and was accused of killing another drinker in a brawl.

Reviews were poor. *Variety* (April 22, 1959) wrote, "Ladd elects to play his role so stoically that he is likely to leave even his diehard fans feeling balked." The *Hollywood Reporter* on the same date commented, "Ladd, delivering an uninspired and pedestrian performance, fails completely to bind the two halves of the story together into a complete dramatic whole."

≈

Lana Turner was a client of Paul Kohner at the time, and when we discussed our UA plans with Paul, he proposed a project for Lana, *The Blonde on the Boulevard,* which never materialized. Later on we did make a picture with Lana Turner, *By Love Possessed.*

Harold and I also talked about projects with Doris Day, whose name was in our initial announcement. We never did make a picture with Doris, although we developed *Roar Like a Dove* for her.

We talked to Tony Curtis about doing a film with us, since we had a relationship with Tony going back to the time when Moulin had financed *Beach Head,* in which he had starred. Later, of course, Tony would be Billy Wilder's choice for *Some Like It Hot.*

11

Billy Wilder and
Some Like It Hot

illy Wilder told us that he was interested in doing a film about an all-girl orchestra, the premise of which had been utilized many years before in a German film, *Fanfare der Lieben*, or *Fanfares of Love*. He proposed that we acquire the rights to *Fanfare*. It became a real test for the attorneys to find the then-owners of the film and to acquire the right to remake it. In his screenplay, Billy used little material from the original film, except the idea of two men who disguise themselves as women so they can get jobs in an all-girl band. Nearly everything else was original. Billy wanted to work on the script with I. A. L. Diamond, with whom he had worked for the first time on *Love in the Afternoon*, so we made a deal for Iz to collaborate with Billy on what was later titled *Some Like It Hot*.

Billy Wilder had made *The Seven Year Itch* with Marilyn Monroe in 1955, and now he conceived the brilliant idea of creating for her the role of Sugar Cane, a vocalist in an all-girl band, in *Some Like It Hot*. *Fanfare der Lieben* had now became the story of two Chicago musicians during the Depression who happen to witness the St. Valentine's Day massacre. Being pursued by the perpetrators, whom they can identify, they decide to disguise themselves so that the pursuing gangsters can't find them. They dress themselves as women and get jobs in an all-girl band that has been contracted to play at a Florida luxury hotel. It was Billy's idea to cast Tony Curtis and Jack Lemmon as the musicians.

He created a satire of movie gangsterdom and sought to populate it with stereotypical gangsters. He chose George Raft to play Spats Columbo, the heavy, and Pat O'Brien to play the pursuing cop. From the very beginning he wanted Edward G. Robinson to play Little Napoleon, who was a satirized Little Caesar. We kept hoping that Robinson would play the role. To tempt him, Billy cast Edward G. Robinson's son in the picture, as one of the thugs, but Robinson wouldn't be drawn into it, despite all of our pressure. Finally Billy cast Nehemiah Persoff to play Little Napoleon. I've always regretted that Little Caesar didn't play Little Bonaparte.

There is no question that Billy wrote the role of Sugar for Marilyn Monroe, and certainly no one else could have played the part. Fortunately for us, no one else did. Marilyn was married to Arthur Miller at the time, and they were living in New York. They came to Southern California when we started production in September 1958 at the Del Coronado Hotel in San Diego, which stood in for a luxurious Florida hotel of the 1920s. The difficulties of working with Marilyn Monroe have been told and retold. Certainly this was a troubled period in her life. For one thing, she suffered a miscarriage while we were shooting. For another, she had been seeing a psychiatrist in New York, on whom she had become quite dependent, and she would ask to go to New York on weekends so she could visit her doctor. The weekends sometimes became protracted, and we had to keep adjusting our schedules to work around her absences. She had great difficulty remembering her lines, and we would sometimes get up to forty or fifty takes of a scene.

Billy showed remarkable patience through it all, and I don't think he ever compromised. He didn't try to work around her dialogue readings, but he just stuck with her until she finally got it right. Paula Strasberg, Lee's wife, was her drama coach, and Marilyn insisted on having Paula on the set with her while she was working. After each reading she would look over at Paula and await her approval. Billy showed the most incredible tolerance of this process. Jack and Tony told me that the multiple takes were driving them around the bend. Jack once said to me, "My worst nightmare is that we're going to be on the fiftieth take, and Marilyn is finally going to get it right, and I'm gonna screw it up."

Billy Wilder made his oft-quoted remark that if we no longer could tolerate what Marilyn was putting us all through, he had this sweet aunt in Vienna. Her name was Lena. "She's the most wonderful lady in the world. She'll be here every day on time, she'll work all night long if we ask it of her. We'll have no trouble whatsoever with her, but who wants to see her in a movie?" His patience was certainly rewarded.

Finally the film was finished, and like all of Billy's films, which are shot with a minimum amount of coverage, you see the first cut shortly after the production is finished. We weren't disappointed. We knew we had something really wonderful.

At one point, Billy wanted to call the film *Not Tonight, Josephine,* but eventually he decided upon *Some Like It Hot.* That title had been used on a 1939 Bob Hope picture, and we had to get permission to use it from Universal, which now owned the rights. We rather sweated out the process of getting it cleared and getting the right to use it.

For some reason, the picture opened rather slowly in March 1959. It even got some poor reviews! The notice in the *Los Angeles Times* was headed "SOME LIKE IT HOT Not So." Others were absolutely glowing, and the picture soon caught on and was hugely successful.

It was the first giant hit for The Mirisch Company, and it helped propel us into the next group of our pictures on an entirely different level. The film elevated our standing in the industry, and its value to us as producers was incalculable.

Some Like It Hot was photographed in black-and-white because Billy felt that it should be done in the medium of its 1920s period. Second, and I think even more important, was the fact that the makeup and the costumes of the two men are in one way or another more acceptable in black-and-white than they would be in more realistic color. Black-and-white somehow helps create the illusion that the other characters are seriously accepting the two men as girls. If one wanted to make *Some Like It Hot* today, I don't think it could be done any better. Neither the style, nor the casting, nor the writing or direction could be improved upon. It was nominated for six Academy Awards and surprisingly won only one, for costume design.

After the film had opened, a correspondent for the *New York Times* interviewed Billy, and he finally unburdened himself about Marilyn Monroe's behavior. After the article appeared, he called me one day and said, "You have to come over here." I walked to his office, and he showed me a telegram he'd just received from Arthur Miller, who had read the interview in the *Times* and was outraged at Billy's insensitivity to Marilyn and his lack of appreciation of her great contribution to his picture. Billy replied to Miller's wire with an appropriately witty communication. Miller replied to that, and it became a marvelous exchange of correspondence that is quoted in *The Bright Side of Billy Wilder, Primarily,* by Tom Wood, the unit publicity person on *Some Like It Hot.*

Some Like It Hot became a milestone picture, not only in the history of The Mirisch Company but also in the history of United Artists. It was budgeted at a little over $2 million dollars and eventually cost more than $3 million. However, when we looked at the film, we were immensely enthused and genuinely felt that this was a truly wonderful comedy. I don't know that I would have believed then that it would stand the test of a half century and make motion picture history, but I sure thought it was good.

Later I produced another television pilot with NBC, which was based on *Some Like It Hot* and written by Herb Baker. In its first scene, Jack Lemmon and Tony Curtis are being chased by gangsters still trying to kill them, when Tony says to Jack, "You know, there's only one way for us to get these guys off our backs."

Jack asks, "What is that?"

We cut from that to a scene in a hospital, on two adjoining beds with two figures, whose faces were all swathed in bandages. When the bandages came off, they revealed the two actors (Vic Damone and Dick Patterson) who play the leads in the television show. Our plot paralleled the movie, and Jack and Tony were very generous to do that first scene for us. The Marilyn Monroe role was played by Tina Louise. It was funny, but this pilot failed to make the airwaves.

12

John Ford and
The Horse Soldiers

Generally I function as a producer in the traditional style of David Selznick, Samuel Goldwyn, and Hal Wallis, producers who came out of an earlier period, when the producer found the material, arranged to acquire it, or else initiated the story himself. Many films I have produced were based on story ideas of my own or properties that I acquired or that I developed. I employed writers, with whom I worked on the screenplays, and then selected a director, cast the film with him, and supervised the production of the film, while working with the director in shaping the picture as it was being filmed. In post-production, I would help guide the film through to its release, along with the director.

I would often sit at the back of a soundstage watching the director at work. If it were obvious that the director was unhappy with my presence, I would leave. If I had a suggestion or a criticism to make, I would always take the director to one side and never discuss anything with him in front of the cast or crew. I was almost always present with the director during the projection of the rushes.

I did not initiate *The Horse Soldiers*, which was brought to us as a development project by well-known screenwriter Martin Rackin. The book, written by Harold Sinclair, was a Civil War action story centering on a conflict between two strong men, one the commanding officer of a

Union force ordered to make a raid in Southern territory and the other a physician who is assigned to his unit. Marty Rackin wanted to collaborate on the screenplay with John Lee Mahin, a well-known writer who had many outstanding credits. Marty and John also wanted to produce the picture. They told me that they had discussed the project with John Ford and that he was interested in directing it. Naturally I hoped that if it appealed to John Ford, it would appeal to John Wayne. Marty and John began to write the script and were successful in securing a commitment from John Ford to direct.

We met with Ford, one of the all-time great American directors, whose credits included *The Grapes of Wrath, The Informer, How Green Was My Valley, The Quiet Man,* and *Stagecoach,* and who was probably the best director of Western pictures in the history of American films. Among his great cavalry pictures are *Fort Apache* and *She Wore a Yellow Ribbon,* both masterpieces. I was thrilled that he wanted to do *The Horse Soldiers,* and I hoped that it would become a film in that tradition.

John Ford was tough. He was a man of relatively few words, remarkably self-assured, generally wearing a large slouch hat, probably to cover his balding head, along with an eye patch that had become his trademark. He slouched. I can still see him, sitting in his chair, with his hat perched on his head and his glasses on his nose, his black eye patch covering one eye, a handkerchief or a stub of cigar that may or may not have been lit clenched on one side of his mouth.

I talked to him about how pleased I was that he liked *The Horse Soldiers* and that he was going to do it. I said, "I think we'd better start talking about casting."

He replied, "Well, Duke. Duke."

I said, "Really, that would be great. There's nobody else that could play the commander as well as he." And, besides, Marty and John had obviously written it for him. I said, "We really need to make this picture in the spring or summer, because it's almost entirely exterior. So we must be able to submit the script to Wayne for his approval as soon as possible, so that we can get an answer from him as to whether he will be available when we're ready to shoot."

Ford said, "When I'm ready, he'll be there." And he was. John Wayne appeared when required.

We wanted William Holden to play the other male lead, and we made an offer to him that he accepted, but there was a problem about getting him in the film. This was near the peak of Holden's career, and we were excited about the possibility of having both of these exceedingly popular male stars in an action cavalry film to be directed by John Ford. But, at the time, Holden was embroiled in a contractual dispute with Paramount. In September 1958, the studio sought an injunction against his appearing in *The Horse Soldiers,* claiming he was in default of his contract. Fortunately, the court declined to issue the injunction, and Holden was permitted to appear in our film. His role was that of the doctor assigned to a raiding party of Northern troops operating behind Confederate lines, while Wayne played the commander of the group. The personal conflict in the story, between the commander and the doctor, arose from various disagreements between them as the raiders progressed southward.

The Horse Soldiers contains one of my favorite, but perhaps over-sentimentalized, John Ford sequences. It's an episode that takes place at a Southern boys' military academy. A warning is brought to the academy that our party of Northern troops is crossing their grounds, and the commandant of the academy assembles his corps of cadets to resist them. These boys vary in age from nine to fifteen, but with their banners flying and their drums playing, they march off to do battle with the veteran, hard-bitten Northern troops, led by the unconquerable John Wayne. The cadets approach the entrenched positions of the Northerners, and as we wait for John Wayne to give the order to fire, he pauses and reflects for a moment, then turns to his bugler and says, "Sound retreat." The Northern raiders retreat before the oncoming cadets.

We suffered a most tragic experience during the production of *The Horse Soldiers* in Natchitoches, Louisiana. Forty-eight-year-old Fred Kennedy, a veteran Hollywood character actor and stunt man for more than twenty-five years, died of a broken neck on Friday, December 7, during filming. He was injured when, doubling for John Wayne, he threw himself from a horse during the final scene, where the script called for him to fall from his horse and feign an injury so he could elicit sympathy from the leading lady, actress Constance Towers. Constance, acting out the scene, leaned over to kiss Kennedy and found he was gasping for breath and unable to speak. Kennedy was rushed to the

Natchitoches Parish Hospital, but he was dead on arrival. The accident occurred on a wooden bridge. Despite the fact that we had tested the bridge to make sure that it was firm, there was some concern about whether or not it would support a really spirited ride, but the stunt man thought there would be no problem with it. Real-life tragedy is also sometimes a part of moviemaking.

There was also a good deal of gossip, as well as an editorial in *Variety,* about the huge salaries that we were paying to John Wayne and William Holden. The editor of the trade paper wrote that the salary structure of the industry was being destroyed because we were paying the incredible sum of $750,000 apiece to John Wayne and William Holden. The salary structure of motion pictures has endured many escalations since then, and the industry has still not been destroyed.

The Horse Soldiers received excellent reviews, and I thought it took its place among Ford's other great cavalry films, although time has not been as generous to this film as it has been to *Fort Apache* and *She Wore a Yellow Ribbon.*

We tried something interesting in the advertising campaign for the picture. The week before the film was to open, there was going to be a world heavyweight championship fight between Floyd Patterson and Ingemar Johansson. Someone got the idea that the picture should sponsor the fight's radio broadcast, since it was assumed that the fight was going to appeal principally to a male audience that would probably be the same audience that we would want to reach with our film. So we contracted to sponsor the broadcast. Unfortunately, the fight ended in a knockout in the third round, cutting short our advertising blurbs. The film was not a commercial failure, but it wasn't the big success that we had hoped for.

13

John Sturges and
The Magnificent Seven

Soon after we had made our arrangement with United Artists and had asked Billy Wilder to join us, Harold and I felt that we should try to secure other first-rank directors for our films. We tried to find projects for the men we knew and with whom we had previous associations, such as William Wyler and John Huston.

John Sturges, however, was a director with whom I had been very impressed and had wanted to attract to our company immediately after its formation. Among his outstanding credits were *Gunfight at the O.K. Corral* and *Bad Day at Black Rock*. I tried to interest him in our philosophy and our working system, and, happily, I was able to make a deal with him to join our company, take offices with us, and develop projects together. His contract provided that I was to be the executive producer on all the pictures that he produced. I brought *The Magnificent Seven* project to him and took credit as executive producer.

Our company had chosen to be represented by the law firm of Kaplan, Livingston, Goodwin and Berkowitz. It was headed by Leon Kaplan, who called me one day and told me that a client of his, Yul Brynner, was interested in the possibility of doing a Western film that would be based on the well-known Japanese film *The Seven Samurai*, made by the great Japanese director Akira Kurosawa. I questioned him about the nature of Brynner's involvement and what role he saw for himself in the project. He told me that the idea had been originally broached to Brynner by Anthony Quinn, who had directed a film, *The Buccaneer,* in which Yul had starred some years earlier. Quinn had suggested *The Seven Samurai* as a Western project for the two of them. With the passage of time, there had been a falling out between them, and Quinn had now dropped out of the project. I thought the idea had excellent possibilities. I arranged to get a print of the Japanese film, ran it alone in a projection room, and began to visualize it as a Western. I then became even more enthused about the project. Having recently made our arrangement with John Sturges, I called him and told him the idea. I suggested that we run the film together. We did and had a most stimulating session. One idea led to another, and we became very excited about the possibilities of the project.

We explained the concept to United Artists. The company was pleased at the idea of doing a film with Yul Brynner, although certainly the concept of doing a Western with Yul seemed quite contrary to his usual screen persona. John suggested that we sign Walter Newman to write the script of *The Magnificent Seven,* as we were now calling it. We assigned the task of acquiring the rights to *The Seven Samurai* from Toho, its producer, to Leon Kaplan and his team of lawyers. They finally were able to arrange for us to acquire the rights.

Walter Newman worked at the studio and progressed at a snail's pace. One day he came to my office and said, "I have to ask you about something I've been thinking about, and I don't know if it's crazy or not, but I've got to talk it over." He continued, "Now these two men are out there, challenging one another, as we have seen so often in Westerns, except that one guy has a gun and the other guy has a knife. Do you think that a knife can travel as fast as a bullet?"

I said, "No, it can't, I'm positive it can't."

He said, "That's what's worrying me, but just think about it."

I reflected for a moment, and I said to him, "You know, let's do it anyway."

The script was finally finished, and we began to talk about the possibilities for casting. John Sturges suggested a young actor named Steve McQueen, with whom he had worked in a film he had directed for

MGM called *Never So Few.* Steve had played a supporting role to Frank Sinatra and was now playing the lead in a Western series, *Wanted— Dead or Alive.*

I arranged to see *Never So Few* and was impressed with the young, charming, and dynamic Steve McQueen. I asked his agents, Abe Lastfogel and Stan Kamen of the William Morris Agency, to arrange a meeting with Steve, and it was set up at a restaurant on Ventura Boulevard, close to the Four Star Studio where Steve was shooting *Wanted—Dead or Alive.* He had already read our script and told me of his great respect for John and of his conviction that he could do full justice to the role of Vin. We also discussed the difficulties of arranging for Steve's services, because his television show was still in production and would be for some time. There would obviously be a scheduling conflict.

We had already decided to shoot the film in Mexico, which is the story's locale. We had sent our production manager, Chico Day, to check out locations and make arrangements for our shooting. He had suggested the town of Tepoztlan, near Cuernavaca, as our principal location, where he had selected a site for the construction of a Mexican village. Our preparations were now moving very quickly. We had also given a start date to Yul Brynner that we could not alter. So we told Steve that there was nothing we could do about changing our production schedule.

We proceeded with the rest of our casting. I suggested James Coburn, who had played the heavy in the first episode of *Wichita Town,* to play the knife fighter. I also suggested Charles Bronson, whom I thought was an ideal choice for O'Reilly.

I had met Charles Bronson some years earlier, when I was planning the production of the 3-D film *The Maze.* A friend had invited me to observe the shooting of a film that was being shot in 3-D at Warner Bros., titled *House of Wax,* directed by André de Toth, who was most hospitable to me and explained the process in great detail. I remember being amused at the fact that de Toth, who unfortunately had but one eye, described 3-D effects to me, which he was unable to see himself because of his disability. Charles Bronson, who was then called Charles Buchinsky, was working on the set, and de Toth introduced us. I had been interested since then in monitoring his development as an actor, and the O'Reilly role seemed perfect for him.

We interviewed many other actors and made our choices for the other parts. We selected Robert Vaughn, Brad Dexter, and Horst Buchholz to complete our magnificent seven. Billy Wilder had seen Horst Buchholz in German films and thought that Horst could well become a star. He had decided to cast Horst in *One, Two, Three* and encouraged John Sturges to cast him in *The Magnificent Seven*. We worried a great deal about his German accent, but we finally came to believe, or else convinced ourselves, that he could do a Spanish accent that would be believable.

About four weeks before the start of our production, the situation with Steve McQueen had still not been worked out. On a Friday night, at about nine o'clock, I received a telephone call at home. It was from Tom McDermott, the president of Four Star Productions, who told me the *Wanted—Dead or Alive* company was having a terrible time with Steve on their set. They needed to finish a show that evening, and Steve was in his dressing room, wouldn't come out, and was behaving very badly. He told the director that he wasn't happy with his lines, and besides that, he was angry that Four Star hadn't worked out a way for him to do our film. McDermott suggested that if I spoke with Steve and asked him to finish their show, which had an airdate in a week or ten days, he would listen to reason.

I told Tom I sympathized with his problem, but I didn't think that it was appropriate for me to intervene, since the problem was between him and Steve. Later I heard that this situation continued for a couple of hours, until McDermott agreed that Steve could do *The Magnificent Seven*. Steve appeared and finished their show before midnight. I wasn't sympathetic to Steve's methods, and I became the victim of other ploys of his in later years, but he did get his way, and he came along with us to Cuernavaca to begin shooting *The Magnificent Seven*.

John Sturges suggested Eli Wallach for the role of Calvera, the Mexican bandit. I was dubious about it at first, but I quickly saw how right he was for the role. Parenthetically, when my wife, Pat, arrived in Cuernavaca to spend some time with us, she and I found ourselves one day having lunch with Eli. During the course of our conversation, she said to him, "You know, I'm a great fan of your work, but don't you think your career would be advanced if you didn't have that gold tooth in the front of your mouth?"

Eli looked at her tolerantly and said, "Pat, this gold tooth cost your husband a great deal of money in dental bills." It was, of course, part of Eli Wallach's transition to Mexican banditry. His bravado and his demeanor were just marvelous, and he proved to be a brilliant heavy.

We had an outstanding group of actors down in Cuernavaca, each of whom was trying to improve his own role. They were all concerned lest they be overshadowed by the others, with Steve McQueen probably the most concerned of all. There was constant pressure to rewrite. John and I decided to bring Walter Newman to Cuernavaca, where he could help us field the requests and ideas coming from our actors. We also hoped that we could perhaps make the script even better. Unfortunately either Walter Newman had some reason why he couldn't come or he didn't want to be put in the middle of the pressure we were getting, and he declined to join us. John suggested another writer who could be politic and diplomatic, was a good enough sport to deal with our temperamental cast, and also was able to do whatever writing might be required. William Roberts came down to join us and helped us deal with our problem. At one point I proposed that he put a suggestion box outside of his hotel room.

John Sturges and I talked about various musicians to score the film, and among those we considered was Elmer Bernstein, to whom we ultimately gave the assignment. Elmer was certainly a happy choice, since he contributed one of the most memorable and famous scores in film history.

An interesting incident occurred during our shoot, which gave me an insight into the personalities of two of our stars. While we were in Mexico City, working in the Churubusco studio doing interiors, I was in the projection room one day with Yul Brynner and Steve McQueen, looking at some dailies. As chance would have it, the film we looked at that day was of Horst Buchholz pretending to be a bullfighter and cavorting about with some sad-looking old milk-cow. Steve McQueen recoiled from this and said, "You see, Yul? That's what I was telling you, that kid's trying to steal the picture."

Yul, who was very cool, replied, "No, he's not, Steve. That's not gonna happen."

Steve responded, "How do you know that?"

At lunch on the set of *Bomba, the Jungle Boy* with director Ford Beebe and cameraman Bill Sickner in 1947. Reproduced courtesy of Warner Bros.

A still from my first film, 1947's *Fall Guy*. Reproduced courtesy of Warner Bros.

With Errol Flynn on the set of *The Warriors* outside of London in 1954. Reproduced courtesy of Warner Bros.

At a gala occasion, my father Max Mirisch's eightieth birthday party in 1954. From left to right: Harold, Irving, Dad, myself, and Marvin.

With Steve Broidy at the Allied Artists Studio in 1955.

Celebrating a new association with United Artists in 1957. From left to right: Arthur Krim, myself, Max Youngstein, Harold, Marvin, and Bob Benjamin. © 1957 Metro-Goldwyn-Mayer Studios Inc. All rights reserved.

Joel McCrea and myself having a little script disagreement in 1958 on the set of *The Gunfight at Dodge City*. © 1958 Metro-Goldwyn-Mayer Studios Inc. All rights reserved.

Gary Cooper, iconic "Man of the West," and myself in 1958. © 1958 Metro-Goldwyn-Mayer Studios Inc. All rights reserved.

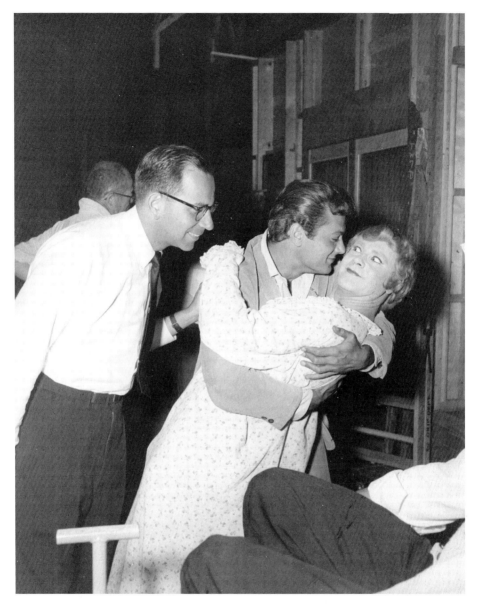

A frolicking moment on a set of *Some Like It Hot* with myself, Tony Curtis, and Jack Lemmon in 1958. © 1959 Metro-Goldwyn-Mayer Studios Inc. All rights reserved.

Top left: Not alone but deep in thought on the set of *Man of the West* in northern California in 1958.

Bottom left: Intimate moment on a set of *Man of the West* in 1958. From left to right: Gary Cooper, Julie London, Anthony Mann, and myself. © 1958 Metro-Goldwyn-Mayer Studios Inc. All rights reserved.

Joel McCrea and myself on a set of *Wichita Town* in 1959. Reproduced courtesy of Mirisch-McCrea Television.

Top left: Tony Curtis, Marilyn Monroe, Marvin, myself, and Harold celebrating the start of production of *Some Like It Hot* in 1958. © 1959 Metro-Goldwyn-Mayer Studios Inc. All rights reserved.

Bottom left: Birthday party in 1959 on a set of *The Apartment*. In front row: Harold, I. A. L. Diamond, Shirley MacLaine, honoree Jack Lemmon, myself, and Billy Wilder. © 1960 Metro-Goldwyn-Mayer Studios Inc. All rights reserved.

Yul Brynner, director John Sturges, and me near Cuernavaca, Mexico, on a set of *The Magnificent Seven* in 1959. © 1960 Metro-Goldwyn-Mayer Studios Inc. All rights reserved.

Top right: Alone and deep in thought on the set of *The Magnificent Seven* near Cuernavaca, Mexico, in 1959.

Bottom right: Harold, William Wyler, Shirley MacLaine, and myself taking a few moments to talk on a set of *The Children's Hour* in 1961. © 1961 Metro-Goldwyn-Mayer Studios Inc. All rights reserved.

Oscar night in 1962 with *West Side Story,* the Best Picture winner. From left to right: Robert Wise, Natalie Wood, and Jerome Robbins. © 1961 Metro-Goldwyn-Mayer Studios Inc. All rights reserved.

Myself and Elvis Presley on a *Kid Galahad* set in 1961. © 1962 Metro-Goldwyn-Mayer Studios Inc. All rights reserved.

My mother and father, Josephine and Max Mirisch, at his ninetieth birthday in 1964.

Top left: Director George Roy Hill and myself are very serious on the set of *Toys in the Attic* in 1962. © 1963 Metro-Goldwyn-Mayer Studios Inc. and Claude Productions. All rights reserved.

Bottom left: Julie Andrews and me, enjoying a moment's conversation on the set of *Hawaii* in 1965. © 1966 Metro-Goldwyn-Mayer Studios Inc. All rights reserved.

A favorite picture of The Mirisch Corporation on our tenth anniversary in 1967. From left to right: Harold, me, and Marvin.

Yul, very nonchalantly, answered, "I know because I've read the script."

In its initial domestic release, the business on *The Magnificent Seven* was not outstanding. But it was released abroad shortly afterward, and the business was immense. The foreign gross was five to six times the domestic. Although *The Magnificent Seven* played over twenty thousand individual U.S. theater engagements, its domestic gross was disappointing, but the foreign gross was so big that it became an exceedingly profitable picture for United Artists. Subsequently we made three sequels, all of them profitable. The title has become part of our language. The picture was also exceedingly well reviewed. It reflected marvelously well on me, as well as on all the other people involved in its production. And it was a big boost to our company in its relationship with United Artists and with exhibitors, and it was instrumental in building the mystique that grew up around The Mirisch Company.

14

The 1960s

U nited Artists had film production arrangements with many producing entities, and among them was one with Seven Arts Productions. Seven Arts was an independent producing company that was partly owned by Eliot Hyman, who many years before had been involved with us in the financing of *Moulin Rouge* and *Moby Dick.* Eliot was a hard-driving, entrepreneurial pioneer in motion pictures for television. He had acquired rights to studio libraries and entered into a partnership with Ray Stark, formerly a successful agent, to produce new films. Seven Arts had produced a number of movies and now had a financing and distribution arrangement with United Artists, but there soon developed a serious breach between Seven Arts and United Artists, and the two agreed to terminate their contract.

However, Seven Arts had three expensive properties that United Artists had acquired for its account: these were the Broadway hit plays *West Side Story* and *Two for the Seesaw,* and the best-selling novel *By Love Possessed.* United Artists approached The Mirisch Company to tell us that they were repossessing these properties from Seven Arts, and asked us if we would take them over and produce them. We enthusiastically agreed.

I flew to New York to view the two plays. I saw *West Side Story* for the first time at the Winter Garden Theater, and I found it stunning, one of the most exciting pieces of theater I'd ever seen. I then went to see *Two for the Seesaw,* which starred Anne Bancroft and Henry Fonda, a beautifully written and played drama but with serious problems for films, primarily due to the fact that it has two actors alone on the stage from beginning to end.

By Love Possessed was a book by the Pulitzer Prize-winning novelist James Gould Cozzens, a sudsy melodrama about the personal lives of upper-class attorneys.

After seeing the plays, I returned to Los Angeles. I thought that *Two for the Seesaw* would be an excellent property for Billy Wilder, and at my earliest opportunity, I discussed the play with him. He said he hadn't seen it as yet, but that he was planning to be in New York shortly and would see it.

We began to discuss the casting possibilities of *West Side Story* in terms of a director and actors. We determined early on that we wanted to avail ourselves of the services of Jerome Robbins, who had choreographed and directed the play, to participate in the production of the film as director. His lack of experience in film production led us into deciding that we should seek, as co-director, someone who would be exceptionally well suited to handle the dramatic elements of the material. With Robbins aboard, the musical side of the picture would clearly be in the most talented of all possible hands.

We had for some time been discussing—with his agent, Phil Gersh—the prospect of having Robert Wise join our company with a deal similar to that which we had with John Sturges. Bob and John had long ago worked together as film editors at RKO. Bob's experience in gritty subject matter was persuasive, and we thought he would be an excellent choice to co-direct *West Side Story*. With the concurrence of United Artists, we offered the film to Bob Wise, to co-direct with Jerome Robbins. Bob was most enthusiastic about the project and accepted our offer.

Billy Wilder now came back from New York, after having seen *Two for the Seesaw.* He told me that he had given the play a great deal of thought, but "I think I can do us a better picture." And, for the first time, he told me the story that became *The Apartment.* He said he wanted to work again with Iz Diamond, and with everyone's approval they set off to do a screenplay.

The problem of *Two for the Seesaw* and *By Love Possessed* still remained, and I determined to try to get them underway as soon as possible by employing writers to prepare screenplays.

In 1958, the William Morris Agency submitted the manuscript of James Michener's *Hawaii* to a number of potential purchasers, including The Mirisch Company, packaged with the commitment of Fred Zinnemann to direct. We thought this was a project of tremendous potential. Fred was one of the great film directors in the world, and we recommended to United Artists that they agree to do the film under our deal.

United Artists paid $1 million for the rights to the book, and we negotiated a deal for Fred to supervise the preparation of the screenplay and to direct the film. We agreed with him on the selection of Daniel Taradash, who had previously written *From Here to Eternity* for him, to write the screenplay.

I had a great deal more difficulty finding a suitable writer for *By Love Possessed*, but finally I arranged for the services of Charles Schnee, who had written *The Bad and the Beautiful* for MGM. Now the preparation of all these properties was underway, with outstanding writers assigned to each of them.

For *The Apartment*, Billy decided that Jack Lemmon would be his protagonist. He had enjoyed a wonderful experience with Jack on *Some Like It Hot*, and he tailored the role of C. C. Baxter for him.

Shirley MacLaine was in the early years of her career. She had started as a dancer on Broadway and had been brought to Hollywood by Paramount, under contract to Hal Wallis. Her first screen role was in Alfred Hitchcock's *The Trouble with Harry*. She clearly was an unusual and most interesting actress, represented by Herman Citron of MCA, the same agent who represented Billy Wilder. Billy met with her and determined that Shirley would play Fran Kubelik. The script was written specifically for her and Jack.

Alexander Trauner, who had been the production designer on *Love in the Afternoon*, was also enlisted to design *The Apartment*. Trauner had been born in Budapest, although he had been living and working in Paris for many years. His English was excellent, and he came to Los Angeles and did the production design. From Trauner came the incredible insurance company set that is still a stunner, as one looks at the tiny cog, Jack Lemmon, in the midst of a huge office complex and sees the

Jack Lemmon, Shirley MacLaine, and a tennis racquet in *The Apartment* in 1959. © 1960 Metro-Goldwyn-Mayer Studios Inc. All rights reserved.

image of the little man who tries to emerge from the herd and climb the ladder of success. The Trauner contribution to *The Apartment* was very great indeed.

The film was edited by Daniel Mandell, who had been Samuel Goldwyn's editor for most of his career. It began shooting on location in New York, then returned to Los Angeles and resumed production at the Goldwyn Studio. It was a happy shoot, as distinguished from *Some Like It Hot* and the problems that arose on many of Billy's later pictures.

Another most felicitous decision was made by Billy Wilder in the casting of Fred MacMurray as J. D. Sheldrake. The role is pivotal in the movie, and Billy, who had worked with Fred in *Double Indemnity*, knew what he could do with the role. It took some effort on Billy's part to persuade Fred MacMurray to assume that most unsympathetic role, but he certainly played it brilliantly.

The next inspirational choice of Billy's in *The Apartment* was the selection of Adolph Deutsch, a brilliant musician, whose contribution is immense. While attending the scoring session and listening to the piano solos being played by the studio orchestra pianist, John Williams, I met John for the first time. It was a privilege to get to know a man who later on contributed so mightily to a large number of our films, as well as many others.

In my opinion, *The Apartment* is one of the funniest, most moving, touching, and socially relevant films ever made. It was nominated for ten Academy Awards and won five. It was exceedingly successful commercially and was also the first Mirisch film to win a Best Picture Academy Award. Billy Wilder won Oscars for writing, directing, and producing. The Academy Awards were a gigantic thrill and a most exciting climax to all of our work and efforts and to the philosophy that underlay our whole approach to picturemaking. Billy Wilder's contribution to the success of The Mirisch Company in its early years was enormous, with *Some Like it Hot* in 1958 and *The Apartment* in 1960.

Billy was very disciplined. He came to the studio every day and worked in his office. Iz Diamond would join him in the morning; they would have their coffee, look at the newspapers, and then set to work. They worked all day long, and they worked together. Iz would sit in front of his typewriter and Billy would pace back and forth with a blackboard in front of him, writing dialogue, polishing it, or stopping to discuss points of characterization or construction.

Iz was a man of strong opinions, and Billy had great respect for him. Iz also sat on the set with Billy during the shooting of all their pictures. Billy listened to his comments, and they discussed problems while Billy was shooting, or they might make some changes that they would both agree upon. In terms of the writing, they were exceedingly collaborative, with a great deal of respect on both sides.

Iz Diamond had been brought to the United States by his Romanian parents when he was an infant. He grew up in New York City and attended Columbia University, where he studied journalism. He wanted to be a writer, and he worked on the school paper. Though his parents were Romanian, he was completely American, whereas Billy Wilder was an adult when he came to America and had to overcome a language difficulty. When he arrived in 1934—as a refugee from Nazi Germany, where he had worked at the UFA Studio in Berlin as a writer—he taught himself English, mainly by reading and listening to the radio.

Billy soon began working with friends who were also expatriates and had come here before him. He worked occasionally with a close friend, Walter Reisch, a writer whom Billy knew in Germany. Reisch collaborated with Billy and Charles Brackett on the screenplay of *Ninotchka*, which was directed by Billy's idol, Ernst Lubitsch, whom he considered his mentor. The story is told that Billy Wilder and Willy Wyler were at Lubitsch's funeral. After the funeral, Billy said to Willy, "Well, I guess that's it, no more Lubitsch."

Willy said to Billy, "What's even worse, no more Lubitsch pictures."

By 1960, I was thirty-nine years old, and our company had won its way to the forefront of motion-picture production. We were leading the way in a style of independent picturemaking that succeeded the old big-studio, production-line methods. As we moved into the 1960s we had the prestige and the wherewithal—with the support of United Artists, which itself had become affluent—to enter the new decade with confidence.

By Love Possessed, however, remained a troubling project. We had a great many script difficulties. Finally I thought we had progressed with it about as far as we could, and I decided it was time to submit it to a director. John Sturges and I had worked closely on *The Magnificent Seven*, and John had worked before with our writer, Charles Schnee, on *Jeopardy*, a film that starred Barbara Stanwyck. When I told John about the project, he read it and said he would like to do it.

Paul Kohner, the agent with whom we had done much business, was then representing Lana Turner. At my request, Paul gave the script to her, and she agreed to play the leading role. However, she wanted some script changes, and Charles Schnee began to make those revisions that we had agreed upon.

Efrem Zimbalist Jr. had been successful in a popular TV series, *77 Sunset Strip*, and we hoped that casting him with Lana in our picture would make him a motion-picture star. We then tried to people the film with outstanding supporting actors. Jason Robards Jr. agreed to play Lana's husband. Thomas Mitchell, Barbara Bel Geddes, Paul Kohner's daughter Susan, and George Hamilton were also in the cast.

Lana never let up wanting additional script changes. Charles Schnee finally lost patience with her and the need to accommodate her requests while retaining our concept of the film. At this point, Isobel

Lennart, who was working on the script of *Two for the Seesaw*, did me a big favor and did further work, hoping to compromise Lana's concerns and polish the dialogue. The script ultimately departed from Charles Schnee's draft, and he asked that his name be taken off the credits. We did so, and a pseudonym, John Dennis, was used on the film.

John Sturges was certainly more at home with male-oriented, action subjects than soap opera. I was well aware of that, but I was guilty of ignoring my own misgivings and of wanting to keep him involved in one of our projects rather than letting him accept an assignment elsewhere while we were doing the script preparation on *The Great Escape*.

There wasn't any stage space available at the Goldwyn Studio at that time, so we leased stages at the Columbia studios. While the picture was shooting, John and I often used to eat lunch in the Columbia executive lunchroom, where we were exposed to Harry Cohn presiding over his minions. I had never met him before, but I became a witness to shocking displays of bad manners and awful humiliations imposed upon his staff.

The lack of success either artistically or commercially of *By Love Possessed*, like many films I was involved with both before and after it, was a psychological and emotional blow as well as a huge personal disappointment. On an individual basis, it was always difficult for me to accept the fact that not all of one's films can be successful, despite the immense investment of creativity and self that goes into each of them. The chemistry that comprises the composition of a successful film is maddeningly difficult to achieve. Most often because of that complicated chemistry or because the tastes of varied audiences throughout the world are constantly changing, success is highly elusive.

I'm a baseball fan, and I would often remind myself that Babe Ruth didn't hit home runs every time he came to bat and that the best hitters in baseball are those who, on the average, get hits about three out of every ten times they come to the plate.

The best filmmakers, historically, have been those who have achieved reasonable averages of success—either artistically or commercially or sometimes, miraculously, both—and have done it often enough to instill confidence in their audiences, their financiers, and themselves. Ultimately, their commercial successes, not necessarily numerically more than their failures, must yield returns that will far exceed the losses of their unsuccessful films if they are to be privileged to continue their work in this amazing combination of art-business. I learned the lesson very early on that one really successful film can more than make up for the losses of many unsuccessful ones.

15

West Side Story

Bob Wise suggested that Ernest Lehman, who had previously written *Executive Suite* for him at MGM, write the screenplay of *West Side Story*. Billy Wilder, whose counsel I sought, also recommended Lehman, with whom he had worked on *Sabrina*. Bob and I met with Ernie Lehman and talked about the construction of the play. A number of interesting notions developed, in terms of the placement of some of the musical numbers; it was an excellent interview. We proceeded to hire him to write the screenplay.

We chose Saul Chaplin, who had a great deal of experience in the MGM musical department, to serve as associate producer to help us organize the musical elements of the picture. He suggested that we employ John Green, with whom he had worked for a long time at MGM, to become the musical director and to conduct the orchestra in the pre-recordings and the post-recordings. As chance would have it, John Green was also an old friend of Leonard Bernstein's. John, besides having been head of the music department at MGM for many years, was a well-thought-of composer and conductor, and we were delighted to be able to secure his services.

It was always our intention, with the concurrence of United Artists, to roadshow the picture, which means to merchandise it on a so-called hard-ticket, two-a-day plan, with reserved seats. Under this plan, the audience buys their seats in advance. They enter the theater and are seated in designated seats. The picture is presented like a live theatrical program, and an overture is played for stragglers who might be late entering.

The first problem in the production of the film was a disagreement between Jerome Robbins on the one side and Bob Wise and myself on the other. Bob had suggested the idea of doing the prologue ballet in New York, on the streets. I thought that was a wonderful idea and an exciting opening for the film. Robbins had grave doubts. He felt that the dancers would look ridiculous doing ballet on the streets, since ballet is so antithetical to reality. What would bystanders think were they to see classical dancing on real streets?

Jerry felt that the prologue should be done on stylized sets, whereas Bob Wise and I didn't want the film to look like a photographed stage play. Robbins acknowledged the problem, but he felt that effect was preferable to what might seem like a clash between reality and stylized dance. One day Jerry asked me to watch him rehearsing the dancers, while they danced on the pavement around the perimeter of a sound-stage. He said, "Come and look at this with me, and just imagine this on the street." He and I watched the prologue, with the Sharks dancing around the outside of the stage. But Bob Wise and I still didn't agree with him. This became a very serious point of difference and only increased in intensity as we approached the starting date of the picture.

However, by this time we had come upon a very fortuitous piece of luck while seeking locations in New York. We found a site on West 60th Street that was shortly to be razed to make way for Lincoln Center. Two blocks of tenement houses had already been vacated, and the next step was to tear down the buildings so that Lincoln Center could be built. We were fortunate to be able to arrange to work in those streets prior to the demolition of the buildings. The windows had been taken out, but we replaced them. Those West Side streets with unoccupied buildings were made exclusively available to us, just as if we had built a huge set. It was a great stroke of luck. It also convinced us that we had a marvelous site to stage the prologue.

Finally, I took a huge gamble and told Robbins that if he would agree to shoot the prologue on the streets in New York, we would edit the sequence on our return to Los Angeles. If he still didn't like it, we would redo it on a stage. With that understanding, he agreed to stage the prologue on the New York Streets.

Cinematography on *West Side Story*, in 65mm, was by Daniel Fapp. Our music editor was Richard Carruth, Thomas Stanford was our film editor, and Boris Leven was our production designer. Allen K. Wood again was our production manager.

When we began production in New York, we started the shooting with the helicopter shots of Manhattan that open the picture. We saw the dailies of the first day's work in a little projection room in the basement of what was then the Rivoli Theater. The Rivoli, coincidentally, was where the picture opened in New York City. Sitting in that little projection room, looking at those now-famous straight-down shots on Manhattan, was thrilling.

Casting had presented us with difficult decisions. Whether to cast stars or unknowns was long debated. There were those who thought we should offer the role of Maria to Elizabeth Taylor. There was a United Artists executive who thought we should offer Tony to Harry Belafonte. I thought they were both too old for the roles. I had hoped to emulate *Romeo and Juliet* and have two truly young people.

We began to make screen tests. We tested Larry Kert, who had played Tony on Broadway, and Carol Lawrence, who had played Maria. Unfortunately, we felt that they were both too old by then to repeat their roles on the screen. We tested a large number of candidates for these roles and simply never did find anyone who pleased us.

We began to think about Natalie Wood. Certainly she was not ideal as a Hispanic, but she was the right age for Maria, and a good actress. I had known Natalie since *The Rose Bowl Story*, so long ago, and had watched her career develop. Now she was playing the lead with Warren Beatty in Elia Kazan's *Splendor in the Grass*. We decided to offer her the role of Maria and were pleased when she accepted. She strongly wanted to do her own singing in the picture, and we did record her singing a few songs. However, her renditions didn't compare with Marni Nixon's, whose voice we finally used on the soundtrack.

Richard Beymer, by that time, had been in a number of pictures. He was boyish and young although some critics found it difficult to accept Richard as the tough, New York tenement–bred leader of the Jets. But, unfortunately, we didn't find another actor who we felt had all the other requisites and who was also qualified to contribute the dramatic performance that was required. We decided that we would revoice him in his singing sequences.

West Side Story in 1961 with Richard Beymer and Natalie Wood. © 1961 Metro-Goldwyn-Mayer Studios Inc. All rights reserved.

Rita Moreno, who is Puerto Rican, was cast as Anita. George Chakiris, who is of Greek extraction, was cast as Bernardo. Riff was played by Russ Tamblyn.

The shooting of *West Side Story* proceeded slowly. We fell into a pattern where Bob and Jerry would have long discussions about shots before we made them. When they agreed, we would move on to the next setup. The process moved a lot slower than it would have with one director. There was just more talk, more indecision, more choices. We also had weather problems in New York, and we ran a great deal over schedule and budget. We returned to California without shooting certain scenes that we had intended to film in New York, but we finally decided we could pick them up in Los Angeles.

We pressed forward with the editing of the prologue. Bob Wise worked on it whenever he could with Tom Sanford, the editor. When Jerry Robbins saw it, he agreed it was excellent and didn't ask us to reshoot it. I breathed a sigh of relief.

The production delays continued, and we fell further and further behind schedule. We were under great pressure from United Artists. I did everything I could think of to expedite the shooting. We concentrated on getting as many of the musical numbers shot as early in the schedule as we could, until we decided the only way to accelerate our shooting pace was to dispense with the two-director plan.

I discussed it with Bob Wise. He said he was perfectly satisfied to go on and finish the picture with Jerry. He thought Jerry was making a great contribution to the picture. As he was! I didn't disagree with that. But we were under so much pressure from United Artists and its financiers since we were so far over budget, that we simply had to do something radical to try and move the shooting along faster. All of the musical numbers had been intensely rehearsed by Jerry Robbins, and we felt that his assistants could carry through with Bob in the staging of the musical numbers that still remained to be shot.

I talked to Jerry Robbins's agent, Jay Kanter of MCA, and told him what we were planning to do. I asked him to talk to Jerry, and he said he wouldn't do it. He said, "You'll have to do it yourself."

I made an appointment with Jerry over a weekend, and Harold and I went to see him at his home. We told him what our problems were and what we intended to do. He was, of course, hurt, furious, and insulted. It was a terrible scene. But we stuck to our decision. We acknowledged that his contributions to the play were immense, and his contribution to the picture was equally great.

He told us that if he was let go, he wanted to take his name off the picture. I didn't want him to do that and replied, "Of course, that's your prerogative. But I suggest that you wait until the picture is finished, and then decide whether or not it is so far afield from what you would have wanted it to be that you still want your name removed from the credits." He agreed.

He left the picture, Bob continued on alone, and the pace of production picked up some. However, it was a very difficult picture to shoot, and it continued to fall behind schedule. Perhaps not as far behind as it would have under the two-director format, but it was a logistical struggle straight through to the end.

Daily Variety (December 7, 1960) quoted Bob Wise on the abandonment of the co-directorial arrangement: "It was merely a matter of time, not of artistic differences or personal friction. . . . It took too much time to coordinate our thoughts. . . . It became unwieldy and time-consuming, and it got to the point where it became unmanageable." The *Variety* writer, Larry Tubelle, continued, "How about the booming budget? Originally labeled a five-million dollar effort, it is now projected at about six-mil. Originally mapped for a December wrap, it now should extend into February."

It finally cost about $6.75 million. This was immensely expensive at the time. We struggled on, but as we watched the dailies every day and saw what we were getting, I kept thinking, "This will be a truly great movie! And we just have to tough it out." Which is what we did. We finished shooting the picture, and when I finally saw its first cut, it just flew off the screen at me in a way that no other film ever had. There was so much energy, so much vitality, so much excitement in *West Side Story*, that it surpassed my greatest expectations. It was difficult to bring to fruition, but a remarkable film resulted. After seeing the film, Jerome Robbins elected to retain his credits.

There's a whole school of thought, and I've heard directors and producers enunciate it, that friction and conflict all push everybody working on a film to their limits, and better work results from it. I don't agree. I suppose that can happen, but great work can also come from camaraderie, compromise, and cooperation. With people being excited about what they are doing and having confidence in themselves, their material, and their director, picturemaking can also work superbly, as happened with *The Apartment* and *In the Heat of the Night.* Yet *Some Like It Hot* and *West Side Story*, on the other hand, were both troubled.

Midway through the shooting of the picture, Leonard Bernstein happened to be in Los Angeles, and Johnny Green told me that he wanted to have a party for Bernstein at his home. He said that he had just put a whole new recording system with the quality of dubbing-room sound into his house. He wanted permission to run the pre-recorded music tracks at the party so that Bernstein could hear them. He invited the crème de la crème of Los Angeles society, the Philharmonic people, the social lions of the city, and the important movie stars, directors, and executives. The party list finally got so long that he moved the soirée to the rooftop restaurant of the Beverly Hilton Hotel.

After the party, everybody went back to Johnny's home, where there were speakers strategically positioned through the whole house. After Johnny introduced it, the overture of the film began to play. Bernstein listened to it intently, as I watched his every reaction to it. He was very serious and contemplative. When the first selection was over, he turned to John Green and said, "Johnny, how the hell could you have done it so badly?"

It was just terrible to see a man so devastated in front of his peers. The music that Bernstein listened to that night is the music that is in the picture. Johnny later said, "I suppose he wouldn't have liked anything if he hadn't done it himself." He was probably right.

West Side Story had its world premiere at the Rivoli Theater in New York on October 18, 1961. Bosley Crowther in the *New York Times* described the film as "nothing short of a cinema masterpiece." In the *Saturday Review,* Arthur Knight wrote that "the effort throughout is toward quality, the same kind of quality that the stage production brought to Broadway and, at least in my opinion, it has not only succeeded, it has exceeded the original." Discussing the camera technique in *Limelight,* Jack Holland wrote, "Sure, it's been done in a way before, but not with the compelling urgency found in *West Side Story.* Perhaps I'm reading much more into all this than there is actually present. For the first time in years I found myself being startled and excited by these techniques, and the net effect was like seeing a motion picture for the first time. At any rate, *West Side Story* is a motion picture of which all Hollywood can be justifiably proud. Our bow to photographer Daniel Fapp." The critics were unanimous in their praise.

The picture was shown at the Rivoli for sixty-eight weeks, becoming the highest-grossing film of 1962, with some $19 million of film rental domestically. By 1963, according to *Variety,* it had become the fifth-highest grossing film ever released. It also broke tradition for all American musicals and earned huge grosses abroad, grossing in its initial release over $30 million in film rentals throughout the world. Since then, in re-release, television, home video, DVD, etc., this film has gone on to entertain countless millions of people.

West Side Story won the best picture award of the New York Film Critics, as well as similar awards from the Directors Guild and the

Producers Guild, among numerous others. It received eleven Academy Award nominations and won ten Oscars, including Best Picture. A special Academy Award was voted to Jerome Robbins, which was presented to him by Gene Kelly. Most fitting was the presentation of the Best Picture award to Bob Wise by Fred Astaire.

The Mirisch Company had been in existence for four years and produced two consecutive winners of the Academy Award for Best Picture. Not many major companies have accomplished anything like that. We were very proud. United Artists gave us an appreciable bonus, over and above our contractual financial arrangements, to express its appreciation.

By 1960, in the midst of the huge workload that I was carrying, my family had become complete. My daughter Anne was then nine, my son Drew was seven, and our third child, Larry, was three. Pat was thirty-six, and the two of us were engaged in our most important production, namely the rearing of our family. I tried and succeeded in spending as much time with my family as any professional person could. Those were busy and exciting days as we watched our children develop and grow. We tried hard to keep them living relatively normal lives, and they all attended public schools.

In addition to the Producers Guild, I also undertook other industry affiliations. I became president of the Permanent Charities of the Motion Picture Industry and served in that capacity for a year. Through the whole of my career, I was constantly increasing my relationships with people in other areas of the industry.

While participating in some of the special occasions of that era, I was invited, along with the presidents of other guilds, to the reception that was held at the Twentieth Century-Fox studio for Nikita Khrushchev, the Soviet premier, when he visited Los Angeles. After lunch had been served, Spyros Skouras, in introducing Khrushchev, spoke of his own immigrant beginnings and described how he had been brought to this country by his Greek parents as a very young boy, and proudly said that America was a great country in which a young man of his background could work and rise and become the president of a great, worldwide motion-picture company.

In responding to him, Premier Khrushchev said that he felt obligated to point out that he had been born a poor boy in the Soviet Union and had worked very hard and had pulled himself up by his bootstraps, and he was now the leader of the Union of Soviet Socialist Republics!

16

One, Two, Three and
Other Projects

Billy Wilder's next picture, *One, Two, Three,* might be called inevitable. Finally he had to have his say on the screen about postwar Germany, in a way that reflected his own wit and brilliance. As the vehicle for his satire, he chose an old Molnár play, *Eins, Zwei, Drei (One, Two Three)*, and he changed almost everything about it but the title. Cary Grant was the original preferred casting for the role of MacNamara, the Coca-Cola executive in postwar Berlin. It played off Grant's characterization in the *Front Page* remake, *His Girl Friday,* where Grant played fast-talking editor Walter Burns to Rosalind Russell's reporter Hildy Johnson.

When Cary Grant proved to be unavailable, Billy immediately sought out James Cagney. Cagney was sixty years old at the time, near the end of his career, and didn't work again after *One, Two, Three* until his very old age, twenty years later. Billy wanted the picture to be exceedingly fast-paced. He wanted it to move like an express train, and he knew Cagney could give him that. Cagney later said that he wasn't happy with Billy. He felt that Billy was too rigid in following his script and didn't allow Cagney as much leeway as he wanted in developing his role. However, I don't think that affected the film at all.

It was shot, partially, in Germany. And as luck would have it, during the production of the picture, the zones between East and West Berlin were closed as a result of international problems. We were filming in Munich at the time, but we finally brought the picture back to California, where we picked up all the scenes in the Goldwyn Studio that we had not been able to shoot in Germany.

When the picture was previewed, audience laughter covered up the soundtrack. That might have been a mistake, since it didn't leave space for either important dialogue or other possible laughs. Its rapid-fire pace hurt *One, Two, Three.*

Billy is Austrian and had lived in Berlin, where he had worked as a newspaper reporter for a time. Then he started to work in silent pictures, as a writer at the UFA Studio, where his best-known credit was on the film *Emil und der Detektiv.* When the Nazis came to power, Billy made his way from Berlin to Paris, en route to the United States, having decided that he wanted to work in films in Hollywood. The Holocaust was very personal and painful to him. Members of his family were trapped in the Holocaust; his mother was sent to a concentration camp and was killed. His revenge was in his films *Stalag 17, Foreign Affair,* and *One, Two, Three.*

Unfortunately, *One, Two, Three* was not a commercially successful film. I was surprised. I thought it was going to be successful. The previews were marvelous. The theaters rocked with laughter. It was one of three or four pictures in my career that I expected to be successful and then was very disappointed.

By 1961 we had delivered to United Artists *Fort Massacre, Man of the West, The Gunfight at Dodge City, The Man in the Net, Some Like It Hot, The Horse Soldiers, Cast a Long Shadow, The Magnificent Seven,* and *The Apartment.* Awaiting release, or in various states of post-production, were *West Side Story, By Love Possessed,* and *Town without Pity.* As a result of this production record, we extended our deal with United Artists for an additional three years.

Eric Johnston, who in 1961 was president of the Motion Picture Association of America, asked me if I would agree to serve as the American delegate to the Cannes Film Festival. In those years, the Cannes Festival was treated as an international conference, and foreign nations were invited to participate by the French government. I discussed the invitation with Pat, and we thought it would be fun to accept.

Eric Johnston recommended me to the State Department, and I was appointed by Secretary of State Dean Rusk to represent our country. I was asked to go first to Washington, where I was briefed by various people in the State Department about whom I would be meeting at Cannes, primarily the representatives of other governments. The State Department people were mainly interested in the delegates from the Communist countries, who would be representing Russia, Poland, China, and other Communist-bloc countries, and what situations I might expect to find myself in with them. It was very interesting for a motion-picture person to be thrust, in this oblique way, into the world of international diplomacy. I was supplied with a diplomatic passport and met at the airport in Paris by an embassy car with American flags on both front fenders. It was a very heady experience.

It was at this festival that I encountered Fred Zinnemann. Fred had been selected to be a member of the award-granting jury at Cannes. So Fred and I became allies in flying the American flag.

The American entry in the Cannes Festival that year was *Raisin in the Sun,* with Sidney Poitier. Sidney came over at the time the film was being shown, and I had an opportunity to renew my acquaintance with him. We had been introduced when he was working in *Porgy and Bess,* which had been shot at the Goldwyn Studio. He had told me at that time that he had hoped *Porgy and Bess* would finish shooting on schedule because he had been offered a marvelous role in a Broadway play, *Raisin in the Sun,* and he had hoped that he would be able to accept it. He did, and was a great success in it. Lifelong relationships with Fred Zinnemann and Sidney Poitier grew from this period at Cannes.

The festival was exciting and time-consuming. As American representatives, Pat and I were invited everywhere, and we were assisted by an aide from the U.S. Office of Information, Howard Simpson, who was very efficient in navigating us through all of the diplomatic potholes that lay before us. There were parties every night into the wee hours and film screenings every day and every night. It was an exhausting two and a half weeks.

Finally the Soviet minister of culture, Madame Ekaterina Furtseva, appeared at the festival, and the Soviet delegation hosted a big party for her. We of the American delegation felt obliged to reciprocate.

Unfortunately, we had no funds budgeted for such reciprocation. I contributed some money, and our Information Office man, Simpson, contributed his wits. There was an American aircraft carrier on station in the Mediterranean not far from Cannes. Simpson, somehow or other, arranged to buy liquor at PX prices and other food stuffs to serve at our reception, and we managed to put together a reasonably respectable affair, at which we proudly flew our flag.

As we came to the end of our stay, I was pleased when I was told by the festival officials that the French had voted to award a medal to Gary Cooper, who was then suffering from cancer and terminally ill. He was awarded the medal of the Order of Arts and Letters, and to my immense surprise, I was awarded the same decoration at the same time. Coop wasn't in attendance, and Fred accepted the medal on his behalf. The French minister of culture had come from Paris for the occasion, and in a very solemn ceremony at the Carlton Hotel, he made a presentation to me, accompanied by kisses on both cheeks. It was an exciting climax to the festival for Pat and me.

After the festival was over, I flew to Munich, where Billy Wilder was shooting interiors on *One, Two, Three,* and spent some time with him. While there, I was introduced to W. Somerset Maugham, who was having dinner at the Four Seasons Hotel where we stayed. I was anxious to return home, where the development of *Hawaii* awaited me.

By the time I had returned from Cannes and Munich, Dan Taradash, whom we had chosen to write the script of *Hawaii,* had finally become available. We scheduled our first meeting with Fred Zinnemann and Dan, at the latter's house, to discuss his approach to the script. The writing problem was formidable; it involved taking a thousand-page novel and condensing it into a normal-sized script for a film. My brother Harold had indicated that he would like to sit in on the first meeting and hear the original discussions about conceptual approaches to the screenplay. I said, "Fine."

I drove to his house, to pick him up. On arriving there, I found that he had been taken very ill. His wife, Lottie, had already called his doctor and an ambulance. He was taken to the Mount Sinai Hospital, and we learned that he had suffered a serious heart attack. This was the beginning of constant cardiac problems until his death in 1968. He experienced numerous attacks between 1961 and 1968, for which he was hospitalized, followed by long convalescent periods. During those years he spent a great deal of time in Palm Springs, where his physicians felt that he might be in a less pressured atmosphere. I tried to relieve him of much of the work he was doing, as did Marvin. Undoubtedly we lost the value of many things that he could have or would have contributed, if he had been well. But we closed ranks.

His doctor felt that his involvement in business should be minimal. When he was feeling well, he was anxious to become more involved. When he was feeling poorly, he retreated quickly from work. It was more difficult for him than for anyone. He was a man of extraordinary ability, marvelous in his relationships with people, and his incapacity was a serious blow to our company. He and I were exceedingly close. We talked over everything we were each doing, we saw one another every day, and in the evening we talked on the telephone. We spent many vacations together.

He never saw himself as a producer or as a picturemaker. His name never appeared on a movie credit. He usually didn't want to sit in on story conferences or casting sessions. But he was a brilliant executive, and he was a great dealmaker. When we were faced with exceedingly difficult deals—such as how to accommodate the deals for John Wayne, William Holden, and John Ford in the same movie, or for Billy Wilder, Jack Lemmon, and Shirley MacLaine—he would devise formulas acceptable to all. He dealt with the agents, and he also managed the brunt of our relationship with United Artists, getting approvals from them for the things we wanted to do.

He was able to operate over the phone from Palm Springs to a certain extent, but that also sometimes caused problems. He would get into certain matters, but by the time he was in the middle of them, he felt ill and then didn't want to be involved any further. We never quarreled about it. I think I can say fairly that we loved one another deeply and we tried to work our way through it, and largely did, without anything terrible happening either to our work or our relationship. Marvin took over most of the negotiating that Harold had been doing.

In 1960, Paul Kohner called Harold and proposed a project, *Town without Pity*. There was already a script. Gottfried Reinhardt was committed to direct it, and Kirk Douglas had agreed to star. An Austrian company, Gloria Films, was to provide the below-the-line costs, and we were asked to invest $1 million, which was to be paid to Kirk Douglas, to Reinhardt, and to the writers. With only a limited exposure for us, we read the script and agreed to propose it to United Artists. The company would have distribution in the Western Hemisphere and in many other territories. I felt that the project was promising but that the script required a lot of work.

I met with Gottfried Reinhardt and then with Kirk Douglas. Kirk also felt that the script needed work and proposed that Dalton Trumbo be hired. Dalton had already done *Spartacus* for Kirk, and he arranged for us to meet.

Dalton was an extraordinary man. He was a great raconteur and, considering all he had been through during the blacklist years, a man with a wonderful sense of humor. He was the kind of friend that you could truly say you enjoyed. Although he ultimately received no credit on *Town without Pity*, I certainly thought that he deserved it. He accomplished a great deal in improving the script. Later he asked that the scripts be submitted to the Writers Guild for arbitration. It was done, and the arbitrators decided to award him no credit. He was furious about it and wrote a most extraordinary letter, brilliantly devastating the arbitration committee. Parenthetically, Dalton Trumbo was one of the great letter writers that I have known in my lifetime.

Town without Pity was based on a novel by Manfred Gregor, and the original script had been written by George Hurdalek and by Gottfried's wife, Silvia Reinhardt. The plot revolved around four American soldiers stationed in Germany who are accused of raping a German girl. Kirk Douglas played their defense attorney. This sensitive subject led to a great deal of controversy with the Production Code Administration, but finally, with compromise and re-editing, the film was granted a seal of approval. *Town without Pity* gave a reasonably good account of itself commercially, spawned a very successful song that was nominated for an Academy Award, and was responsible for starting valuable relationships for me with Dalton Trumbo and editor Ralph Winters.

Two for the Seesaw by William Gibson was the third property in the Seven Arts package that had included *West Side Story* and *By Love Possessed.* It had been directed by Arthur Penn, who had previously directed *The Miracle Worker,* Gibson's other big success with Anne Bancroft. *Two for the Seesaw* was a cinematic challenge because there were only two people in the cast and the play was performed in two adjoining sets;

it was largely a play of character and dialogue, both brilliantly written by Gibson. The question the material posed was whether or not the talk between two disparate people, who meet and fall in love, would be interesting enough to hold the attention of a film audience.

I made an attempt to get William Gibson to write the screenplay, but he declined the offer. I then chose a well-known screenwriter, Isobel Lennart. I felt that a woman writer would be particularly suitable for *Two for the Seesaw,* which is centered on the female character, Gittel Mosca. Isobel had a long and successful career as a screenwriter, almost exclusively at MGM, and agreed to do the script. Isobel, who later became one of my closest and dearest friends, was marvelously suited to *Seesaw.* I had to wait for her to finish another assignment, and so there was a long delay. Later she wrote the play *Funny Girl* and still later the screenplay for the screen version.

Casting became our next serious problem. We discussed at great length whether or not to offer the role of Gittel to Anne Bancroft, who had been truly wonderful in the play. I wanted to offer it to her. I had seen her do the play and knew how good she was. She was Gittel Mosca. But United Artists wouldn't approve her. Her movie career had not yet begun, and they wanted a major movie star. We now began to consider Shirley MacLaine.

Having made *West Side Story,* and with a deal in place with Bob Wise, with whom we were already developing other material, he became a serious candidate to direct *Seesaw.* He had emerged as a major director, and judging from other films that he had done, I considered that *Seesaw* was material for which he was well suited. I offered it to him, and he liked it. He knew Isobel, since he had directed her script of *This Could Be the Night,* and he agreed to do the film.

Shirley MacLaine was considered a major star after *The Apartment.* Although she was and is a marvelous actress, with wonderful gamine-like personality, she certainly was not the Jewish beatnik of Gibson's play. Bob Wise, Isobel, and I wrestled with that problem, and we finally agreed that it could be overcome. I talked with Shirley about *Seesaw,* and she, like everyone else, had been impressed by the play, and with *West Side Story* and Bob's work. She agreed to do the film.

Henry Fonda was another problem. His career in films had come to a standstill. He had not made a picture in a number of years and had returned to New York to work on the stage. He had acted in *Two for the*

Good friend Robert Mitchum, meditative in *Two for the Seesaw* in 1962. © 1962 Metro-Goldwyn-Mayer Studios Inc.

Seesaw for quite a while. He was by then older than we wanted Jerry to be, and United Artists pressured us to secure a bigger, more current movie star than Henry Fonda was at that stage of his career.

When transposing a successful Broadway play to the screen, you can't please everybody. If you use the cast of the original, you're criticized. If you don't, you're criticized. I have done it both ways. I used the leading performers of the play in *How to Succeed in Business without Really Trying* and was criticized. I used none of the stage cast in *Toys in the Attic* and was criticized. The granddaddy of them all, though, was the decision not to cast Zero Mostel as Tevye in *Fiddler on the Roof.*

After failing to get Paul Newman to play Jerry, the idea of casting Bob Mitchum in *Seesaw* was suggested. I had mixed feelings. He was the right age to play Jerry. He was vital, had great sex appeal, and you could see that sparks would come from a relationship between him and

Gittel. In 1948, Bob Wise had worked with Bob Mitchum in *Blood on the Moon,* and he encouraged the idea of casting him.

Mitchum was a pro. He was serious about his work, although he was self-deprecating. He said he didn't know much about acting, he just learned the words and came in and said them. But despite that modesty, real or pretended, he brought an honesty that came through in most everything he did in a long, extraordinary career. I truly liked him. Years later he did me a big favor when he played a cameo role for me in *Midway.*

Seesaw now began production, with Bob Wise directing Shirley MacLaine and Robert Mitchum. Ted McCord was selected to photograph the picture. Boris Leven, who had done *West Side Story,* did the production design, and Stuart Gilmore edited. To compose the score, which I always felt was going to be immensely important to the picture, I was fortunate enough to secure the services of André Previn. He also wrote a song, with lyrics written by his then-wife Dory Previn. With some exteriors shot in New York, the film was photographed mainly in sets at the Goldwyn Studio. The shooting was largely untroubled.

I had great expectations for the success of *Two for the Seesaw.* The night before the review was scheduled to appear in the New York morning papers, I was terribly nervous about it. I had called a publicity person at United Artists and asked him to get an early edition of the *New York Times* and to call me at home with the review. I waited and waited, until finally I called him and was told, "The paper's not out yet."

Finally Pat said, "I'm not going to wait for this any longer." She telephoned the *New York Times* and got someone at the paper, at that hour, to read her the review. Unfortunately, it wasn't very good, and I was crestfallen.

Although it was not commercially successful, I'm proud of having produced *Two for the Seesaw.* André Previn's score and Ted McCord's photography both received Academy Award nominations.

17

William Wyler, Elvis Presley, and John Sturges

From the beginning of the formation of our company, we had made strenuous efforts to find a vehicle that would be mutually agreeable to ourselves, United Artists, and William Wyler. The experience on *Friendly Persuasion*, despite the fact that it was an expensive film and not commercially successful in its own time, had not in any way damaged the personal relationship that Harold and I both enjoyed with Willy Wyler. We talked to him, whenever possible, about finding a project for him to do, and he always said he was eager to work with us again. I had offered him *Two for the Seesaw*, and after some consideration, Willy, who had been most successful in bringing many Broadway plays to the screen, finally decided he didn't want to do it. Many of our conversations took place while he was directing *The Big Country*, which he shot at the Samuel Goldwyn Studios. When we could get him away from his production work, we would talk about other projects, until he was offered *Ben-Hur*, which he decided to accept and which occupied him for two years, mainly in Italy.

We did, however, acquire some material that he said he would be interested in producing and directing. A play by Sidney Sheldon, *Roman Candle*, had been brought to his attention. He encouraged us to make a deal with Sheldon to write a screenplay, which we did. Later, he said that he wanted to do the screen version of his great friend Lillian Hellman's play, *Toys in the Attic,* and so we also acquired the rights for him.

However, prior to the delivery of screenplays of these projects, he came to us again with another idea. He now wanted to remake his 1936 film *These Three,* which Lillian Hellman had also written and which was based on her play *The Children's Hour.* Willy said that he believed that we had now come to a period when a more honest depiction of lesbianism, the subject matter of the play, could be shown on the screen. When the original screen adaptation had been made, starring Miriam Hopkins, Merle Oberon, and Joel McCrea, the lesbian angle had been completely omitted and the gossip about which the movie revolves concerned a heterosexual triangle, to meet the Code requirement of the day. Now Willy was anxious to do *The Children's Hour* as it had originally been written. He was persuaded that he could do a newer version of the play that would be true not only to the spirit but to the letter of the original. Many years had passed since *These Three,* the censorship doors were opening wider all the time, and Willy and Lillian Hellman thought that they could now overcome that problem.

Willy also had, for some time, been looking for another vehicle to do with Audrey Hepburn. He had directed her great breakthrough success, *Roman Holiday,* and she was most eager to work with him again, and he with her. He felt that *The Children's Hour* would present an ideal vehicle for her.

When we discussed who should be the screenwriter of *The Children's Hour,* I naturally assumed that Lillian would do the script. However, she was either occupied at that particular time or else felt that she would prefer to have a fresh mind work on the script. She would come back to it later, reinvigorated by a fresh approach, and do a final polish. Willy agreed to that, and he suggested that we employ John Michael Hayes, who had written the screenplays of numerous successful films, including Alfred Hitchcock's *Rear Window, To Catch a Thief,* and *The Trouble with Harry.*

In discussing who else should be in the cast, the name of Shirley MacLaine was suggested. We still had one remaining film in our contract with Shirley. Her career was at a high point, and Willy was pleased to add her to the cast.

We had many conversations about who should play the male lead. Finally, Wyler said to me, "You know, what I really want is a tall, great-looking cowboy, like Joel McCrea was when I cast him in the original picture."

That rang a bell with me, and I said, "That's James Garner!"

At that point, James Garner had been starring in the successful Warner Bros. television show *Maverick,* but finally, after a number of years of great success in the medium, he had a falling-out with Warner Bros. He refused to continue in the series, and the matter of his contract with Warners had become a subject of litigation.

I arranged for Willy to see the *Maverick* television show so that he could see Jim. After looking at a number of episodes and meeting Jim, he said to me, "He's exactly right, he's just what I want."

We now got in the middle of the Garner-Warner litigation. Jim was able to extricate himself from his contract with Warners with a compromise agreement that he would appear in a certain number of theatrical films for them. Willy Wyler got the leading man he wanted, and I was able to conclude what I felt was a reasonable deal with James Garner, plus securing options for two further films with him. Our getting in the middle of this melee proved valuable to all of us, except perhaps to Warner Bros., which had to recast the lead in its hit television series.

The Children's Hour was photographed by Franz Planer. I made a heroic effort to get Aaron Copland to do the score, but we couldn't arrange that and finally it was composed by Alex North. Robert Swink edited the film, and Robert Wyler was associate producer. Robert Relyea was assistant director, and the production designer was Fernando Carrere.

On the first day of shooting, Willy Wyler called me from the set and asked me to come down to see him. I did, and he took me aside and said, "Walter, I think we made a terrible mistake. I think we should not have cast Shirley."

This was the same experience that I had gone through with him on his casting of Dorothy McGuire in *Friendly Persuasion.* Frankly, this time it troubled me less than it had previously, because I now attributed it to normal second-thought doubts. I encouraged him to continue to work with Shirley. I told him I was sure he would become more comfortable with her performance, and he did. He didn't complain further about it, and I don't know to this day whether or not that kind of insecurity troubled Willy on other films. But I don't think either the casting of Dorothy McGuire in *Friendly Persuasion* or of Shirley MacLaine in *The Children's Hour* was wrong.

Clearly the problem with the whole project was that when the play was originally written and produced on Broadway, it was very daring and had a considerable amount of shock value. Willy felt, now that the original could be shown on the screen, that it would enhance the dramatic conflict between the characters. The big error we all made was that not only had the time come when this material would be considered daring, but it had also passed. We made the mistake of not realizing that it needed to be much more daring than it was. As a consequence, it tended to be something of a period piece, still having the feeling of a 1930s play but set in 1960. Despite the fact that it was beautifully shot and certainly well acted by its principals, it was unsatisfying to contemporary audiences. *The Children's Hour,* which was the last film that I was privileged to work on with the great William Wyler, was not financially successful.

However, the production afforded me the opportunity to meet and work with Lillian Hellman. We later also collaborated on *Toys in the Attic,* and we continued to be friends until her death.

The reviews of *The Children's Hour* were mixed, although the *Hollywood Reporter* (December 8, 1961) wrote, "William Wyler's new version of *The Children's Hour* is a shattering, realistic drama of tangled lives and tangled emotions, superlatively acted and directed, one of the most honest films ever made in Hollywood. It will be a strong box-office attraction, probably one of the year's biggest. It should also be rewarded with general critical acclaim."

After two consecutive Best Picture Oscars, and with the encouragement of United Artists, which increasingly looked to us as the supplier of their A films, we continued to seek out other directors with whom we could make deals similar to those we now had in place with Billy Wilder and John Sturges.

We had completed a multiple-picture deal with Robert Wise, and we became involved with him in the development of a number of other properties, including *The Haunting of Hill House,* a novel by Shirley

Jackson. Another property we developed with him was a screen treatment of the life of the famed photojournalist Robert Capa, and we employed Nelson Gidding to write the screenplay.

The effort to attract other directors to our banner continued over the years, and noteworthy among those with whom we had arrangements was Fred Zinnemann, who by now was working with Daniel Taradash on the development of the screenplay for *Hawaii.* Later on, multiple-picture deals were made with David Miller and, somewhat later, with Franklin Schaffner, Peter Yates, Mark Rydell, and Sydney Pollack.

Last, but certainly not least, was our effort to attract Blake Edwards to our company. We felt that Blake Edwards was a spiritual heir to Billy Wilder, and that his potential as a comedic director was great. We also felt that he was an individual with whom we could have a long and successful relationship. Blake came with a great deal of enthusiasm and a large number of projects that interested him. One was *Love, Love, Love,* to be written by Owen Crump; other projects were *The Battle of Gettysburg, The Great Race,* which we also put into development, and, some time later, an original idea that Blake had developed with Maurice Richlin, tentatively titled *The Pink Panther.*

Over this period, there were numerous other properties that we developed that came from varied sources. Some of them I was interested in and developed screenplays myself with writers, hoping, when they were completed, to submit them to our directors or to others whom we might attract to our organization with them. One of those, for example, was a book, *633 Squadron,* the story of an aerial mission carried out by the wooden Mosquito bomber that was used by the British in the early years of World War II.

In the 1950s, Abe Lastfogel, the president of the William Morris Agency, spoke to Harold about the teenage phenomenon Elvis Presley and the excitement that he was generating in the concert world. He told Harold that he had already made an arrangement with Hal Wallis for Presley to appear in a number of pictures that would follow his first picture, which was a Fox project, *Love Me Tender.* We watched the Presley phenomenon develop. On one occasion, Abe Lastfogel called and told me that Presley was going to be appearing in concert in Los Angeles at the Pan-Pacific Auditorium near Fairfax Avenue and Beverly Boulevard. He insisted that I attend the concert, and I did. It was an extraordinary event. I don't know if any of it was staged or not, but the teenage audience went absolutely wild at Elvis's performance. Clearly he was an extraordinary talent.

Lastfogel told us that they had a spot open in Elvis's schedule and were looking for another film. We met his manager, Colonel Tom Parker, the former snake-oil salesman, who was quite different from most other managers I had met before. I told him I had some ideas about possible vehicles for Elvis. He said to me, "I'm not interested in that at all, young man, that's your job. You're supposed to know about picturemaking. You pay us the money, and we'll trust you to pick the vehicle and make the picture. Don't bother me with that. I just sell him." I was astounded at this, but I looked for a vehicle that I thought might be a good showcase for Elvis, as well as give him an opportunity to sing.

By this time, United Artists had acquired the pre-1948 film libraries of RKO and Warner Bros. I combed these libraries, looking for a vehicle that could be tailored to Elvis's talents. I chose two.

One was an old Warners film, *Kid Galahad,* that had been made in the 1930s with Edward G. Robinson and Bette Davis. Wayne Morris played the title role, and it was directed by Michael Curtiz. I thought that the boxer role would be well suited to Elvis, and I began preparation of the screenplay with writer William Fay.

I also chose a film out of the RKO library that starred Ginger Rogers and James Stewart, *Vivacious Lady,* which I also thought might be a possible Elvis vehicle and which I determined to develop.

The deal with Elvis was simple. We paid him $1 million flat. He received no participation, just cash. By this time, *Love Me Tender* had been successfully released, as had *Jailhouse Rock.*

I hoped that we could develop properties in which the below-the-line cost of the pictures would not be too high and, even including the $1 million that he was being paid, would allow us to make the picture at an overall reasonable cost. That is exactly what we accomplished in both the films we produced with Elvis.

We were preparing the *Kid Galahad* script when another script, *Pioneer Go Home!,* was brought to me by an ex-agent, Sam Jaffe, who intended to produce it himself. I was taken by it. I thought it offered an ideal vehicle for Elvis and could easily be tailored to his talents. *Pioneer* became *Follow That Dream,* and Charles Lederer, its original screenwriter, did the script revisions.

I talked to Elvis about the script. He was polite and respectful and said he thought it would work out just fine. We discussed, in greater detail, the placement of the songs. We agreed that he and his team of composers and lyricists would supply the songs through his publishing company, Hill and Range. For his scoring sessions, he used a scoring stage at Radio Recorders, located at 7000 Santa Monica Boulevard.

He selected the musicians, and he and the composers seemed to work out the songs as they went along. This was really quite unique for me, with the arrangements seemingly happening before my eyes. Elvis would be plucking on the guitar, and someone would come up with something, and they'd pick up on it, and the lyrics would be interpolated. One of the songs was "Follow That Dream." Liking the song, and hoping it would become a hit, we used it as the title of the picture.

These were very busy times for me. Having gotten the screenplays in the works for the Presley pictures, I looked about for somebody to produce the pictures, go on location, and supervise on a day-to-day basis. I was just too involved in all the rest of our program. I chose David Weisbart, a man I had known for some time, who had previously produced Elvis's Fox picture, *Love Me Tender.*

David proposed that we employ Gordon Douglas to direct *Follow That Dream.* Gordon had worked for David previously, although I had never met him before. He had a long list of credits, and I agreed to the selection.

Follow That Dream was shot on location in Florida, in Tampa, Ocala, Yankeetown, Inverness, and Bird Creek. I never went to the locations. I saw the dailies, and I talked regularly on the telephone with David. We shot the interiors at the Goldwyn Studio. Elvis had his group of friends, "The Memphis Mafia," present to keep him company, but neither he nor they presented any problem while we were working. Nor did Colonel Tom Parker, who was credited as technical advisor.

I was pleased with *Follow That Dream.* I thought it was a good picture and that it stood on its own even without the presence of its great star. It disappointed me in that it wasn't a really big grosser. It did well, but not nearly as well as I had hoped it would. Unfortunately, we didn't get a hit title song out of it. We needed a "Love Me Tender." If we'd had one, I think the picture would have been a big hit.

On *Kid Galahad*, we didn't get a hit song either, and the picture performed at the box office pretty much the same as *Follow That Dream*. However, as the Elvis mystique grew, the library value of these films remained high, enhancing their residual values.

As we approached the production start date for *Kid Galahad*, David Weisbart told me that his doctor had informed him that it was absolutely imperative that he undergo the then-rare and risky open-heart surgery procedure, so we lost his services. I arranged that he get his whole fee and profit participation in the picture, despite the fact that he would be gone during the entire pre-production, production, and post-production of the picture. I undertook to supervise the picture myself, so there would not be a doubled producer's fee attached to it. In order to facilitate that, I chose Phil Karlson to direct.

I had known Phil for a long time, since he had directed a number of pictures that were made at Allied Artists while I was in charge of production, among them *The Phenix City Story*. Phil had directed one of the first pictures that I observed being shot when I went to work at Monogram. He had also directed many Charlie Chan pictures there. Over the years, we continued to be in touch and talk about projects, and I felt very confident with him.

Kid Galahad did not have the long, distant location that *Follow That Dream* had. We shot the exteriors in the environs of Idyllwild, up in the same mountains where, years before, we had shot *Fort Osage* and other Westerns. The production company wasn't on location very long before it returned to the studio, and with Phil directing and the film proceeding without any serious problems, it wasn't too difficult a shoot.

Kid Galahad had an excellent supporting cast. Charles Bronson played the Kid's trainer, Gig Young played the Edward G. Robinson part, Lola Albright played the Bette Davis part, and Joan Blackman was the ingénue.

My first recollection of *The Great Escape* was John Sturges proposing it to me as a vehicle for a future film. He gave me a copy of the book by Paul Brickhill, who had been trained as a fighter pilot in Canada, flew with a squadron in England, and was shot down over the Tunisian desert in 1943. He spent the rest of the war in Stalag Luft III, the prisoner-of-war camp that was the setting of his book. I investigated the book, which had been published in 1949, and discovered that it was represented by a Hollywood agent, H. N. Swanson. I ascertained that the book was available for films. I read it and thought it incorporated marvelous material for a movie. It was not a novel, and it did not have personal stories. It would require a great deal of invention to take its background material, plus some interesting personalities, and create a screenplay and a film from that raw material.

I was concerned about the subject matter because the escape itself, as described in Paul Brickhill's book, had been utilized as background for other films, the most recent being *The Password Is Courage*, a black-and-white British film that starred Dirk Bogarde. We chose not to be deterred and plunged forward.

With some difficulty, we were able to acquire the rights to the Brickhill book. I had some conversations with Rod Serling about writing the screenplay, but, after our experience with Walter Newman on *The Magnificent Seven*, John and I decided to approach Walter and propose the project to him. He responded enthusiastically and set out to dramatize the material.

Walter was a very slow writer, and this process took a good deal of time. John Sturges left us during this period and directed a film for another company. When we received Walter Newman's version of the script, John and I were both disappointed in it. It was rambling and didn't have either the excitement or the tension that we felt the material needed. We decided to employ another writer.

The idea of employing Bill Burnett then arose. I had not worked with Burnett before, and I'm not sure if John had either, but as W. R. Burnett he was a distinguished novelist, responsible for *Little Caesar*, *The Asphalt Jungle*, and many others. So, with high hopes, we employed Burnett to do another version of the script. Unfortunately, this didn't pan out too well either, and we still didn't feel that we had a script with which we wanted to proceed. Neither of these scripts had the structure and the interplay of characters that made the final film so completely unique. The balancing of the number of stories that are told in *The*

Great Escape is really exceptional and has not often been matched. We felt a great deal of disappointment when Burnett also failed to come up with the script that we were looking for, but we persevered and convinced United Artists not to lose heart. We wanted to try again, and we decided to ask James Clavell to do a version.

Jim Clavell was Australian. He had been a prisoner of war in the infamous Japanese prison Changi and later he wrote a novel, *King Rat*, based on his experiences there. He had lost a leg while he was in the prisoner-of-war camp and now availed himself of an artificial limb. He had come to Hollywood and had begun to write and direct inexpensive films for a small company, Lippert Productions. His own background and experiences seemed to us like an ideal match for *The Great Escape*. He finally accomplished what we had been looking for and created the structure and the characters of *The Great Escape* as we now know them. His script was the one that we determined was ready to be filmed.

We did some preliminary budgets based on the idea of shooting it abroad. We planned to shoot in Germany and hoped to achieve some savings in this way. But the film budgeted at a good deal more than we had hoped. At this stage of preparation, we had been talking about casting the leading roles with big stars. John and I discussed doing the picture with Kirk Douglas playing the role of Hilts and Burt Lancaster playing the role of Hendley. Both Kirk and Burt had appeared in John's film *The Gunfight at the O.K. Corral,* and we were confident that we could put that combination together. These two major male stars were close to the peak of their careers, and their salaries reflected it.

The Great Escape was on the agenda for a meeting that was held at the Beverly Hills Hotel with Arthur Krim, Bob Benjamin, and Bob Blumofe of United Artists, and Harold, Marvin, and myself. Adding the salaries for major stars to an already-high below-the-line cost created a very expensive film. Given all the other problems inherent in this subject, the United Artists group wouldn't agree to go ahead with the film, feeling that it was simply too expensive. I was terribly disappointed.

Fortunately, I had a backup plan, which I had previously discussed with John. That idea was to cast it with Steve McQueen and James Garner rather than Kirk Douglas and Burt Lancaster. When I had made the original deal to put Steve McQueen in *The Magnificent Seven,*

I had insisted with his agents that The Mirisch Company be given options on his services for three more films at reasonable salaries. The first of these options was at $50,000 for the film.

When I had cast James Garner in *The Children's Hour*, I had also negotiated future options for Jim's services at nominal salaries. I proposed to United Artists that we exercise the options we had on these two actors. The difference in cost between the combination of McQueen and Garner as against the combination of Douglas and Lancaster was over $1 million.

The United Artists group was rather concerned about this approach. They felt that the second cast simply didn't have the box-office appeal of the first, and they were hesitant to do it with actors who had not yet carried major movies on their own. Steve had made a real impact in *The Magnificent Seven*, but clearly his role was part of an ensemble. Jim had made even less of an impact, although he was probably as well known because of the huge success of *Maverick*. We were now proposing a film that might cost twice as much as *The Magnificent Seven*, but without Yul Brynner, who was a big star when that film was made. With much talking, persuasion, and cajoling, we finally got a green light from United Artists to proceed with *The Great Escape* starring Steve McQueen and James Garner.

In short order, we arranged for the services of James Coburn and Charles Bronson, who were still nominally paid supporting actors. For the key role of Big X, we arranged for the services of the well-known English actor Richard Harris.

We proceeded with plans to shoot the film in Germany, at the Bavaria studios in Munich. We chose an American production designer, Ferdie Carrere, and he planned to build the prison camp on the back lot of the studio. Most of the rest of the casting was done in London, with English actors Donald Pleasance, David McCallum, James Donald, and Gordon Jackson. The German actors were cast in Bavaria.

Preparations proceeded swimmingly until about four weeks before the start of production. We were then advised that Richard Harris, who was appearing in *This Sporting Life*, was not going to be finished in time to start our film. We were compelled at the last minute to recast his role. After much scurrying around and last-minute submissions, we finally arranged for the services of Richard Attenborough to take over the role of Big X.

Production began in Germany and went along reasonably well until we began to have Steve McQueen problems. Steve, as was his wont, began to feel that his role was not developing as importantly as it should. He had grave misgivings that he was going to be overshadowed again, as he thought he might be by Horst Buchholz in *The Magnificent Seven*. He became quite agitated and told us that, until we could come up with some solution to his concerns, he would not continue to appear in the film. He was irreconcilable.

I sent for his agent, Stan Kamen, of the William Morris Agency, to come to Munich. He wasn't able to reason with Steve. The situation continued to deteriorate while we kept shooting around him for as long as we could. Steve was very fond of John Sturges and had great respect for him, but even John couldn't prevail on him to return to work. We were rapidly approaching the time when we would have to stop shooting. Neither John nor I nor anyone else was able to come up with any suggestion to overcome Steve's concerns.

We canvassed writers in London to determine if we could get any help from some new quarter. Fortunately we came upon Ivan Moffat, and Ivan suggested an idea that worked very well. It was a takeoff on a situation in *The Bridge on the River Kwai*. Ivan suggested that we have Big X come to Steve's Hilts character and suggest that he attempt an escape alone and, if he is successful, to proceed to the German border. Then, in an act of selflessness, Hilts will allow himself to be recaptured and returned to the prison camp. He can then inform the whole group, who are going to attempt the major breakout, about what they can expect to find on the outside and what their problems will be. In *Bridge on the River Kwai*, William Holden's character is blackmailed into returning to the prison camp by his superiors. Ivan's suggestion was that Steve's motivation would be selfless, putting himself through the ordeal of an escape just for the good of the whole group.

Steve liked the idea and agreed to return to work. The new sequences were written and incorporated into the picture. Unfortunately, they also added eighteen minutes to the running time, which made an already long film even longer. The final film ran two hours and fifty-three

Legendary motorcycle jump by Steve McQueen in *The Great Escape* in 1962. © 1963 Metro-Goldwyn-Mayer Studios Inc. All rights reserved.

minutes, and clearly its running time adversely affected its gross. We were limited to one show per night in theaters instead of two.

Steve, a great motorcycle fan and an excellent driver, felt that he could do the jump over the fence at the end of the picture himself. We were concerned that he could have an accident that might delay the completion of the picture. We insisted that a stuntman, Bud Eakins, execute the jump. However, though I did not see it nor do I know if it's true, I was told that the day after we shot the stunt, Steve went out to the location and jumped the fence himself on a motorcycle.

The Great Escape is one of my favorite movies. It's a movie movie. It is one of those films in which all of the casting seems impeccable. Yet it also has some important things to say about what the will of men can accomplish when tested. The fact that ninety men were able to accomplish an incredible escape, and to compel the Germans to mobilize great numbers of people to find them, was an extraordinary feat of bravery. Then, finally, the horror of the mass-murder retaliation, also based on fact, reminds us again of Nazi barbarism and the necessity of preventing it from ever happening again. *The Great Escape* accomplished that most successfully. The defiance and quiet heroism of Steve's extraordinary routine, of sitting on the floor of his cell and throwing a baseball against a wall, remarkably captured the unquenchable spirit of free men.

Our contract with John Sturges stipulated that John would be the producer of the films that he made for us, and I would be credited as executive producer. I was so credited on *The Magnificent Seven*. When we came to *The Great Escape,* I suggested to John that I not take credit on the picture although we worked together on it in the same way as we had on other films, and that he, who had made such a great contribution to it, have the only producer credit. I was greatly appreciative of his great contributions, and as I looked forward to having a long career making films with John, I wanted him to have the limelight exclusively.

The film was invited to be shown at the Moscow Film Festival. John was unable to attend, but I went to Moscow with the film, along with my brother Harold, Jim Clavell, and Elmer Bernstein. Elmer's score for *The Great Escape* contributed mightily to the film, just as his towering score in *The Magnificent Seven* had done. In Moscow, it was run in a palatial theater in the Kremlin, with simultaneous translations into Russian while the film was running. It was greeted with a great ovation.

The festival ran *West Side Story* too, which was also well received. We presented it to the Russians as an example of Americans' right to criticize shortcomings in their society, in their art, and in their media. We were, I suppose, proselytizing. But that's only fair since the Russians were doing the same for their philosophy.

18

A Big Hit and a Few Misses

By 1962, Billy Wilder had made *Some Like It Hot, One, Two, Three,* and *The Apartment,* the first and last of which had been smash hits for us. *One, Two, Three* had not been a box-office hit, but it certainly was a most interesting and worthy effort. Billy now suggested that his next film be based on a musical play that was currently running in London, *Irma La Douce* starring Elizabeth Seale and Keith Michel. The English version had been translated from the French. The score had been written by a famous composer, Marguerite Monot, and the book was by Alexandre Breffort. The score was beautiful, in the style of the romantic French music of the 1950s and 1960s, and the ballads — "The Language of Love," "Irma La Douce," and "The Bridge at Caullencourt" — are lovely. "Dis-Donc" is an audience rouser.

We investigated the rights to the material and learned that they were involved in a myriad of complex claims and counter-claims. Billy was eager to do the film, and we conveyed our interest in acquiring the property to United Artists, but they expressed little enthusiasm for the project.

Irma is a story about *poules, flics,* and *mecs:* prostitutes, cops, and pimps. The title character is the most beautiful of the poules and is harassed by the flics while she pursues her love for her mec. He is an ex-flic who falls hopelessly in love with her and wants her for himself. In order to assure himself of her love, he impersonates another person, pretending to be a client, so that he can test her love for his real self.

Our lawyers began to try to untangle all of the property's ownership problems. Harold also enlisted the services of an old friend and former associate of his, Edward Alperson, who knew some of the parties who were involved in the play in France. Alperson took it upon himself to try and clear up the rights situation. He went to Paris and devoted himself to bringing all the interested parties, or their heirs, into some kind of agreement. Harold was ill at the time, but Alperson cobbled together a deal that I asked United Artists to approve so that we could acquire the property.

When finally faced by a concrete proposal, Arthur Krim, who probably thought that we could never work out all the ownership problems, finally said he didn't want to finance the acquisition of the property, about which he had had misgivings from the beginning. The deal involved payment of $350,000 against future considerations. Arthur expressed to me his concern that this was a picture that would never be made, since he was convinced its story problems would finally discourage Billy Wilder. He would not approve the acquisition.

I was already out on the end of a limb with Billy. I had a real feeling for his enthusiasm for the material and for the approach that he was bringing to it, and I did not want to disappoint him. Nor did I want to drive him into the hands of others who might be more agreeable to doing the deal and breaking up our relationship with him.

I finally suggested to Arthur that if UA would advance the funding for the acquisition of the property, our company would indemnify United Artists for half of the money so that, in the event the film was not subsequently made by Billy, its exposure would be cut in half. Arthur advised me against indemnifying UA but agreed to go along with the arrangement if I insisted.

Finally we acquired the rights and, under an arrangement we made with Edward Alperson, agreed that he would have a participation in the picture, as well as a cash payment, and he would share our presentation credit on the picture.

Billy Wilder was delighted. He and Iz Diamond began work on the screenplay. Billy felt it was important that Nestor, the mec character played by Jack Lemmon, be made sympathetic. The original role, that of a pimp, is certainly not that. But Billy finally conceived the idea of beginning the film by dramatizing Jack Lemmon's character as not an ordinary Paris policeman, but rather a most extraordinary one, an honest one. It is only by virtue of the fact that he refuses to be corrupted that he is dismissed from the police force. Then, unable to find other employment and against his own better judgment, he is convinced by Shirley MacLaine's prostitute character, Irma, to assume the role of her pimp. This ploy accomplished a great deal of what Billy hoped to do, and also gave us an amusing opening for our film.

After considerable discussion, Billy also agreed to photograph the picture in color. Billy had not made a film in color since *The Seven Year Itch* in 1955 and had, in all of our previous films, always opted for black-and-white. But we all agreed that this material certainly called for color photography.

Billy decided that he did not want the film to be a musical. He felt more comfortable doing it as a straight farce. He had done only one musical, *The Emperor Waltz* with Bing Crosby, and it had been unsuccessful. He intended to utilize the score of *Irma* only as background, and André Previn did a marvelous job of adapting the Marguerite Monot music for that purpose. One short number that Shirley MacLaine does, "Dis-Donc," is all that remained of the singing from the original.

Most of the film was shot interior, on stages at the Goldwyn Studio. The streets were creatively designed by Alex Trauner, but unfortunately the acceptability of that kind of production design had passed, and audiences expected the real thing. Effective as some of those sets were — such as Pigalle, and Les Halles, the produce market — I wished even then that they had been done on actual exteriors. We did undertake a rather short location shoot in Paris, but I've always regretted that we didn't do more there. The picture would have benefited from it.

Billy had worked with Charles Laughton years before on *Witness for the Prosecution* and was a great Charles Laughton admirer. From the very beginning, it had been his idea that Laughton should play Moustache, the owner of the bistro in which most of the action of the story takes place. Laughton, when presented with the role, was enthusiastic about doing it but, unfortunately, was suffering from cancer. It soon became clear that he was not going to be able to work again. Billy subsequently chose Lou Jacobi to play Moustache.

The production proceeded somewhat more slowly than Billy usually worked, but not seriously so. The film cost about $5 million. When we screened the completed film for the first time for the United Artists executives, I sensed they were very cold to it. One of them even asked if we thought that we could find another distributor who might take the film over and reimburse UA for its investment. We felt that would be injurious to the film and didn't want to make such an overture. An excellent advertising campaign was devised, and the film opened. *Irma La Douce* proved to be an exceedingly profitable picture both domestically and in the foreign market for United Artists, despite its own misgivings.

Like *The Great Escape, Irma La Douce* was a long film, running 143 minutes, which limited theater exhibition to one showing per evening rather than two, and which reduced what the gross might have been had the film been shorter. Nonetheless, it grossed $15 million in film rental, becoming Billy's highest grossing production.

🐟

Toys in the Attic had been written by William Wyler's good friend Lillian Hellman, and he professed great eagerness to do it. It was in the mold of the Tennessee Williams plays of the period, concerned with southern families riven with sexual problems that played themselves out in melodrama. The play had been produced on Broadway, starring Jason Robards Jr., and had been moderately successful. United Artists and our company were both eager to develop a continuing relationship with William Wyler, and we thought this would be a piece of material that could lend itself to a highly successful film in the vein of *A Streetcar Named Desire, Come Back Little Sheba,* and *The Glass Menagerie,* all of which films had been made from Broadway plays of the period. However, upon completion of *Ben-Hur,* Wyler told us that he had changed his mind and would prefer to do a new version of *The Children's Hour* rather than *Toys in the Attic.* We had a considerable investment in the latter, and in discussions with United Artists, it was decided that we should try and put together a film based on the play, despite the fact that Wyler had dropped out of it.

Hoping to use an attractive motion-picture figure in the lead, we decided to offer the role to Dean Martin. We felt that he would bring humor to it, as well as an audience that might expand the normal constituency of that type of film. I chose a young television director, George Roy Hill, with whom I had been impressed and whom I felt could be a successful movie director. We employed a screenwriter, James Poe, who had previously written screenplays of Tennessee Williams's *Cat on a Hot Tin Roof* and *Summer and Smoke*.

Between the time that we began preparation of *Toys in the Attic* and the time the film was made, George Roy Hill was employed by Metro-Goldwyn-Mayer to direct a film version of *Period of Adjustment*, based on another Tennessee Williams play. That film had been adapted by my friend Isobel Lennart and starred Jane Fonda and Anthony Franciosa.

For the roles of the sisters in *Toys in the Attic*, we chose two brilliant actresses, Geraldine Page and Wendy Hiller, who were supported by Yvette Mimieux and Gene Tierney. It was a well-made film of its genre that probably appeared at the end of a cycle. We had attempted to re-suscitate this property, after it had been abandoned by Wyler, and as so often happens, it did not turn out well. It's a grim story. It was not well reviewed and was not financially successful.

I will always connect the shooting of *Toys in the Attic* with one of the most enjoyable and exciting experiences of that whole period. The film went into release in the fall of 1963, and as chance would have it, the baseball World Series was being played at that same time. The Los Angeles Dodgers had won the pennant in the National League and they were pitted against the New York Yankees, who had won the American League pennant. This was the era of the great Dodger pitchers, Sandy Koufax and Don Drysdale, and they had both enjoyed superlative seasons. Sitting with Harold one afternoon, he suddenly mused, "I wonder what the odds would be if one were to make a bet that the Dodgers would beat the Yankees in four straight games."

I said, "Well, I don't know, but I'd guess they'd be very high. You have two great teams, and four straight is almost unheard of in the World Series."

He then continued to muse, took a pencil and a piece of paper, and said, "I wonder what would happen if one were to make a bet on the Dodgers to win four straight, assuming that, with the great Sandy Koufax pitching the opening game, they would at least win the first of the four. If that were to come to pass, then one could hedge the four-straight bet by betting on the Yankees in each of the following three games, so as to mitigate the loss if the Dodgers didn't win four straight. The odds on the four-straight bet should be great enough so that, even if all the losses on the hedging bets were deducted, one would still wind up with a tidy profit." The more we discussed this, the more excited we became about the concept. We told it to some other people, and pretty soon we had collected a small syndicate of potential partners in the bet. Harold said, "I wonder where one would place such a bet?"

I said, "I have an answer to that." I phoned Dean Martin and said, "Dean, do you know anybody in Las Vegas who might be willing to book a bet on the World Series?"

He replied, "That shouldn't be too much trouble. I'll let you know."

Sure enough, he shortly gave me the name of a person to call in Las Vegas, and we booked the bets. The following Yankee-Dodger games were the most exciting baseball games that any of us had ever followed in our lives. Yes, the extraordinary, almost unbelievable, did happen, and the Dodgers won four straight in the series.

✺

I had gotten to know Stuart Millar quite well when he had worked as Willy Wyler's assistant on *Friendly Persuasion*, many years ago. He and his producing partner, Larry Turman—who had, up to that time, been an agent working for the Kurt Frings agency—proposed a project to us that would be a remake of the Bette Davis film *Dark Victory*, which was included in the pre-1948 Warners library then owned by United Artists. Millar and Turman told us that they had discussed this as a vehicle for Susan Hayward and that she was interested in doing the film. Susan Hayward was a fine actress who had already won an Academy Award for *I Want to Live!* Certainly she seemed to be an excellent candidate to play the Bette Davis role. They proposed making the film in England, where it could qualify for subsidies under the Eady Plan. The Eady Plan was a law in force at that time which stipulated that films produced in England with largely English casts and crews would qualify for a subsidy based on the theatrical gross of the film in the UK. The remake of *Dark Victory* seemed like a worthwhile project. They recommended a fine English director, Lewis Gilbert. Stuart suggested that Joseph Hayes—who had written both the play and the movie that Wyler had directed for Paramount some years before, *Desperate Hours*—write the screenplay of the remake. We arranged with United Artists to make the right to remake *Dark Victory* available to us, and we then began the preparation of the film that, at that point, had been retitled *Summer Flight.*

As the project developed, most of the original elements were changed. For some reason, Lewis Gilbert dropped out of the project and was replaced by Daniel Petrie, then an outstanding television director. Joseph Hayes was replaced, and Stuart brought in Jessamyn West, another old friend and associate from *Friendly Persuasion,* to write the screenplay.

The leading male role was played by an English actor, Michael Craig, and Diane Baker played the role of the friend, played in the original by Geraldine Fitzgerald. The film, eventually released as *Stolen Hours,* was not particularly well reviewed. It was unfavorably compared with the original, as often happens with remakes, and it was not commercially successful. However, it wasn't an expensive film. The Eady benefits were helpful, and it created another film with a well-known star for the United Artists library.

❦

Kings of the Sun was suggested to me by Arnold Picker, the executive vice president of United Artists in charge of its foreign sales. He had read an article about the Mound Builders of Mexico and told me that he had discussed the idea with Yul Brynner, who had indicated an interest in doing such a film. I had some concerns about it, but Arnold was eager for us to undertake the project. I talked with Yul Brynner, who confirmed to me that he had told Arnold that he thought it was interesting and something that he would like to do.

I discussed these conversations with Elliott Arnold, a writer who also expressed interest in the idea. He did a good deal of research on the subject and then wrote a treatment and later a screenplay.

I wasn't pleased with the screenplay, and I next contacted another writer, James Webb, whose credits included *Trapeze, The Big Country,* and *How the West Was Won.* Jim was challenged by it, accepted the assignment, and finally was able to get a workable script out of the subject, based on the culture and history of the Mayan builders of the pyramids of Yucatan.

I called Lewis Rachmil, who had been a producer for numerous companies over many years and was a top-flight production person, and asked him to go to Chichén Itzá to scout locations in Mexico. He did and advised me that it was a highly feasible location.

We next enlisted the services of J. Lee Thompson, an English director who had, by then, directed *Taras Bulba* with Yul Brynner and the very successful *Guns of Navarone.* Lee Thompson had been suggested for the assignment by Arnold Picker. I never went to Chichén Itzá while the picture was being shot, but Lew Rachmil went there and was in charge. Shirley Anne Field, who played the female lead, was an English actress strongly recommended by Lee Thompson. Richard Basehart and George Chakiris were also in the cast.

Kings of the Sun was not successful, either artistically or commercially. It wasn't made for the right reasons, and that is most often an insuperable handicap. Our creative team lacked passion for what we were doing, and its commercial values could not overcome that. Not being enthusiastic about it, I should have taken a position. By just letting the project move from one stage to the next, I allowed it to progress further than it should have. Arnold Picker was enthusiastic and kept pushing it, but the problems of making the film and its content were not his responsibility. I always blamed myself for its failure. I had thought of it as a vehicle for the star power of Yul Brynner, who was an important international star by then. But that was not a good enough reason for doing a film about which I had serious misgivings.

19

Blake Edwards and
The Pink Panther

One of the early targets of The Mirisch Company's campaign to
attract talented directors was Blake Edwards. I had met
Blake many years before, when he was still an actor and I
was just beginning my career at Monogram. Blake was acting in *Pan-
handle*, a film that he and John Champion produced for Monogram, directed by Lesley Selander. Later Blake wrote a number of low-budget
films for Columbia and finally began to direct. Among his most successful films were *The Days of Wine and Roses* and *Operation Petticoat*.

We succeeded in making a four-picture producing and directing
deal with Blake, and he came to us with an idea for a film that he and
his collaborator on *Operation Petticoat*, Maurice Richlin, had developed.
The Pink Panther is the name of a precious jewel that a famous thief—
called the Phantom, who is much like the Cary Grant character in *To
Catch a Thief*—plans to steal. Blake suggested that the film be made in
Italy and also proposed that an ex-agent of his, Martin Jurow, come
aboard as producer. They went to Rome, surveyed the area and budgeted
the film, and we proceeded with the casting of the picture.

He selected Claudia Cardinale to play the Princess from whom the
jewel would be stolen, and Robert Wagner to play the nephew of the
jewel thief, who aspired to the success of his uncle in the jewel-stealing
business. David Niven was to play the jewel thief. As the bumbling

detective, Inspector Clouseau, Blake chose Peter Ustinov, and to play the detective's wife, who is the lover of the Phantom, he chose Ava Gardner.

The script was excellent, and we were able to put this expensive group together within the parameters of our budget. We thought the project had all the elements for a funny, sophisticated, outrageous comedy.

As chance would have it, before the film went into production, Ava Gardner chose to drop out of the cast. Charles Feldman, an important agent of the time, convinced Blake to use an actress named Capucine to replace her. Blake acceded to this request and asked us to approve her for the role. Capucine had been in a number of films by then; she was very attractive and certainly adequate to the demands of this particular role. We agreed.

This replacement did not please Peter Ustinov, who advised us that he did not want to act in the film with Capucine and chose to withdraw from the cast. The role of Inspector Clouseau was critical to the film, and losing Ustinov was most serious. We instituted a lawsuit against him and were terribly worried that the picture had been irretrievably injured. After feverish discussions with Blake Edwards, we finally selected Peter Sellers to replace Ustinov. Sellers, whose international career was just beginning, was delighted to get the role.

Blake altered the screenplay as shooting progressed and he began to see the breadth of Peter Sellers's comedic talent. The role expanded far beyond what it had been in the original version. With improvisation, Peter also elaborated on his character and made the film even funnier. It took this extraordinary combination of circumstances for one of the comic geniuses of his era to find his way to a role for which he may have been born. *The Pink Panther* caught lightning in a bottle. The cherry on the cake was Henry Mancini's score, which has also passed into the realm of the historic. The blending of all these elements produced a great comedic film.

We had decided to have an animated main title for the film. To execute it, we chose a new firm that had been set up by the great Friz Freleng, who was one of the animation geniuses of Warner Bros. cartoons and, along with Chuck Jones, the heart and brain of Bugs Bunny and the Roadrunner. Friz had gone into business with David DePatie, and they were just beginning to organize an animation studio. We assigned them the task of creating the main title. They responded brilliantly and created the figure of the Pink Panther, which soon assumed a life of its own. Although the Pink Panther in the film is a jewel, most people now think of it as a sophisticated animated figure.

The film was shot in its entirety in Rome. As the shooting of the picture progressed, it soon became clear that Peter was going to dominate the film and play a much greater part in the telling of the story than the original script called for. The public reacted the same way to the film we did, and Peter Sellers, who had appeared in a number of films before this, finally broke through in *The Pink Panther,* becoming a major comedic screen star.

The title sequence also created a tremendous amount of comment from critics and reviewers, as well as audiences. The idea of having an animated title sequence was not unique. It had been done in numerous other films, but there weren't many that were as amusing as the one DePatie-Freleng created for this film. We began to talk about the possibility of using the figure of the Pink Panther as the lead in a cartoon series. Our original thought was to try it out as a six-minute cartoon supplement to a long film or a roadshow attraction. DePatie-Freleng, who became partners with us and Blake Edwards in the enterprise, assumed the responsibility for creating the first Pink Panther cartoon, and so was launched *The Pink Phink.*

We hoped that if *The Pink Phink* were successful we could convince United Artists to produce twelve six-minute cartoons per year. United Artists agreed to our plan, and we began the production of *The Pink Phink,* which turned out to be an absolutely first-rate cartoon. It was readily booked. It cost about $30,000 to produce and won an Academy Award as the Best Animated Short Subject in the year of its release. United Artists enthusiastically agreed to finance and distribute twelve Pink Panther cartoons a year. We looked toward the theatrical release of the cartoons with the hope that eventually we would find another home for them on television, which subsequently happened.

It was part of the mystique of the cool character the Panther developed that he didn't need to speak. And he didn't speak for thirty years, until we produced a package of 120 twelve-minute cartoons for television syndication, which appeared in the early 1990s. The earlier cartoons were supported by the release of subsequent Pink Panther pictures and by the endurance of Henry Mancini's "Pink Panther Theme." That music is forever identified with the film and with the cartoon character. It continues to be played and recognized all these years after its original appearance.

The animated panther continues to find big audiences. He has appeared on television in Saturday morning cartoon shows and in daily TV syndicated shows and he has been merchandized in many products. In the 1980s he also appeared in a new cartoon show for ABC, *The Pink Panther and Sons,* in which he co-starred with his two young panther nephews, Pinky and Panky. A new show, *The Pink Panther and Pals,* will be telecast in 2008.

These cartoons also spawned other cartoon series. The television networks, when they bought a so-called Pink Panther show, often requested that we create new characters, so that a half-hour would not be composed of just Pink Panther adventures. Other series that were generated are *Roland and the Rat Fink, The Ant and the Aardvark, The Texas Toads,* and *Mr. Jaws.* All these shows added to the body of what was called the Pink Panther animation library, which by now contains close to five hundred cartoon subjects. The cartoons are distributed and merchandised now by Metro-Goldwyn-Mayer, which acquired United Artists and all its properties in the late 1980s. This entire library developed out of that short main title, all those many years ago.

❧

For some time, my brother Harold had been talking to Anatole Litvak about his doing a film for us. Litvak finally came to us with the proposal that we acquire the rights to a recently opened, highly successful Broadway play, *A Shot in the Dark,* which had been based on a French play by Marcel Achard, *L'Idiote,* and had been adapted for the American stage by Harry Kurnitz, with Walter Matthau playing the lead on Broadway. We saw the play, a suspense comedy, and we agreed to acquire it. Anatole Litvak proposed Alec Coppel to write the screenplay.

As the project developed, Litvak succeeded in securing the interest of Sophia Loren to play the lead. When the script was finished and was submitted to Loren, she and her husband, producer Carlo Ponti, advised

Peter Sellers as bumbling Inspector Clouseau in 1964's *A Shot in the Dark*. © 1964 Mirisch-Geoffrey Productions.

us that she did not approve it and would not do our film. We agreed that it needed more work, and we employed Norman Krasna to do a rewrite. It still disappointed us.

With the picture uncast and the script not yet satisfactory, Anatole Litvak told us that he wished to withdraw from the project. Clearly, this was very upsetting, since by then we had made a substantial investment. But we hoped to find a way to salvage it. We decided to discuss the project with Blake Edwards and see if he would become involved.

It was Blake's idea to convert it into a vehicle for Peter Sellers and his Inspector Clouseau character. It was a marvelous idea, and it salvaged the whole project. Blake and I went to New York, met with Peter Sellers, and explained the project to him and the idea of incorporating the Clouseau character. We succeeded in convincing him. He agreed to play the Clouseau character within the framework of a completely re-written *Shot in the Dark* script, which Blake undertook to do himself, along with a collaborator of his choosing. *Shot* was now a Peter Sellers/ Inspector Clouseau project.

Blake chose William Peter Blatty to collaborate with him, and Blake said they would like to go by ship to London, where the picture was to be produced. They planned to write the script while they were aboard ship and hoped to have a version that could be budgeted five days later, when they arrived in London. They didn't achieve quite that, but they did accomplish a great deal of the writing en route from New York to London.

We were able to arrange for Elke Sommer to play the role that had originally been intended for Sophia Loren. George Sanders, Herbert Lom, and Graham Stark were also cast in the picture. Using the springboard of the original play, Blake and Bill Blatty designed *Shot in the Dark* to be a showcase for Peter and his talents, and it worked out beautifully.

The film was shot in London, amid a great deal of controversy between Edwards and Sellers. After its completion, we screened the picture for Peter Sellers in Los Angeles, and he was very upset by it. He told me he thought it was terrible, and that it shouldn't be released. He said that if we would agree not to release the picture, he would refund the entire cost of the picture to us, over a period of years, because he didn't want the film to be shown. We respectfully declined.

The film was marvelously reviewed and much more financially successful than the original *Pink Panther.* Peter's offer, and his feelings about the film, were soon forgotten.

We repeated the cartoon main-title motif on *Shot in the Dark,* for which DePatie-Freleng created a cartoon version of the Inspector.

Because *Shot in the Dark* was completed after a stormy relationship between Blake Edwards and Peter Sellers, they both vowed never to work together again. I hoped that time might heal that breach, since the Pink Panther was a franchise that deserved to be continued, and they were both indispensable to it. However, Blake wanted to do other things, and we developed more material with him. *The Great Race* was a favored project of his, and we agreed to undertake its development.

At approximately the same time, with Blake's acquiescence, I engaged Tom and Frank Waldman, who had been frequent collaborators of his and knew the Clouseau character well, to work on a possible third Clouseau picture. We hoped to develop a script that, after their quarrel had abated, would interest Peter and Blake. The actual production of this picture, *Inspector Clouseau,* was finally accelerated by the emergence of Alan Arkin in *The Russians Are Coming, the Russians Are Coming,* for which he received an Academy Award nomination.

I thought Alan Arkin could become a successful comedy star, perhaps along the same lines as Peter Sellers. Certainly he seemed to me a good choice to play Clouseau. At first I had some misgivings about offering the role to him. I thought there was a good chance that he would not want to risk comparisons with Sellers, and that he wouldn't accept the part. However, I was pleasantly surprised when he said he would like to take on the challenge. I again asked Blake if he would change his mind and if he would direct the film with Alan, and he declined.

Looking about for another experienced director of comedy, I offered the film to Bud Yorkin. Yorkin was already a partner with Norman Lear in Tandem Productions, and they had made a number of successful comedies together. He was enthusiastic, and we planned the picture for production in 1967 in Switzerland, Paris, and London. Just prior to the start of production, I received a telephone call, late one night, from Peter Sellers in London. He said to me, most irately, that he had learned that a film was going to be made titled *Inspector Clouseau,* and that it was scheduled to start production shortly. He was furious at me and said, "How could you do this without me?" I reminded him, as gently as I could, that I had, on numerous occasions, asked him to play the role. He brushed all this aside and said something to the effect that Clouseau was his role, and I had to dismiss Alan Arkin and do the film with him. That is, after he had seen the script.

I told him that we were close to starting production and that what he was asking was not possible. Replacing Arkin with Sellers would convert a go project into a new script development, at a very high cost, with no assurance of the mercurial Peter ever really doing the film.

I went to London for the final preparations for the film. The cast, except for Alan, was completely British. I remained in London until just after the picture went into production; Lewis Rachmil stayed on for the shooting. Our cameraman was Arthur Ibbetson, the production designers were Michael Stringer and Norman Dorme, Ken Thorne did the score, and the film editor was John Victor Smith.

I had high hopes that we could bring about a switch in leading actors that would enable us to continue this exceedingly popular series of pictures with an actor who was more professional than Peter Sellers.

Unfortunately, Sellers was right, and we were not able to make the transition from one actor to another, as the Bond pictures accomplished so well. The film was not successful commercially, and the Pink Panther and Inspector Clouseau remained dormant theatrically for six years, until 1974.

Interestingly, the critic in *Life* magazine (August 23, 1968) wrote,

> *Inspector Clouseau* is, in its little way, a historic film, proving not only that the title character is now so well established that his name alone can lure us into the theater, but that his spirit can survive delightfully unscathed the transmigration from Peter Sellers, in whom it resided so comfortably in *The Pink Panther* and *A Shot in the Dark,* to Alan Arkin. Arkin has something of the late Buster Keaton about him, the same implacability in pursuit of seemingly impossible goals, the same unflappability in the face of endless self-inflicted chaos, the same sublime, unfathomable, and greatly exaggerated faith in himself and his power to cope with the maniac challenges the gods of chance fling before him. I am not saying he is better than Sellers was in this, the best characterization of his not-completely-happy years of international stardom, but he is every bit as good, and that is very good indeed.

The *Hollywood Reporter* also loved the film, and predicted it would be a big hit. Instead, it was a great disappointment.

The Party was conceived by Blake Edwards, who suggested the idea of Peter Sellers playing a bumbling, accident-prone Indian actor. We had seen Peter do an Indian character before in *The Millionairess*. It sounded funny, and it was Blake's idea to follow this character, who is mistakenly invited to a fancy Hollywood party where he proceeds to make an utter shambles of it. Despite Blake and Peter's vow never to work with one another again after *A Shot in the Dark,* once Blake got the idea for *The Party* he felt there was nobody else but Peter who could do it. He told the idea to Peter, who became enthusiastic. These two men, who had vowed not to work together again, now couldn't wait to get started.

Because of his health problems, as well as his unpredictable conduct, Peter gave pause to many movie financiers. And Blake himself had achieved a reputation as a very expensive director, particularly after *The Great Race.* When *The Party* was proposed, Blake assured me it would be a controlled picture. He said he thought we could find an appropriate house to rent for the duration of the production and actually shoot most of the picture there. Consequently, we would have inexpensive set-construction costs. He estimated that the film could be produced for $3 million. We were most enthusiastic about the picture. We thought it could be a tour de force for Peter, and certainly there would be no better director for this kind of a picture than Blake Edwards. I pushed hard for the project with United Artists while Harold was having one of his periods of illness. To make the project more palatable to United Artists, I succeeded in getting Peter and Blake to agree that if the cost of the picture exceeded $3 million, they would pledge their salaries toward the completion of the picture.

We and United Artists both felt that if Blake and Peter were going to have their own money at risk, it would be a deterrent to a cost over-run. Peter wanted to work, and I supposed that he felt it was important to work again with Blake, with whom he had made his greatest successes. In addition, they both believed strongly in the material.

The rental house location never worked out, and we ultimately built a house set on a stage at the Goldwyn Studio. The screenplay was written after the deal was put together. The idea for a swimming pool sequence came up and it, too, was put on the stage at the Goldwyn Studio. Of course, we finally wrecked the house in the picture, and if we were using an actual home we would have had to rebuild it when the film was completed anyhow.

The other important roles in the film were played by Claudine Longet, Denny Miller, Gavin McLeod, and J. Edward McKinley. The picture was photographed by Lucien Ballard. Ralph Winters edited it, and Henry Mancini, who scored every film Blake made for thirty years, did an excellent job.

The safeguards worked well, and the picture came in close to budget. I thought *The Party* was going to be very successful financially, as well as critically, but it proved to be disappointing. It has, however, developed a good deal of cult status over the years.

Neither Blake nor Peter had to forego any of their fees toward completion. However, in the years following *The Party*, Peter's career did not flourish. Nor did Blake's. Toward the late 1960s or early 1970s, as The Mirisch Company was coming close to the end of its relationship with United Artists, Blake suggested making another *Pink Panther* film.

This was now about seven or eight years after the release of *Shot in the Dark*. He had written fifteen or twenty pages of an outline, entitled *The Return of the Pink Panther*. I was very enthused about the idea, but I could not convince United Artists to take another chance with Peter, Blake, and the Pink Panther.

Many years later, after we had sold our interest in the Pink Panther live action films and our contract with United Artists had expired, a situation developed where Julie Andrews, the wife of Blake Edwards, had made a deal with Lord Lew Grade to appear in a series of weekly variety television shows to be shown on ABC. As part of her deal to do those shows, Grade agreed to finance two movies in which she would appear. The television show, *The Julie Andrews Hour*, did not do well in the ratings and was canceled after thirteen weeks. However, according to an associate of Lew Grade, Blake now told Grade that Julie wished to do a film, *The Tamarind Seed*, which he would direct.

As he was obligated to do, Grade financed the film, but, unfortunately, it was unsuccessful. Having been badly hurt with *The Tamarind Seed*, Grade suggested that for the second film, perhaps they should do a comedy. Blake now proposed to him that they do *The Return of the Pink Panther*, from that same treatment that I had seen all those years before.

Peter's career had not flourished during that period, and he was quite ready to return to one of his past great successes in the hope that it would give a new momentum to his career. Grade, too, was pleased with the idea. He told United Artists that if it would allow him to license the rights for one film, he would finance the picture completely and give United Artists worldwide distribution and a share of the profits.

The Return of the Pink Panther was produced and became the greatest commercial success of all the films in the series. The motion-picture business had mushroomed since the first *Pink Panther*, and grosses had grown tremendously. The methods of distribution had changed, ancillary markets had developed, and the potentials for successful films had expanded enormously. Through an extraordinary set of circumstances, United Artists had backed into one of its most profitable films of 1974 and resuscitated one of its most valuable franchises.

20

The Academy of
Motion Picture Arts
and Sciences

I was first elected to the Board of Governors of the Academy of Motion Picture Arts and Sciences in 1964, an election that marked the beginning of a lifelong association with the Academy. In 1966, I was elected assistant treasurer, and two years later I became treasurer.

When I first joined the board, the president was Arthur Freed, the legendary producer of MGM musicals. The executive secretary was Margaret Herrick, who had been with the Academy since a few years after its inception in 1927 as one of its first librarians. Regular meetings were held at the Academy headquarters, which were then located in an old theater building at the corner of Melrose Avenue and Doheny Drive, formerly called the Melrose. The auditorium was used for Academy screenings, and a small library and boardroom had been improvised upstairs. It was crowded and certainly didn't provide much shelf space for what was publicized as the Academy's library. The board considered all matters of business coming before it, such as rules, dues, publicity, public relations, and the planning of the Academy Awards ceremonies, as well as the vigilant protection of the Academy's name and world-famous Oscar figure.

Having outgrown its quarters by the late 1960s, many of the Academy's activities had to be conducted in rented facilities, away from its headquarters. Most of its library collections were kept in storage. The *Academy Players Directory* had its own quarters, and the theater was very old by then, requiring a great deal of maintenance. We wanted to increase our staff so we could expand our services, but we had no room whatsoever in which to grow. The need for a new facility had become increasingly apparent to the board. The theater, which produced a certain amount of income when it was rented out for film company press screenings, could no longer compete with the new venues that were being built in the city. For example, the Directors Guild had constructed a new building on Sunset Boulevard, which had a state-of-the-art theater. The Academy Theatre also suffered from the worst of all possible afflictions in Los Angeles: it provided no parking. There was only a small empty lot alongside that accommodated about a dozen cars. It is certainly difficult, if not impossible, to operate a theater that provides no parking facilities. When screenings were held for the membership, or when it was rented out, people had to scour the neighborhood to find parking places.

When Steve Broidy was chairman of the Building Committee in the late 1960s, he had been approached with a proposal for the Academy to enter the Century City development, located on the former Twentieth Century-Fox back lot, which had been sold to William Zeckendorf Sr., a partner in the Webb and Knapp Company. Zeckendorf later went bankrupt and disposed of the property to Alcoa, which continued to develop it. The idea was that the Academy would become part of what was called the ABC Entertainment Complex. They proposed an area kitty-corner from the twin towers, fronting on the mall, where they would construct a headquarters building and a small theater, while also giving it some entrée to the Shubert Theater in the Center for the Academy Awards shows. It would also have the use of the Century City underground garage. Over the years, the Academy Awards presentations had moved from the Biltmore ballroom to the Chinese Theater to the Shrine Auditorium to the Pantages Theater and later to the Santa Monica Civic Auditorium.

In 1970, I was appointed chairman of the Building Committee by President Dan Taradash, at which time the Academy was presented with a proposal from Universal Studios, which was interested in developing its studio tours. It was seeking new attractions to help bring people to visit its back lot, its rides, and its studio. Universal offered the Academy its choice of any available site on the studio back lot, comprising some four hundred acres. We began to talk about a site that would be furthest removed from the studio proper, probably out near a point that, as you see it from the freeway, is the tip of the Universal property as you turn to go to Burbank. The studio agreed to pay all the costs of building a thousand-seat theater, as well as a modest headquarters building. The Academy could still do the Awards show wherever it chose.

The Universal proposal was almost irresistible to many people on the Academy Board of Governors. Lew Wasserman, then chairman of MCA, offered it to the board at a special meeting, in which he presented an elaborate brochure with visualizations of the edifice that could be constructed.

There were, however, still a number of governors who had concerns about the proposal. Despite its obvious benefits, there was a feeling among some that the independence of the Academy might be attacked if its home was on the property of a particular studio. Others felt that the location might not be central enough for the Academy. The proposal was debated very heatedly on a number of occasions.

I opposed the proposal. I felt the Academy should not appear to be captive to a particular studio that had been financially generous. Since certain segments of the press constantly sought to find reason to impugn the integrity of the Academy, I felt that the Academy must always be purer than Caesar's wife, despite the fact that there might be no ulterior motives in Universal's proposal. Its benefit would have been merely proximity to the Universal Studio tours. Later, if the Academy Awards were to emanate from a reconstructed Universal Amphitheater, the publicity value of the announcement that the Academy Awards were being held in Universal City might have been of some worth to the tour business.

Hal Wallis, a member of the Building Committee, wrote a letter to Daniel Taradash, dated February 16, 1971, in which he recapitulated: "As to the Universal site, it is possible that, if we go this far from Hollywood or Beverly Hills, we might find alternatives, but I doubt that any of them could be bought for the price that has been agreed upon by Universal," which was a dollar per year for the land and a ninety-nine-year lease. "I must make it clear that I am not influenced by my association with Universal, but only because of the amount of land, three or four acres. The fact that Barham Boulevard will be widened to six or eight lanes, and all of the parking will be ground-level parking at no cost either to the Academy or members, the whole project makes more sense to me than others we have discussed, taking our financial situation into consideration." He concluded, "I do not say that the Universal site is the only one we should consider. I do say that economically, and thinking within our budget, it is the only one that comes close to what we are able to do." Hal Wallis was a highly respected producer and a renowned real-estate expert. He was most articulate, a giant in the industry, and influential with the board. My arguments against him were largely on the basis of maintaining absolute purity. Fortunately, the Board of Governors backed me, and our quest for a new location would continue.

🐟

In its early days, the Academy Award ceremonies were closed industry banquets. In March 1945, for the first time, a full radio broadcast of the ceremonies emanated from Grauman's Chinese Theater. It continued as an annual radio program for a number of years, until 1953, when the show was telecast on the combined television and radio facilities of ABC and the Armed Forces Radio Network overseas. Television income from the Awards shows now became highly significant to the Academy and has continued to fuel the expansion of its many programs and services.

When Gregory Peck became president of the Academy in 1967, he was persuaded that the reach of NBC was greater than that of ABC since, at that time, it had more affiliated stations and consequently could deliver bigger audiences. During Peck's tenure, a contract was signed to move the Academy Awards shows from ABC to NBC. The show remained with NBC from 1971 to 1975 before moving back to ABC in 1976.

Gregory Peck and I were both on the first board of directors of the Center Theater Group, which governs both the Taper and the Ahmanson theaters. We had become involved in both the construction and the operation of the theaters. The Dorothy Chandler Pavilion, the third theater of the L.A. Music Center complex and the home of L.A.'s symphony orchestra, was clearly the most beautiful venue in the city. We thought it would be a wonderful place to move the Academy Awards.

In pursuit of that goal, I became involved in arranging for the Academy to lease the theater. I tried to convince Dorothy Chandler and Los Angeles County Supervisor Ernest Debs, the supervisor of the central city area, of the public-relations benefits that would accrue to the county if the Awards emanated from this theater, despite the fact that it presented a great many scheduling problems to the Los Angeles Philharmonic Orchestra, its principal lessee. It involved moving the orchestra out of the theater for a period of two to three weeks while the Academy show was being loaded in and out. Finally, pressure was put on the management of the Music Center by the County Board of Supervisors, which administers the Music Center's property. It was finally arranged, and starting in 1969 the Dorothy Chandler Pavilion became a most elegant venue for the Academy Awards for many years. The Pavilion's support areas have also been excellent, and the ability to have the Governors Ball in a tent on the plaza made the Music Center a marvelous home for the Award shows. Its only problem was the relatively limited three thousand seats it provided. Consequently, in recent years the Academy Awards presentations have moved, from time to time, to the Shrine Auditorium, which has nearly six thousand seats and offers more possibilities for accommodating most all of the Academy members who wish to attend, and more recently, to the Kodak Theatre in Hollywood.

🐽

The new Academy headquarters at 8949 Wilshire Boulevard came about as a result of an approach from a personal friend, Bram Goldsmith, who was partnered with George Konheim in a real-estate company, Buckeye Properties, which operated mainly in Beverly Hills. Goldsmith told me about the availability of a site at Wilshire Boulevard and La Peer Drive. This land, which was owned by Alice Faye, could be acquired for about $300,000. It encompassed not quite all of the frontage of a whole block on Wilshire, from La Peer to Almont drives. However, the property presented a serious problem because of its inability to provide ground-level parking facilities.

Fortunately, Buckeye was in a peculiarly advantageous position to deal with this problem. It had constructed and owned a number of office buildings, all within the same area. It proposed covenanting to the Academy, in perpetuity, evening parking rights in these adjoining structures at one dollar per car per evening. The company felt that if we brought this arrangement before the planning committee of the Beverly Hills City Council, we might well receive an approval. Buckeye would agree to construct the building based on architectural plans that would be subject to our approval and capped at a ceiling price, with any additions to this ceiling caused only by changes or modifications that would be made at the Academy's request. The total cost of construction—based on a design that had been prepared by the architectural firm of Maxwell Starkman and that our committee, with some modifications, had approved—was presented to us at a cost of about $2.2 million. Our plan envisioned a seven-story building, in which would be included a theater with seating for approximately one thousand, a library, executive offices, quarters for the *Academy Players Directory*, employee parking, and exhibition space.

I found the Wilshire Boulevard location attractive and favored the proposal. The Academy had $1.5 to $2 million in its treasury at the time, and I estimated that our present quarters could be sold for somewhere between $200,000 and $300,000. There would also be another year or two of Academy Awards show profits to augment the building fund, and I hoped that we would find a donor who might provide whatever shortfall we might have. Therefore I became a great proponent of the Wilshire Boulevard site, and I was able to convince the Building Committee, and ultimately the board, to vote in favor of that proposal, despite the fact that many of the people who were involved in the decision were conservative and did not want to go that far out on a limb. I felt very strongly that the time and the site were right for the Academy, and I believed that if I provided determined leadership I could bring the other members of the Building Committee and the board along with me.

Phyllis Seaton, at that time a member of the Beverly Hills City Council—and the wife of distinguished writer-director George Seaton, who was an ex-president of the Academy—became an ally. She helped with advice and counsel about our negotiations with the Beverly Hills Planning Committee and City Council. We then tried to retain our hold, via option payments, on the site while we navigated through the corridors of the Beverly Hills bureaucracy. When it was finally approved by the city council, the Academy board agreed to proceed. Following that decision, I was elected president of the Academy in August 1973.

We then proceeded with the contract with Buckeye, under which it would do the construction at a guaranteed price. It provided the basic structure, and we made modifications and changes, which they costed out before finally providing the fixed figure with which we started construction. That figure was now in the neighborhood of $3.5 million.

Hal Wallis recommended that the Academy employ its own architect to go through all the plans and help in liaising with Buckeye's architect on what changes we would want. He suggested an architect of his acquaintance, Harold Levitt, who became our consultant and helped to keep us on course.

Many problems arose as construction got underway. One was the acoustical treatment of the theater. I proceeded to employ the best acoustician that we could find, Veneklasen and Company. I appointed Gordon Sawyer, an old friend, formerly the head of the sound department at the Samuel Goldwyn Studios and one of the most respected sound engineers in the industry, to serve as a consultant on equipping the theater. I appointed production designer Robert Boyle to serve as consultant on the interiors, and Bob worked with set decorator Walter Scott. They, too, provided invaluable services. Then came the changes, and these all wound up in change orders, which added to our original fixed cost.

Veneklasen devised an unusual plan for the acoustical treatment of the theater. He recommended that there be no ceiling and that we leave an empty space from the floor up to the roof of the theater. I was quite concerned about the concept and commissioned a model to be made of the interior of the theater so that we could get a look at it and see what kind of treatment we could give the false ceiling. It was his idea to create sails, suspended over the audience, which still exist in the Academy's theater. The ceiling, which is actually the roof of the theater, is painted black, and the sails hang in the air above the audience. Veneklasen was right. The acoustics in the theater are excellent. The consulting services and the care given to acoustical fidelity were expensive, but the results in our elegant theater completely justified them.

Despite the fact that we had provided a large area for our library, I felt that we needed to have a plan for its expansion, since libraries must grow. We finally conceived a plan whereby the library—which would be adjacent to the roof of the theater auditorium, on the fourth floor of the Academy's seven floors—could possibly expand out onto the theater's roof. I was told that the roof would have to be re-stressed in order to support such an expansion, and I was given a figure of approximately $100,000 to accomplish this. I felt it was critical to take this step, and although this expansion never happened and the Academy later moved the library to another venue, I believed it was the right decision to make at the time.

Cost increases became burdensome as we approved more change orders and, as in most construction, the price began to escalate. From the beginning, I had hoped that we could manage to construct the building without having to secure a mortgage. Our financial people said that no buildings are built without mortgages, and that our ultimate recourse was to secure a reasonable mortgage on the property. I recognized that possibility, and Jim Roberts, our executive director, had some discussions with our bankers, who said they would be interested in making a loan any time we required it. I was probably paranoid about not wanting the Academy to be saddled with mortgage payments, always feeling that if the Academy were in dire straits or if there was somehow no Academy Awards show one year there might be pressure to license the Oscar figure to some commercial enterprise. I knew this was all far-fetched, but I wanted the Academy to own an unencumbered building. I determined to try and ease the Academy's financial needs by securing an advance from NBC, the network on which the Academy Award shows were being televised.

Prior to my election as president, I secured Dan Taradash's approval for me to talk to the Los Angeles NBC people about the possibility of extending its license for the Academy shows, in return for which I requested an advance payment to be utilized in the construction of the building. Ultimately, I discussed this request with Herbert Schlosser, then the head of the NBC network. He told me that he would prefer to wait until the next Awards show had been telecast before deciding on extending the agreement. Seeing my whole plan to secure the money to guarantee the completion of the building falling to pieces, I said to him,

"You know, regardless of what the ratings are on the next telecast, this show will be on the air every year, long after you and I are both gone. If you think that the ratings on next year's show are going to be so significant, you may not be the right network for the show."

He said, "Well, it's not going to be too long; we'll talk about it later."

However, I was still anxious to get an advance and get it quickly. I was going to New York on business, and I phoned Leonard Goldenson, the chairman of ABC, which by then had added affiliate stations to provide roughly the same coverage as the other networks. I told him I would like to come to see him. He agreed. I went to his office, and I assumed that Leonard, whose roots were in the movie business and who had been an executive of Paramount Theaters, would feel some identification with the Academy Awards and would be interested in what I had to propose. I asked him how he would like to have the rights to broadcast the Academy Awards show. He responded by asking what he had to do to get them.

I told him first that he would have to wait two and a half years, because the next two shows were already committed to NBC, and he would have to wait for the expiration of that contract. However, if that didn't deter him, I wanted him to advance $1 million the following week, interest free, to the Academy, which would secure for him a three-year contract for ABC to telecast the Awards show, to begin at the expiration of the NBC agreement. That contract would also provide for reasonable increases over the fees that had been contracted for in the NBC deal.

Leonard didn't quibble about it. He said, "I want to make the deal. Let's talk about the numbers." I stipulated that the advance had to be recouped over three years, and he agreed.

So began a relationship between ABC and the Academy that has endured for over thirty years. The ABC affiliation with the Academy has proven to be very felicitous. When one contract expired, another was negotiated, and ABC continues to be the telecaster of the Academy Awards shows, now contracted for until the year 2010. Following my presidency, all the subsequent presidents of the Academy have asked me to serve on the committees negotiating extensions of that original agreement.

On the day that I negotiated the first deal with Leonard Goldenson, he invited Elton Rule, the president of ABC, and Martin Starger, in charge of its entertainment division, to join us, and he told them what we had been talking about. They were all very enthusiastic and invited me to lunch with them in their dining room. Howard Cosell was also lunching there, and I was introduced to him. He started to laugh, and I asked, "What strikes you so funny?"

He said, "Well, I was broadcasting the early-knockout-shortened Johansson heavyweight championship fight, on which *The Horse Soldier* was being advertised. After the knockout, all of the announcers laughed and joked about those poor guys who had sponsored the show! Nice to finally meet you."

🐎

In financing the building program, I always had in mind that we had an important naming opportunity, and I began to address the problem of seeking a donor who would make a gift to the Academy for the naming rights to the theater. The Academy's library had already been named for Margaret Herrick, its longtime executive director.

As chance would have it, Samuel Goldwyn had begun suffering what turned out to be a lingering illness during this period. I had known him for a long time, being the principal tenant of his studio. I knew of his commitment to the industry and to its institutions, primarily to the Motion Picture and Television Fund, to which he had been most generous. He had also given the Motion Picture Permanent Charities its headquarters building in Hollywood. The Academy had recognized Goldwyn with its Best Picture Award for *The Best Years of Our Lives,* and he was also an Irving G. Thalberg Award and a Jean Hersholt Award recipient. Until myself, he was the only person to have won all three awards. I planned to talk to him at an appropriate time about making a gift to the Academy.

Samuel Goldwyn loved the industry and felt he owed a great deal to it. He wanted to serve as a statesman and make his experience useful in combating what he thought were its great problems. He was concerned with pornography and violence in pictures, and he feared that exploiters would use pornography and violence to so antagonize the press, as well as religious and family groups, that they would rise up and try to use those excesses to interfere with the freedom of the screen.

There is a story about Samuel Goldwyn that is a good indicator of the character of the man. Lillian Hellman and I had become friends after we had done *The Children's Hour* and *Toys in the Attic,* and I was in the habit of calling her when I was in New York. She would generally invite me to tea at her apartment. On one such occasion, I asked her what she was writing. She replied that some time earlier she had received an advance from a publisher to do a book. A great deal of time had passed, and she still hadn't decided what should be the subject, although she had already spent all of the advance money. She seemed somewhat troubled about the problem.

"You know, Lillian," I said, "you ought to do a book about Sam Goldwyn. You're the one person who can really write that book. You've done so many films with him and you know him better than anyone."

She said, "Well, we haven't talked in years." They'd had a terrible argument over some film or other, and she said, "I think it probably would be too painful for me to do that."

Then she added, "Let me tell you a story. About a year ago, Willy Wyler was in New York, and we were having dinner together when he said to me, 'Lillian, Sam Goldwyn's very ill now, and it would be wonderful if you called him up and just said hello.' I said, 'After all our quarrels and anger, that would be the height of hypocrisy.'

"Willy said, 'I've had more than a few fights with him myself, but every once in a while I go over and sit with him for a half-hour or so. What's the good of nursing all those old grievances?'"

She replied, "That's the trouble with you, Willy, you're too goddamn sentimental."

As time passed, Willy's suggestion kept bothering her until one day she thought, "Maybe I'll call him." So she dialed his number, and Mrs. Goldwyn's voice came on the other end of the phone. She said, "Hello, Frances. This is Lillian, Lillian Hellman. I've called to ask about Sam."

"It's wonderful of you to call," Frances Goldwyn said. "I know he'll be thrilled. I'm sitting at his bedside now, while he's having his dinner. Sam," she heard her say, "you'll never guess who is on the phone. It's Lillian Hellman and she's calling to ask about you."

Lillian next heard Sam Goldwyn's squeaking voice come through the phone, saying, "Tell her to go and fuck herself." Lillian Hellman said that in all the time she had known him, she never respected him more than she did at that moment. Old and sick as he was, he was still sticking to his guns.

After Sam Goldwyn's death, I waited for an opportunity to talk to Samuel Goldwyn Jr. about naming the Academy's new theater in honor of his father. As chance would have it, I was at a dinner party one night at Delbert Mann's house, and Sam Jr. was there. We were talking, and finally I thought, "Maybe I'll do it now." I told Sam that I would like to talk with him privately, and so we went into another room, where I told him my suggestion, that the Goldwyn Foundation make a gift to the Academy and that the Academy name the theater in its new building for his father. He was immediately enthusiastic about the idea. When he asked me what size gift I was thinking of, I told him I thought they should give the Academy $1 million. He said he would get back to me shortly.

I hoped that only the theater in the Academy would be used as a naming opportunity, and even that would be handpicked. I felt that Goldwyn's name represented quality movies and was respected both in the industry and with the public generally. I thought that using his name for the theater would not be compromising any of the Academy's integrity but would reflect honor on both. Fortunately, I was able to accomplish my goal with my first choice. The Goldwyn Foundation agreed to a gift of $750,000, and the theater was named for Goldwyn.

🐦

Since $330,000 per year of the payments due from ABC under our new television contract would have been paid in the form of the advance, there would be a diminution of operating revenue to the Academy during those three years. Consequently, after the ABC deal was done, I called Leonard Goldenson and told him I needed to ask him to buy some additional programming from the Academy.

He asked, "What are the programs going to be?"

I suggested to him that the first would be a program to be called *Oscar's Best Movies,* which I conceived of as a film to be made up of clips from all the Best Picture Academy Award winners. I said we would enlist some stars who would serve as hosts. ABC agreed to pay us over $1 million for that two-hour show. That sale cushioned the spread of the money that was needed for our operating expenses.

Later we did some other specials for ABC. One was *Oscar's Greatest Music,* which utilized clips of the musical portions of old shows, with

Jack Lemmon hosting. Then came *Oscar Presents the War Movies and John Wayne* and *Oscar's Best Actors,* which aired in 1978. These shows became a new and valuable source of income as the Academy entered its modern era and continued the expansion of its activities.

With the advent of the new building, it was clear that all of the Academy's costs would rise. The size of the library would grow, and more staff would be needed. Security, insurance, telephone, air conditioning, lighting, as well as the scope of our programs, would increase. The Academy would no longer be a mom-and-pop operation. My idea for the theater was to make it a meeting place for people in the industry, a mecca in which to congregate and exchange ideas and where films would be run frequently. The old Academy Theater wasn't conducive to fulfilling that function. The new Academy has done so beautifully. It is a place that people like to attend. It enlarged its screening schedules for members and became very popular with the studios for their trade showings. That was what I believed the Academy should be about.

As I saw the structure developing into an elegant, first-rate edifice that would make an important contribution to the whole industry, I told Jack Valenti, then president of the Motion Picture Association of America, that I thought the film companies should all make gifts to the Academy, spaced over a five-year period, to help underwrite the additional services that we were going to be providing to the entire industry. Jack agreed, and although I had hoped that he would undertake this mission for me, he declined and asked me to take on the task of talking to the heads of each of the film companies individually.

Most of the companies agreed to make gifts of $50,000 apiece, over a period of five years, so that we received $10,000 a year from each of them. This also helped to expedite the transition of the Academy into its new era.

I also hoped to acquire a small piece of property on a narrow slice of ground adjoining the Academy building. The parcel isn't large enough to build a structure on, nor can it provide for its own parking. I had been quoted a price of $300,000 to acquire the ground, and I asked two people if they would buy it and make a gift of it to the Academy. They both declined. I didn't really have any particular use in mind for the property, but I wanted to control it, so that nothing that might be embarrassing to the Academy could appear there. However, being concerned that we were on the edge of our financial capabilities, I didn't want to invest further in acquiring land that might only lie unimproved for a long time. Feeling that we would deal with it at another time, I let it go, although I still regret it. I wish we had stretched ourselves and acquired it.

I had been elected Academy president on August 23, 1973, and groundbreaking for the new Academy building on Wilshire Boulevard began in September 1973. My visibility on the Academy Board of Governors increased during the period when I was chairman of the Building Committee and the planning was being done for the building. Clearly I was the person who was spearheading it, so I was the natural candidate to become president if we were going to proceed with the building of the structure that I had planned and espoused. It was one of the major developments in the history of the Academy, which now assumed a new sense of importance and dignity within the industry.

In July 1973, twelve special governors were elected, either people who were under thirty-five years of age or who had been Academy members five years or fewer. This was an effort by the board to force the representation of new and younger members in its governing body. Elizabeth Allen, R. Andrew Lee, Charles F. Wheeler, Tom Gries, Ned Tanen, David Bretherton, Fred Karlin, Burton Schneider, Sid Ganis, Robert Kurtz, Leo Chaloukian, and Lorenzo Semple Jr. were those twelve new governors.

The other officers, besides myself, who were elected at that time were Howard W. Koch, first vice president; Robert Wise, vice president; John Green, vice president; Marvin Mirisch, treasurer; and Hal Elias, secretary.

The groundbreaking ceremonies were held on September 18 at the northeast corner of Wilshire Boulevard and Almont Drive in Beverly Hills. Past presidents of the Academy who were present included George Seaton, Frank Capra, Gregory Peck, and Dan Taradash, as well as Los Angeles Mayor Thomas Bradley and Beverly Hills Mayor Phyllis Seaton.

As we came closer to the time when our new building would be ready for occupancy, I began to think about making some disposition of our old quarters. I had always anticipated that we would realize some money from the sale of the building, and I had an idea that perhaps one of the talent guilds might be interested in a property that had screening facilities such as ours. The Directors Guild had already erected a building on Sunset Boulevard, but the Writers Guild evinced interest in our property. Michael Franklin was the executive director, and he negotiated a deal with the Academy to acquire the Melrose Avenue building.

The Writers Guild employed lawyers to do the negotiating for them, and we gave them all the documents they requested. Finally the deal was closed, and the Writers Guild agreed to assume occupancy as soon as we moved to our new quarters. We received about $200,000 for the building. However, before the Writers Guild took possession, they discovered something that they should have discovered before they bought it. Apparently, years earlier, when the building on Melrose had been acquired by the Academy, the city had agreed to waive the requirement that parking facilities be built to accommodate the theater during the Academy's tenancy. When the Writers Guild took over, they discovered that they couldn't get a certificate of occupancy without providing parking. There was no place in the area to construct parking, so they had to dispose of the building to a developer who tore it down. The Writers Guild later acquired another theater on Doheny Drive, just south of Wilshire Boulevard.

The Academy Board of Governors decided to have special opening ceremonies for its new building. We had, by that time, finished the film *Oscar's Best Movies,* and we decided to have a premiere of that film for our members as well as other local dignitaries. We scheduled five opening nights and invited our entire membership to come, one-fifth of them each night, or about a thousand people per evening. Pat and I hosted each of the premieres. We also provided tours of the building, refreshments were served, the film was shown, and all of our members had an opportunity to see what we had wrought.

On the first night of the Academy's opening, all past Academy Award winners were invited as special guests, and a large number of them appeared. The new Academy building and its facilities proved to be an instant success. The members were delighted, and I enjoyed a tremendous sense of pride at what we had been able to accomplish.

☙

The Academy shows continued on NBC for the first two years of my presidency. As the choice of the show's producer is made unilaterally by the president, I chose Jack Haley Jr. to produce the show that was telecast in 1974. Jack arranged for Burt Reynolds, Diana Ross, John Huston, and David Niven to serve as co-hosts. Jack Haley had a great deal of experience as the producer of various kinds of documentary and industry-oriented shows and had excellent credentials for this kind of job.

In 1973, the Academy board voted an honorary Oscar to Groucho Marx, who was then in the twilight of his career. Since he had never been recognized before, and since Harpo and Chico had already died, it was felt appropriate to recognize the contributions of this great comedic team. Henri Langlois, the founder and guiding spirit of the Cinémathèque Francaise in Paris, was also awarded an honorary Academy Award for his service to motion pictures on the European continent.

The Thalberg Award, recognizing a consistently high quality of motion-picture production, was voted that year to Lawrence Weingarten, who had been a producer of many classic films during the MGM golden era. Larry had been Irving Thalberg's brother-in-law, and had produced a number of the great Spencer Tracy–Katharine Hepburn movies. Larry had become a friend of mine at the Producers Guild and had succeeded me as president of that organization. Tragically, in 1974 he was terminally ill, and the Academy board wanted to accord him this honor while he was still among us.

After the board voted to present the Thalberg Award to Larry Weingarten, I called and told him the news. He was thrilled, and I asked him whom he would prefer to make the presentation to him. He said, "Kate Hepburn, of course, I would want her to do it."

Wanting to please Larry, if I could, and also savoring the coup of finally getting Katharine Hepburn to appear on an Academy Awards show, I decided to call George Cukor, a close friend of Katharine Hepburn and Larry Weingarten, and the director of some of the Hepburn-Tracy films, as well as a board member of the Academy. I told Cukor that since I was not acquainted with Miss Hepburn, I would appreciate it if he would call her and ask her if she would make the presentation. He demurred immediately and said, "No, I suggest you ask Larry's wife, Jessie. She swims with Kate every day. Ask her."

I knew that George Cukor, the Weingartens, and Katharine Hepburn lived next door to one another on a street in Beverly Hills and had all been close friends for a long time. I called Dr. Jessie Marmorston

Weingarten, Larry's wife, who was also physician to Katharine Hepburn and George Cukor, and I asked her if she would talk to Katharine Hepburn for us. She also demurred. However, she did say, "I'll give you her phone number." That was the best I could do with Jessie.

I phoned Katharine Hepburn, identified myself, and told her the reason for my call.

She replied, "Yes, I think that's right. I think I am the person who should make this presentation to Larry. But I'm not going to do it."

"What?"

She said, "Well, I just can't do that. You know I've won before, and I've never come to the ceremonies. It's hard for anyone to believe, but appearing on a stage, like that, without lines to read, that's not what I do. Besides, I'm recovering from a broken hip and I'm walking with a cane."

I said, "We'll arrange that. We'll open a curtain and reveal you on the stage, and you won't have to walk."

She replied, "No, I don't care about that. I don't care if I walk with a cane."

"Well . . ."

"Call me back in a couple of weeks."

This went on for a while. I called her again in a week, and told her that we needed to know whether she was going to appear or not. She said, "I just can't do it. Besides, I don't have a thing to wear."

Hearing that she was already thinking about what she would wear, I thought that she had given me an opening. I immediately said we would get someone to take care of her clothes. At which point she said she had an outfit that she thought might work all right, but it needed mending. I said, "Well, perhaps we could get a seamstress."

She answered, "No, I can sew it myself."

It took another phone call before she agreed that she would come to a rehearsal. I told her she had to be rehearsed, so the director would know where she was coming from and where she was walking to. She said she would come to a rehearsal, but she didn't want anybody to be in the theater except the director and the cameraman. I said, "All right, come to a rehearsal during the lunch break."

As we came to the last week before the show was to be aired, I explained the situation with Ms. Hepburn to Elizabeth Taylor, who was also going to be on the show. She sympathized with me and agreed that in the event that Hepburn didn't appear, she would make the presentation. However, having Katharine Hepburn on the show would be a great coup, and I wasn't willing to give up the chase.

Katharine Hepburn came to a rehearsal on the appointed day. She arrived during the lunch break, and I introduced her to the director and the cameraman. Some of the other people who were on the show, including Liza Minnelli, were squirreled away in the balcony, just to see what was happening.

After talking for a few minutes, she asked, "What do you want me to say?"

I handed her the material that had been prepared and said, "You might want to look at this, and then perhaps adapt it so that you're comfortable with it."

She looked at it and said, "This is terrible. Do you have a typewriter?" So we got a typewriter for her. She set herself up in front of it and started to hunt and peck for a while. That didn't take long, and she hadn't gotten far, when she said, "All right, I'll manage with this."

She took her papers and put them in her purse and came onstage. Her introduction was worked out, where her talk would be made and where Larry would come from, and how she would exit. Breathing a sigh of relief, I walked with her toward the stage door. I said to her, "That's great, and I know Larry will be delighted. I'll see you tomorrow night."

I shall never forget the next moment. She continued to walk a step or two toward the door without replying to me, and then in that marvelous manner of hers, with that great head of hers held high, it swiveled halfway back to me and she replied, "Maybe."

On the day of the show, I left the rehearsals in the afternoon and went home to get dressed and to escort Pat, Anne, Drew, and Larry to the Dorothy Chandler Pavilion. On returning, I was told by Jack Haley Jr. that Burt Reynolds, who was our first emcee, had decided during my absence that he was going to tell a story on air that Jack thought was inappropriate and censorable.

I said, "Well, did you tell him not to do it?"

"I didn't want to get into an argument with him, and I was waiting for you to get here. I need you to talk to him."

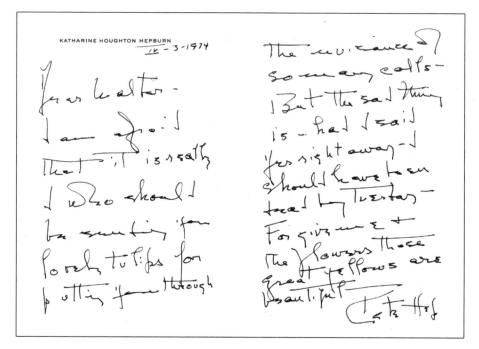

A note from Katherine Hepburn after her Academy Award appearance in 1974. Reproduced courtesy of Katherine Hepburn's estate.

I didn't even hear the story, but I accepted Jack's judgment. I didn't want the evening to be marred at its opening by a questionable story, and I sought out Burt Reynolds. We became involved in a heated argument about whether it was appropriate or not. He and I were still vigorously arguing when someone came up to me and tapped me on the shoulder and said, "You're going to be on in one minute, and you have to go to your holding place."

With my mind consumed with the argument I'd just had, I was standing in the wings, waiting to go onstage to make the president's talk at the top of the show. A stagehand, seeing how disturbed I appeared to be, came up to me and said, "Don't be nervous. There's only a billion people going to be out there watching you." If there was anything I needed to calm me down, it wasn't that. I went out and made my first presidential talk on an Academy Awards show.

Katharine Hepburn arrived at the theater on time, and I greeted her with a sigh of relief. She wore a black suit. When her name was announced, there was a standing ovation that must have lasted for three or four minutes. It was memorable. She made an opening remark that endeared her to the audience immediately: "I'm living proof that a person can wait forty-one years to be unselfish." Then, she spoke warmly and honestly about Larry.

It was clear from the tears in Larry's eyes how meaningful this moment was for him. He said, "To have Katharine Hepburn here, and an Academy Award at the same time, is an emotional package that I simply can't cope with." The presentation of the Thalberg Award was followed by Jack Lemmon's presenting the honorary Oscar to Groucho Marx.

On the day following the Awards, I sent flowers to Katharine Hepburn and she wrote me the charming note which is reproduced on these pages.

Susan Hayward, a great lady of so many marvelous screen performances, had also agreed to be on the show. She was in the late stages of cancer and weighed only eighty-five pounds. But her trademark red hair, now in a wig, sat on her head, and with great bravado she appeared and did what she was called upon to do, to great acclaim. *Variety* (April 10, 1974) noted, "For the trade, one of the most dramatic moments of the night came with the appearance of Susan Hayward, who, together with Charlton Heston, presented the Best Actress prize. Nature of her recent illness and its severity have been rumored for almost a year, and Niven introduced her as being 'no illusion.'"

As David Niven moved to introduce Elizabeth Taylor, who would present the Best Picture award, a naked man suddenly appeared and streaked across the stage while showing a peace sign with his hand. David Niven, caught completely by surprise, showed the most extraordinary aplomb and made one of the most imperishable remarks ever uttered on an Oscar show. "Just think, the only laugh that man will probably ever get is for stripping and showing off his shortcomings." He brought down the house. It was so good, *Variety* and others thought the whole thing was planned, but it wasn't. The streaker, who owned a pornography shop in San Francisco, had somehow eluded the security people and made his way backstage, dressed as a stagehand.

Niven resumed his duties and introduced Elizabeth Taylor, who commented, "That's a pretty tough act to follow." She went on and announced *The Sting* as the winner of the Best Picture Oscar.

The evening had begun with a great deal of tension for me. This was the first show to be produced during my presidency, and I was anxious for it to be successful. It certainly was. At subsequent Academy shows during my presidency, I tried to choose themes for the president's address that seemed to be of current interest. I reiterated from time to time that the Academy is about more than awards, and there are many other areas in which the Academy functions. I didn't want it to be perceived as just a once-a-year award-giving institution, but that, in fact, it strives to be what a classic academy is supposed to be. I made that explanation early in my talk at the Academy Awards in 1974. I also took note that Samuel Goldwyn had died. In respect to him and to the great movies that he had brought to the screen, I dedicated the evening to his memory.

In later years, I talked about the Academy's fiftieth anniversary, about America's two hundredth anniversary and the place of motion pictures in that history. After my first appearance I overcame my nervousness and became quite confident about what I wanted to say and my ability to say it effectively. I appeared on nine shows in all, as a president, presenter, and recipient, and found them all enjoyable and exciting experiences.

Howard W. Koch, whom I selected to produce the 1975 Academy Awards show, chose multiple hosts again: Sammy Davis Jr., Bob Hope, Shirley MacLaine, and Frank Sinatra. This sparked an evening of great controversy. Bert Schneider, the producer of the feature documentary *Hearts and Minds* about the Vietnam War, won the Best Documentary Award early in the show. He accepted and then used the occasion to read a communication from the Vietnamese delegation in Paris, who were negotiating peace with the Americans. To many people, it seemed to be an act of Vietnamese propaganda, and the critical tenor of the communication led to a most extraordinary political division backstage that went on during the entire show. The conservatives argued with the liberals about what needed to be done about this seemingly pro-Vietnamese statement that had been read by Schneider.

Bob Hope was infuriated by the remarks and insisted to Howard Koch, backstage at the time it occurred, that the Academy make a disclaimer. Shirley MacLaine said, "Don't you dare." Soon they were all writing drafts of what they thought should be said. I was in the audience and didn't find out about it until afterward. In succeeding years, I made it a practice to go backstage periodically, although I didn't want anybody to feel they were being monitored or censored. I've always regretted that Howard Koch did not send for me when the controversy erupted. Bob Hope, with Howard's agreement, finally asked Frank Sinatra to read the disclaimer, and he did. Shirley MacLaine continued to complain, and the incident became a tempest in a teapot.

Sinatra said, "I've been asked by the Academy to make the following statement regarding a comment made by a winner. The Academy is saying, 'We are not responsible for any political references made on the program, and we are sorry they had to take place this evening.'" The announcement was met with both boos and applause. Clearly what was happening backstage was happening in the audience as well. Some people thought that the disclaimer should have been made, and others felt not. I'm sure the same sentiments were felt throughout the country.

At the Board of Governors Ball, following the *Hearts and Minds* incident, there was no end of controversy. Some people thought Schneider's comments were outrageous. Others felt similarly of Frank Sinatra's remarks.

The Godfather, Part II won the Best Picture Award at the Academy Awards held in 1975, besting *Chinatown*. Ellen Burstyn and Art Carney were chosen Best Actress and Best Actor. There was no Thalberg Award, and the Hersholt Award was voted to Arthur Krim. I had left United Artists by that time and made a deal to produce pictures for Universal, but I respected Arthur for his achievements, both in his motion-picture career and in public service. I thought he was a most deserving recipient, and I was pleased that the honor came to him during my presidency of the Academy. Frank Sinatra presented the Hersholt Award to Arthur.

There was also an honorary Academy Award for Jean Renoir, presented by Ingrid Bergman, and for Howard Hawks, presented by John Wayne.

The next Academy Awards show during my presidency was broadcast on March 29, 1976, and was the first show televised on the ABC network under our new contract. It was hosted by five emcees, instead of the usual four: Goldie Hawn, Gene Kelly, Walter Matthau, George Segal, and Robert Shaw. The Thalberg Award that year was presented to Mervyn LeRoy, the Hersholt Award to Jules Stein, and an honorary Oscar was awarded to Mary Pickford, "in recognition of her unique contributions to the film industry and the development of film as an artistic medium."

Jules Stein had been involved in many extraordinary philanthropic activities, primarily the Jules Stein Eye Institute at the UCLA Medical Center, to which he gave leadership and great sums of money. Mervyn LeRoy had been a director and a producer all the way back to silent films, and his credits ranged from producing *The Wizard of Oz* to directing *Little Caesar*. The long and successful career of Mervyn LeRoy was thereby recognized.

Mary Pickford was quite aged and, unfortunately, not in good health at the time. She had won the second Best Actress Academy Award, for *Coquette,* in 1928. She had been "America's Sweetheart," a great star of silent films, and a leader in the industry as a founder of the Motion Picture Relief Fund and as an organizer and co-owner of United Artists. I was concerned about her ability to come to the theater and appear live on air. I discussed the matter with her husband, Charles "Buddy" Rogers, who acknowledged she wasn't in good health. I decided we should tape the presentation to her, so that we would not be subjecting her, and our show, to all the possible embarrassments of a live ceremony. Buddy wanted her to be on the show in person, but I insisted that we do the presentation on tape, and he finally agreed.

One afternoon before Academy night, we took a camera crew to her famous home, Pickfair. I wore black tie, and we waited a considerable period of time for the lady to appear. She was helped down the stairs by a nurse. She was then seated in a chair by the nurse and Buddy. She had been made up for the occasion and wore a robe with a feathered collar that covered her neck, along with a very obvious blonde wig. She was very nervous. Even more nervous than I was.

Hoping to relax her somewhat, I tried to make small talk with her prior to the turning on of the lights and the camera rehearsal. She still seemed quite flustered by everything that was going on around her. I tried to get her attention on some subject or other, but she kept looking at the lights and all the people who had invaded her living room. Clearly she very much wanted to do this well and had grave concerns about her ability to accomplish it. How glad I was that we hadn't tried to present the award live on the stage of the Dorothy Chandler Pavilion.

We realized that we couldn't give her any lines to say, and that the whole thing would have to be improvised. I suggested to director Marty Pasetta and the camera crew that they just keep the camera rolling. I would then try to get some kind of responses from her that might be worthwhile, rather than stopping and starting, which would only add to her nervousness. We did just that. I kept talking to her, trying to elicit some interesting remarks, until we felt we had some good moments.

She ultimately was quite sweet and charming. I said something to the effect that Oscar hadn't changed very much in all the years since she had received her first Academy Award. She replied, "Oh, I hope not!"

I said, "It's been a long time since then, but here's another." She looked at it and was obviously very pleased and excited. As she took the Oscar, a visible tear came to her eyes. I was proud to have participated in the Academy's recognition of this lady, in the twilight of her life, who had contributed so much to motion pictures. We also shot some footage of Pickfair, showing the house and the grounds and a lovely painting of Miss Pickford in her youth. Gene Kelly, most effectively, introduced the segment on the air.

The following year's show, the last during my term of office, was telecast on March 29, 1977, again on ABC. This time I selected William Friedkin, a well-known director as well as a member of the Board of Governors, to produce. Billy had directed the enormously successful *The Exorcist,* and I hoped that he could bring a certain amount of freshness to the evening. He also chose to use multiple hosts, namely Richard Pryor, Jane Fonda, Warren Beatty, and Ellen Burstyn.

This year was also notable for the release of the film *Network,* which was Paddy Chayefsky's not-quite-sympathetic view of how television networks operate. It had been the Academy's practice, for a number of years, to run excerpts from the nominated Best Pictures. That year, I received a telephone call from a high executive at ABC, asking me if I would police the excerpt that was being used from *Network,* so that it was not one of those that were strongest in their vehemence against the television industry.

I was quite shocked by the call. I responded that I had no intention of doing that, and the choice of the excerpt was entirely up to the producer. I also told him that I intended to forget that I had ever received his phone call, and I suggested that he forget that he had ever placed it. I also said to him, "I wouldn't be surprised if, in a couple of years, a network, possibly yours, makes an arrangement to license this film and runs it in its entirety." Of course, that did happen, and the film was shown on the networks.

Billy Friedkin succeeded in making some innovative changes. He eliminated the concept of dual presenters and their scripted patter. He wisely eliminated the "envelope please" routine, and he opted for a clean, somewhat futuristic set. Unfortunately, the evening hit an early low with Marty Feldman, who had been chosen to give the Best Short Subject awards and made a few God jokes, which undoubtedly offended myriads of viewers. Then he proceeded to make anatomical reference to Oscar's private parts. Finally he smashed an Oscar statue to the floor and gave half to each of two winners in a disastrous interlude.

The Thalberg Award was presented that year to Pandro Berman, the legendary producer of the great Astaire-Rogers musicals, who had also become a friend of mine back in the Producers Guild days. There were no honorary Academy Awards voted, and no Hersholt Award.

The Best Actor Academy Award was given to Peter Finch, posthumously, for his performance in *Network,* marking the first time such an Academy Award was ever given. I was pleased that Peter, whom I had known since he played the villain in my film *The Warriors* with Errol Flynn, so many years before, had won. Whenever I had occasion to see him, he would regale me with Errol Flynn stories. Peter Finch's award was accepted by Paddy Chayefsky, the writer of *Network,* who immediately asked Peter Finch's widow to come to the stage and say a few words. This was completely unexpected and, again, became one of those great moments that come out of unanticipated happenings on an Academy Awards show. She was very gracious and spoke of the appreciation that she was sure Peter would have had for his recognition.

Faye Dunaway won an Oscar for Best Actress for her performance in *Network.* I was standing in the wings as she came off the stage, holding her Oscar. She seemed terribly flustered. I put my arm around her, to reassure her, and she seemed to throb with excitement. I had known Faye since *The Thomas Crown Affair,* and I said some comforting words to her until the excitement of the moment had subsided and she could move on to the press interviews.

The 1977 broadcast was also notable as the lowest Nielsen-rated Oscar show to date. However, I believed the Oscar ratings during this period have to be evaluated in the context of the immense changes that were taking place in network television. The competition of cable was being strongly felt, and viewing habits were changing. In the early days of network television, the three major networks would generally attract 90-odd percent of the television viewers, but by the late 1990s that number had declined to 50 to 60 percent. The emergence of Fox, the fourth network, and later the CW, as well as the strong competition of the cable networks, all affected the ratings of network television. It would have been naive not to expect fall-offs, even in the great shows such as the Academy Awards. Despite periods of declining ratings, the desirability of the show to advertisers has not lessened.

Certainly the ratings are also a function of how much interest the public has in the pictures that are competing in any given year. For example, in 1997, when *The English Patient* won the Best Picture Award, the ratings were relatively disappointing. A not unfair conclusion would be that there wasn't a great deal of interest in that particular film or in its stars. The following year, in which *Titanic* was a nominee, resulted in some of the highest ratings the show had ever had. So, to some extent, the shows tend to reflect the popularity of the major contestants. It is instructive to remember we are always watching a horse race. A lot of the popularity of a particular race will be based on which horses are in contention.

In 1977, there was also some comment in the press about the sexual and double-entendre content of the show. Richard Pryor used a routine about the competing nominees, who were shown on camera at the time of the announcement of the winner of the Academy Award. He admonished them, "So don't say . . ." Then he silently mouthed an obscenity.

The limits of what is acceptable and what is not, on a family show, is constantly moving. The kinds of things that are acceptable on network television have also changed from year to year. *Roseanne,* after starting in later time slots, ultimately became an eight o'clock show. There were other shows with sexual content, such as *Mad about You* and *Friends,* that also became very-early-in-the-evening shows. Many subjects that, in an earlier period, would have been considered completely unacceptable for family audiences finally did become acceptable. What the networks tolerate is changing all the time, and the boundaries of sexual content are clearly being pushed. On the other hand, there are many within the community who feel that television is assailing the morals of the young. This conflict continues to this very day, on television and elsewhere, and is necessarily also reflected on Academy Awards shows.

The 1977 Awards show marked my final presidential address at an Academy Awards ceremony. I spoke about the approaching fiftieth anniversary of the Academy and our pride in what it had been able to accomplish during a critical period in both the history of our industry and the history of our country.

The following month, on May 11, 1977, the Academy celebrated its golden-anniversary year. The occasion was marked by a luncheon that was held in the Los Angeles Biltmore Bowl, the site of its original organizational banquet on May 11, 1927. Gathered again, in that same room, were the survivors of the thirty-seven original founding members, who were the Academy's honored guests. Bob Hope, who had hosted numerous Academy Awards shows, was the master of ceremonies. All sixteen of the still-living members who joined the Academy in its first year were granted lifetime memberships. Mayor Tom Bradley of Los Angeles was present, as was Chip Carter, representing his father, President Jimmy Carter. We had a fiftieth-birthday cake, a slice of which Bob Hope shoved into my mouth for the photographers. The occasion received a great deal of publicity throughout the world.

The following year, after I had completed the four years of incumbency allowed to any individual under the Academy's constitution, Howard W. Koch succeeded me as president. I was pleased that my colleagues had seen fit to accord me the maximum tenure that an Academy president can have, and I felt that I had been privileged to bring the Academy into a new era, which began with its occupancy of its new quarters. In the future, the Academy would take active roles in many more areas than it ever had before. Its new quarters allowed it to become a meeting place for industry people where, with great pride, they could show their theater, their library, and their history to visitors from all over the world.

The Academy Awards shows were growing in popularity. Despite that fact that ratings seesawed, I took pride in the fact that license fees from the network were only going up. The Academy was wealthier, more independent, and more influential than it had ever been, both within the industry and with the public. The value and the esteem of Oscar were as great, if not greater, than they had ever been. I took pride in looking back on my tenure as president as a turning point in the history of the Academy as it entered a new and ever more far-reaching era.

One of the most cherished experiences of my tenure as Academy president was my proposal to the Board of Governors in 1976 that it vote to correct an injustice that had been done to Dalton Trumbo twenty years earlier. While blacklisted, Dalton had written the script for the film *The Brave One,* under the nom de plume Robert Rich. The film won the writing award in 1956, and it was common gossip that the writer was, in reality, Dalton. Nothing had been done about this until my proposal to the board. The Academy sought and received affidavits from the director and producers of the picture that Robert Rich was indeed a pseudonym for Dalton Trumbo. The board now voted to present the award to the man who had earned it.

I phoned Dalton, who was then suffering from a terminal illness, and I asked him if I might bring the Oscar to his home. He asked me, "How soon can you get here?" When I arrived with his award, he was visibly deeply moved. He said to me, "I've laughed at and put down the Oscars for most of my life, but now I can't describe to you just how much this means to me." Nor can I describe how much it meant to me to share this moment with my old and dear friend.

Following my presidency, I served four more years on the Academy's Board of Governors, until I retired from the board in 1982. It is the practice of the Academy to award life membership to ex-presidents upon the completion of their terms. This is done in the form of an elegant gold-plated membership card. There is an inscription on the back of mine, of which I am very proud: "For unparalleled contributions to the Academy's well-being and growth, and for outstanding leadership as President of the Academy, 1973–1977."

During the 1970s, I was also honored to receive a number of meaningful awards. The Will Rogers Award of the Beverly Hills Chamber of Commerce was presented to me in 1976. In 1977 I was chosen as the recipient of the Cecil B. De Mille Golden Globe Award from the Hollywood Foreign Press Association for "outstanding contributions to the entertainment field." The United Motion Picture Association named me Producer of the Year in 1974 at its Show-A-Rama convention in Kansas City, Missouri, and the National Association of Theater Owners presented its Producer of the Year award to Marvin and me at its convention in Bar Harbor, Florida, in 1972.

21

633 Squadron, a New Corporate Entity, and Unrealized Projects

One of the first properties The Mirisch Company had acquired was *633 Squadron,* a novel by Frederick E. Smith. It is a fictional World War II story about the British Royal Air Force Mosquito bombers, which were built of plywood and were the only wooden airplanes flown in combat.

The project remained relatively inactive until I proposed it to James Clavell. He wrote a good script, and we began to prepare it for production. Jim then went on to London, where he wrote and directed *To Sir, with Love.* Later his novel *King Rat* came out and launched Jim on what became his ultimate career, as a novelist. He subsequently wrote *Tai-Pan* and many other adventure novels.

It was always our intention to produce *633 Squadron* as an Eady Plan picture. However, I wanted to stock it with as much American talent as I could. I was fortunately able to secure the services of Cliff Robertson to play the lead. There was a character role in it that fit George Chakiris—with whom we still had options dating back to *West Side Story,* for which George had won an Academy Award—and we considered having him in the film would be valuable.

To direct it, I chose an old college friend, Walter Grauman, who was enjoying a successful career in television. He was eager for an opportunity to direct a feature film, and as he had piloted a B-25 bomber during the war, I thought this would provide an appropriate opportunity.

I asked Lewis Rachmil, a capable producer, to go to London to oversee the production. I was quite overloaded with work at the time, and I felt I couldn't go abroad and be separated from the rest of our program. I also enlisted Bob Relyea, my right arm—who had been with us since working as a first assistant director on *The Magnificent Seven,* and who had also worked on *West Side Story, The Children's Hour,* and *The Great Escape*—to go to London. Cecil Ford, who received credit as producer on the picture, was principally a production manager of English films and had grown up in the British film industry. He had been the assistant director on *The Bridge on the River Kwai* and had done many outstanding films. Cecil had also worked as production manager on my Errol Flynn picture, *The Warriors.*

Cecil Ford became the producer of record, because that was required under the terms of the Eady Plan. We were permitted to exclude the salaries of only three non-British people from the computation of the labor cost of the picture, which determined its qualification for Eady benefits.

We chose an ex-RAF airfield at Bovington as the principal exterior location. An ex-RAF officer assisted us in collecting a squadron of Mosquito bombers, and we ultimately assembled twelve of these antique airplanes. Of these, only three could fly, and the rest remained earthbound and were used mainly for background set dressing.

At one point, the technical advisor, Group Captain T. G. Mahaddie, told me that he had been looking at a list of the world's air forces and had noted that our air force, composed of these twelve rather sad Mosquitoes, constituted the world's fourteenth largest. He asked me how I felt being the commander of this armada. I told him I felt uncomfortable with it, and I hoped we could dispose of it as soon as we were through shooting.

I had gone to London to see the film launched and to sit in on the casting. A few days before we started production, I was awakened in my hotel room at seven o'clock in the morning by a phone call. Cliff Robertson had just arrived in London and he told me he needed to see me immediately. Although we had discussed this film at great length in Hollywood, after he had read the script and accepted it, he now told me that he had been too hasty, and on reading it again on the airplane he found that there were a number of things that now troubled him. He simply couldn't do it in its present form. He thereby provoked a real crisis, immediately prior to the start of production. I became quite alarmed. I could see us getting into a serious delay by his being so difficult that morning. I tried to conciliate him, until finally I asked, "Are you quitting the picture?"

Fortunately, he retreated from that. It was somewhat daring of me, to throw down the gauntlet to him. But, for whatever reason, and it may well have been financial, he said no, he wasn't quitting. Yet he wanted to know that we would make changes in the script. When I saw that we were not going to have to face the necessity of recasting his role and delaying the start of production, I said I would agree to employ another writer and make changes that we would mutually agree upon. He, in turn, agreed to commence production. I now saw myself remaining in London longer than I had anticipated.

I finally discovered that Howard Koch, a Hollywood writer, not the producer, was a resident in London. He had written many films, principally at Warner Bros., the most famous of which was *Casablanca,* for which he shared screen credit. Later on he was blacklisted during the Hollywood witch hunt. He agreed to work with me in making changes in the Clavell script that would maintain the integrity of the piece while meeting Cliff Robertson's concerns. I began to work with Howard at his flat, and when scenes were completed I would bring them to the set and discuss them with Walter Grauman, the director, and with Cliff. The latter now settled down, the rewriting continued, and production on the picture was never delayed.

We rented three German Messerschmitt ME-109 fighter planes and arranged for the use of an old B-25 bomber as a camera plane. We did our aerial photography off the coast of Scotland, simulating the Norwegian fjords that are the principal location of the action sequences of the film. Bob Relyea supervised the aerial photography. Lew Rachmil oversaw the physical production of the picture with the assistance of Cecil Ford.

Maria Perschy was employed to play the leading female role. Angus Lennie, Harry Andrews, Donald Houston, Michael Goodliffe, and

John Mellion completed the cast. The picture was produced relatively close to its budget, which was approximately $1.3 million. The stirring musical score was composed by Ron Goodwin. The film was edited by Bert Bates, who subsequently did a number of other films with us.

633 Squadron was very successful at the box office, principally in the United Kingdom. The musical theme became exceedingly popular, and we had the extraordinary experience of earning almost the entire cost of the film out of the Eady Plan receipts in the UK, so the film was practically cost-free when it began its distribution throughout the rest of the world.

In fact, it was so successful that it led me to propose a program of pictures to United Artists, which would all comply with the Eady Plan requirements, would all be made in the $1 million cost bracket, and would all have a military theme, which appeared to guarantee a reasonably good playoff in the very patriotic UK of those years.

United Artists agreed, and I undertook to prepare a program of films that would follow in *633*'s path. The first of these was *Attack on the Iron Coast*, starring Lloyd Bridges, followed by *Submarine X-1*, starring James Caan, *Hellboats*, starring James Franciscus, *Mosquito Squadron*, starring David McCallum, *The Thousand Plane Raid*, starring Christopher George, and *The Last Escape*, starring Stuart Whitman. Each of the films had a recognizable American personality in the lead, they were Eady pictures, and they all had American directors. None was as successful as *633 Squadron*; however, they all produced Eady revenue and were held close to $1 million to produce. They were action pictures that found a ready market throughout the world and continue to play to this day.

✽

On March 1, 1963, we completed a deal whereby ownership of The Mirisch Company went to United Artists in a stock transfer worth close to $2 million. It involved some twenty films, including the as yet unreleased *Irma La Douce, Toys in the Attic,* and *Stolen Hours.* The three of us—Harold, Marvin, and I—would continue our UA production activities under two other established corporate setups, Mirisch Pictures Inc. and The Mirisch Corporation, both of which we owned 100 percent.

We retained our ownership in *West Side Story, Two for the Seesaw,* and *By Love Possessed,* which we had taken over from Seven Arts and owned through a company we called Mirisch Pictures. The terms of our arrangement with United Artists for this group were different from our other pictures, and that was the reason we put them in a separate company.

We had arrived at an understanding with United Artists that The Mirisch Company—which owned all the films that had been made up to that time and were all cross-collateralized—would be sold to United Artists. The sale was on the basis of a formula, derived by taking 2 percent of the gross of the whole program of our pictures, profitable and unprofitable, yielding a dollar number, which would then be converted into its dollar equivalent in shares of United Artists stock. In that way, we, the owners of the stock in The Mirisch Company, were able, on a tax-free basis, to exchange our stock for the stock in United Artists, which was publicly traded and which, hopefully, would have a good upside. We thereby exchanged the equity that we had in our product for a security that could be freely bought and sold. Later on, when Transamerica acquired United Artists, it exchanged the United Artists stock for Transamerica stock.

Not quite a year later, there were discussions about our making a distribution deal with Paramount. We met with Barney Balaban, the chief executive of Paramount at that time, and his principal corporate officers, and we discussed a deal whereby we would assume responsibility for managing its studio and its total output, as well as, alternatively, just setting up a unit to produce films for its distribution, as we had for United Artists.

We informed United Artists that we were considering moving, and Arthur Krim and Bob Benjamin made a concerted effort to get us to remain. Out of that negotiation, a new deal was made with United Artists. It was, in the aggregate, a ten-year agreement, including the three years from 1963 to 1967, concluding in 1974. The basis of this deal was the same formula as we had arrived at in the earlier deal, so that it would again culminate in an exchange of stock, which, at the time, seemed to be advantageous to us.

As fortune would have it, these turned out to be very bad deals for us. It cost us the ownership of maybe ten or twelve all-time classic films, whose longevity and value we could not even have hoped to anticipate. In 1963, we felt that, four, five, or six years after a film's initial release, its income-producing potential was pretty well exhausted. We have discovered that was not so, and the invention of the VCR and DVD and the development of cable television throughout the world created additional markets for film libraries that has completely revolutionized the value of film negatives.

Our movies comprised a relatively small library, but in themselves their ability to continue producing revenue is extraordinary. *In the Heat of the Night*—which was included in this deal and was sold based on a percentage of its gross up to that time—spawned a television series of 138 one-hour shows that were on the networks for eight years! We received nothing from them. *The Magnificent Seven* has also been a one-hour television series. MGM has remade *The Thomas Crown Affair* and *The Pink Panther* as feature films and is now talking about remaking others of our films.

By the middle 1970s, our Transamerica stock had plummeted from $40 to $5 per share. We made these deals hoping for appreciation in the value of Transamerica stock, but unfortunately the stock went down instead of up. For all these reasons, what seemed like a very shrewd arrangement at the time didn't turn out that way at all.

We developed a number of other properties in 1963 and 1964 that we "turned around," a term that describes a situation when a company that has financed the development of a particular project decides it doesn't want to proceed with it. The company then gives the person or persons who developed it the right to set it up elsewhere. *The Haunting of Hill House* was a project of Bob Wise's, and Nelson Gidding wrote the screenplay. We liked it, UA didn't, and Bob was given the right to take it elsewhere, and he produced and directed *The Haunting* for MGM.

In the late fifties, I had acquired the rights to the novel *The Sand Pebbles* as a possible vehicle for Steve McQueen and developed a script with screenwriter Robert Anderson. When it was completed, I gave the screenplay to Bob Wise. He was most enthusiastic about it and wanted to make the film. He insisted, however, on going to Asia to do the film, where it clearly was going to be much more expensive than it would have been if it was filmed in a more controllable location. In order to maintain our relationship with Bob, we allowed him to have a turnaround on *The Sand Pebbles*. He took it to Twentieth Century-Fox, and while he was working there, a situation arose where he was offered *The Sound of Music.* We never did get him back to do any more films for us.

Bandoola was an adventure film project that required many elephants. We surveyed locations for it in Ceylon, and a script was written. We finally felt that it was both too expensive and too risky a project, and we decided not to go ahead with it.

We made an overall deal with John Frankenheimer during this period, and he proposed a project, *The Confessor.* The story of a compulsive confessor, it was to be tailored to star Tony Perkins and Henry Fonda and to be produced by Edward Lewis. A script was written by Lewis John Carlino, and we attempted to do a deal with Henry Fonda to play the leading role in it. Unfortunately it didn't work out, and the film was abandoned.

The Mutiny of Madame Yes was involved in a deal to develop material with Ronald Neame. He proposed the property, and we developed it to a certain extent but finally decided to abandon it. *High Citadel* was a book about an advanced transatlantic airship. It was submitted to us as a possible project by Richard Fleischer, and together we developed a screenplay, with Earl Felton writing. We later decided not to proceed with it. *Lydia* was developed with producer-director David Miller. John Gay did a screenplay, and we finally decided it simply wasn't good enough to make. Kingsley Amis wrote the book *The Egyptologists,* which was submitted to us by Bryan Forbes. We commissioned a script, but, again, we were disappointed. We didn't make it. *Richard Sahib* was an idea by John Sturges for an adventure film to be made in India. It had come out of discussions that John had with James Clavell. Jim wrote a screenplay, but it too simply wasn't good enough, and it never found its way to the screen. *The Great Japanese Train Robbery* was another David Miller project that also failed to reach the screen during the 1960s.

22

The Start of a Jinx
and Cinerama

After having written, produced, and directed the immensely successful *Some Like It Hot*, *The Apartment*, and *Irma La Douce*, as well as *One, Two, Three*, for The Mirisch Company, Billy Wilder had developed an adaptation of an Italian play, *L'Ora Della Fantasia* by Anna Bonacci, which he called *Kiss Me, Stupid.* It was his idea to cast Dean Martin as a famous pop singer, Dino, around whom the plot revolves. He wanted a meek, introverted character to play off of the highly extroverted Dean Martin character, and he saw that as a role for Peter Sellers, who readily agreed to play it. Dean Martin eagerly accepted the role of Dino. Billy chose Kim Novak to play Polly the Pistol, a Marilyn Monroe type role. Alex Trauner again did the sets. Billy was still adamant about not shooting in color, and Joseph LaShelle was his cinematographer. Again, Danny Mandell was the editor.

Someone had brought to Billy's attention some songs that had been in the files of Mrs. Ira Gershwin, on which George and Ira Gershwin had collaborated. I was uncertain about them, although I didn't want to pour cold water on the idea since Billy was so enthusiastic about it, but I always felt there must have been a good reason why the brothers hadn't published the songs. As arranged for *Kiss Me, Stupid*, they finally worked out quite well.

The story revolves around a famous nightclub singer driving from Las Vegas to Los Angeles. His car breaks down in the small town of Climax, Nevada, and he needs to have it repaired. There's a lot of excitement in the town when he's recognized, particularly by the Peter Sellers character, Orville, a music teacher, who has written a song. He and his lyricist, who runs the gas station, get excited about their opportunity to interest Dino in singing their song and possibly catapulting them into fame and fortune, and they do everything in their power to keep him stranded in town until they can convince him to sing their song. Dino is furious about being delayed and tells the Sellers character that unless he sleeps with a woman every day he gets terrible headaches, so he needs to find a lady to keep him company until the part needed for his car arrives on the following day.

We recognized that this picture would present serious censorship problems, but Billy reassured us that he could deal with those problems and ultimately work out any objections that the Production Code Administration made. The PCA objected to the script when it was submitted to them and wrote frequent letters. Billy replied to the letters and made some changes. He dealt with the PCA people himself, since he completely controlled the material as writer, director, and producer.

He chose Felicia Farr, Jack Lemmon's wife, to play Zelda, Orville's wife. The picture had the feel of a Preston Sturges vehicle to it, even in the names of the characters. Orville was certainly an Eddie Bracken part. The film is a kind of homage of Billy's to Preston Sturges.

From the beginning, Peter Sellers and Billy Wilder did not get along. Their styles were completely different. Peter Sellers was an improviser. Billy Wilder was a by-the-script picturemaker, which is not to say that he didn't give any latitude to his actors, but being the writer as well as the director, he had a strong allegiance to the written word as he had scripted it. He was not as receptive to Peter's improvisations as Peter would have liked or to which he had become accustomed. He and Billy became very cool to one another.

The production had been in progress for about three weeks when Peter suffered a massive coronary thrombosis, and we had to close down the shooting. He was hospitalized and put in intensive care, and his life literally hung by a thread. As his condition stabilized, it became clear that he couldn't continue in the picture, certainly not without a long delay. Billy didn't want to wait, or perhaps he'd just had enough of Sellers. Since the picture was covered by cast insurance on Peter, it was up to us to choose whether or not we wanted to wait for him to recover or to recast the role. Billy opted to recast.

There were conversations with Danny Kaye to take over the role, but he was involved with a popular weekly television show, and the timing didn't work out for him. The next possibility that arose, and of which I became a great proponent, was for Jack Lemmon to play the part. At that time, Jack was appearing in a picture for Columbia, *Good Neighbor Sam,* and Jack said that if Billy would wait until he was finished with the picture, he would play the role. I thought that was the best solution to our problem and tried to press it on Billy. But he didn't want to wait the couple of months it would take for Jack to become available. Billy then surprised us all by suggesting Ray Walston.

Ray had been in *The Apartment* and was excellent in it. He was a fine actor, with a great deal of stage and screen experience, but I felt that the role required a so-called big name motion-picture star, and I was disappointed when Billy elected to cast Ray Walston. That is not to take anything away from Ray, or from the way he played the role; it's just that I thought it needed the charisma of a big star. The production continued, with Ray Walston playing Orville, and from that point on proceeded without any difficulties.

The final film was considered very censorable for its time. The Production Code Administration wouldn't pass the picture, and United Artists couldn't distribute it without a seal. Eventually, United Artists took its name off the picture, and it was distributed through a subsidiary company, Lopert Pictures, which had been formed as a distributor of foreign and art house films, or of non-PCA-accepted films, that were acquired for distribution by United Artists. So the label "distributed by Lopert Films" was attached to *Kiss Me, Stupid.*

The Catholic Legion of Decency gave the film a "Condemned" rating, which was very serious at that time. United Artists, as a distributor, was under no obligation to the Legion of Decency. It was, of course, under obligation to the Code Administration of the Motion Picture Producers Association. But the condemnation undoubtedly hurt the film. On the other hand, there have been pictures that have been condemned and have done very well. Sometimes that even seemed to make a film more titillating to particular audiences. Lopert distributed *Never on Sunday*, which had also received a Condemned rating and was very successful.

I couldn't believe that we would not eventually be able, somehow or other, to reach a compromise with the PCA. Ever since I had first made films I'd been dealing with them, and we had always been able to work out differences, but not this time. The Legion of Decency had considerable influence with Geoffrey Shurlock's PCA, but he was usually able to hold the Legion at bay and as we were compromising with him, he was able to get the Legion to accept the compromises that we would make. This time, however, both were just completely unbending. Certain newspapers even refused to accept our advertisements. It is ironic that only six years later, when the ratings system was introduced, *Kiss Me, Stupid* was rated PG. The film was not well reviewed and did poorly at the box office, which was disappointing to us, to Billy, and to United Artists.

Our next film, *The Satan Bug*, was released in March 1965. It was a Mirisch-Kappa Production, produced and directed by John Sturges, with a screenplay by James Clavell and Edward Anhalt, based on a novel by Ian Stuart, a pseudonym for Alistair MacLean. It held the promise of being an exciting action picture. John was getting impatient to get back to work, and we agreed to develop *The Satan Bug* with him. The novel was set in England, but John changed the locale to the United States. He liked collaborating with Jim Clavell, and they undertook the writing of the screenplay. Later on, he brought in Edward Anhalt, who had worked with him when he was making pictures for Hal Wallis, and he did a rewrite.

We were disappointed that we were not able to get a major star to play the leading role, but finally the idea of using a young actor named George Maharis was suggested. George had been in *Route 66*, a successful television series, and since we hadn't been able to get an important star, John pressured us to cast him. I had felt the subject required a major action-adventure star. George Maharis wasn't that, nor did he ever become a major movie star.

After shooting for about two weeks at a Palm Springs location, John called and told me he was very dissatisfied with Joan Hackett, the leading lady he had chosen. He asked me to get in touch with Joan and explain to her that we were going to replace her. I arranged to meet her for lunch, and it was a painful experience for both of us. We then chose Anne Francis, who had worked previously for John in *Bad Day at Black Rock,* to play the role.

The film had a story not too dissimilar from that of *The Andromeda Strain,* which *The Satan Bug* preceded. It worked quite well, but it never developed any momentum on its release and wasn't successful commercially.

By the mid-1950s, widescreen processes such as CinemaScope had exploded and expanded the screens of American theaters. These reached their zenith with the Cinerama process. Like other companies, we cast about looking for material that might be suitable for production in that process. John Sturges seemed to be the ideal director to create such a film. His most successful films were action vehicles and male-oriented. He had an excellent visual eye and was a superb storyteller. We asked John to give some thought to finding a subject that might be suitable for Cinerama production. He brought us a novel, a comedic Western, by Bill Gulick, *The Hallelujah Trail.* It offered action and comedy, and we were persuaded that it contained the elements for what could be a very successful film in the new process. We acquired the property and engaged the services of John Gay to write the screenplay.

I have always been somewhat wary of comedic Westerns, despite the fact that many of them have been successful. I always felt the Western is a genre that doesn't take well to being spoofed. The story of *The Hallelujah Trail* concerned a shipment of whiskey being brought to Denver on a wagon train. The temperance leaders in Denver, learning of the shipment, try to keep it from entering their city. Finally the shipment is hijacked by Indians.

John was most enthusiastic about the subject and was able to put together a first-rate cast to appear in the picture: Burt Lancaster, Lee Remick, Donald Pleasance, and Jim Hutton.

We embarked on the production on location outside of Gallup, New Mexico. We were plagued with rain and suffered many delays in the shooting because of weather conditions. But the worst moment came when a stuntman was killed during the filming. Bill Williams, forty-three years old, was fatally injured when he tried to leap from a wagon before it plunged off a cliff. People making films become absorbed in their work and the importance of a particular shot. Suddenly that importance becomes minuscule when a horrible accident deprives someone of his life.

The film opened at the Cinerama Dome Theater in Hollywood and simultaneously in other Cinerama showcases around the country. These were a group of theaters that had been built specifically to accommodate the proportions of the Cinerama process. Unfortunately, the film was not well reviewed and was not successful. It proved a real disappointment to all of us, despite the fact that *Variety* (June 15, 1965) reported, "This whole concoction has been so expertly blended, and with such consummate attention to utter chaos on the western plains, that it emerges as one of the broadest comedies of the year. It should meet with appropriate reaction at the box office, where it's headed for road showing, packaged in eye-filling Ultra Panavision and Technicolor." That was exactly what we set out to do. Unfortunately, audiences didn't agree with *Variety*'s assessment.

⚍

At about the same time as the *Hallelujah Trail* premiere, we re-entered television production with the formal launch on March 30, 1965, of Mirisch-Rich Productions, financed by United Artists, of which Lee Rich was president. Negotiations for three projected series already had been initiated with the networks. As Harold explained, "Our objectives in television will be the same as our objectives in motion pictures, to provide the public with the very best in entertainment. Toward this end, we feel that we have already taken a major step forward in allying ourselves with Rich, whose stature in the TV industry is based equally on his own abilities and his respect for the talents of others."

Because of the relationships that we had developed, through our motion-picture company, and the reputation that we had been nurturing, we felt that a natural expansion of our activities into the fastgrowing television business should again be attempted. We had earlier made twenty-six half hours of *Wichita Town*, with Joel McCrea, for NBC, and we had produced twenty-six half hours of *Peter Loves Mary*, with Peter Lind Hayes and Mary Healy. After those unsuccessful attempts to gain a foothold in television, I became completely involved in our feature-film production, until Harold developed a relationship with Lee Rich, who had a long, thirteen-year experience in the advertising business with the firm of Benton and Bowles. Lee was housed at the studio with us, and he began to develop a group of subjects for presentation to the networks.

Within a year, we had three new shows on the air. The first was a comedy, written by Garry Marshall and Jerry Belsen, titled *Hey, Landlord*. The second was an action-adventure series, *The Rat Patrol,* created by Tom Gries and starring Christopher George in a story of a small American reconnaissance group operating out of a jeep during the North African desert war in World War II. The third was the animated *Super 6,* created with DePatie-Freleng, which became a Saturday-morning show. This was an extraordinary achievement by Mirisch-Rich, and Lee deserved a lot of credit for the quick launch he had made.

Hey, Landlord was on the air for one year, after which it was canceled. *Super 6* also was not renewed. *The Rat Patrol* was picked up and continued for a second year. Like most television series, it required deficit financing, which is to say that the films cost more than the license fee that was paid by the network for its two runs. Consequently, the financier of the show had a deficit, which he would have to recoup from domestic syndication after the completion of the network runs and from the foreign market.

Probably the deficits on *The Rat Patrol* were greater than had been anticipated, and certainly greater than United Artists, which was deficit-financing these shows, had been willing to bear. It became disturbed about the amount of deficit financing that was required.

During the first year, we produced the series in Almería, Spain, on the assumption that episodes could be done more economically abroad than domestically. In the second year, we moved the production of the shows back to Los Angeles, and they were mainly shot within the Los Angeles area and in the desert around Palm Springs.

The ABC network, which was running *The Rat Patrol,* wanted to renew the series for a third year, but United Artists, disillusioned with being deficit-financiers, wanted to discontinue the show. At UA's request, ABC agreed to take the show off the air, despite its own desire to renew.

Besides representing our thrust to become a force in the television business, our venture also offered United Artists an opportunity to become a factor in the television business. But it didn't have the mind-set, or the capital, for the economics of that business. Over the years, *The Rat Patrol* continued to find markets in syndication. It was run and rerun domestically and abroad, and all of the deficits were recovered by United Artists, along with ultimate profits. The network run could have continued for a number of years, and the total package would have been much greater in number and consequently much more valuable in syndication and DVD distribution. But it was unfortunately aborted.

UA decided to discontinue our television operation, and Lee Rich joined the Leo Burnett advertising agency in Chicago and waited for an opportunity to re-enter production. Within a couple of years, he returned to Hollywood and formed Lorimar Productions, which became immensely successful in the television business. Had United Artists not retreated from *The Rat Patrol,* we and they, with Lee, might have created and owned a company like Lorimar, which was eventually sold to Warner Bros. for a huge amount of money.

The next feature film released by The Mirisch Company was *A Rage to Live,* based on a best-selling book by John O'Hara. The picture, unfortunately, was an attempt to duplicate the success of *Peyton Place,* which had appeared a few years earlier and seemed to create a market for soap opera. The original screenplay, written by Wendell Mayes, was written in period, as was the original novel. We later decided to contemporize the story, and John Kelley did the rewrite.

Like a lot of subjects one initiates, when you begin it you think, "If I can get this done, and out to market shortly, there's an audience for it," by the time you finally get it made, that audience's interest has gone on to other things.

We had purchased the rights to *A Rage to Live* back in 1959 with the intention of developing it as a vehicle for Natalie Wood, at the time of her appearance in *West Side Story.* That plan did not work out. After a number of years, I gave the script to Walter Grauman, who had directed *633 Squadron.* I was looking for another vehicle for him when Suzanne Pleshette agreed to play the lead and United Artists consented to do the film. Ben Gazzara, Peter Graves, and Brad Dillman filled out the cast, and the film was shot mostly at the Goldwyn Studio.

The story is about a wealthy young girl in a small Pennsylvania town and how she manages to make a mess of her life and relationships. It was no worse than many others of this genre that were made at the time. The unfortunate thing is that it wasn't any better than the others. The time for that kind of soap opera had passed.

I had first met J. Lee Thompson, an English director of considerable talent, many years before, when he was making films for Associated British Pathé back in the Allied Artists days. He later directed the successful action film *Guns of Navarone* and then a marvelous suspense film, *Cape Fear.* He proposed a book to me, *Return from the Ashes* by Hubert Monteilhet. The story was about a French woman who had been sent to a concentration camp during World War II. After her release from the camp at the end of the war, she returned to her home in Paris to find that her second husband, a professional chess master younger than she, was now living in her home with her stepdaughter. I thought that the complications ensuing from this somewhat bizarre but quite exciting plot held much promise.

Lee Thompson had interested Gina Lollobrigida, a major international star at the time, in the idea of playing the leading role in the film. We also conceived of the film as a subject that would lend itself to production in England, as an Eady Plan quota film. All of those elements seemed to recommend it. The film was a confined suspense story. It lent itself mainly to interior photography and seemed to be a film that could be made at a reasonable cost with major international personalities.

We succeeded in interesting a highly talented writer, Julius Epstein, in preparing the screenplay. We recruited Cecil Ford to oversee the production, even though Lee Thompson received producer-director credit. We also arranged for Samantha Eggar, a rising young English actress, to play the daughter and Maximilian Schell to play the husband.

Preparations proceeded until a few weeks before the commencement of production. A problem arose with Gina Lollobrigida. Neither the script nor her salary were in dispute, but her agent, George Chasin of MCA, made requests for a number of perks and fringe benefits on her behalf. We felt they were unreasonable requests and rejected them. She was to be paid a very considerable salary for doing the film, and I couldn't believe that she would walk away from that salary just because of our rejection of her requests for these fringe benefits. Consequently we took a hard stand and were surprised when she informed us that if we didn't accede to these requests, she would withdraw from the film. We held our ground and she held hers, and we found ourselves coming up to the start of our production schedule without a leading lady.

We scurried about at the last minute and tried desperately to find a replacement. We ultimately decided to employ a Swedish actress, Ingrid Thulin, who had appeared in a few of Ingmar Bergman's films and had played a leading role in Vincente Minnelli's *The Four Horsemen of the Apocalypse*. She was not a big star and certainly not at all comparable to the magnitude of Gina Lollobrigida at that time in her career.

There was a sequence in the picture involving a murder in a bathtub, and the UA publicity people latched onto that as an exploitation ploy, hoping to create a comparison to the shower sequence in *Psycho*. UA vice president James Velde explained in a press release, "We are fully aware that we cannot impose a rigid exhibition policy on motion-picture theaters, but because of the extraordinary suspense qualities of this fascinating and dramatic film, we are urging that exhibitors subscribe to the following policy, 'No one may enter the theater after Fabi enters her bath.'"

Return from the Ashes received reasonably good reviews, particularly for the acting, but it was not successful at the box office.

23

Hawaii

The Mirisch Company and United Artists were both enthused by the pairing of Fred Zinnemann with James Michener in *Hawaii*. By 1965 the book had realized our fondest hopes and become a huge best-selling novel. It also offered the sweep and the promise of a film spectacle on a par with *Gone with the Wind*. The novel personalizes the story of Hawaii from its beginnings up to the present. Consequently, the length and scope of the material presented a serious compression problem from the outset. We chose to tell the story by following its key characters, Abner and Jerusha Hale, a missionary and his wife, and how they and their descendants influenced the history of Hawaii.

Fred Zinnemann, our producer-director, was a brilliant filmmaker at the peak of his career. He had, by this time, made *From Here to Eternity*, *High Noon*, *The Men*, and *The Nun's Story*. We were delighted to have attracted him to our company and believed that he was as well suited as any director in the world to make a classic film out of *Hawaii*.

He chose Dan Taradash, who had previously worked with him on *From Here to Eternity*, to write the screenplay. A great deal of time was spent trying to condense the material in the book and still retain its essence and its sweep, and it took a long time for Dan to complete his first draft of only the first half of the script. Among our group, the Mirisches, Fred Zinnemann, and United Artists, there was dissatisfaction with Dan's material. We felt that it required condensation far beyond what he had accomplished and also generally felt dissatisfied with his treatment. We decided to replace Taradash with Dalton Trumbo.

Following his blacklisted period, Trumbo had proved his command of epic material with credits on *Spartacus* and *Exodus*. He expressed enthusiasm for the material and, taking the Taradash script as a starting point, used it as a gauge of what to do and what not to do. Amusingly, Dalton referred to himself thereafter as DT2. Dalton did a mammoth amount of work. The writing took so long that Fred Zinnemann took another assignment, directing *Behold a Pale Horse* while Trumbo worked on *Hawaii.*

Dalton Trumbo was one of the most interesting, talented, engaging intellects that I have ever encountered. He was a man of great taste and a man who had suffered much. I came to know him well, and we became good friends. Over the course of our friendship, he told me stories of what he had gone through during the period of the Hollywood blacklist, the wrenching decisions that he had to make, his strong conviction not to testify before the House Committee on Un-American Activities, the terrible time of his prison sentence, and the difficulties of supporting his family following his return from prison when he found that he was not employable. Many of his friends had left the country, but Dalton chose to remain.

He worked in a bakery, on the night shift, in Glendale. During the day he would write screenplays, which he would deliver surreptitiously to the people who had commissioned them, and he was paid as little as $100 or $200 for a script. During this period, one of his great screenplays, *Roman Holiday*, which did not bear his name, was produced, as was *The Brave One*, which won a Best Screenplay Academy Award for the fictitious Robert Rich.

His wife, Cleo, was a remarkable woman, wonderfully supportive of him, and had been a tower of strength through all of his travail. He had persevered during those awful years until Kirk Douglas, who had employed him to write *Spartacus*, insisted that he be accorded his rightful screenplay credit.

I first met Dalton when we were working on *Town without Pity.* Kirk Douglas wanted Dalton to do a rewrite of that script. An arbitration panel of the Writers Guild had ruled against his receiving any credit on the film, although he did write a masterful letter to the Screen

Writers Guild objecting to their decision. Parenthetically, Dalton Trumbo was one of the most extraordinary letter writers that I have encountered in my life. He loved to write letters and expressed himself beautifully. His letters were a pleasure to read. Oftentimes, when sending me script pages, he would write a long letter as an introduction, outlining his thoughts and his musings about them.

He would send me pages when he had finished a particular scene or group of scenes, and there was no warning about when these pages might arrive. Rather different from most writers, he was anxious to have me or Fred read them as quickly as possible, so that he could get immediate feedback. A messenger might ring the doorbell to my house at ten or eleven o'clock on a Sunday night, and there would stand an older, rather gnarled man. He'd hand me the pages and say, "This is from Sam Jackson," which was a pseudonym that Dalton had used during the blacklist period. The messenger would hand me an envelope, turn his head, and wink. I would wink back. On one occasion, I opened the envelope and eagerly started to read, only to be met with a profusion of profanity and satire, until I came to a line he had written in a descriptive passage saying, "Well, has that awakened you yet? Now let's begin." That's the kind of wit, humor, and talent that Dalton Trumbo had.

Fred returned from directing *Behold a Pale Horse* in Paris. He read and liked the Trumbo script, which found ways to get into the story a great deal sooner than the Taradash version. Dalton wrote an interesting montage of shots, covered with narration, that beautifully and poetically established the background for the original settlement of the islands. That narration is still the opening of the film.

Fred began to select the people he wanted working with him. He chose Cary Odell, who had been with him at Columbia on *From Here to Eternity* as his production designer, and Emmett Emerson, who was a production manager with whom he had worked before.

We had been contemplating Alec Guinness playing the role of Abner Hale, the missionary, and Audrey Hepburn playing his wife, Jerusha. Fred began discussions with both of them. There was also talk of Rock Hudson's playing Rafer Hoxworth, the romantic sea captain.

At about this time, Fred became convinced that the script had to be done as two films. He was pleased with the Trumbo script, but he wanted to break off the missionary story into one film and the Chinese story into another film. He wanted to shoot both films continuously. After the two films were completed, he envisaged their being exhibited in two separate theaters at the same time, with the hope that an audience, having seen one film one night could, on the next night or shortly afterward, see the continuation of the story in the second film, in another theater. In a sense, it would have been a theatrical miniseries. I don't believe that policy had ever been followed before or since, but that was the way Fred visualized doing *Hawaii*.

United Artists, the financier, didn't want to be committed to the second film if the first film was not successful. Consequently, it would not agree to that arrangement with Fred. All of these exciting prospects, Fred Zinnemann, Alec Guinness, Audrey Hepburn—and even David Lean, whom Fred had talked to about directing some of the picture—disappeared when United Artists decided not to accept Fred's new concept of how he would do the film. He told us that if he couldn't do it his way, he would retire from the project. On February 6, 1964, he announced that he was leaving the picture.

I deeply regretted the loss of Fred Zinnemann's services to produce and direct *Hawaii*. I had thoroughly enjoyed the intellectual challenge of working with him. I found him the most stimulating director I had worked intimately with since William Wyler. I had been looking forward to continuing our work together through the production and post-production of the picture, and I was crestfallen when he decided to withdraw.

We had an excellent script, although it still needed condensation to force it within the parameters of one picture. I hoped to attract another outstanding director to the project. I had tried hard to convince Fred to eliminate the Chinese story and hold it for a potential second film if the first film was successful. But he wouldn't hear of it. He felt that the Chinese story was integral to the material, and I never could change his mind. I hoped that I could convince the next director to do just that.

It was my suggestion, following the departure of Fred Zinnemann, to offer the project to George Roy Hill. Two months later, in April 1964, he agreed to direct *Hawaii*, with my producing it.

I had worked with George Roy Hill on *Toys in the Attic* and found him a man of great taste, high intelligence, and considerable talent. He had, by that time, directed two other films, *The World of Henry Orient* and *A Period of Adjustment.* He expressed great enthusiasm for the *Hawaii* project, and I thought that he would be an excellent choice to take over the direction of the picture. In discussing the length problem, and the Chinese story, he had great confidence in our ability to effect compressions that would permit the inclusion of the latter.

I trusted, contrary to a director of the prominence of Fred Zinnemann, George Stevens, or Willy Wyler, that George might have been more amenable to accepting the budgetary constraints that were being imposed on us by United Artists and agreeing to do whatever was necessary to meet them. He was confident that we could do the picture on a $10 million budget. I introduced George to Dalton, and the three of us now began anew, with ideas of George's that led to further rewrites on the screenplay.

As time went on, the possibility of effectuating the Audrey Hepburn-Alec Guinness casting dimmed. Either Audrey Hepburn had other commitments or her enthusiasm waned when Fred dropped out of the project, and she was lost to us. Then we talked about Tom Courtenay playing Abner Hale, and Julie Andrews, who had by then emerged as a major star, playing Jerusha. Julie was signed for the picture in December 1964.

George and I now began to have serious disagreements about the script. I was concerned that the beginning of the script was overwritten, and that the amount of time being devoted to the journey to Hawaii was disproportionate, and also far more expensive in the overall design of the film than it should be. George felt that it would play much shorter than I thought it would, and he tried to allay my concerns. He insisted that he was absolutely confident about his ability to bring in a film whose running time would be two to two and a half hours.

I voiced again the concerns that had caused the retirement of Fred Zinnemann, namely that the arrival of the Chinese characters in Hawaii would be too difficult to contain. George felt strongly otherwise and was exceedingly confident that we could manage it.

He proposed a marvelous casting director, Marion Dougherty, and Marion began to look for characters in the Far East to play the Chinese as well as some of the Hawaiian characters. She recommended two English-speaking Chinese actors who were working in Hong Kong at the time, Jeannette Lin Tsui and Peter Chen Ho. We saw film of both and hired them.

Marion also found Jocelyne La Garde, the 350-pound woman who played Malama, the so-called Alii Nui of our piece, who came from Tahiti. She spoke only French, and we employed a tutor to teach her English before she was to begin work in the picture. She learned English, and she was taught her dialogue. However, for casting a nonprofessional person, Marion's choice was extraordinary. Jocelyne La Garde was nominated for an Academy Award for her performance.

Marion also recruited Manu Tupou, a Fijian, for the role of Keoki, the son of Malama, who joins the missionaries. Ted Nobriga, who played Malama's husband, was a police officer in Hawaii. Their daughter was played by Elizabeth Logue, an employee of Hawaiian Airlines. We interviewed countless people in Hawaii and selected a large number of them to play smaller roles. We chose one young woman, Bette Midler, to play a missionary's wife. Gene Hackman was selected to play John Whipple, one of the missionaries, and Carroll O'Connor played Jerusha's father.

We struggled with the casting of Abner Hale until George became enthusiastic about the idea of casting Max Von Sydow, who had made his mark in Ingmar Bergman films, was fluent in English, and had by then nearly completed his role as Jesus in *The Greatest Story Ever Told*. Max is a marvelous actor and a wonderful human being. Abner is a most difficult role. He is a man so stern, so unforgiving, so unsympathetic, that he would try any actor's skill. Max accepted the role with great enthusiasm. We then contracted with Richard Harris to play the part of Rafer Hoxworth.

The budget of the picture, prepared by Emmett Emerson, a production manager who had worked for George and me on *Toys in the Attic*, was $9.9 million, just on the edge of the $10 million limit that had been set by United Artists.

Included in that budget was the construction cost of a ship to portray the *Thetis,* in which the missionaries travel from New England to Hawaii. The ship was built in Norway to our specifications and was sailed from Norway through the Panama Canal to Hawaii, under the command of Alan Villiers, a well-known sailing captain, with a small crew.

In Hawaii we had great difficulty in finding an open beach without a hotel or a development sitting on it. We visited all the islands and scouted many beaches. We finally were able to work out an arrangement on an open beach, Makua, which was under lease to the Air Force for target practice and as a training site. We housed our cast and crew in the Ilikai Hotel in Honolulu, one of the few hotels that could provide accommodations for a company as large as ours. From the Ilikai to the Makua beach, where most of our sets would be erected, was an hour-and-a-half drive that proved to be both exhausting and tremendously costly.

We enlisted Russell Harlan, a marvelous cinematographer, and Stuart Gilmore, who had previously edited *Toys in the Attic* for us. Dorothy Jeakins designed the wardrobe and played a small role as Abner's mother. Elmer Bernstein was selected to score the picture.

The size of the picture was so huge that I decided I needed help in running this big company, and so I asked Lew Rachmil to act as associate producer and largely manage the below-the-line elements of the picture.

George and I continued to quarrel about the script and about the length problem. He frequently reassured me that he would agree to cuts later on that would allow us to complete the picture within our allotted schedule. We weren't making much progress in that area as we came close to production.

We had our first serious run-in a couple of weeks before we were to begin shooting in Old Sturbridge Village, a model Colonial village in Sturbridge, Massachusetts. We were planning to use this set as the little New England town that was Jerusha's home. We were to begin shooting early in April, and George Roy Hill went on ahead to Sturbridge to prepare. I was planning to come on a little later and be there for the start of production. He phoned me in Los Angeles terribly troubled. Contrary to our expectations, there were as yet no blossoms on the Sturbridge trees. The whole idea of going to Sturbridge was to establish the New England spring locale. He wanted to delay production until the trees began to bloom.

I went ballistic. I said, "That's impossible." With all of our production problems and cost problems, we simply could not delay the start of the picture for a week or more and sit idly in Sturbridge waiting for the trees to bloom. I said, "We'll use artificial flowers attached to the tree limbs on the town common where we are going to shoot." He wouldn't hear of that, and the quarrel became bitter. I insisted we were going to start, and he said he wouldn't shoot artificial flowers.

I reported the problem to David Picker, United Artists vice president in charge of production under Arthur Krim. David tried to mediate between George and me. He talked separately to George and finally suggested that I come to New York where the three of us would meet. At the meeting, George agreed to start production on the date that we had chosen, with the artificial flowers, if necessary.

When shooting began, the screenplay still contained the Chinese story, and I was concerned, because I was now dealing with a much less compromising George than I had ever before confronted. Although this first serious quarrel had been finessed, we had a long, hard shoot in front of us, and I was concerned that when other problems emerged, George would be unwilling to make any of the concessions that would be necessary if I was to meet the commitment that I had made to United Artists that the picture would be as close to the budgeted cost as possible.

We were to commence shooting on a Monday morning. After the conference in New York, which took place on Saturday, I drove to Sturbridge on Sunday evening. Driving up, I began to see snow hitting the windshield of the car. By the time I arrived, we were having a full-fledged snowstorm! George wanted blossoms on the trees, and on April 19 it snowed. A townsman told me it hadn't snowed in April in Sturbridge in a hundred years. Sam Gordon, who had been the prop man for most of my pictures all the way back to the Monogram days, had by now already prepared himself with bushels of blossoms with wires on the end that he was going to attach to the limbs of the trees on the common in Old Sturbridge Village.

George and I had dinner together that Sunday night, and we decided to begin the picture with some scenes that could be shot in the snow. We now opened the picture with a scene of a young boy running through the snow, carrying a letter that has just arrived for his brother, Abner Hale, advising him that he has been accepted as a missionary to be sent from the Yale divinity school to Hawaii. That scene was the first one that we shot.

By the time George had made the opening shots with the boy in the snow and taken him into the interior of the Hale farmhouse, the sun began to appear. As it melted the snow, our crew went out on the common and hosed it down. The prop men, with all the laborers they could hire, were soon up on ladders while our company was at lunch. By the time we finished eating, the sun was shining, all the snow had been hosed away, and the trees were filled with flowers that had been wired onto them. George then began to rehearse the next shot, which is a scene of Abner and Jerusha walking down the common, in which he proposes marriage and asks her to share his life in Hawaii.

After completing our shooting at Sturbridge, we returned to Hollywood and began to shoot the interiors of the *Thetis* on its voyage to Hawaii at the Goldwyn Studios. We built part of a ship on rockers in a tank on a soundstage, and there we shot the exterior and interior material of the terrible storm that the ship went through as it navigated the Cape of Good Hope. Other scenes that were shot at the studio included Jerusha's home, Abner's arrival there, and his meeting Jerusha's family. We did a picnic exterior with Jerusha and Abner at the Disney ranch. The interior shots, including all the dump tanks of water engulfing the deck, were time-consuming and went much more slowly than we had anticipated.

After many sailing problems, the *Thetis* arrived in Hawaii, where it required considerable repair. We managed to have it ready to shoot by the time our company moved from Hollywood to Hawaii, where we first photographed the arrival of the missionaries. The seas were heavy, and nearly everybody on the crew and the cast became seasick. We had a difficult time, but finally we shot the arrival, and George did it beautifully, with Malama in her royal canoe coming out to greet the arriving missionaries.

The shooting continued to go slowly. We had hoped that once we got off the ship and on to our beach it would improve, but then other problems arose. Airplanes flew over us frequently. Hawaii is characterized by clouds passing in front of the sun, and we were getting light changes in too many of our shots. We often had to reshoot to eliminate them. Our location at the Makua beach was approximately an hour and a half drive from the Ilikai, where the crew lived. The cast largely lived in the Kahala district, which is a half-hour drive beyond that. The travel was tiring and also shortened our workdays.

The United Artists executives, who had been badly hurt by the cost overruns of *The Greatest Story Ever Told*, exercised a great deal of surveillance over how much we were spending and how much we were exceeding our budget. I was very strongly made to feel the pressure of meeting that budget. United Artists representatives countersigned all our checks and monitored everything that was happening. David Picker, in charge of production for United Artists, made his presence felt constantly and came to visit on a number of occasions. We had a very long script, and the problems of delay only exacerbated the normal problems of our huge canvas.

What was also happening—which I had anticipated, and about which George had told me he felt I was unduly concerned—was that our film was going to run far too long, and that the problems of failing to edit the script properly would grow to even bigger proportions when trying to edit the film, where the cuts might not be as seamless as they would have been in the script. We were now coming to the point where the script supervisor's timing of the amount of film we were getting was accumulating and going far beyond what it should have been, considering the number of pages that had been encompassed by that much film. Generally I've been what we used to call a minute-a-page person. We were far exceeding that. Extrapolating the length of our first cut, if we were to continue on the road on which we were embarked, yielded an estimate that the first cut of this picture would run between four and five hours. I kept returning to the old bugaboo, the Chinese story, whose excision would allow us to make a script cut of about thirty pages. None of that story had as yet been shot.

I was in Los Angeles and called George on the phone one night. He must have been exhausted, and I'd probably had a hard day myself, and we got into a heated argument about my concerns. I thought the time had come to confront our problems.

I next told United Artists that I didn't think we could come close to finishing the rest of the picture on budget, even after the over-the-budget that had already been expended was added to it, if George continued to direct the picture. I also said that I thought there was a reasonable chance that someone else could maintain the quality of what we were doing, were we to replace George. United Artists agreed that we should replace him.

I went to Hawaii and told George that we'd come to the end of the line, that United Artists wouldn't allow us to continue to exceed the amount of money that had been budgeted for the making of the picture, and that we were going to replace him.

After telling him that, we stopped production, and I returned to Los Angeles and started to look for another director. The Directors Guild agreement provides that one cannot approach a new director until the previous director has been informed that he has been taken off the picture. George was obviously very angry. He said things like, "You people don't understand the problems. I don't have time to work on cutting because I'm too busy shooting, and when I'm not shooting I'm driving to location, and my weekends are busy with preparation." We were working six days a week, and it was a brute of a job. I continued to press for the elimination of the Chinese story. He replied, "How can I take it out? I don't have time to think about how to take it out."

Dalton Trumbo was on another picture, in Europe, but I said, "I'll bring Dalton here to work on it." He said, "I've no time to work with him!" George strongly resisted eliminating the Chinese story. He wanted it in the picture just as Fred Zinnemann wanted it in the picture. And I wanted it in the picture, except I was the one who was pressing to cut it because I was the one who had to answer the questions of the financier. I came back to Los Angeles and talked to Arthur Hiller, whom I thought might be able to take over the direction, provide the kind of quality that we were getting from George, and still keep us reasonably close to budget.

Before returning to Los Angeles to find another director, I had invited Julie Andrews, Max Von Sydow, and Richard Harris to have lunch with me, and I told them all that had transpired between George and myself. I assumed that George had probably told them his side of the story by then, but I explained that I felt that we didn't have any alternative and, sorry as I was to see George go, that we had been forced to take the step. I told them I needed their cooperation in continuing to give their best efforts to whatever director took over the picture. All three were saddened but supportive. They were all fond of George and had the highest regard for his talent as a director. They said they wished the situation hadn't come to this, but they were all professionals and agreed to go on with whoever replaced George.

Arthur Hiller had worked with Julie on *The Americanization of Emily,* a most successful picture, and I thought the fact that they had a previous relationship would be helpful. I expected we would lose a week's shooting when we made the replacement, but I undertook to take what seemed to me to be the most responsible course, difficult as it was. It certainly would have been a lot easier not to do it. Obviously, everything I was doing was subject to the approval of United Artists. Certainly I couldn't replace the director without UA's approval, and so the company was intimately involved in everything that was happening. By that time, UA was convinced that it must do everything it could to avoid having another *Cleopatra* experience, which had brought Twentieth Century-Fox to the verge of bankruptcy in 1963.

Arthur Hiller and I returned to Hawaii on August 1, 1965, where I discovered some new developments. Jocelyne La Garde, who played Malama, and Manu Tupou, who played Keoki, now stated that they would not agree to continue in the film unless George remained to direct it. These two nonprofessional actors, one from Tahiti and one from Fiji, had been proposed to us by Marion Dougherty, our casting director and an old and dear friend of George Roy Hill's. I assumed their decisions reflected her influence.

I arranged to meet Jocelyne, hoping to persuade her to continue in the picture. My brother, Marvin, had come back to Hawaii with me when I returned with Arthur, and he and I met with her. It was a difficult meeting. She spoke little English, and we had to converse with her in French. My French is collegiate, and Marvin's was somewhat better. We had a long meeting and tried to persuade her of the professionalism that was involved. We also had the same kind of a meeting with Manu. What we were saying was of little meaning, because both of them had said they had no interest in careers in films beyond this picture. They felt they owed their loyalty to Marion and to George, and they certainly exhibited it. They were completely unbending. They couldn't care less about disciplinary actions against them by the Screen Actors Guild or American law courts.

Next, a fire broke out on our set, which we were told had been started by Hawaiian extras who were indicating their dissatisfaction with the dismissal of George. So now the newspapers called the fire part of the "revolt of the natives." Some 175 extras signed a petition in support of George.

I went back to the hotel and talked to Arthur Hiller. Our options were either to replace Jocelyne and Manu with other actors and reshoot scenes that had already been shot, or else to consider the possibility of dropping one or the other out of the story. I didn't think that either of these options were real possibilities, and so I was left with the conclusion that there was no way to go on with the picture and maintain any of the quality or integrity of what we were trying to do.

At this point, I had to face the possibility of writing off a $10 million investment. I spent one of the most terrible nights of my life.

Amazingly, I received a phone call the next morning from John Ford. John, whom I'd known and worked with some years before on *The Horse Soldiers,* happened to be in Honolulu. He owned a beautiful yacht, which he kept at the marina in Honolulu. He had read the newspaper accounts of our travail, called me, and said, "You know, I've been reading all this stuff, and this is crazy, Walter. I want to have a meeting with you and George and see if we can't straighten this thing out."

"Well, I don't know if he wants to do that."

He said, "Give me his phone number and let me call him." I didn't know if John Ford knew George at that point, except certainly George knew who he was. Ford called me back and said, "George says it's fine with him, and he asked if we could meet at his house. Can you be there at twelve o'clock?"

I said, "Fine, I'll be there." I went to George's house, and while we were waiting for Ford to appear, we made some small talk. John Ford soon arrived, accompanied by a friend of his, Willis Goldbeck.

We all sat down, and it soon became pretty clear that Ford was by now deep in his cups. He asked George if he had some beer in the house. Holding a bottle of beer in his hand, he started to murmur. I'm not quite sure what he said. Neither was George. But he went on like that for a while, and then he started to snooze. The two of us looked at Willis, and Willis threw up his hands and smiled, "You know, we're on vacation."

After a while, we got Ford up, all three of us helped him into his car, and Willis drove off with him. Taking advantage of the opportunity, I thought I would make a last effort to reason with George, and I said, "You know, the final result of all this is that United Artists will probably have to junk the picture. But somehow or other they'll absorb the loss, and go on and make lots of other pictures. But this is not good for me, and it's not good for you. I don't know if we can do anything to pick up the pace of our shooting, but the one thing we can do is to give you less to shoot."

He said, "The Chinese story."

I said, "I can get Dalton to come here. He and I will work on how to delete the Chinese story, and on Sundays we'll go over our ideas with you, and Dalton will continue to work in the hotel."

He said, "Well, there are other things . . ."

Then he started to bargain for other things that he wanted. He asked me to provide a helicopter for him, to take him to and from the set, to cut down the amount of his travel time. I said, "Okay, you've got a helicopter." He asked me to agree not to shoot on odd Saturdays, so that he would shoot only two Saturdays a month and not four, which would give him more time for working on the script. I agreed to that. Having won these points, he agreed in principle to cutting the Chinese sequence out of the picture.

Dalton Trumbo was in London working on a picture. But he was completely cooperative and worked it out so that he could come to Hawaii. I can't say enough about how supportive he was in helping me manage the situation. George and I agreed that we would resume production on our new basis upon Dalton's arrival in a few days. After that, we would reschedule the picture, deleting the Chinese story. We rebudgeted the picture, because we'd now shortened the shooting schedule.

We had to pay off the Hong Kong actors, who had already been hired. The Mirisch Company settled its arrangement with Arthur Hiller, and we paid him some money. He was cooperative and decent about the whole thing. He was quoted in the *Los Angeles Herald-Examiner* (October 9, 1966) as saying, "Well, at least I got a trip to Hawaii . . ."

Richard Harris's contract provided that we would not materially alter his role from the script that had been submitted to him, which he had approved. His role, Rafer Hoxworth, appears throughout the Chinese story. At the beginning of the controversy, I had said to Richard, "I need to talk to you about this. We may have to cut a lot of scenes that you're in."

Richard said to me, "You do what you have to do." Implicit in that, I suppose, was that he would then do what he had to do. Later he sued United Artists for a large sum of money for materially altering his role. The suit dragged on for a while, until finally he was paid a not-unreasonable amount to withdraw it.

Dalton Trumbo came to Hawaii, and he and I and George began to have talks about how to implement the script cutting that we had discussed. We began the process of putting our shooting company together again. First, there were some celebratory events. Arthur Krim flew from New York to Hawaii to be present and wish us all well on the resumption of production. Obviously he and all of the United Artists executives had been apprised of everything that was going on by telephone. John Ford insisted on having a big party for our whole company aboard his boat at the marina in Honolulu. We also had a luau at a Hawaiian restaurant. Then we resumed production. I spent a great deal of time in a hotel room with Dalton. We gave George pages that Dalton had rewritten and then had further meetings with George on the set or on Sundays at home. When shooting resumed, it wasn't any faster paced than before. But fortunately now there was a great deal less to be shot, which made a significant difference. The picture was originally budgeted at somewhat under $10 million, and its final cost was over $14 million.

When the picture wrapped, we had a party at the Kahala Hilton, where Julie Andrews entertained and sang the whole repertoire of her great hits. She remarked amusingly that it had been so long since she'd done any singing that she wasn't sure she'd remember the lyrics of all of her old standards. But she did, and she was wonderful.

We moved back to California for post-production. Stu Gilmore moved as quickly as he could to arrive at a first cut, which ran somewhere around the four-hour mark. I shudder to think what the length would have been if we hadn't eliminated the Chinese story. George Roy Hill said he now wanted to work with Gilmore in preparing his director's cut, and the two of them went to work.

We spent considerable time discussing the prologue and finally determined that we would have one that would be semi-documentary in approach, telling of the changing of the gods in Tahiti and the emigration of the settlers from Tahiti, who traveled in longboats to Hawaii. We chose documentary filmmaker James Blue, who shot the material to dramatize the narration that had been written by Dalton. It was edited by Stu Gilmore with George's help, and it worked out quite well. It's not too long, and I think it gives the film a feeling of size. It was always intended that *Hawaii* be a road show and be exhibited with an intermission.

The first preview of the film was to be held in Santa Barbara, at a running time of 186 minutes. George called me when we were making arrangements about the preview, and having been a Marine flier in the Korean War, he invited me to fly up with him in a biplane of World War I vintage, which was his latest acquisition. I told him I was afraid that, en route, he might remember how angry he had been at me in Hawaii, and consequently I'd rather meet him at the theater.

The preview went very well. We made some changes and then decided to have a second preview, in Minneapolis. We had a good preview again, and plans were made for the road show openings of the picture at the De Mille Theater in New York, on October 10, 1966, and two days later at the Egyptian Theater in Los Angeles.

There was a gala premiere in New York for the benefit of the Will Rogers Hospital, with many celebrities in attendance. I thought the film was playing quite well, but as it approached the intermission, I became terribly anxious to see the *New York Times* review, which I was told would be out at approximately that time of the evening. I left the theater and walked out on Broadway, looking for a newspaper kiosk at a subway station, where, as I arrived, the newspapers were being delivered. I bought a copy of the *Times*, to find a devastatingly uncomplimentary review, which destroyed the rest of the evening for me. I tried to remember other films that had been badly reviewed by the *New York Times* and had gone on to be immensely successful. I remembered *Dr. Zhivago*, but it didn't much help. Critic Vincent Canby wrote of *Hawaii*, "One comes out of the theater not so much moved as numbed by the cavalcade of conventional, if sometimes eye popping, scenes of storm and seascape, of pomp and pestilence, all laid out in large strokes of brilliant DeLuxe color on the huge Panavision screen." There were a lot of reviewers who agreed with Canby. There were also many who were enthusiastic about the film. Unfortunately, one tends to dwell on the negative reviews, hoping always that everything will be positive and complimentary. But they weren't.

However, audiences liked *Hawaii*. They liked it a lot. The advance sales were excellent. We opened in theaters throughout the country, always on the two-a-day, reserved-seat basis. It looked as if our film was going to be financially successful, which—after all of the heartache that had gone into it, and the disappointment of some of the major reviews—helped make the whole project appear to be worthwhile.

At the Oscars, the film received seven nominations, a considerable number for one film, and a great deal of attention was given to that in the press. It was a great disappointment to me when it won none. However, the picture now appeared with an aura of success, and I began to think of the possibility of doing another *Hawaii* film and to make notes as to how that might be executed when the time was right for it. On its first release, *Hawaii* earned film rentals of about $19 million domestically. The foreign rentals were probably about the same, which was an excellent result. So the catastrophe that I had feared didn't happen, and somehow or other we managed to bring this ship to harbor without any fatalities.

24

A New Relationship
with Norman Jewison

O ur next release, *The Fortune Cookie,* was considerably less expensive and took place in a quite different locale, Cleveland, Ohio. *The Fortune Cookie* probably stemmed from the
fact that Billy Wilder was a great football fan and a regular viewer of
Monday Night Football. He postulated an accident happening to the
football sideline cameraman, who happens to be cursed with a brother-
in-law who is a shyster personal-injury lawyer. Billy's idea, from the beginning, was to tailor this vehicle to the respective talents of Jack Lemmon and Walter Matthau.

Walter had played the lead on Broadway in *Shot in the Dark* and
then had done the play *The Odd Couple,* which vaulted him into stardom as a comedic actor. The role of Whiplash Willie, the shyster lawyer, to be played by him, seemed like a probable tour de force in a film
that could be a comedic romp. We eagerly embraced the concept. It certainly didn't present the censorship problems of *Kiss Me, Stupid,* and
what could be more American than apple pie, motherhood, and football? We thought this would be a noncontroversial comedy with tailor-
made roles for two superb actors.

I was disappointed that Billy didn't choose a better-known actress
than Judi West for the leading female role. Billy had seen her in Arthur
Miller's play *After the Fall* and became enthusiastic about her. He felt

confident that he could get a good performance from her, but I felt that had the role been played by a more recognizable film name, the combination of two men and a woman would have been more attractive to audiences. Both *Some Like It Hot* and *The Apartment* had that two-men-and-one-woman combination.

Art Modell, who owned the Cleveland Browns, was most enthusiastic about cooperating with us, and we began production of the picture in Cleveland. It went along well, and we soon moved the company back to Los Angeles to do the interiors when, catastrophically, Walter Matthau suffered a severe heart attack. This occurred about three-quarters of the way through production. Walter's condition was precarious. In the beginning, his doctors weren't sure he would survive. The film was insured and the actors were covered by cast insurance, but it was clear from the dailies that Walter's performance was outstanding in a once-in-a-lifetime role.

Jack Lemmon's role didn't give him a chance to do very much. He was confined to a wheelchair, which limited him terribly. I'm sure he accepted the role primarily out of respect and friendship for Billy Wilder. As it developed, he began a friendship and a partnership with Walter Matthau that endured throughout their lifetimes, and they became close friends. Jack recognized that Willie was a marvelous part for Walter, and he was happy to play the secondary role in order to support Walter in the bravura performance that he contributed to *The Fortune Cookie*.

Walter Matthau's illness incapacitated him for three to four months, but fortunately our cast-insurance policy paid the costs of holding together all of those elements that had to be maintained until production could be resumed. Those essential elements consist of sets, wardrobe, set dressings, props, furniture, and cast. Even with all this, the financial burden of the delay to the insurance company was not terribly heavy.

However, neither was Walter Matthau when he was finally able to return to work. As a matter of fact, he was about forty pounds lighter than he was when he was taken ill. To this day, if I happen to see the picture playing on television, the difference in his before and after weight jumps out at me. But apparently no one else was seriously troubled. Walter resumed his role, and the film was completed.

After his experiences with Peter Sellers on *Kiss Me, Stupid,* Billy Wilder was beginning to think he was jinxed. But it didn't happen to him again until his next picture. I thought *The Fortune Cookie* was going to be both critically and commercially successful. It was not another *Some Like It Hot* or *The Apartment* or *Irma La Douce,* but I thought it would do very well and that Walter Matthau's performance would carry it. Unfortunately, it was only mildly received. We had been spoiled by Billy Wilder. We considered *Kiss Me, Stupid* as an unfortunate glitch. Although *The Fortune Cookie* was disappointing at the box office, I was delighted that Walter, after all he had gone through, was awarded the Best Supporting Actor Oscar.

≋

Everyone then alive remembers where he or she was on the day of the assassination of President John F. Kennedy. On the morning of November 22, 1963, I found myself in the offices of Ted Ashley, Yul Brynner's agent. I had stopped by to discuss with Ted the possibility of doing a sequel to *The Magnificent Seven,* which would again star Yul. When I arrived at Ted's office and approached the desk of his secretary, she excitedly said to me, "Have you heard the news about the assassination of the president?" We were all shocked to hear the details, and we remained glued to a television set for quite a while, listening to the latest developments. We decided to defer our discussion to a later time when we agreed to a deal under which Yul would again play the role of Chris, in a sequel tentatively entitled *The Return of the Seven.* I chose a writer, Larry Cohen, who had done some outstanding television work on the popular series *The Defenders,* and Larry began preparation of a script.

As I was heavily involved with *Hawaii* at that time, I chose a producer, Ted Richmond, to supervise the project. Ted had enjoyed a long career as a producer of action pictures, most recently at Universal. He and I discussed the possibility of securing the services of Burt Kennedy, a writer-director who had been doing some good Westerns, to direct, and we submitted Larry Cohen's script to Burt. He reacted favorably to the project but wanted to do a rewrite of the script himself, and we agreed. He did so, although he didn't receive a writing credit. Ted Richmond had produced *Solomon and Sheba* in Spain, which also starred Yul Brynner, and for budgetary reasons he proposed shooting the film there. We had been looking for an economical place to make the film, and as labor costs were considerably less in Spain than they were in either in the United States or Mexico, we determined that it might provide the most reasonable locations to shoot the picture.

When it came time to cast *The Return of the Seven,* we investigated the possibility of reuniting as much of the original cast as we could. But aside from Yul Brynner, we were unable to do so, either for reasons of increased salary demands or unavailability, or simply a desire not to repeat their previous roles. Failing to get Steve McQueen to play Vin again, we looked to reconstitute the chemistry of the first picture and chose Robert Fuller, who had played the lead in a successful television series, *Wagon Train,* just as, years before, Steve McQueen had emerged from *Wanted—Dead or Alive* to play in our film. Failing to get James Coburn, I chose Warren Oates. This was quite early in Warren's career and the first time that I worked with him. It served me in good stead when it came time, a few years later, to cast *In the Heat of the Night.* Claude Akins and Jordan Christopher were also selected, and the rest of the casting was done in Spain, notably with Emilio Fernandez and Julian Mateos. The production proceeded quite uneventfully.

The post-production was done in London, where it was scored and dubbed. Elmer Bernstein repeated his music from the original, except that this time it received an Academy nomination. The film was not very successful in America, but like its predecessor, it was exceedingly well received abroad, and the combined worldwide gross of the picture produced a tidy profit. The film was generally not well reviewed, except in the *Hollywood Reporter,* which gave it a rave.

At that time, I had no plans for a third film in the series. I didn't think there was much chance that Yul Brynner would want to play Chris again, and changing the leading actor in a series is always risky, although the title had developed a charisma that could not be denied. However, as time went by, I would sometimes give thought to the possibility of doing still another film based on the concept and its magic title.

We had enjoyed considerable success with Blake Edwards in *The Pink Panther* and *A Shot in the Dark,* but unfortunately his *Battle of Gettysburg* project was not working out. A long treatment had been prepared, but it ran even longer than the battle and would have been more expensive to produce. I loved the idea of doing *The Battle of Gettysburg.* I enjoy that kind of film, and Blake was enthusiastic about it. I was disappointed when we had to give it up.

Blake had also proposed *The Great Race* to us, and we financed the script. It seemed like an ideal subject for him. But a budget was prepared, and it, too, was immensely expensive. United Artists asked us to pass on the film, and we agreed that Blake could submit the project to another company. He succeeded in placing it quickly. He arranged to produce the film with Jack Lemmon, Tony Curtis, and Natalie Wood for Warner Bros.

After *The Great Race*, Blake Edwards became enthusiastic about making *What Did You Do in the War, Daddy?* a comedic film with a war background. He wrote the script with Bill Blatty, who had been his collaborator on *A Shot in the Dark*, based on a story by Maurice Richlin and himself. All these auspices were good. Although the picture was to be shot locally, it was clearly an expensive picture, but we hoped the cost would be controllable within the parameters of the budget that had been approved.

The film starred James Coburn and Dick Shawn, hardly big comedic box-office attractions. They were fashionable, but not the personalities who would promise an audience a big comedic romp. I think its casting certainly affected its grossing potential. Unfortunately, it also went considerably over budget. Its review in the *New Yorker* (September 10, 1966) was of small comfort:

> One keeps hearing, and one keeps having more and more reason to fear, that Hollywood just doesn't know how to make those good old-fashioned slapstick farces anymore. Mr. Edwards has struck several sharp blows against this notion . . . and he knocks it into a cocked hat. The first two-thirds of his picture is so continuously and relentlessly funny that it would almost be true to say that I spent the entire fraction laughing. Oh, I may have stopped for breathing a few times, and I recall a couple of ugly moments when somebody clambered past me on his way to a seat, and I couldn't see the screen. But otherwise I remained in a state of helpless, joyous breakdown. In the last third of the picture, the plot thickens to the point of threatening to become unstirrable, but Mr. Edwards pulls himself together and rounds everything off in a neat, clattery, cuckoo climax. Nearly all contemporary pictures are too long, and length is, of course, a particular enemy of comedy.

❦

In 1961, an agent at William Morris and a friend, Stan Kamen, called and told me he would like to bring a young director by to meet me. I had known Stan from *The Magnificent Seven* days, when he was still representing television personalities and was Steve McQueen's agent. Stan handled the deal with Four Star Productions that made Steve available to do *The Magnificent Seven*. Stan and I had maintained a friendship ever since then, and I valued his judgment. If he thought I should meet this young director, Norman Jewison, I certainly wanted to do so.

Stan and Norman came to the Goldwyn Studio, and I met with them and found Norman to be a most articulate young director with a long and impressive background. He is Canadian by birth and had begun his career working for the CBC. From there he went to New York, where he had done some outstanding television work.

At the time, we were in production with *The Children's Hour*, and I mentioned that, as we spoke, William Wyler was shooting downstairs on an adjoining soundstage. Norman said that he would like nothing better than to visit the set, meet Mr. Wyler, and hopefully have an opportunity to observe him working. I gladly acceded to his request, and after our positive and enjoyable meeting, I took him down to the stage, introduced him to Willy, and found him a chair. He spent a good deal of the afternoon there, watching Willy directing Audrey Hepburn and Shirley MacLaine.

We continued to talk with Stan about the possibility of working out some kind of a producing-directing deal with Norman, who, at that time, was engaged to do a film at Universal, *Forty Pounds of Trouble* with Tony Curtis. We finally did work out an arrangement, along the lines of our formula producer-director deals. We needed to position it around his other commitments, mainly *The Thrill of It All*, released by Universal in 1963, *Send Me No Flowers*, released by Universal in 1964, and *The Art of Love*, released by Universal in 1965.

As the basis for his first Mirisch Company project, he proposed Nathaniel Benchley's book *The Off-Islanders*, which became *The Russians Are Coming, the Russians Are Coming*. I responded to it immediately, and we acquired the rights and discussed possible screenwriters. We agreed that the best writer for the project would be William Rose.

Bill Rose was an American who, since the end of World War II, had been living in England, and who later moved to the Isle of Man. His first great success was the British film *Genevieve,* and subsequent to that he had done a couple of other outstanding comedies for Ealing Studios. We sent him the material, and he was most enthusiastic about it, although, because of his commitments, we had a long wait before his services could begin. Another delay also developed at this time. Norman was asked to produce and direct the Judy Garland television variety shows, and he wanted to take the assignment. It required his going to New York for quite some time, but it helped to rationalize our long wait for Bill Rose.

Bill worked slowly but finally sent us a long treatment. It was marvelous. We were delighted and felt that he had really broken the back of the project, and he then proceeded to write a script that, after his long treatment, appeared in a reasonable amount of time.

At this juncture, Norman received an offer to take over the direction of a film starring Steve McQueen that was in production at MGM, *The Cincinnati Kid.* It had begun production with Sam Peckinpah, but he had been discharged. Norman told me he thought *Kid* had a marvelous script, and he would like to do it. It again resulted in a further postponement of *The Russians Are Coming, the Russians Are Coming.* I didn't want to interfere with Norman's being able to do a project that he thought so highly of, so we acceded to the further delay. Norman completed *The Cincinnati Kid* in about four months, and we embarked on casting and production plans for *The Russians.* We had hoped to shoot it on the Massachusetts coast during the summer, but we couldn't get ready to begin production until September 1965.

The delay forced us to reconsider our original plan for a New England shoot, and we now began to consider locations on the West Coast. We finally settled on the Fort Bragg area in Mendocino County, in Northern California. We needed a submarine for the picture and tried to make arrangements with the U.S. Navy to make one available to us. We didn't require it for very long, and I was amazed that the Navy would not agree to cooperate. Failing with the U.S. Navy, we made a request that we didn't expect to have accepted, to the Russian Embassy, asking if they would make one of their submarines available to us. We were not quite as surprised when they rejected our application. We finally rented a 165-foot-long unifoam and plywood replica that Twentieth Century-Fox had built to portray a Japanese sub in their film *Morituri*.

Looking for new faces, Norman went to New York, interviewed many actors, and photographed his interviews with them. He phoned and told me that he was enthusiastic about one in particular. He said, "I don't want to tell you any more about it, but you'll be seeing the film tomorrow, and you'll see for yourself." The film to which he referred was an interview with Alan Arkin. Alan assumed a Russian accent, and it was one of the funniest standup pieces I had seen in a long time. Once we had screened that interview, we knew that he was the man to play the Russian submariner.

Carl Reiner, who played the husband and father in the film, had worked with Norman in *The Art of Love* at Universal. Felicia Farr, Mrs. Jack Lemmon, had been chosen to play the wife, but prior to production she dropped out because of pregnancy and was replaced by Eva Marie Saint. We had a lot of weather problems on location, but otherwise the picture went well in its shooting phase.

There was great enthusiasm among our group as we watched the dailies. We sensed that this was going to be an uproariously funny comedy with quite serious overtones just as, later on, *In the Heat of the Night* had something important to say and was cloaked in the guise of a murder mystery. Alan Arkin was both funny and moving, as was Brian Keith. Tessie O'Shea, Michael J. Pollard, Jonathan Winters, and Paul Ford were also excellent. I thought it was a wonderful film, and I was very proud of it.

The Academy and the public agreed. The picture received a Best Picture Academy Award nomination, as well as nominations for Alan Arkin, J. Terry Williams and Hal Ashby for film editing, and William Rose for his screenplay. Sadly, it won none. The press reviews were uniformly excellent, and the picture was tremendously successful, grossing $12 million in film rental in its first domestic release on an investment of less than $4 million. The *New York Daily News* commented, "There is already some talk that *The Russians Are Coming* . . . will be a strong contender for the Nobel Peace Prize," and the editorial was inserted into the *Congressional Record* by Senator Ernest Gruening of Alaska.

The Russians Are Coming, the Russians Are Coming fulfilled most of the things that I hope for in a picture. It has something to say, it entertains, it is commercially successful, and it is recognized by one's peers for its values. Those are the four bases that it touched, and I think that's a home run. It received the third Mirisch Company Academy Best Picture nomination in the nine years that we'd been in business.

≋

Sometime in 1964, *Cast a Giant Shadow* was brought to my brother Harold by Herman Citron, an agent at MCA, who represented Mel Shavelson, its writer-director. Shavelson had enjoyed a long and successful career as a comedy writer and director, having started out as a writer for Bob Hope and collaborating often with Jack Rose. Finally he became a director and began to direct their work, mainly at Paramount, and was enjoying a most successful career when he came upon the book by Ted Berkman. It told the story of Colonel Mickey Marcus, a Jewish decorated hero of World War II who, after returning to civilian life, had been enlisted to go to Israel and help the Israeli army in its 1947 war of independence.

Mel was enthusiastic about the story and had succeeded in interesting John Wayne in playing an American general who presumably was a friend of Marcus's and was instrumental in convincing him that the cause of the Israelis was one that he should take up. Wayne was still one of the most highly sought-after actors in the industry, and his promised presence in the film was a great inducement to develop the property. His role was only a cameo, but later the idea to incorporate other cameos in the film was suggested, so that we could create the aura of an all-star cast. We developed the script and submitted it to Kirk Douglas, who consented to play Marcus.

Arthur Krim, who was very involved with the youthful Israeli state and had many friends and connections in Israel, also became enthusiastic about the film. There seemed to be a great deal of sentimental interest in telling this story of a man who, having finished his own war, extended himself to give the benefit of his training and experience to his coreligionists fighting a war of independence halfway around the world.

The shooting took two months in Israel and then six more weeks at the Cinecitta Studio in Rome, where it was completed in late July 1965.

John Wayne undoubtedly believed the film was a worthwhile project. However, in addition to his nominal compensation, he and his company secured a position in the production. His son, Michael, received a credit as co-producer, and Wayne's company had a profit participation. Unfortunately, the film didn't do well at the box office and was a disappointment, although it did have an important story to tell.

✽

On one of the many trips that I made to New York during the 1960s, I attended the Broadway production of *How to Succeed in Business without Really Trying*. Abe Burrows and Frank Loesser had written the show based on a book by Shepherd Mead. It starred Robert Morse and was a funny, fast-moving satire on American business, with a first-rate musical score by Loesser. We had not produced a musical picture since *West Side Story*, and I gave a great deal of thought to the possibility of our doing *How to Succeed* as a film. I talked it over with Harold and Marvin, and we discussed it as a possible project with Arthur Krim and Bob Benjamin. They agreed to our making the picture if we could produce it at a cost of $3 million, including the acquisition of the property, despite the fact that it had limited foreign appeal because it was a musical film.

In order to see whether or not that would be possible, we opened negotiations with the Dramatists Guild, which represented the creators of the show. We soon learned that we could acquire the motion picture rights for $1 million, which left us only $2 million to produce the film. *How to Succeed* was presold, to a certain extent, and the music score was exceedingly popular. But our problem was how to put together a team to make this film on the rather limited budget that we had agreed to with United Artists.

We decided from the outset that because of cost reasons and also because he really was so outstanding in the play, we would repeat the casting of Robert Morse as J. Pierpont Finch. We hoped the film would make a movie star of him. The casting of a relative unknown didn't loom as a big problem to us. We felt that the property was the star of our film. We didn't have big stars in *West Side Story*, and that didn't present any detriment to its box-office success.

We were contacted by an agent representing David Swift, who advised us that he was interested in the property. He had been a television writer, had written some good movies, and had directed the successful Disney film *The Parent Trap*. He had recently completed a film with Jack Lemmon entitled *Good Neighbor Sam* for Columbia. We talked with David, an exuberant man, full of enthusiasm for the project, who indicated that he would want to write the screenplay himself. We explained our budget constraints to him and the kind of schedule that would be necessary in order to produce the film within those parameters, and he agreed to them. We negotiated a deal, and he undertook the writing of the screenplay.

Michelle Lee had played Rosemary in the Broadway production. She was young and attractive and sang well. We decided to cast her as well as Rudy Vallee and Maureen Arthur from the Broadway cast. We selected Robert Boyle as our production designer, Ralph Winters as editor, and the cameraman was Burnett Guffey. We started production on location in New York to infuse a feel of the real city into the beginning of the picture. Then, after a short shoot, the film returned to the Goldwyn Studio, where the major part of the film was shot on soundstages. It was completed close to schedule and close to budget.

We enjoyed excellent previews of *How to Succeed,* and it was booked to open at the Radio City Music Hall in New York. Richard Schickel reviewed it for *Life* (March 31, 1967):

> We must thank whatever gods may be for David Swift's unconquerable vulgarity. Had he allowed one moment of what is customarily regarded as good taste, or the balanced view of life, to intrude on *How to Succeed in Business without Really Trying,* which he adapted from the stage musical, directed, and produced, he probably would have spoiled the whole thing. As you may remember, the purpose of the exercise is to satirize, in the broadest possible terms, the bumptious tenacity which some of us, say about 99 percent, pursue the bitch goddess these days. It is a vulgar and exhausting process, and it requires a vulgar and exhausting style to illuminate it. Consider it illuminated, in white-hot arc lamps. . . . *How to Succeed* is noisy, edgy, harsh, and raw, but it does have the courage and humor of its own crude convictions.

All of the reviews were good, and most judged it to be the best musical to be released that year. Although it is an immensely entertaining film and was well reviewed, it was very disappointing at the box office. I never have understood why it was not more popular, particularly when *The Secret of My Success,* with Michael J. Fox, a nonmusical with virtually the same springboard as *How to Succeed,* was a huge success not too many years ago.

25

In the Heat of the Night

In 1965, Martin Baum, an agent who represented Sidney Poitier, brought me the book *In the Heat of the Night* by John Ball and said that it had been submitted to him by a literary agent, H. N. Swanson, who represented Ball, as a possible vehicle for Sidney Poitier. At that time, Sidney was the preeminent African American actor in American films. Swanny, an astute literary agent, recognized that selling a property in which the leading man was an African American detective had little or no chance to succeed at that time unless he could couple it with an important personality. Sidney's was the first name that would have come to mind.

I read the book and found it wanting in many areas, although there was a marvelous relationship between the detective, Virgil Tibbs, and the southern redneck sheriff, Bill Gillespie. That relationship just crackled. However, most of the situations that surrounded it were rather disappointing. The plot revolved around a musician, who came to the little town of Wells, Mississippi, to conduct a concert. We later changed the musician to a developer coming to build a factory that would open up the sleepy, bigoted, southern town, thus giving the story socioeconomic implications that it didn't originally have. There is a conflict between the forces of conservatism in the community—as represented by the Larry Gates character Eric Endicott—and the progressive people, led by the mayor, who want to open up the town and unleash forces that would seek racial equality by upsetting the status quo of a community that has remained relatively undisturbed since the Civil War.

I had met Sidney Poitier many years before, shortly after the formation of our company and our move to the Goldwyn Studio. Samuel Goldwyn was then in production with his last film, *Porgy and Bess,* in which Sidney played the title role. A publicity man, Leon Roth, introduced Sidney to me in the commissary one day, and we talked for a while. I was very impressed by him. He is an extraordinary man, who has built his life and career by overcoming the tremendous handicaps of poverty and prejudice while remaining a man of great intelligence and charm.

When I met him, he talked about how *Porgy and Bess* was running over schedule, and he was troubled because he had been asked to do a play on Broadway. He was enthusiastic about it and was afraid that he might lose the role if he weren't available by the time his services would be required. Fortunately, he was finished in time, and he contributed an extraordinary performance to the great success of *Raisin in the Sun.* When *Heat* was presented to me, I was very receptive, since I had hoped that a project would appear on which he and I could work together.

I told Martin Baum that we would acquire an option on the book and develop it with the hope that we could get a screenplay that would please us all. Baum would not commit Sidney to the project until such time as we had a script that was acceptable to him. I also told Baum that I wanted Sidney to be involved with me in the development of the screenplay, since I wanted to take advantage of his intelligence and sensitivity to the material. He would then also have a personal investment in the screenplay and would presumably be more agreeable to playing Virgil Tibbs when the script was finished.

We discussed writers; Marty suggested, and United Artists and we agreed, that we would make a deal with Robert Alan Arthur. Arthur was a well-known television writer who had written many successful shows for *the Philco TV Playhouse,* including one that starred Sidney, *A Man Is Ten Feet Tall.* Arthur wrote a long screen treatment, and I was in Hawaii when I received it. I made a lot of notes, and I was ready to call him when he phoned me and told me that he had just received an offer to work with John Frankenheimer on *Grand Prix,* which was going to

be shot in the south of France. John wanted him to come to Nice immediately and bring his whole family. They would have a house for him,
and he would spend the whole summer there! He continued, "I told
John I have this commitment to you. What should I do?"

I said to him, "What any sane man would do. Quit this job and go to
the south of France!" I was really sorry to lose him, because he had come
up with some excellent ideas. He told me later that he had enjoyed a
wonderful summer on the Riviera, and I told him it had cost him an
Academy Award.

I then talked to Marty and Sidney, and the name of Stirling Silliphant was suggested. I hadn't met Stirling before, but he had been
doing some very good work, including *The Slender Thread*, in which
Sidney starred. We arranged to meet him and discuss the project. He
had great enthusiasm for it, and we made a deal for him to take over the
writing.

As the script progressed, I arranged for Sidney, Stirling, and me to
meet whenever it seemed advisable. We discussed current events, the
civil rights movement, and the complexities of our characters and story.
Although this was 1965, we didn't want our movie to seem like a po-
lemic. We wanted the environment to play only its normal role in the
telling of a personal and melodramatic story. I was delighted with the
screenplay when it was finally finished, and Sidney indicated that he
was ready to come aboard.

Just about that time, I was in an airplane, en route to a preview of
Hawaii in Minneapolis, sitting alongside George Roy Hill, and I was
reading the script of *In the Heat of the Night* and making notes. This was
after all of the problems that George and I had gone through together
on *Hawaii*. He suddenly said to me, "What are you reading?"

I replied, "It's a script called *In the Heat of the Night*."

He said, "What's it about?" So I synopsized the story for him. He
said, "That sounds like something I'd like to do."

I thought, "Do we want to do this again?" I didn't reply, but I'm sure
he would have done a wonderful job. There had just been so much that
we had gone through that I thought we shouldn't work together so soon
again. As a matter of fact, we never did work together again. His career
wasn't hurt by it. Shortly after that he did *Butch Cassidy and the Sun-
dance Kid* and later *The Sting*. He did fine without me.

We had, by that time, completed *The Russians Are Coming, the Russians Are Coming,* and I felt I wanted to offer the screenplay to Norman Jewison. We had a multiple-picture deal with him, the first film of which was *The Russians.* I wanted Norman to remain with our company while we developed other properties, but mainly I felt that Norman was an exceedingly talented director and would do an absolutely first-rate job of directing *Heat.* I gave him the script. I told him that I had developed it myself, that Sidney Poitier had already seen it and had agreed to appear in it, and that I would be producing it. Although Norman's deal with us called for him to be producer-director on all the films he made for us, I told him that as I had been so intimately involved with this project and had brought it to the point of what I felt was an excellent screenplay already packaged with the preeminent star to play the leading role, I wanted to produce the film myself. He quickly read the script and then called me to say he wanted to do the film.

I had intended, when the screenplay was finished, to offer the role of Sheriff Bill Gillespie to George C. Scott. I shared this proposal with Norman and Sidney, and they were both enthusiastic. We contacted Scott and were delighted when his agent told us that he would like to play the part. Negotiations with him were pretty nearly worked out when I got a call from his agent, who said that Scott's then-wife, Colleen Dewhurst, had been offered a role in a Broadway play, and she wanted him to do it with her. The dates for the play conflicted with our shooting dates, and he asked if he could withdraw from our film.

Norman and I then considered other possibilities for the Gillespie role and agreed that Rod Steiger was the actor to whom we should offer the role. We did so and were delighted that he responded positively.

We had originally planned to find a location for the film somewhere in the South. However, after discussing it with Norman, Sidney, and Jim Henderling, whom we had selected to be our production manager, we decided that we shouldn't risk running into any racial problems by going into the deep South. From the outset, we understood that we were dealing with a piece of material that might not be shown in the South. The United Artists executives were concerned that many southern theaters might not want to play the film for fear of creating racial unrest. There might be picketing or disturbances that could result in violence or, at the least, having our play dates canceled. I had argued the

Thematic moment from *In the Heat of the Night* with Sidney Poitier and Rod Steiger in 1966.

case with United Artists that this was a film that could be made for a disciplined price that would give a good account of itself even if they were not able to distribute it at all in the South. "The big industrial cities in the North are going to play it, and we've got a good chance that it's going to be successful there." Given the risks, they agreed to go forward with the picture if we could produce it at a cost of no more than $2 million.

I had told Norman, at the outset, that he couldn't expect to get more than some forty-odd days to shoot. He was very upset at that. I said I'd given my word to United Artists, and that it really wasn't an open question any longer. Sidney Poitier was paid $200,000 and 20 percent of the profits, and Rod Steiger received $150,000.

Our location people now proposed shooting the film in the little town of Sparta, in southern Illinois, near Belleville, Missouri. Norman, on seeing the town and seeing all the signs reading Sparta Feed and

Grain and Sparta Hardware, decided we'd call our city Sparta. So it was no longer Wells; it was now Sparta. The town worked just fine for us. We flew to St. Louis and drove to Sparta.

We then resumed our casting. For the pivotal role of Endicott, one actor in whom we were interested was Lew Ayres. For some reason, that casting didn't work out. I remembered Larry Gates, who had been in *Invasion of the Body Snatchers* and *Toys in the Attic*, and I thought he would be just fine. We asked him to come in for an interview, and Norman became enthusiastic about him.

Norman suggested Lee Grant, who hadn't worked in a long time, largely because of the blacklist, and we cast Lee in the small role of the murder victim's wife, but she made it much more than that. Warren Oates, William Schallert, James Purdy, and a newcomer, Scott Wilson, completed the excellent cast.

The preparation of the picture was a constant struggle with the budget. I felt the obligation of my commitment to United Artists strongly and tried as hard as I could to adhere to it. We were anxious to do one sequence in the Deep South. We wanted to show cotton fields and a plantation house that would definitely stamp the southern locale of the picture. We planned to do this sequence, namely the visit of Tibbs and Gillespie to the plantation home of Endicott, in Dyersburg, Tennessee. It opened up the film, to a certain extent, and allowed us to include a real southern feel to the picture. I thought this was important, and so we had to accommodate the additional cost of that location trip.

We learned that when we were scheduled to return to Hollywood, we would not be able to have space at the Goldwyn Studio, where we had shot virtually all of our locally based films. Its stages were completely booked during the time we would require them, so we arranged to shoot at a small rental studio in Hollywood, which at that time was called the Producers and is now the Raleigh Studio. The picture was finally budgeted at $2.05 million, and we embarked on production in Sparta.

The shooting of many films is accompanied with a great deal of Sturm und Drang. This was not one of those. Everybody got along well together. The locations were excellent, and the production was well planned. Norman tried to adhere to the schedule, and all things considered, it went very well.

During the shooting of the sequence in which Tibbs and Bill Gillespie have a relatively quiet time in a discussion in Gillespie's house, a certain amount of questioning came up about the dialogue. Norman encouraged some improvisation with the two actors, which actually led to a considerable improvement in the scene. It finally became one of the best scenes in the film, when the two men are able to let down their guard to a certain extent with one another and see each other as individuals and not as stereotypes.

The sequence in the greenhouse, where Tibbs slaps Endicott in the face, is a stunner. The last scene, where Gillespie says to Tibbs, "You take care, y'hear," is a triumph of understatement and the bonding of the two men. Haskell Wexler's photography made a huge contribution. Hal Ashby, who edited the film, made interesting and innovative edits. We even changed the continuity in one place. By the time the editing process was completed, the picture fairly sparkled.

We were extraordinarily well served by Quincy Jones's musical composition and by Ray Charles, who sang the title song. The lyrics were brilliantly written by Alan and Marilyn Bergman in their first movie assignment.

I arranged a screening for Sidney Poitier one evening when the picture was finished. I wasn't present, but he called me at home after he'd finished seeing the film. I shall never forget his excitement, his enthusiasm, and his pleasure. I felt a tremendous sense of fulfillment.

The film was released in the summertime of 1967. In New York it opened at the 6,000-seat Capitol Theater, one of the biggest in the city. The lines went completely around the block. It was a huge opening, and I sat in the theater as it played before an immense audience. We got laughs wherever we had hoped we would, even in some places where we thought they might be problematic. When the film transitioned to seriousness, you could hear a pin drop. It was an absolutely marvelous reaction.

The business was great, and everybody was thrilled with the results. When the distributors extended the picture into other regions of the country, particularly in the South, we had no demonstrations whatsoever against it. The business continued to be uniformly excellent.

Incidentally, the final cost of the picture was $2.09 million.

As the year began to wind down, it appeared either near the top or at the top of most best picture of the year selections. The Academy competition that year was formidable, including *Bonnie and Clyde, The Graduate,* and *Guess Who's Coming to Dinner?* We were fortunate to be chosen as the best picture of the year by *Film Daily,* the New York trade paper, Best Drama by the Golden Globes, and by a number of other groups. I went to New York for the New York Film Critics Award dinner at Sardi's restaurant. It was presided over by the then-president of the New York Film Critics Association, Bosley Crowther, the respected critic of the *New York Times.* Senator Robert Kennedy was there, and he made the presentation to me of the best picture of the year plaque.

Before recognizing the best film, the critics made an award to the best director of the year. I was terribly disappointed that Norman wasn't chosen. Mike Nichols was given the Critics Award for *The Graduate* by Crowther, who admonished him not to become too self-satisfied now that he had won this prestigious award, reminding him that John Ford had won it three times in a row. Despite my disappointment that Norman hadn't won, the fact that they did choose *Heat* as the best picture was a great lift to us all.

The award season was now in full flower, but unfortunately it coincided with my father's final illness. He was, by then, ninety-four years old, had been suffering from cancer, and was, by the early part of the year, spending a good deal of time in a hospital. I was invited to go to London to attend the British Film Academy Awards, but I decided not to go. I didn't want to be away during this critical time of my father's illness. I was very close to him, and it was a most difficult period for me. I finally was persuaded to go for one day. My father's physician told me that he didn't expect anything immediate to occur, and he felt I could certainly be gone for one day. So I made the trip to London.

I arrived there in the afternoon. The ceremony was held in a hotel, and the Best Film of the Year Award was presented to my friend Fred Zinnemann for *A Man for All Seasons,* which had in the previous year been eligible in the United States and had won the Best Picture Academy Award. I was, however, exceedingly pleased that the United Nations Award was voted to *In the Heat of the Night,* and that Rod Steiger was chosen as the best actor in a foreign film. A lovely piece of appropriately inscribed black Spode statuary was presented to me, and I returned home the next day.

The next big award hurdle was the Academy Awards. Because our picture had been released some nine months earlier, I persuaded the United Artists' distribution people to rent a theater and run the picture in Beverly Hills for a month before the casting of the ballots, so that it would be available to Academy members who might want to see it. During this period, *Heat* was also presented with an award from Mass Media Ministries, an ecumenical organization headquartered in Baltimore, and the Stanley Isaacs Award by the New York chapter of the American Jewish Committee. It was heartwarming and fulfilling to see this little picture, which had grown from such unimpressive roots, travel all the way to the pantheon of great films.

As the week of the Academy Awards approached, my father's condition deteriorated dramatically. He died on April 5, the Friday preceding the Monday of the Academy Awards presentation. I was forty-seven years old, and he was a nonagenarian who had lived a long and full life. But this was the first time I had lost a parent, and as it is for most people, it was a very difficult time for me. My grief—and my family's grief, because he was truly a beloved patriarch to his four sons and daughters-in-law and to his ten grandchildren—was very great.

Since moving to Los Angeles in 1960, it was his custom to be driven by his housekeeper to the studio every morning at about eleven. Impeccably dressed, he would sit in either my outer office or Harold's, where he would read the newspapers or attend to the payment of his household bills. If either Harold or I was not otherwise involved, he would come into our offices and talk for a while. If we were free for lunch he would join us; if we weren't, he would lunch with Harold's secretary, Sylvia Kantor, or my secretary, Jessie Ponitz, both of whom adored him. If we had a picture in production he would sit on the set for a while after lunch and then return to the office for a short nap before he was called for by his housekeeper at about four. My favorite story about him during this period took place one day after he had finished lunch and was walking out of the dining room. He stopped at my table where I was sitting with Rod Steiger. I immediately introduced him to Rod. I said to him, "You remember, Dad, you told me how much you enjoyed seeing Mr. Steiger in his picture *The Pawnbroker*." His hearing, which was failing at the time, betrayed him and he said, "Oh, yes, yes, a pawnbroker, that's a good business you're in, Mr. Steiger." We all enjoyed a hearty laugh that day.

I decided I wouldn't go to the Academy Awards. It simply felt inappropriate to me.

That same week, on April 4, as fate would have it, Martin Luther King was assassinated. And for the first time in many years, the Academy Awards were postponed in deference to that national tragedy. Gregory Peck, the president of the Academy, announced that the Awards presentation would not be held until after Dr. King's funeral on Tuesday. The Awards were now rescheduled to Wednesday, April 10. By then, nearly a week had gone by since my dad's death, and about three days since his funeral. I decided to attend the Awards ceremonies, which were held that year at the Santa Monica Civic Auditorium.

Bob Hope was again the master of ceremonies. When the Best Director Award was announced, I was again disappointed when Norman Jewison was not voted the Oscar, and I was filled with foreboding. Lovely Julie Andrews, from my *Hawaii* adventures, had been selected to bestow the Best Picture Award, and it was from her lips that I heard that *In the Heat of the Night* had been voted the Best Picture of 1967.

Many people have described their emotions at winning an Oscar. Fewer people have described the emotions of winning the Best Picture Oscar. I stood up, I was somewhat transfixed or enraptured, I don't quite know how to describe my emotion. I do remember thinking, "At this very extraordinary moment, all these people, fellow workers, people whom I respect, have selected this piece of work that was my project, and on which I was able to assemble some remarkable collaborators, have chosen our film as the best piece of work of this whole year. And they have now placed it alongside forty of the best pictures ever made." I was experiencing an intoxicating sensation.

On arriving at the microphone, I looked squarely at my wife, Pat, with whom I had been sitting, and tried to concentrate on just talking to her. To paraphrase my remarks, I said the usual thank-you's, most particularly to Norman Jewison for his extraordinary contributions to making the film what it was. I was deeply moved and spoke from the heart. I concluded my short remarks by thanking the Academy for its acceptance of our picture and of the lesson of *In the Heat of the Night*.

I was somewhat flustered, and I turned from one side of the stage to the other, not knowing whether to walk off at stage left or stage right. I saw Sidney Poitier, who had been a presenter that night, standing in the wings with Rod Steiger, who had previously won the Best Actor Award. I immediately went to them and threw my arms around Sidney and kissed him, and then I threw my arms around Rod and kissed him. We were, all three of us, truly transported.

In the final count we won five awards that evening: Best Picture, Best Actor, Best Film Editing, Best Screenplay Based on Material from Another Medium, and Best Sound. Five Academy Awards for our little labor-of-love picture was a munificent reward for all of our efforts. I couldn't understand then and I still don't understand why Norman didn't win the Best Director Award.

People have tried to explain what Oscars mean to the film community, not only to the people who are awarded them but also to those who aspire to them. There are many descriptions. I like Walter Matthau's particularly: "The great thing about winning an Academy Award is that you are one of the favored few who know in advance what the first line of your obituary is going to say." It also means that, for a moment in history, or in the history of your craft, something that you did was considered by your peers to be the very best of that year. You also have a memento of that decision to remind you that, for a moment, you had ascended to the pantheon or had your day in Camelot. Anyway, it was an extraordinary experience.

Winners move on something like a conveyor belt, progressing from one press group to another, to be interviewed following their acceptances. That was all pretty much of a blur to me, and I don't really remember much of what I said. I returned to my seat to find Pat absolutely thrilled, as thrilled as I've ever seen her. We kissed and enjoyed our marvelous moment in the sun together. I phoned my children to hear their congratulations and share the moment with them.

We decided to drive straight home because I was eager to show our new Oscar to my children. Arriving there, I found them exultant. After remaining for a short time, Pat and I left to go to my mother's apartment, where I wanted to share the thrill with her. It was still not quite a week since my father's death, and it was a difficult time for her. She cried, and we embraced, and it was certainly a memorable occasion.

During the course of the evening, I had also phoned Marvin and Harold, neither of whom were at the ceremony. I told Harold that I was going to my mother's, and he asked me to meet him at Chasen's restaurant. My mother's apartment was not very far from there, and I agreed to meet him. We arrived at the restaurant, and it was jammed, since, in deference to Dr. King, the Academy had cancelled its customary Governor's Ball. We had a great deal of difficulty getting a table. Finally one was found for us in the bar room. The restaurant was filled with people who had come from the Awards ceremony.

There was a big party being held in the private dining room of the restaurant, hosted by Warner Bros. in honor of its nominees, who were mainly the people involved in the production of *Bonnie and Clyde*. As I walked into the restaurant, I saw Warren Beatty standing near the door of the private room. I walked over and congratulated him. He, in turn, congratulated me. I then said something polite about the record-breaking business *Bonnie and Clyde* was doing. Warren said thanks; then, putting his hand on my Oscar, which still remained firmly clutched in my grasp, he said, "I'd rather have that."

I left and rejoined Pat. Interestingly enough, Steve Broidy happened to be in the restaurant, and I thought it particularly fitting that he, who had contributed so much to the early years of my career, was there. He extended his congratulations, which I certainly appreciated. Harold arrived shortly thereafter, though he was not feeling well. I was pleased that he had come.

An interesting sidelight that Arthur Krim later related to me was that he and Mrs. Krim were having dinner that night with President and Mrs. Johnson at the White House. After dinner, he told the president he would like to look at the Academy Awards ceremonies on TV. The latter agreed and the two couples watched our victory together in the president's sitting room. After my acceptance speech, President Johnson asked Arthur to extend his congratulations to me. Later in the month I was pleased to give Arthur the Best Picture of the Year plaque presented to me by the New York Film Critics Association, which remained on the wall of his office for as long as he occupied it.

It was a marvelous night in many ways, tinged with a certain amount of sadness. I regretted so much that my father had not been able to share it. I regretted that Norman hadn't won the Best Director

Oscar. But this film had now changed my professional life for all time.

In the Heat of the Night became immensely profitable. The social and cultural effects of the picture I cannot judge. But I would like to think that it contributed in some small measure to the enlightenment of racial policy in our country.

The Mirisch Company had now won three Best Picture Academy Awards in a period of seven years.

26

A Western, a Comedy,
a Drama, and a Caper

Following *In the Heat of the Night,* the next release of The Mirisch Corporation (our new corporate name) was *Hour of the Gun* in October 1967, produced and directed by John Sturges. The story of *Hour of the Gun* began where John Sturges had left it ten years earlier in his film *Gunfight at the O.K. Corral.* John had found a book, *Tombstone's Epitaph* by Douglas D. Martin, that described the events of Wyatt Earp's life following the gunfight at the O.K. Corral, most particularly his attempt to revenge himself on the Clantons for the killing of his brother.

It seemed like a first-rate idea. If there were still a market for Western pictures, John Sturges certainly was the ideal director to test it. He chose Edward Anhalt as his writer for a script titled *The Law and Tombstone.*

We discussed the idea of trying to reunite Kirk Douglas and Burt Lancaster in their roles of Wyatt Earp and Doc Holliday. We didn't succeed in this attempt, but we still had an option left on the services of James Garner dating back to the time when we had cast him in *The Children's Hour.* It seemed a natural idea to cast Jim in a Western, since he had earned his initial stardom in the Western television hit show *Maverick.* When John and I filmed *By Love Possessed,* we had come to know Jason Robards Jr. as a brilliant actor, although one with problems.

During that production we'd had difficulties a number of times with Jason's drinking. However, we agreed that he would be ideal for the role of Doc Holliday. I thought we had a great modern combination with Jim and Jason, and you couldn't have asked for a better director to do the film.

We were also fortunate in being able to secure Robert Ryan to play Ike Clanton, the heavy. Clanton had been played by Walter Brennan as sort of an addled hillbilly in John Ford's Wyatt Earp picture, *My Darling Clementine*. But in our scenario, Clanton is clearly more of a match for Earp.

We began our film by showing the great gunfight at the O.K. Corral, the climax of the previous film, and we hoped that we could make the rest of the film exciting and suspenseful enough to retain the audience's interest. Our challenge was to accomplish that, and success or failure would hinge on it. Unfortunately, we did not succeed. Probably also playing a large role in the reaction to the picture was the continued loss of interest by audiences in Western pictures. I was again guilty of thinking that this trend would reverse course and that Westerns, led by a hit picture, would return to favor stronger than ever. I was wrong. As a new generation arose, their interest in Westerns had been satiated, probably by television, and they now embraced the so-called *Easy Rider* period of moviemaking. America now entered the era of the flower children and the Vietnam War, and somehow or other, as one genre of pictures has followed another, Westerns have still not returned to the favor that they once enjoyed. *Unforgiven*, with Clint Eastwood, which won the Best Picture Academy Award in 1992, is a notable exception.

The Law and Tombstone, now retitled *Hour of the Gun*, was filmed in Mexico, mainly for budgetary reasons, and there weren't any special production problems. Supporting roles were played by Jon Voight, Monte Markham, William Schallert, William Windom, Robert Phillips, and Michael Tolan. Cinematography was by Lucien Ballard, editing was by Ferris Webster, and Jerry Goldsmith composed the score.

❧

Our Christmas film, released in December 1967, was *Fitzwilly*, based on the book *The Garden of Cucumbers* by Poyntz Tyler, given to me by Isobel Lennart. She and I were always looking for subjects on which we could again collaborate. The Broadway play and film of *Funny Girl* kept her busy over a long period of time, but at one juncture she read *Garden of Cucumbers* and was most enthusiastic, thinking it could be a charming romantic comedy. We acquired the rights to the property and Isobel and I had a most enjoyable time working on the script.

I am often reminded that during a Writers Guild strike of that period, I arrived at the main gate of the Samuel Goldwyn Studio one morning to see a large assemblage of writers carrying placards and picketing the entrance to the studio. I went to my office and phoned Isobel, telling her about the pickets, and I said to her, "I was terribly disappointed this morning not to see you here picketing me." Without skipping a beat, she replied, "I only awakened a short while ago, and I'm rushing to Elizabeth Arden's to have my hair done, but I'll be at the studio in time for the afternoon shift." That was Isobel Lennart.

Cucumbers is a fairy tale about a delightful old lady philanthropist who lives in an elegant Fifth Avenue mansion, in the highest of style, attended to by a large staff of servants, presided over by her attentive and loving butler named Fitzwilliam, or Fitzwilly for short. We discover, shortly after having met these people, that the old lady has no tangible means of support, and that she is supported in her elegant fashion by various cons that are perpetrated by her staff, who are devoted to maintaining her in the manner she has lived her whole life.

I saw *Fitzwilly* as an ideal role for Cary Grant. Like all picturemakers, the hope of producing a film with Cary Grant was a tremendous stimulus, and in 1961, when we acquired the property, I hoped that *Cucumbers* would fit the bill. As time went on, and I waited for Isobel to become available, Cary Grant was coming closer to the end of his great career. Sometime during this period he announced his retirement. This was a great blow to me. However, I continued to believe that, with a wonderful script by Isobel and my own persuasive powers, Grant could be encouraged to make at least one exception to his retirement.

I was successful in arranging a meeting with Cary Grant, and I told him the story. His hair had turned completely gray by that time, but all of his charm was intact. He told me he had enjoyed a wonderful career, but he felt the time had finally come to end it. I reminded him this was a role that didn't compel any kind of specious relationship for him with a young woman, but he replied that—although the story sounded charming to him and he wished me great luck with the picture—it would have to be done without him.

At about this time, Abe Lastfogel, of the William Morris Talent Agency, talked to Harold and me about the possibility of our making a multiple-picture deal with Dick Van Dyke. Dick had become one of television's biggest stars as a result of *The Dick Van Dyke Show* and had already appeared in the films *Mary Poppins, Lt. Robin Crusoe U.S.N.,* and *Divorce American Style.* We thought that Dick, still youthful and charming and certainly well known throughout the country, might be an element around which we could make some successful comedies. We also thought he could be of value in our arrangements with Blake Edwards and Billy Wilder. With the enthusiastic agreement of United Artists, we now concluded a three-picture contract with Dick Van Dyke.

When we finally accepted that Cary Grant was not going to be in *Fitzwilly,* we naturally began to consider that this might be a vehicle for Van Dyke. I talked to a number of directors and finally hit upon the idea of Delbert Mann doing the film. I had known Del for many years. I had met him shortly after he came to California after doing *Marty,* and we had discussed projects from time to time, none of which came to fruition. Del had made two successful romantic comedies with Doris Day, *That Touch of Mink* with Cary Grant and *Lover Come Back* with Rock Hudson. I gave him the script of *Garden of Cucumbers,* and he was most enthusiastic. We discussed Dick Van Dyke's participation, and Delbert thought he was an excellent choice.

We proceeded to the balance of the casting. When the idea of Dame Edith Evans appearing in the picture was brought up, we all embraced it. Barbara Feldon, an attractive comedienne, had been successful as Agent 99 in the television show *Get Smart,* costarring with Don Adams. We cast her in the leading female role. Next we selected a group of excellent comedic supporting actors—John McGiver, Norman Fell, John Fiedler, and Cecil Kellaway, as well as Sam Waterston in his first role in a film.

When shooting was completed, I thought it would be ideal musical casting if I could persuade André Previn to do the score. By then, he had done five films for us. When I told him about the project, he said it sounded like something he would like to do, but unfortunately he was overcommitted, and it would be impossible for him to undertake. However, he said, "I think John Williams is ready to do a score, and I wish you would give him this picture."

I had originally met John Williams when we were scoring *The Apartment*. At that time he was the pianist in Adolph Deutsch's studio orchestra. It was John who played the piano solo of that incredibly beautiful theme. His rendition was so outstanding that I had naturally made it my business to make his acquaintance, and now I thought seriously about André's suggestion. I talked to John and finally decided to give him the picture. John responded by contributing an outstanding score to *Fitzwilly*. It is melodic, lends fun to the picture, and adds charm. It also includes a lovely song with lyrics by Alan and Marilyn Bergman, "Make Me Rainbows," which I thought might have a chance to become a pop hit. I was delighted at the way John Williams's score turned out.

The film contained a good deal of fun, and the premise is so outrageous that I thought it would appeal to audiences. Possibly it was too outrageous or, for its time, it wasn't outrageous enough. It wasn't terribly successful critically, and commercially it was also a disappointment. However, I made some good friends among the people who worked on the film with me, and I often worked with them again, including John Williams, Ralph Winters, Del Mann, Joseph Biroc, and Bob Boyle.

As a sidelight, it is amusing to note that *Fitzwilly* had its New York premiere on the third floor of Gimbel's Department Store at Broadway and 33rd Street, following in the footsteps of *Bomba, the Jungle Boy*'s premiere in the Chicago Zoo for Bushman the gorilla, and the premiere of *Flat Top* on the flight deck of the USS *Princeton*.

🎵

In our effort to keep our producer-director corps fresh, we continued to look for other candidates to fit into the formula established in our Billy Wilder, Blake Edwards, John Sturges, and Norman Jewison deals. Our Robert Wise arrangement had come to an end after *Two for the Seesaw*, when he took his turnaround properties to other companies. As we considered new people, Phil Gersh, Wise's agent, suggested to us another of his clients, David Miller.

David had made a number of successful films by then, most recently *Captain Newman, M.D.* with Gregory Peck and *Midnight Lace* with Doris Day and Rex Harrison, and we thought that he would fit into our organization well. We provided offices for him at the Goldwyn Studio, and he proposed three projects, namely *Lydia, The Great Japanese Train Robbery,* and *The Bells of Hell.*

British novelist Roald Dahl had written the last under the title *Oh Death, Where Is Thy Sting-a-Ling-a-Ling,* later retitled *The Bells of Hell Go Ting-a-Ling-a-Ling.* It revolved around a World War I effort to cart a disassembled airplane in secret across Switzerland; the airplane had to be disassembled because of Swiss neutrality, and it had to be in a particular place at a certain time in order to execute a specified mission.

David Miller was very enthusiastic about the project, and he interested Gregory Peck in playing the lead. The film was planned for production in Switzerland, since it required snow-covered mountains, and was scheduled to begin shooting in the summer. We had a tight schedule that would allow us to photograph all the necessary exteriors so that we would finish them before the snows came.

Lew Rachmil and David Miller went to Switzerland and organized a company for the shooting in alpine locations. But various delays pushed back the start of production until early fall. When it finally commenced shooting, the company moved at a snail's pace, and the scheduled work simply didn't get done. There were those who blamed it on the director. But, in any case, after a week in production we were nearly a week behind schedule. We continued to fall outrageously behind. I was not on the location myself, but I was on the phone constantly with Lew Rachmil. We tried to move things elsewhere, in order to shorten the list of scenes that we had to photograph exterior, but there were numerous things that simply had to be done on those mountains before the snow came. We finally fell so far behind that we had to accept the fact that we couldn't shoot the required exteriors in Switzerland until the following year!

Along with David Picker on behalf of United Artists, I flew to the Chateau d'Oex, in the little Swiss town where the picture was based. We had some painful discussions about our options. After reviewing all of the possibilities, we finally decided to discontinue production.

United Artists paid Gregory Peck his full salary, and we had to assume a big write-off on the project. *The Bells of Hell* is the only picture in which I have been involved that was started and never finished.

≋

In 1966, Norman Jewison told me that he had been given a script by his agent at William Morris entitled *The Crown Caper*. He asked me to read it, warning me in advance that it had been written by a nonprofessional. It was not written in orthodox script form. It had a lot of dialogue, a lot of description, and a lot of prose. But it also had a great germ of an idea, the story of a successful Boston businessman who, bored with his life, determines to rob a bank just to prove that he can do it without anyone being hurt, thereby showing off his ability to outsmart the establishment.

Alan Trustman, the writer of *The Crown Caper,* was a practicing attorney and a partner in the Boston law firm of Nutter, McClennen, and Fish. He was quoted as saying, "I had never written a line, except for law briefs. One Sunday afternoon in 1966 I got bored watching TV. It was too early in the season to go skiing, and suddenly, for no apparent reason, I thought it would be fun to write a screen story. I worked Sundays and a few nights, and in two months *The Crown Caper* was done." After he completed the script, he didn't know what to do with it, but was advised by a friend to contact the William Morris Agency, which, he believed, had an office in New York. Alan called the agency and said that he wanted to talk to somebody about a screenplay he had written. The script traveled from one hand to another, and ultimately it found its way to Norman and to me.

We thought it could be an exciting picture, and we secured the approval of United Artists to acquire it and develop it for production.

As the development of the script proceeded, our first choice in casting was Richard Burton to play the elegant gentleman who is the unlikeliest of bank robbers. When we couldn't get Burton, we determined to try to interest Sean Connery in the role. Norman and I went to New York to meet Connery. We lunched with him at the Regency Hotel, where we had a long talk. We then went upstairs and talked further, for most of a Saturday afternoon, with no success. We couldn't convince him to play the role. Many years later when I ran into Connery at a UCLA basketball game, I said, "We met before, when Norman Jewison and I tried to convince you to play in *The Thomas Crown Affair.*"

He said to me, "Yes, I remember that." He added, "You know, I should have played that part."

We were crestfallen when we failed to convince Sean Connery. But Steve McQueen also knew about the project, and Norman finally sent him the script.

Norman and I both felt that Steve was completely wrong to play Thomas Crown. "Steve McQueen should not wear a necktie on the screen," we agreed. "He needs to wear a blue denim shirt!" That generally summed up our thinking.

Finally Stan Kamen, who represented Steve, said, "You have to talk to him about it. Meet with him."

In our conversation with Steve, we expressed these very same sentiments. But he replied, "You fellows don't understand, I can do this!" I had, by then, made *The Magnificent Seven* and *The Great Escape* with Steve, and Norman had directed him in *The Cincinnati Kid,* all very successful films. We finally concluded that Steve could do the role, differently from Burton or Connery, but he could do it. We came to believe he would be even more interesting than our other choices.

Audiences didn't expect Steve McQueen to wear a necktie and a vest, with a Phi Beta Kappa key hanging from his watch chain, but he was wonderful. He later commented, "I had thought of changing my screen image for more than a year. I felt it was time to get past those tough, uptight types. When Norman Jewison showed me the Crown part, I grabbed it. . . . I couldn't get used to the key either. My fraternity emblem should be a couple of hubcaps hanging from a tire chain."

We had a great deal of difficulty deciding on an actress to play the leading role of the insurance investigator. Very early on, I suggested Faye Dunaway. I had seen Faye on the stage in a play, *Hogan's Goat,* and she was marvelous. I'd always had in mind that, one day, a role would come along that Faye Dunaway could play for us. I thought this was it. Norman had concerns about it, so we went on and considered other people, but finally he too came around to Faye.

The Mirisch Company still had two options left with Steve McQueen, going back to *The Magnificent Seven* deal. His agent and

Steve McQueen in one of the best and most uncharacteristic performances of his career in 1967's *The Thomas Crown Affair*. © 1968 Metro-Goldwyn-Mayer Studios Inc. All rights reserved.

manager made a big fuss about the nominal salary provided for in our second option. To settle the argument, I agreed to pay him the salary called for in the third option, as well as to cancel that last option. His agent agreed to accept these concessions. I recognized that we really should be paying him more than the price stipulated in the option. Also

I felt that trying to enforce the third option would be difficult, if not impossible. We paid Faye Dunaway, who had by then appeared in *Bonnie and Clyde*, a larger salary than Steve. However, Steve's agents were eager to avoid litigation, and it was worth a great deal to him to cancel the last option. In addition, Thomas Crown was a part Steve wanted very much to play; the director was someone with whom he felt at ease, so it worked out fine for all of us.

For *The Thomas Crown Affair*, we reassembled many of our cast and crew from *In the Heat of the Night*, with Haskell Wexler as cinematographer, and Hal Ashby now sharing credit with Ralph Winters and Byron Brandt as editors. Thea Van Runkle did the costumes. However, the major share of the credit for the film belongs to Norman Jewison, because the picture's success, both artistically and commercially, was largely due to the high style that he imparted.

The concept for the multiple-screen sequences was Norman Jewison's, and it was executed brilliantly by visual designer Pablo Ferro, who had also done the title sequence for *The Russians Are Coming, the Russians Are Coming*. Describing Ferro's contribution, Norman Jewison wrote to the Nominating Committee on Special Visual Effects of the Academy of Motion Picture Arts and Sciences, concerning the three areas of the film in which multiple-image effect was used:

> First, to introduce on the screen at the same time six different characters, and to establish their interrelationships with a bank robbery. . . . The second special-effects section deals with a polo game. Again Mr. Ferro has used not only out-of-focus and soft-effect panels, but has also at one point involved over fifty separate panels on the screen simultaneously. The third section of the film involves yet another bank robbery, which Mr. Ferro treated with a multiple-image technique. During the actual robbery itself the amount of film used in relationship to the amount of screen time was probably in the ratio of four-to-one.

The film began production on locations in the Boston area. Steve McQueen made it a point to make sure that two of his motorcycles were aboard the prop truck that was driving cross-country carrying our equipment, so that immediately upon his arrival he would have his required bikes.

At this time, too, Steve was concerned about some letters of a threatening nature that he said he had received. He wanted the company to have his rented house guarded because he was concerned about his children's safety. It preyed on his mind a great deal during the shooting of the picture. I never saw the letters, and I'm not even sure they really existed. He may have just been concerned and wanted the company to provide a security detail for his home. But, in either event, whether it was real or imagined, it was serious to Steve.

The shooting of the picture proceeded well. I very much enjoyed being in Boston again, twenty-five years after I had attended college there. During the shoot, some of the people in our company took the opportunity on Sundays to go to Montreal, where the Montreal Expo 67 was in progress. On the day I chose to go there, accompanied by my son Drew, Queen Elizabeth of England was also visiting and it was a most festive respite from our long shooting week.

We filmed *The Thomas Crown Affair* at Old Copp's Hill Cemetery, the Boston Commons, the outdoor markets of Little Italy, Anthony's Pier 4 restaurant, and the dunes near Crane's Beach and Provincetown. The society art auction was staged in the St. James Ballroom of the Jordan Marsh mansion, at 46 Beacon Street.

The great set piece in the film, the chess game, was shot on a set at the Goldwyn Studio. Norman spent a great deal of time shooting it, since it's really a seduction and we were hoping that we would get inspired moments that would give us more than dialogue could. I think we succeeded. It's an exceedingly stylized sequence in a picture that is, itself, an exhibition of style. We hoped to dazzle the audience with the multiple panels and the chess game, the photography and the music.

We really struck pay dirt with the score, and with our theme song, "The Windmills of Your Mind," composed by Michel Legrand with lyrics by the Bergmans. It was sung by Noel Harrison, Rex Harrison's son, and it certainly helped the film tremendously. The Michel Legrand score was nominated for an Academy Award, and "Windmills of Your Mind" won the Oscar for Best Original Song.

In production, *Thomas Crown* was a happy film, and when it was in post-production we changed its title. It had originally been *The Crown Caper,* then *Thomas Crown and Company* for a short time. But, at lunch one day with Norman, we finally decided on *The Thomas Crown Affair.*

I think the film has stood the test of time pretty well. The motivation of the central character is rather special. Viewing it in the perspective of

Steve McQueen's entire career, it is so different from anything else he ever did that it must be considered an extraordinary and spectacular performance. Similarly, I think it is one of the most outstanding pictures of Norman Jewison's career. If, as it has often been said, it is style over substance, it constitutes an even greater contribution from the director who created that style. The film was remade with Pierce Brosnan and Rene Russo in 1999.

27

Personal Matters — Familial and Corporate

By 1963, my oldest brother, Irving, was also living in Los Angeles. He had been running the Theaters Candy Company in Milwaukee for a long time but felt that without an infusion of a great deal of capital it was impossible to expand the business. He became anxious to sell it. He and Harold owned the major share in the company, and they agreed to dispose of it when he found a customer. Irving had become lonely in Milwaukee, and he wanted to move to Los Angeles and join the rest of his family. It was also an exciting time for his brothers, and I think he wanted to share more closely in their activities. He had moved to Los Angeles briefly in the 1940s, when he had come to open a branch of the candy company. It wasn't successful, and finally he gave it up and moved back to Milwaukee. But he liked living in Los Angeles — as did his wife, Frances, who had been born and raised in Long Beach — and they both wanted to move now that their children were grown and had left Milwaukee. Without much delay, he sold the candy company, moved to Los Angeles, and retired.

Now, with my parents, Irving, and Frances living in Los Angeles, our whole family was reunited. For the first time in thirty-three years, we were all living in the same city. From a familial point of view, it really was wonderful for us. Frances died in 1966, and Irving later remarried. His children were also reunited in Los Angeles: his daughter Nan and his son David, who has been in the public-relations business for his entire career.

The period 1963 through 1968 was a wonderful time of togetherness for our family, and we truly cherished it. However, this happy time ended in 1968 when my father died at the age of ninety-four. Harold also died later in 1968, and my mother died in 1969. In 1971, Irving died at the age of sixty-seven. Within a period of two and a half years, I suffered the loss of both parents and two brothers. It was devastating.

Ours was a small but close-knit family, and it was now quickly decimated. My father, who was the first to go, had lived a long life. He was not quite fifty when I was born, and I used to amaze myself by remembering that he was born only nine years after Lincoln was shot. He had seen a lot of changes in the world and had a difficult but finally fulfilling life. He possessed a marvelous disposition. He was always cheerful, positive, and wise. His life was completely wrapped up with those of his four sons. He took a great deal of pleasure, not only in the success that our work brought us and the achievements that we had enjoyed but mainly in the kind of people we were.

My mother died of heart failure at the age of seventy-eight, although she hadn't previously suffered from heart disease. In her late thirties, she had become diabetic. When I was a young boy, I remember her giving herself insulin shots, and she continued that treatment all of her life. But it led to many other problems, and she had been in fragile health most of her years. Considering all the illness she had endured, she enjoyed a relatively long life.

During the period between 1961 and 1968, my brother Harold had suffered a number of heart attacks, which were followed by hospital stays and convalescences. He had sought the best medical advice he could find. He had gone to the Mayo Clinic for evaluation, where he was told he was being treated correctly. People talked about bypass surgery at that time, but it was still experimental, and he was absolutely set against being experimented on. He was also relatively inactive, businesswise, during this whole period. Marvin and I would discuss with him projects, casting, and the deals that had to be made with actors or directors, and he was helpful in proposing compromises. He had great connections within the industry, and when he thought he could help in a particular situation, he would do so. But he was actually living most of

Julie Andrews has just presented the Best Picture Oscar to me for *In the Heat of the Night* in 1968. Reproduced courtesy of the Academy of Motion Picture Arts and Sciences.

The *In the Heat of the Night* winner's circle. From left to right: film editor Hal Ashby, director Norman Jewison, Rod Steiger, and myself on April 10, 1968. Reproduced courtesy of the Academy of Motion Picture Arts and Sciences.

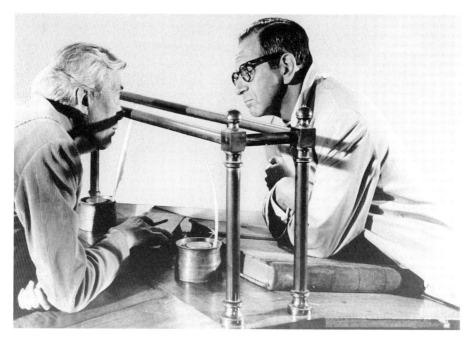

In deep conversation with John Huston on the set of *Sinful Davey* in Ireland in 1968. © 1969 Metro-Goldwyn-Mayer Studios Inc.

Billy Wilder and me in serious conversation on the set of *The Private Life of Sherlock Holmes* in London in 1969 while I. A. L. Diamond considers. © 1970 Metro-Goldwyn-Mayer Studios Inc. and Phalanx Productions, Inc. All rights reserved.

Alone and still deep in thought on the set of *The Hawaiians* in 1969.

Shooting *Fiddler on the Roof* near Zagreb, Yugoslavia, with director Norman Jewison in 1970.

In 1970 on a London set of *Fiddler on the Roof,* discussing the dream sequence are Topal and
Norma Crane.

On the set of *The Spikes Gang* in Almeria, Spain, with Lee Marvin in 1973. © 1974 The Mirisch Corporation of California. All rights reserved.

Chatting on the *Mr. Majestyk* set with Charles Bronson and Richard Fleischer on location in La Junta, Colorado, in 1973. © 1974 The Mirisch Corporation of California. All rights reserved.

Looking at a rendering of the Academy's new headquarters building with Samuel Goldwyn Jr., who endowed its theater in honor of his famed father in 1974. Reproduced courtesy of the Academy of Motion Picture Arts and Sciences.

Top right: Director Jack Smight and myself on the deck of aircraft carrier USS *Lexington* while shooting *Midway* in 1975. © Universal Studios. All rights reserved.

Bottom right: Impromptu story conference on a dockside set of *Midway* in 1975. From left to right: Henry Fonda, Robert Wagner, Charlton Heston, myself, script supervisor Bob Forrest, Hal Holbrook, and director Jack Smight in the foreground. © Universal Studios. All rights reserved.

Party on the set of *Same Time, Next Year* in 1977. From left to right: director Robert Mulligan, myself, Alan Alda, and Ellen Burstyn. © Universal Studios. All rights reserved.

Presenting an honorary Oscar to Mary Pickford on March 29, 1976, while I was president of the Academy. Reproduced courtesy of the Academy of Motion Picture Arts and Sciences.

Jessie Ponitz, my indispensable assistant for more than thirty years.

Righting a great wrong by giving Dalton Trumbo his long overdue Oscar on May 16, 1975, while I was president of the Academy. Reproduced courtesy of the Academy of Motion Picture Arts and Sciences.

Bob Hope and me, enjoying Oscar's fiftieth birthday party on May 12, 1977. Reproduced courtesy of the Academy of Motion Picture Arts and Sciences.

What a thrill it was receiving the Academy's Thalberg Award for the high quality of my career's films from producer-director Stanley Kramer on April 3, 1978. Reproduced courtesy of the Academy of Motion Picture Arts and Sciences.

Receiving the Academy's Jean Hersholt Humanitarian Award from Charlton Heston on April 11, 1983. Reproduced courtesy of the Academy of Motion Picture Arts and Sciences.

Top left: Still talking to one another are myself, Peter Sellers, and Gregory Sierra on a Vienna set of *The Prisoner of Zenda* in 1978. © Universal Studios. All rights reserved.

Bottom left: Smile for the camera—director John Badham, Laurence Olivier, and myself on the set of *Dracula* in London in 1978. © Universal Studios. All rights reserved.

Presenting my longtime and dear friend Sidney Poitier with an honorary Academy Award on March 24, 2002. Reproduced courtesy of the Academy of Motion Picture Arts and Sciences.

Top right: Pat and me on the evening of my UCLA Medal presentation, June 17, 1989.

Bottom right: Our proudest production: Larry, Pat, me, Anne, and Drew in October 1997.

Two veterans of the Pink Panther wars, myself and producer-director Blake Edwards in 2004.

My family in 2006: Larry, Megan, me, Anne, and Drew.

the time in Palm Springs, where he enjoyed a less stressful lifestyle. He had initiated our new television operation in partnership with Lee Rich and spent much time working with Lee on his television deals. Marvin and I tried to see to it that he had enough to do to occupy his mind. I kept him constantly informed about all of our activities. We still spent much of our leisure time together and would discuss every matter that arose in all areas of our company.

However, despite all of his times of illness, I was quite unprepared when the end came. He and his wife were going out to dinner one night with friends. He simply walked into the foyer of their house and collapsed. It was a great shock. He'd been sick all those years, but he seemed to be well during this particular period. When the end came, it happened so quickly that it seemed unexpected. He was still so young and vital at the age of sixty-one. It was terribly tragic.

Billy Wilder composed a eulogy that was delivered at Harold's funeral by Walter Matthau. I quote it in full because of all it says about Harold and about Billy Wilder.

> Over at the Goldwyn Studio, the flag is flying at half-mast, and there is an empty parking space marked "Reserved for Mr. Harold Mirisch." There have been obituaries in the papers, and there will be others in the trades. But the true measure of our loss is in the eyes of those who have lived with him and loved him — not just his family and his friends but the guys in the production office and the policemen at the gate, and the secretaries and the waitresses in the dining room. It was the terrifying suddenness that hit us all so hard — although we knew that he was not a well man. The diagnosis was that he had a bad heart — the cardiograms showed it, and the Mayos in Rochester confirmed it — a heart that sputtered, and ached, and ultimately succumbed to a short circuit. Medically speaking, they may have been correct — but we know better. It was a good heart. In fact, an exceptional one — in a community not particularly dedicated to altruism.
>
> The bare biographical facts are that he started as an office boy at the age of fourteen, that he worked as an usher and a film buyer in the Middle West, that he went on to Hollywood as a minor executive, and that he ultimately wound up as the president of a successful and highly respected independent company. How did he do it? By luck? With a smile and a shoeshine? By elbowing his way to the top? Or was it rather that rare quality called character, or integrity, or class? There was a

fairness and a loyalty about him that superseded tons of legal papers. He was both a sensitive and a sensible man, with a unique gift for attracting the best talent in the industry. He was never a result player. After a great preview, after a triumphant night at the Academy Awards, he would stand in the background with tears of joy in his eyes, letting the picturemaker take the bows and get all the kudos. On the other hand, after a picture had bombed disastrously, he would wander into your office, tell you a little gossip, make a bet on the Dodgers, and then casually say, "We were talking downstairs, Walter and Marvin and I — how would you like to make a deal for six more pictures?" Such was Harold Mirisch. Was that any way to run a company? You bet it was.

As we grieve for his family, we also grieve for ourselves — because he had a much bigger family than he ever thought, and we were all part of it. Let us hope that some of the warmth that was Harold's has rubbed off on us. We will need it — for ours will be a chillier town now that he is gone.

He left behind his wife, Lottie, to whom he'd been married since they were eighteen and twenty-one. They had two children; their elder daughter, Maxine, was by then married to a young assistant director named Jerry Siegel, who spent most of his career working in films as a production manager; and their son, Robert, was an attorney who has spent his career working as a business-affairs executive in the film industry. He also left behind five grandchildren.

✽

Harold's death necessitated a reorganization of our communications with United Artists. From the beginning, one of his principal responsibilities was handling our liaison with UA, primarily with Arthur Krim. Marvin and I also maintained relations with their executives on numerous levels, but primarily with their L.A. production head, first Bob Blumofe and then Herb Jaffe. We all kept relatively informal and personal relationships with the UA executives on all matters relating to our joint interests. The L.A. production heads made decisions at a certain level, but the decisions about green-lighting pictures came out of New York. We decided that Marvin should take primary responsibility for top-level talks.

Harold's disability also coincided with the period during which Arthur Krim had become somewhat more distanced from the closeness of his supervision of United Artists. Arthur had been a fund-raiser for the Democratic Party for a long time, but now he assumed an important position in the top echelon of the party and had a close relationship with President Kennedy and an even closer relationship with President Johnson. This relationship began to take up a large share of his time. He finally bought a house in Texas, adjoining President Johnson's ranch. It was rumored that he had also been offered a seat in the cabinet. At any rate, he became very involved in presidential politics. Consequently, other people became more active in the leadership of United Artists, first Arnold Picker and then David Picker.

Arnold Picker had originally been in charge of foreign sales for United Artists and later became executive vice president. He was a very able film man, and we had an excellent relationship with him. As Arthur Krim became less active, Arnold became more involved in the company's top management. Many people thought that he would succeed to the presidency. However, for his own reasons, he chose not to do that and instead retired, leaving a void that was filled by his nephew, David Picker, who was much younger and who had a great deal of executive production experience as assistant to Arthur Krim. David succeeded to the presidency of the company in June 1969, following by two years the completion of United Artists' merger with Transamerica Corporation.

Not only had The Mirisch Company changed with Harold's death, but United Artists had also changed during this period. Our relations with David were never as cordial as they were with Arthur Krim. Transamerica was a financial-services corporation, principally in the insurance field through its subsidiary Occidental Life Insurance and in the loan business through its subsidiary Pacific Finance. Arthur and Bob Benjamin arranged a sale of United Artists to Transamerica on the basis of a share-for-share exchange of stock and became the largest individual shareholders of Transamerica. In turn, the Mirisches, who had earlier exchanged their Mirisch Company and Mirisch Pictures stock for United Artists stock, now also became shareholders of Transamerica. The Mirisch Production Company, our newest entity, entered 1967 with a new seven-year commitment, expiring in 1974, to produce twenty-eight additional films for United Artists.

The philosophy of our arrangement was that we would benefit from a tax-free exchange that would result in our avoiding paying taxes on individual picture profits. Being gross participants in our overall program and being paid in stock would allow us to eventually convert our payout into the securities of a publicly traded corporation. We hoped that the stock of that corporation would appreciate over time, and that the appreciation would amount to much more than the capital-gain tax that would eventually be payable at the time that we disposed of the stock. Unfortunately, the concept of this arrangement did not work out well for us. The Transamerica stock, which we acquired at a price of about $38 a share, declined over the years, going down to about $5 or $6 a share. So all the potential profits of all the highly successful pictures of our early years dwindled down in the reduced value of the securities we held.

Transamerica, which later sold United Artists to MGM, now owned the negatives of our films. We may not have owned our films, but it was, and remains, a source of considerable satisfaction that they have survived the test of time, finding new audiences on cable, home video, and DVD.

28

Dark Days
for the Film Industry

In February 1969 we announced the election of Marvin E. Mirisch as chairman of our board of directors and chief executive officer. I was elected president, succeeding Harold, and I was to also serve as executive head of production. At the same time the board ratified and authorized execution of contracts with United Artists for the production of a minimum of twenty-eight pictures to be completed by 1974. Other officers reelected were Raymond Kurtzman, vice president and secretary, Jefferson Livingston, vice president for advertising and publicity, Lewis Rachmil, vice president, Morton Smithline, assistant vice president for business affairs and counsel, and George Laikin, assistant secretary. Newly elected officers were Oscar Steinberg, treasurer, and Robert Mirisch, Harold's son, assistant treasurer.

Following Harold's passing, we felt it was important that United Artists make a show of confidence in our new management, despite the fact that nothing much was changing. However, Harold was a commanding figure, and his absence had to result in a change in the perception of our company by outsiders.

Also in February 1969, we sent out a press release listing the films planned or in production:

The One with the Fuzz (Some Kind of a Nut), currently in production at Goldwyn, starring Dick Van Dyke, Angie Dickinson, and Rosemary Forsyth and with Garson Kanin directing and Walter Mirisch producing.

The Private Life of Sherlock Holmes, Billy Wilder to produce and direct, starring Robert Stephens and Colin Blakely, rolling in England, May 5.

The Landlord, with Hal Ashby making his directorial debut on this comedy, to be made in association with Norman Jewison's Simkoe Productions, with Jewison producing, rolling May 15 in New York.

Edge of Fear, with Sidney Poitier starring in the screenplay being written by Al Ramrus and John Shaner, rolling in Los Angeles on May 15.

The Dragonmaster (Cannon for Cordoba), starring George Peppard, to be filmed in Spain, with Vincent M. Fennelly producing and Paul Wendkos directing, beginning July 7.

The Hawaiians, with Charlton Heston starring in the film, based on the second half of James A. Michener's *Hawaii*, rolling July 14 in Hawaii.

The Yards at Essendorf, an original World War II story of an American soldier in Germany, to be produced and directed by John Sturges and shot this summer in western Canada.

The Judgment, a project for Peter Yates, under his recently signed multiple-directorial contract with Mirisch, with a story by Harry Kleiner, set in Mexico, rolling in October.

In addition, the company had several productions awaiting release, including Norman Jewison's *Gaily, Gaily*, John Huston's *Sinful Davy*, *You Don't Need Pajamas at Rosie's* (later retitled *The First Time*), the first production from the team of Roger Smith and Allan Carr, and *Guns of the Magnificent Seven*, the second sequel to *The Magnificent Seven*.

Despite the fact that we now ran into a bad period and not many of those films were successful, there were excellent people involved and we had a right to expect a better fate. But it turned into the least commercially successful period in our history.

Sinful Davy was a project that was suggested to me by James R. Webb, a distinguished screenwriter. Jim had become a good friend and had written *Kings of the Sun* for us, based on an idea that had been proposed by Arnold Picker. Unfortunately, that film didn't turn out to be successful, but Jim later came to me with the story of *Sinful Davy,* a charming, Scottish period romance about a lovable rascal. I encouraged Jim, and he prepared a screenplay.

It was of the same genre as *Tom Jones,* released about five years earlier. Jim and I speculated whether or not enough time had passed to mine this lode again, and we came to think that it had. Jim was an excellent writer and wrote a good script.

I looked around to find a director who might be suited to this kind of material, and I decided to approach John Huston again. It had been thirteen years since the *Moby Dick* experience, and John's stature as one of the preeminent directors in the world had only increased. He had directed numerous films since then and had been reasonably responsible budgetwise. As movie people are often wont to do, we say we'll never work with a particular person again, until we have something that he or she is absolutely ideal for. I approached John and asked him how he'd feel about doing *Sinful Davy.* Despite all of the problems of *Moby Dick,* I was delighted when he responded affirmatively to the material.

John had, in the beginning, only one request, namely that we shoot the film in Ireland, where he was a resident. That didn't seem to be a serious problem, and I acceded. *Sinful Davy* was a reasonably budgeted Eady Plan property, and I was delighted to get a world-class director at its helm.

In early nineteenth century Scotland, young Davey Haggart has one ambition in life, and that is to outdo his father in sinful adventures. John Huston proposed John Hurt to play the title role.

As line producer, I chose William Graf, who had most recently worked on *A Man for All Seasons.* He was American, and I employed him to be the producer of record. However, I retained credit as executive producer and went to London myself to work with John on the preparation and casting of the picture.

John was anxious that we employ his daughter, Anjelica, to play the female lead. Anjelica had been in one picture by then, *A Walk with Love and Death,* also directed by her father. She would have to do a Scottish accent, yet her appearance was rather more Italian than Scottish, and in stature she towered over John Hurt. John and I then had a serious falling out about casting Anjelica. We were arguing about it one day in a hotel room when he said to me, "There's a great wine auction starting soon. Come with me and we can talk en route."

I'd never been to a wine auction before, but it was fascinating. We didn't get to do much talking about *Sinful Davy*, but John did buy a half-dozen bottles of wine. By the time we'd left, I had agreed that we would do a test with Anjelica and John Hurt, and get a sense of their chemistry on film. I felt I was only delaying the problem, although I think I hoped I might be convinced. I wasn't. I felt that it was still wrong, and John remained upset. I remained adamant, and John finally capitulated.

We now chose a young woman, Pamela Franklin, who had done a number of very good things, including Jack Clayton's *Turn of the Screw* and Ronald Neame's *The Prime of Miss Jean Brodie,* to play the female lead. I've always regretted having put John into the position of his having to tell his daughter that she wasn't going to get the role. But, at the same time, I felt that I was being more objective than he.

While looking for locations, the production manager and the lighting cameraman, Ted Scaife, were in a serious airplane accident. Ted was injured and had to be replaced, but we were fortunately able to secure the renowned cinematographer Freddie Young to take over.

We built a Scottish village in Ireland, and the shooting of the picture went along quite well in my absence. I later came back to London to see the first cut of the picture, and I was present at the scoring session, but I didn't like the score of the film, which had been composed by John Barry in a more serious vein then I thought it should be. I then decided to spend the money to redo the music. We employed Ken Thorne, who did a lighter score, which I felt was more appropriate and which we ultimately used.

When the film was completed, we arranged to preview it in New York, despite the fact that John Huston couldn't be there. It was the most disastrous preview I can remember. All the United Artists people were present, and they were naturally disturbed by the audience reaction. Reporting on the showing, I told John and his agent, Paul Kohner, that I felt it was imperative that he be present at the next preview, so that he could see for himself the difficulty that we were having with it. The UA people were clamoring for something to be done to try and help the film.

The next preview was in Los Angeles. Paul Kohner was present, and he told me John had said that he liked it just the way it was. He didn't see any reason to be present at previews. The Los Angeles preview was equally as bad as the New York showing.

I said to Paul Kohner, who now saw our problem for himself, "I have never done anything with this film that I haven't talked out in advance with John, and I don't want to do it now. But he must not abandon the picture. UA is insisting we try and help the picture to play better."

Paul Kohner finally said to me that he had talked to John and explained the situation, but John reiterated his feeling that the picture was to his liking and he wasn't going to be influenced by the preview audiences. Paul Kohner continued, "I think you must do whatever you need to do."

I then supervised the re-editing of the picture until the previews had improved considerably. But it didn't really help. The basic problems with the picture were probably a result of my own misjudgments. The Scottish accents bothered the audience. In retrospect, it probably appeared too soon after *Tom Jones* and wasn't as entertaining as it needed to be to overcome that. I hoped that John Huston could bring elements to it that would make it as good or better. Or perhaps the casting failed, and when I say "the casting," I mean John Hurt. I don't believe the casting of the leading lady was crucial to its success or failure.

John Huston, in his autobiography, said that he was aghast when he saw what I had done in the re-editing of the picture. Responding to preview criticism, I had tried to make it less draggy and more accessible to American audiences.

Vincent Canby in the *New York Times* (June 5, 1969) called *Sinful Davy* "another work out of John Huston's current tired period," also listing *Freud, The Bible, The List of Adrian Messenger,* and *Reflections in a Golden Eye*. John spared himself being present at the previews, and he also spared himself being present at the sessions with the financiers and the distributors of the picture. I didn't have the luxury of sparing myself—I had to respond.

I saw John Huston again on a couple of occasions, many years after the release of *Sinful Davy*, and he was very cold, as I was to him. I thought his behavior in abandoning the picture was unprofessional.

🦅

The First Time was produced by Roger Smith and Allan Carr, who came to us with a script about a group of teenagers determined to lose their virginity before heading off to college, and their effort to achieve that goal. It seemed like an amusing idea. Also partnered with Smith and Carr was director Alex Grasshoff. They had succeeded in interesting Leslie Caron in playing the leading female role. The film was presented to us as an inexpensive project, and in the climate of the 1960s, we judged that there might be an audience for it. In order to produce it as reasonably as possible, we determined that it would be most economical to shoot in Canada. The script was revised in order to accommodate that locale, which also gave us some interesting and fresh backgrounds.

Just prior to the start of production, Leslie Caron asked for major script revisions, and when they weren't forthcoming she dropped out of the cast. But Roger Smith and Allan Carr were able to interest Jacqueline Bissett, and we accepted the substitution.

Production commenced in Toronto, and we weren't pleased by the dailies. I went to Toronto and had a meeting with Grasshoff, which resulted in our decision to replace him. As often happens in such unfortunate situations, it is difficult to find a director who is agreeable to taking over a troubled project. The choices are limited. We were finally able to identify James Nielson, whom I hadn't known before. Roger Smith recommended him, and he took over the direction.

For the casting, I relied on Roger and Allan, who represented a segment of the newer Hollywood community. Roger had worked in television for many years, and Allan was a manager who represented a lot of new young people. Wes Stern, Rick Kelman, Wink Roberts, and Sharon Acker were chosen to complete the cast. Unfortunately, the film wasn't provocative enough, nor was it sensitive or funny enough. None of the areas that it sought to explore were effectively handled.

I had thought that it had the potential to be an amusing story that would appeal to a burgeoning teenage audience. Writing in the *Saturday Review* (April 12, 1969), Arthur Knight commented, "Essentially, it is a joyous, sensitive, and wholly unprurient account of a trio of teenagers who pick up a girl that they, in their innocence, believe to be a prostitute." He was describing the film I hoped it would be, but there weren't too many who felt it succeeded.

Between 1967 and 1970, United Artists experienced a disastrous period. The Mirisch Company didn't alleviate it. In fact, it contributed to it, although UA had much bigger financial failures than we delivered. The entire industry groped about, trying to get a handle on what kind of films to produce during that troubled time. After the UA merger with Transamerica in 1967, Arthur Krim and Bob Benjamin gradually retired from UA's day-to-day operations and devoted themselves to their personal interests. David Picker, at the age of thirty-eight, assumed the presidency of the company in June 1969. UA's gross dropped from $269 million in 1969 to $212 million in 1970. The company showed a pre-tax loss of $85 million, establishing a new industry record. All of the other film companies were experiencing similar reverses, and retrenchment became the order of the day throughout the motion-picture business. Certainly the social turmoil of the late 1960s and the early 1970s contributed to the confusion about what kind of movies to produce. Arthur Krim's absence in 1968 and 1969 undoubtedly also had an effect. By 1970, he returned to UA to resume an active role in the management of the company, and David Picker later resigned as president in October 1973, to be replaced by Eric Pleskow, who had formerly been in charge of its foreign sales.

As for The Mirisch Company, we were also thrusting about, hoping that we could make contact with the difficult audience of that period. In *The Return of the Seven,* which we produced in 1966, Yul Brynner again played Chris in a sequel to our *Magnificent Seven.* It was completely derivative of the original film, but it again proved to be successful. There was undoubtedly some magic in the *Magnificent Seven* franchise, and we continued to mine its lode again and again in future years, and always profitably. In an unpredictable market, we sought further safety in presold material. So, in 1968, we produced a second sequel, *Guns of the Magnificent Seven,* written by Herman Hoffman and produced by Vincent M. Fennelly.

Vince had come from Des Moines all those many years ago to work at Monogram with me. After my brothers and I had left, Vince worked in television for a considerable period of time, most successfully producing the Clint Eastwood television show *Rawhide.* When that show came to an end, he again became available.

Earlier, in looking about for a location where we could produce *Return of the Seven* less expensively than we could in America, we chose

Spain, which had by then been developed by Italian filmmakers as a location for American Western subjects. We decided to return there for *Guns of the Magnificent Seven.*

Unfortunately, we were no longer able to secure the services of Yul Brynner to play Chris, since he wanted to move on to other things. We now chose George Kennedy to play the leader of the seven. It wasn't easy to cast the part, since this was now the third picture in the series. By then, George had received a great deal of attention for his role in *Cool Hand Luke,* for which he had won an Oscar. We endeavored to surround him with as strong a cast as we possibly could, including Joe Don Baker, James Whitmore, Monte Markham, Bernie Casey, Scott Thomas, Reni Santoni, Michael Ansara, and Fernando Rey. We chose Paul Wendkos to direct.

In *Guns of the Magnificent Seven,* our group sets out to liberate a political prisoner from a Mexican prison. It turned out to be an effective film, and it, too, was commercially successful. It utilized the theme music from the original film, which, by then, had grown into a significant sales ingredient of the package, partly because it had been adopted by Marlboro cigarettes as its theme in its advertising campaigns, where it was often called "Marlboro Country."

The production of *Guns of the Magnificent Seven* went well. Vince Fennelly ran a tight ship, and the film was made at a reasonable price. It is a good picture, and it became profitable, both for us and for United Artists, which was especially welcome during a period when a number of our other films did not do well.

Some years earlier, we had concluded a three-picture commitment with Dick Van Dyke, beginning with *Fitzwilly.* I next chose a musical that had been successful on Broadway, *I Do! I Do!* which I thought would be a good vehicle for Dick. United Artists agreed to acquire the rights to do the film, and I made an arrangement with Gower Champion, an experienced and well-known director of musicals on Broadway, to direct.

The musical was based on a dramatic play, *The Four Poster,* about a husband and wife reminiscing on their lives together. It played on Broadway with Robert Preston and Mary Martin as the leads. David Picker, now the architect of United Artists' production program, had grave misgivings about making a musical and reversed his decision about our doing *I Do! I Do!* This left us without a project to fulfill our commitment to Van Dyke.

At this juncture, his agent, Abe Lastfogel, came to me with a script, *The One with the Fuzz*, that he said Dick had read and was eager to do. The well-known writer and director Garson Kanin had written it and also wished to direct. I read the script but wasn't at all enthusiastic. It simply wasn't my cup of tea. But we needed to fulfill our commitment to Van Dyke. I was further seduced into doing the film by the fact that it was relatively inexpensive to produce, and there was also the possibility that Van Dyke and Kanin were right about it and I was wrong.

And so we, and United Artists, decided to proceed. However, like *Kings of the Sun*, the film was made for all the wrong reasons, and it shouldn't have been surprising that it didn't do well, either with the critics or at the box office.

🐦

Norman Jewison had become exceedingly enthusiastic about Ben Hecht's autobiography, *Gaily, Gaily,* which described his youth as a small-town Wisconsin boy exposed to the temptations and sin of turn-of-the-century Chicago. By this time, Norman had achieved an extraordinary record with us of directing highly successful films. He had tremendous enthusiasm for this latest project, and we and United Artists embarked hopefully on the film, agreeing to Norman's choice of Abram Ginnes to write the screenplay.

Norman wanted to make the film on a large scale, and I was concerned about that. I felt that it shouldn't look overproduced for a rather intimate story. But Norman felt that the city of Chicago was a character, which needed to be shown in a burgeoning period of its history. Consequently, *Gaily, Gaily* developed into a quite expensive film.

Norman selected the young Beau Bridges, just embarking on his career, to play the male leading role. For the important role of the madam of a brothel, Norman wished to cast Melina Mercouri. I opposed that selection and tried to convince him to cast Ava Gardner. But he was adamant, and finally UA and we acceded to his wishes.

Gaily, Gaily was a beautifully mounted film, with sets designed by Robert Boyle. The *Hollywood Reporter* (October 10, 1968) wrote of the Chicago exteriors photographed on the Universal back lot:

> Jewison is using a daily average of 625 extras in period wardrobe, 24 vintage cars . . . 24 horse-drawn rigs, plus handcarts, bicycles, and a

three-horse fire engine. Production designer Robert Boyle and set decorator Eddie Boyle worked from hundreds of photographs, with assistance from the Chicago Historical Society. Seven streetcars and two elevated trains have been converted from electricity to gasoline. Sass Bedig and George Brown, of special effects, replaced the power units with modern automobile engines, fabricating special power trains and couplings and installing disc brakes. Construction was handled by personnel from Universal and Goldwyn, except for the elevated railroad. Designed to carry two trains, each weighing fourteen tons, this structural-steel job was farmed out.

All of this was exceedingly expensive, and we ended up with a costly film without an important star. Its commercial results were most disappointing. Certainly UA approved the project because Norman was now its fair-haired director. He had come off of three consecutive hit pictures and had made a lot of money for the company. United Artists was anxious to have his next picture and to retain him for future pictures. As often happened in the past and continues to happen in the present, UA wanted to maintain its relationship, and so it went along, not kicking and screaming but hoping to foster the relationship.

Brian Keith played a tough reporter, George Kennedy had the role of the leader of the "reform" movement, Hume Cronyn was a political boss, Margot Kidder, in one of her earliest roles, was Beau Bridges' romantic interest, and Wilfrid Hyde-White completed an outstanding supporting cast. Having embarked upon the project, and having lost the argument about Melina Mercouri, we hoped that the ensemble cast of outstanding actors would overcome the lack of a marquee star name. We also hoped the film would get marvelous notices and that the picture's critical reviews would become its main attraction. Unfortunately, this did not happen.

Along with the rest of the industry, we endured a bleak commercial and artistic period between 1967 and 1970, when we failed to have a real hit film. Columbia and Twentieth Century-Fox had come to the brink of bankruptcy, and United Artists had the worst year in its history in 1969. Producers and executives were looking at all sorts of non-establishment-type subjects. It came to be called the *Easy Rider* syndrome, taking its name from that surprising anti-establishment film success of the period. There was clearly a cultural revolution taking place during those years, and until it resolved itself, it created problems that were felt throughout the entire industry. It wasn't just The Mirisch Company that was failing, it was the whole industry that simply couldn't connect with its audiences.

After *Gaily, Gaily,* Norman Jewison proposed to us the idea of *The Landlord,* which developed into our attempt to make a nonestablishment kind of film. Written by William Gunn, it was again a young man's coming-of-age story, which we offered to Beau Bridges. Different from *Gaily, Gaily, The Landlord* played in a contemporary setting, with an assortment of characters that we thought would be reflective of the times. It is the story of a rich man's son who buys a tenement in an African American ghetto and becomes involved in his tenants' lives.

While the project was in development, Norman told me that he would like to give it to Hal Ashby to direct, since he thought that, in many ways, Hal could do it better than he, and he wanted Hal, our frequent editor, to have an opportunity to direct. I endorsed the idea. During all the years that Hal had been editing pictures for us, we had discussed the idea of finding a project on which he, eager to become a director, could have his opportunity. Hal was an unconventional kind of man, nonconformist in ways that Norman was establishment, and he probably could have been termed an early "hippie." He was an intelligent man of excellent taste who knew his craft well and who now joined us in the development of *The Landlord.*

At about the same time, writers Al Ramrus and John Shaner submitted a script, *Halls of Anger,* about reverse busing in a high school. Its leading character was a male black teacher. This was another attempt to span the cultural changes that were taking place in our society during this period. For our company, it was a film that signified a marking of time until we could figure out what to make of the changes taking place in our country and in our culture. The Vietnam experience was weighing heavily. The civil rights upheaval was upon us, as was the student revolution.

I chose Paul Bogart, who had a varied live and film television background, to direct. He had a great deal of enthusiasm for the subject and was good to work with. I had hoped that he would get somewhat more out of the material than he did. We cast it with a young African

American actor, Calvin Lockhart, who was called "the next Sidney Poitier" and had garnered excellent reviews in the film *Joanna*.

During this period, when I was deeply involved in the development of new projects, I opted to employ producers of experience and talent to handle the day-to-day production of certain films. One of these was Herbert Hirschman, who I had known for a long time. He had produced a large body of work, principally in television. He knew Paul and had worked with him many times prior to *Halls of Anger*, which I thought presented a good vehicle for him to produce.

In the supporting cast were Rob Reiner and Jeff Bridges, each in one of their early screen appearances. Ed Asner and Janet MacLachlan completed the cast. *Halls of Anger* was an inexpensive picture, costing under $1 million. I had hoped that, with the elements involved and with not too big an investment, it could become a breakout picture, but it didn't.

When the script of *The Landlord* was completed, we decided that Norman should be its producer, since I felt that would help me sell Hal Ashby to United Artists as a first-time director. With Norman involved, and presumably looking over Hal's shoulder, I hoped that UA would feel there was an experienced backup behind our first-time director. United Artists was not enthusiastic about the subject matter, and when it heard that Norman wouldn't be directing the film, its concerns only increased. I went to New York and spent a couple of difficult days trying to convince the company to go forward with the picture and agree to Hal's directing. Finally, UA did agree, on the condition that we get the budget down to $2 million. We complied.

The cast was headed by Beau Bridges, Lee Grant, Diana Sands, Pearl Bailey, Louis Gossett, and Susan Anspach. Our production designer was Robert Boyle, our cameraman was Gordon Willis, our editors were Bill Sawyer and Ed Warschilka, and Al Kooper did the music. The picture was shot in its entirety in New York City.

The production of the picture went smoothly, although slowly. Hal proved to be a meticulous workman as a director. He could not be hurried. As I watched the dailies, I felt he was getting excellent results. But *The Landlord* proved to be one of the great disappointments of my career as a prognosticator. I thought that it would become a big success. I thought it was honest and funny and right for its time. I missed the mark completely. I think we made an excellent film, but it was not a commercial success. I had hoped that the film could be sold to the public with reviews that appreciated how honest and funny it was, and that there would be great word of mouth that would develop into a sales campaign. But that didn't happen. Again, we had great difficulty in connecting with our audience. The same thing was true of most other film companies, all of whom were trying to find the kind of films to which audiences would respond. The industry could not find a footing from which it could address its audiences, and we were no exception.

The principal mainstays of our program were also having great difficulty. Billy Wilder had not had a successful film since *Irma La Douce* in 1963. John Sturges had not been able to deliver for us since *The Great Escape* in 1962. Norman Jewison, after delivering three big hits for us, had failed with *Gaily, Gaily* and *The Landlord*. By 1970, we were making a determined effort to bring in a new generation of directors to create the pictures that would constitute the backbone of our future programs, with the rest of our product developing internally or from other, perhaps short-term, relationships that we would make.

I made a strong effort to conclude a deal with Mike Nichols to come with us but did not succeed. However, I did succeed in making a deal with Sanford Productions, owned by Sydney Pollack and Mark Rydell. They both moved to the Goldwyn Studio and began to develop films for us, while completing other projects in which they were involved with other companies.

I also made a deal with Franklin Schaffner, and we started to develop material with him while he was directing *Patton*. I visited him in Manchester, England, with a writer who was working on our script. I also made a deal with Peter Yates to join us.

I felt that, with Sydney Pollack, Franklin Schaffner, Mark Rydell, and Peter Yates, I had a good crack at the next generation of important directors. Deals with them were based on the formula of the old Billy Wilder–John Sturges–Norman Jewison arrangements. I felt that these alliances would strengthen our company, whether or not we remained at United Artists.

It had always been assumed that Arthur Krim's successor as president of United Artists would be Arnold Picker. We had a good relationship with Arnold, but he surprised everybody by saying he wasn't interested in assuming the presidency. Shortly thereafter, he retired, leaving the field open for his nephew, David Picker. And so in June 1969, when Arthur ascended to the chairmanship of United Artists, David Picker became president. Also rising within the company was Eric Pleskow, who had been vice president in charge of foreign sales and now became executive vice president and much more influential in the overall management of the company.

David Picker assumed a hands-on role in managing production, as Arthur withdrew into semi-retirement. David is said to have made a statement at that time to the effect that it had been generally assumed within the Hollywood community that the best way to make a deal with United Artists was to go through The Mirisch Company, but that this was not so. It appeared that he wanted to deal directly with all the filmmakers and not through our organization. The handwriting was on the wall.

We began to have more difficulty getting material approved. There was one film in particular that I wanted to make that United Artists would not approve. It was *Midway*, based on the great World War II naval battle. My enthusiasm for this project began long before the preparation of *Tora! Tora! Tora!* by Twentieth Century-Fox. I personally financed the writing of a screenplay, trying to convince United Artists of the merits of the subject. Donald Sanford, who had written some of our low-budget World War II action pictures, wrote the script. But despite the fact that I felt strongly about *Midway*, United Artists argued that nobody cared much about World War II any longer and there wasn't much of an audience for this type of film.

Clearly, our relationship with United Artists had changed considerably. David Picker was in charge now, instead of Arthur Krim. We were coming off of a disappointing production period and had not enjoyed a big success for a couple of years. Our corps of producer-directors had not been successful, and I'm sure that also colored UA's point of view. Harold had died in 1968, which also affected the perception of the company. Although Harold had been seriously ill for seven years before he died and had been quite inactive, there were people who said, "Well, you know, Harold's not there any longer."

The relationship that Marvin and I had with David Picker and Eric Pleskow was polite and respectful. They were probably under a great deal of pressure from Transamerica, whose impatience led to considerable instability within the company. The long-range success of the film companies in the so-called golden age was largely based on the stability of managements. When Jack Warner was running his studio, or Harry Cohn or Louis Mayer theirs, they knew they had to perform well, but they weren't in constant danger of being replaced if they had a bad year. They had the opportunity to see the wheel of chance turn and the time to see the results of the good things that they had planned come to fruition.

We had started preparation of our first Franklin Schaffner project, *Nothing to Lose*. *The Judgment* was to be directed by Peter Yates, from a story by Harry Kleiner, with a script by Dalton Trumbo. And *The Bank Robber*, later titled *The Spikes Gang*, started as a project of Mark Rydell, with a script by Harriet Frank and Irving Ravetch. Sydney Pollack, who had just finished *The Shoot Horses, Don't They?*, had moved to offices with us at the Goldwyn Studio, and we were just beginning to talk about projects with him. So we were planning for the future and cultivating the next generation of talented directors.

🐟

Following *The Landlord*, the next film we released was *The Hawaiians*. Its origin was in the so-called Chinese story that had been removed from *Hawaii* when we made the changes that finally settled the rehiring of George Roy Hill. I had always felt that if *Hawaii* was successful, we should make a follow-up film utilizing the excised material. *Hawaii* was successful, and I developed the Chinese story with James R. Webb, who did an excellent job.

Two stars had been proposed to me to play the leading role—Charlton Heston and Clint Eastwood, both of whom were most enthusiastic about the part. We chose Charlton Heston.

We hadn't yet selected a director for the picture when Chuck Heston asked me to look at a film that he had finished not long before, *Will Penny*. He thought highly of the director, and after seeing the film, so did I. It was an absolutely first-rate Western, exceedingly well executed by Tom Gries, who had formerly been an agent and had finally gotten an opportunity to direct.

With Tom Gries directing *The Hawaiians*, the picture was budgeted at about $6.5 million, and we returned to Hawaii to shoot. Whereas the original was shot exclusively on the island of Oahu, *The Hawaiians* was shot on both Maui and Kauai with interiors done at the Goldwyn Studio.

We had a most difficult casting problem in selecting a young woman to play the demanding role of the Chinese girl, Nyuk Tsin. Tom Gries and I went to New York to interview actors and found a young woman there who had appeared in Arthur Penn's *Alice's Restaurant* and who was now working in a medical laboratory. She was intelligent, beautiful, and charming. Her name was Tina Chen. We made a screen test of her and thought she was excellent. She was represented by the ICM agency and married Marvin Josephson, the owner of ICM, a short time after the completion of the movie.

We chose Mako, a well-known Hollywood actor, to play her husband, Mun Ki. The rest of the cast consisted of Geraldine Chaplin, who had been in *Dr. Zhivago*, Alec McCowan, a distinguished English stage actor, and John Philip Law, who had been in *The Russians Are Coming, the Russians Are Coming* and whom I'd hoped to bring along as a young leading man, playing Charlton Heston's son.

The shooting proceeded rather uneventfully. Cary Odell did the production design and Ralph Winters edited. Henry Mancini did the musical score.

I had high hopes for the film, but it was not successful, and I was again disappointed.

🐦

They Call Me MISTER Tibbs! was the second of three Virgil Tibbs films. The great success of *In the Heat of the Night* led us to attempt to do a sequel. I discussed the follow-up story with a number of writers, including Sterling Silliphant and Alan Trustman. We gave the assignment to the latter, and James R. Webb later did a script rewrite.

In *They Call Me MISTER Tibbs!*, Tibbs is now a married San Francisco detective, investigating the murder of a girl in which a street preacher is implicated. I employed line producer Herbert Hirschman to go to San Francisco and supervise the film and Gordon Douglas to direct it. Douglas had enjoyed a long career in Hollywood and had directed the Elvis Presley movie *Follow That Dream* for us some years before. Sidney Poitier approved the choice, and production began. In the deal we had made with Sidney for *In the Heat of the Night*, he agreed to give us options for two more pictures if we chose to continue to make Virgil Tibbs movies. We exercised our first option.

The title comes from the line by Tibbs in the earlier *In the Heat of the Night*, when Rod Steiger says to him, "What do they call you in Philadelphia?" In a marvelous reading, Sidney replies, "They call me *Mister* Tibbs."

Martin Landau appeared in the picture, Barbara McNair played Tibbs's wife, Jeff Corey was his boss, and Anthony Zerbe played one of the villains. Juano Hernandez, Ed Asner, and Norma Crane completed the cast.

In retrospect, I think I may have made a serious miscalculation in this film by not doing a story that included both the Tibbs character and the Gillespie character. A great deal of the success of the first picture was undoubtedly a result of these two men playing off one another. Without that relationship, we were reduced to telling a cop story in San Francisco with Virgil Tibbs. However, I was concerned that if we had done a story, set in the North or South, and used Rod Steiger in the Gillespie character again, the criticism would be that it was only more of the same, and there really weren't any nuances in that relationship that we hadn't either touched on or suggested. We would be damned if we did and damned if we didn't.

MISTER Tibbs wasn't an expensive picture, and I hoped it would have done better commercially. I needed a hit picture badly at the time, but this wasn't it. The film was constructed to be a safe picture during a time of industry uncertainty, and it succeeded in yielding only a small profit.

🦋

In 1969, an agent submitted a script, *The Dragonmaster* by Stephen Kandel, to my brother Marvin. It was a story set in 1912 and revolved around a mission by a group of American soldiers who cross the Texas border in pursuit of Mexican bandits who have stolen an army cannon. Marvin became quite taken with the project, and I encouraged him to submit it to some agents in the hope of attracting an important action star to the script.

George Peppard, who had been starring in a series of action films since his early successes in *Breakfast at Tiffany's* and *The Carpetbaggers*, responded to it. United Artists agreed that if the film were produced on a limited budget, it could be a worthwhile project, particularly in the foreign market.

We decided to produce it in Spain, where we had enjoyed considerable success in filming the low-budgeted *Magnificent Seven* sequels. We chose Vincent Fennelly to produce, Paul Wendkos to direct, and Giovanna Ralli and Raf Vallone to co-star. They delivered a standard action film like other contemporaneous films of its genre, such as *Mackenna's Gold, Murphy's War,* and even *The Bridge at Remagen.* It did not even find acceptance in the foreign markets that we had hoped to win. It was another disappointment for us and for United Artists.

In 1970, Arthur Krim, appraising the wreckage of the period of his semi-retirement, noted, "Thirty-five films placed in production by United Artists in 1968 and 1969, costing a total of eighty million dollars, would lose in the neighborhood of fifty million dollars." In 1969, MGM similarly took a pre-tax loss of $72 million, and Twentieth Century-Fox showed a loss of $65 million. A. H. Howe, a Bank of America executive in charge of production financing, said that the situation in 1970 could be matched "in seriousness, dislocation and change by only two events in film history, the sound revolution of 1930 and the television upheaval of the 1950s." Howe further stated that as of 1969, the seven majors had already lost $200 million. The experience of the little Mirisch Company program during these convulsive years in the industry's history certainly was not unique.

29

Billy Wilder and
*The Private Life of Sherlock
Holmes* and *Avanti!*

Billy Wilder remarked to me one day in the early 1960s, "You know who are the most famous people in all literature? Probably Tarzan and Sherlock Holmes. I think there's a marvelous movie yet to be made about the real Sherlock Holmes." He began to read all of the Sherlock Holmes stories and many of the books that had been written about Holmes.

His original idea was to do the film with Peter O'Toole, who had emerged as a huge star after *Lawrence of Arabia,* as Sherlock Holmes. He wanted Peter Sellers to play Dr. Watson. The idea of Peter O'Toole and Peter Sellers as Sherlock Holmes and Dr. Watson, with Wilder writing and directing, sounded exciting, and that's how it all began. Billy worked on the idea, on and off, over the years but never reached a point where he was ready to start actually writing. Different projects took over, and he made a number of other films during the following years. But he always returned to the Sherlock Holmes project.

We proposed the concept to Peter O'Toole's agents and manager, but they wouldn't commit their client to do the film until they'd seen a script. But that wasn't Billy Wilder's style. He chose not to write a script that was tailored to Peter O'Toole and risk his rejection of the role. And

Billy's unfortunate experience with Peter Sellers on *Kiss Me, Stupid* finished the idea of his doing another film with that Peter.

The exciting casting that we'd been talking about had now disappeared. But Billy, with his great self-confidence and his ability to impart his confidence to others, convinced me that, when the time came, he would produce exciting casting for it.

He attempted to work with some new collaborators in developing the story, including Harry Kurnitz, with whom he had written *Witness for the Prosecution,* and the English writer John Mortimer. I assumed he was looking for something that neither he nor Iz Diamond could contribute and he was looking for somebody else who could. Sometime during those years he finally gave up on other writers, because he wasn't making much progress with them, and started again with Iz Diamond. Finally they wrote the screenplay of the film together.

It had been Billy's custom to produce a new film about every two years. It had now been nearly four years since the release of *The Fortune Cookie,* which was the longest time during which we had not had a Billy Wilder film since the inception of our relationship. But he finally decided that Sherlock Holmes would be his next film, and he labored over the script. He wanted to make a film that both pleased him and that would be successful.

Once he completed the script, he went to London to look for actors, and we budgeted the picture. It was quite expensive, coming in at over $6 million. This time there was no question about whether it would be photographed in color, since by then the entire industry had gone to color.

Billy was convinced that Sherlock Holmes was the star of the film, and that is why he wanted to go to London and find the best casting that he possibly could for the picture. He felt that Sherlock Holmes and the quality of the picture he intended to make would now be the main sales ingredients in marketing it. His idea was that this was going to be the first film that would get into the character of Holmes and the nature of his relationship with Watson, as well as the influence that Holmes's drug habit had on his life. His film would come to grips with the suspicion that Holmes was homosexual, and that there was, perhaps, a physical relationship between him and Dr. Watson. These were all challenging ideas, and we thought that *The Private Life of Sherlock Holmes* was going to elucidate all those fascinating facets of his character, as well as being different and controversial, and consequently would have the elements of what would make for a successful film, particularly in the hands of a master filmmaker.

Billy Wilder, Iz Diamond, and Alex Trauner met in London to begin preparation. I joined them there somewhat later. As was Billy's wont, the screenplay wasn't completed at this stage. He tended to hold it back until after he was in production. After six previous films together, I accepted this custom as a part of his desire to keep the door open for fresh ideas without creating blue pages and to keep his third acts as close to his chest as possible. I had good reason to rely on him, trusting to his talent and responsibility as a picturemaker, and to feel certain that all would be revealed in good time.

The revelation in *The Private Life of Sherlock Holmes* would be that Holmes was not infallible and that he had made miscalculations all through the film. The plot was being masterminded by Mycroft, his brother, who was pulling the strings, with Sherlock being deceived by his machinations.

I arrived in London at about the time that Billy had made up his mind as to his choices for the roles of Sherlock Holmes and Dr. Watson, namely Robert Stephens and Colin Blakely. I was deeply upset about the casting. Although we had given lip service to not using a big-name star cast, I had hoped that we would at least have British actors who were better known than the two he had chosen.

I also arrived in London in time to participate in some rather serious discussions then taking place. Billy and Alex Trauner wanted to construct Baker Street on the back lot at the Pinewood Studio. This was an exceedingly expensive set, and I wanted them to do it on an actual London street rather than undertaking a big construction expenditure. I debated the issue for a long time with Billy, who argued that the convenience of having it in the studio, where he would be protected by cover sets in case of inclement weather, would justify the additional expense. I didn't convince him, nor did he convince me, but we constructed the street on the back lot.

Genevieve Page was cast in the leading female role, and I thought she was fine. My concerns continued to be in the Robert Stephens and Colin Blakely castings, but Billy felt confident about both of them and thought they would give him the special qualities that he wanted. The director of photography was Christopher Challis, who had previously done *Return from the Ashes* for us and was an absolutely first-rate cameraman. Ernie Walter, who edited the picture, had also worked on *The Bells of Hell Go Ting-a-Ling*. Miklos Rozsa, who had scored *Double Indemnity* for Billy, was signed to do the score.

The shooting went slowly, and *Sherlock Holmes* was an expensive film for its time. During the shooting of the picture, there was a delay caused by Robert Stephens's suicide attempt, a result of the breakup with his wife, Maggie Smith. This marked the third consecutive delay caused by actor health problems on Billy's pictures.

The film was scored and dubbed at Pinewood, and we brought it back to Los Angeles for a preview at the Lakewood Theater, near Long Beach. Unfortunately, the preview was disastrous. We had a tremendous number of walkouts. The cards we got at the theater were uniformly bad. Billy was present with his wife, Audrey, and we were all shell-shocked at the end of the performance. I said, "What do you think we should do now, Billy?"

He said something to the effect of, "I don't know. Do whatever you think is best." He was terribly shaken by it, as was Iz Diamond.

I said, "Let Ernie and me run the picture again, and if we can come up with some suggestions, we will submit them to you and see what you think."

And that's what we did. Ernie Walter and I discussed, first, the basic construction of the picture, which was made up of three separate segments intended to be held together by the continuing thread of the presence and characters of Holmes and Watson. We felt that a lot of our problem sprang from the episodic nature of the picture. As each of the segments ended we lost part of our audience and then had to recapture those who remained as we started over again into the next segment. People who had seen a complete segment were not absorbed enough to remain for the start of the next episode. There were originally four episodes, including "The Curious Case of the Upside-Down Room," which we removed entirely, and "The Dreadful Business of the Naked Honeymoon," which we finally intercut with the concluding episode. Ernie Walter and I suggested reconstructing the whole picture to try and make it a single story, with a beginning, middle, and an end. It was difficult.

Finally we submitted notes on the recut to Billy and Iz. They made some contributions to this thinking and finally said, "Let's look at it, and see how it plays in this form." Ernie Walter proceeded to do the re-editing.

In retrospect, it seems that there is a fundamental flaw in the film that no amount of cutting could overcome. Over decades of time, audiences had become accustomed to the perfection of Basil Rathbone as Sherlock Holmes. The vulnerability and imperfection of Robert Stephens wasn't the Holmes that they were accustomed to or wanted. The film has been termed a cynical conception with a romantic execution. The relationship between Holmes and Madame Valodon is romanticized. He's madly in love with her, and she exploits him shamelessly.

We implemented all the changes that we had discussed, and we previewed the new version in Santa Barbara. We had few or no walkouts. We retained our audience from beginning to end, which was, in itself, somewhat of a victory for the recut version. It now ran 125 minutes, which was about forty minutes shorter than the previous version.

Billy Wilder chose not to attend the Santa Barbara preview. I felt that he did not want to expose himself to a possible repeat of the Lakewood preview, which left him very shaken. He asked me to report to him on the details of the second preview, which I did. We succeeded in having the picture booked at New York's Radio City Music Hall, the premiere motion-picture theater in America at the time.

Reviewers felt that *The Private Life of Sherlock Holmes* never really caught fire, but they didn't go so far as to say that it felt incomplete. The lack of plot disappointed the constituency of Sherlock Holmes. The Sherlock Holmes stories are plot-driven, and its lack in our film resulted in a poor commercial response.

On the other hand, perhaps the basic premises of the film had just become overcooked. If the preparation of a particular subject is taking a long time, it's probably because there are a lot of problems in the writing of the script. Oftentimes you come upon a solution, and you're so pleased that you lose sight of the fact that it's not really a good solution. However, you have led yourself to believe that you have found a way to do it. That, of course, is self-deception.

Perhaps, too, the O'Toole and Sellers casting would have made the change in the traditional Sherlock Holmes character more palatable. There would have been much more humor if Peter Sellers had been playing Watson. Peter O'Toole would have brought with him the vulnerabilities and complexities that he delivered so well in *Lawrence of Arabia*. We would have had an entirely different film with Peter O'Toole than we had with Robert Stephens.

In any event, the release of *The Private Life of Sherlock Holmes* started 1970 off inauspiciously for The Mirisch Company.

≋

A couple of years later, we needed a real hit picture, Billy Wilder needed a hit picture, and certainly United Artists needed a hit picture. Billy had enjoyed one of his great successes with Samuel Taylor's *Sabrina Fair* (released as *Sabrina*) and had been interested for some time in Taylor's play *Avanti!*, which had played to mild success many years earlier on Broadway. As expected, Billy had his own ideas about how he would do the film. It promised a light comedy, an area in which Billy was a master. It also presented a ready-made Jack Lemmon role, and Billy and Jack were exceedingly comfortable working with one another. We knew, therefore, we were going to have a major star for *Avanti!*, which we planned to produce in its Italian locales. Again Billy wrote the script with Iz Diamond.

In order to make the film eligible for Italian nationality, which yielded certain advantages in the Italian market, United Artists proposed that we make the film through an Italian company that would give us that eligibility. This necessitated our employing a large number of Italian technicians. Billy welcomed this and even agreed to use an Italian cameraman, Luigi Kuveiller, who spoke little or no English. I asked Billy if using a largely Italian crew was going to be a problem for him. He replied, "Well, why can't I learn Italian?" And he was wonderful. He got some Berlitz records and began to teach himself Italian. This crew, like all crews in my experience with Billy, loved him. He played them like a great violinist plays his Stradivarius. He knew when to tell a joke and when to be stern. The Italian crew liked it and admired him when he spoke his fractured Italian, and I did too.

Avanti! is the story of a stuffy Baltimore millionaire who goes to Italy to claim the body of his father, who has been killed in an automobile crash along with his secret mistress. The millionaire then proceeds to fall in love with the daughter of the mistress. Billy chose Juliet Mills to play the female lead in the picture. He shot the exteriors on the Amalfi coast, at beautiful and picturesque Sorrento and Capri, and the interiors at a studio in Rome. The millionaire, who starts out critical of his father's infidelity, falls into the same pattern and we are led to believe that he and the daughter will continue the tradition of their parents. Billy added many interesting, humorous characters and situations.

He also wrote a cameo role for Walter Matthau as an American diplomat who finally appears to straighten out all of the red tape that surrounds shipping the corpse from Italy back to America. Unfortunately, Walter was not able to come abroad to play the role, and it finally was cast with Edward Andrews.

Billy wanted Juliet Mills to gain a great deal of weight, which rather worried me because I think audiences generally like pretty and shapely leading ladies. He encouraged Juliet to gain fifteen or twenty pounds for the role, because he wrote a lot of weight jokes in the script.

Ralph Winters came to Italy and edited *Avanti!*, which was relatively untroubled in its production and was produced at a cost close to its $3 million budget. Although I like the film very much, at 144 minutes I thought it was far too long. It's difficult to sustain a comedy at that length. I felt that it would play much better if it were shorter, but Billy didn't agree, nor would cutting it have been easy. Billy Wilder's scripts are rather like fine watches. You don't find any extraneous parts in a watch, and it's difficult to remove any of them and still have the watch run. The same thing is true of Billy Wilder pictures. They are all so intricately plotted that it is exceedingly difficult to make deletions.

Stanley Kauffmann, in the *New Republic* (February 24, 1973), after praising the film generally and commenting upon certain general tendencies in Wilder's work, such as his being a specialist in the unconventional meeting, wrote: "There are good things in the film, the way Wilder exploits the feeling of a lovely old hotel, as he did in *Some Like It Hot;* the way he uses vacationland light to make us feel high-spirited, as in *Some Like It Hot;* and, most particularly, the way he sculptures every scene, in script and direction. Every sequence has a sense of architecture, and a final little polishing touch." Kauffmann continued, "Wilder gets a good, sufficiently charming, performance from Juliet Mills, and a smooth, though rather unflavorful, performance from Clive Revill, as the omniscient hotel manager. . . . At least Wilder knows his formal sources, and he is a devout formalist. The structure is traditional farce. The body is in fine shape, it's the blood that's tired."

The *Hollywood Reporter* (December 15, 1972) commented: "Wilder has again chosen to walk a tightrope between slapstick comedy and pathos without falling off even once." It went on to say, "*Avanti!* is a polished example of a commercial Hollywood film. It claims to be neither thought-provoking nor innovative. In fact, except for a few close-ups of Lemmon's bare bottom, there is nothing in its style nor content to indicate *Avanti!* was made in 1972 and not 1962 or even 1952. But this is not a fault. Given the choice, most of us would rather watch a good film from ten or twenty years ago than some celluloid mediocrity whose only virtue is its 'nowness.' Besides, *Avanti!* is entertaining."

There was a strong possibility of *Avanti!*'s becoming a very successful film, despite its length, since there is so much in it that is both moving and funny. But it did only moderate business and was a great disappointment.

It also was the last of our films with Billy Wilder. *Avanti!*'s release occurred close to the end of our relationship with United Artists, which was the umbrella for our contract with Billy. Shortly after, he was offered *The Front Page,* with Jack Lemmon and Walter Matthau, at Universal. He was eager to do that project, and so, without any animus whatsoever between us, this became the first separation between The Mirisch Company and Billy Wilder in fifteen years.

30

Fiddler on the Roof

In September 1964, I went to see the play *Fiddler on the Roof* during the first week of its New York engagement. I was deeply moved and thought it was a wonderful, poignant, human story that said a great deal about people. The play was written by Joseph Stein, adapted from stories by Sholom Aleichem. The score, by Jerry Bock and Sheldon Harnick, was superb. Zero Mostel, who played the lead, was extraordinary.

The following day I told Arthur Krim I had seen the play, how wonderful I thought it was, and what a superb movie I thought it would make. He was very discouraging. He told me that he had already seen it himself, and he too was deeply moved, but he said he feared that there simply was not a worldwide audience for a film that was so ethnically oriented. I remember him saying to me, "If we make this film, it will probably do well in New York, where there are a million and a half Jewish people, but what do we do with it elsewhere?" I conceded that was a problem, but I argued that there was a wider audience for it, that it wasn't simply a Jewish story but would be a film that would appeal to people throughout the world.

We made some inquiries as to whether or not we could acquire the rights. I hoped that some kind of deal could be made where investment could be limited, so that we could hold down the front-end cost of the picture, but apparently that was not to be. The owners of the musical were looking for a great deal of money for the property. They said they were in no hurry to sell the rights, since they expected the play to have a long engagement, and they didn't want the film released while the play was still running. There would be a holdback provision in an acquisition, so one couldn't produce the film for a long time. Because of all those reasons, I was compelled to put the project on a back burner.

Interestingly, Joe Stein, the writer, later told me that his experience with the play had been much the same as mine, only more so. He had read the Sholom Aleichem story many years before, and then he had developed a play and tried to interest people in producing it. After a long passage of time, and numerous rejections, he had also put it on a back burner. However, like so many artists, he figuratively carried it around in his trunk, waiting for an appropriate time, place, or person to uncover it. He finally met the right person when he discussed his idea for doing the play, in those years titled *Tevye and His Daughters,* with Jerome Robbins. Robbins now became the key ingredient. The play began to take new form when Hal Prince became involved with it as producer, with Robbins directing and doing the choreography.

Shortly before the play was to open, they were still searching for a new title. Somebody came up with the idea of *Fiddler on the Roof,* derived from the graphic in Chagall's famous painting. Chagall, I was told, was furious about the lifting of his artistic image, because he felt his permission should have been sought. *Fiddler on the Roof* opened on September 22, 1964, at the Imperial Theater in New York to marvelous notices and became an instant success.

During the ensuing few years, when I was discussing future projects with United Artists, the subject often came up between us. After four years had passed, I began to say, "We must be getting closer to the time when *Fiddler's* New York run is going to come to an end."

In the summer of 1967, while we were shooting *The Thomas Crown Affair* on location in Boston, David Picker came to visit us. I went to dinner with him, and he told me that United Artists had decided that it would acquire the motion-picture rights to two hit musicals, *Man of La Mancha* and *Fiddler on the Roof.* He continued, "I recognize that you have been talking about this to us, but I want you to know that UA is going to acquire the properties for its own account." He meant, of course, without an outside producer being involved. This was revolutionary, because the outside producers who worked with United Artists never wanted to feel that they were competing with the company to acquire projects. But this was really symbolic of David Picker's taking greater control of the production program of United Artists. He told me that he didn't feel that he could offer both of those projects to us, because they had obligations to other producers, but that I could have my choice of either of the two that I wanted. I immediately chose *Fiddler*. At my first opportunity, I asked Norman Jewison if he would be interested in directing, and he said he would.

The rights to the property had cost between $2.75 million and $3 million. The rights to *West Side Story*, nine years earlier, had cost about $400,000. This time the services of Jerome Robbins were not made a part of the arrangement. Norman and I agreed immediately that we would ask Joe Stein, who had written the play, to write the screenplay.

We next began a long and laborious discussion of who should play Tevye. The great problem was that Zero Mostel had created the role and had made it his own. Did one just go along with that casting, or did one give it a second look?

Many years before, while we were shooting *The Party*, Peter Sellers called me one day and said, "You've got to come with me tonight. I want you to see the funniest movie I've ever seen." That evening, he took me to a showing of Zero Mostel in *The Producers*. We both roared with laughter, and Peter was seeing it for the second time. By 1968, Zero Mostel had been in many films, but he had never become a film personality of any commercial consequence. Despite his huge success in *Fiddler*, I expressed to Norman my feeling that his performances were just too big for film. I always felt that, even in his movies, he frequently seemed to be playing to the last row in the balcony, and no movie director had ever been completely able to control that tendency. Marvelous as he was in the play, I felt that his acting style overwhelmed the screen and that we should consider alternatives. Norman didn't disagree with me.

With most of the plays that I have made into movies, I've been criticized either for not repeating the play's casting or, alternatively, for using the same cast. Many critics found fault with our not casting Anne Bancroft and Henry Fonda in *Two for the Seesaw*. When we made *How to Succeed in Business*, and repeated the play's casting of Robert Morse and Michelle Lee, neither of them became movie stars. In *Toys in the Attic*, Jason Robards had played the leading role on the stage but I looked for a commercial movie star to carry this heavy dramatic piece of material and chose Dean Martin, whom I thought could add extra dimensions to the role. Critics would ask why I would not allow the individual who had created the stage role to play the same part in the screen adaptation. *Fiddler* presented an even more difficult decision, because Zero Mostel had made the role so peculiarly his own. He was Tevye. However, Norman and I stuck with our original decision and looked elsewhere.

The names of many actors who were interested in playing the role surfaced, Danny Kaye and Walter Matthau among them, but we didn't discuss the role with them. I was aware that Haym Topol was playing Tevye in the London company of the play. I had first met Topol, an Israeli actor, when we produced *Cast a Giant Shadow*. He played a small role in the film, that of an elderly Arab chieftain, despite the fact that his real age, at the time, was probably no more than thirty.

Norman and I looked again at the scene Topol played in *Cast a Giant Shadow*, and we continued our consideration of other possibilities until, one morning, while looking through the trade papers, I saw an item to the effect that Topol was leaving the cast of the London company of *Fiddler on the Roof* at the end of that week. I took the paper, walked over to Norman's office, showed it to him, and said, "I think we should go to London today." And that's what we did. We left as soon as we could arrange it and flew to London. We arrived there early in the afternoon, London time, got a little sleep, and then went to the theater to watch Topol's performance. We were very impressed with him.

We went backstage after the final curtain, and I introduced Norman to Topol. Haym is a warm and gregarious man, with a strong personality, and he made a decided impression on both of us. As chance would have it, it was rather a pleasant evening, and Norman and I walked from the theater back to our hotel, all the while discussing the pros and cons of casting Topol in the role of Tevye. By the time we'd arrived at the hotel, we had decided to offer the role to him. We asked United Artists, and everybody else who was involved, to agree to our decision, and we boarded an airplane the next morning and flew back to Los Angeles.

We immediately began negotiations with the William Morris Agency, which represented Topol, for his services in the film. Much to my surprise, the negotiations were prolonged. The agents kept insisting that they wanted a participation in the picture's profits for Topol, and we resisted that request. He was not a well-known motion-picture personality, and we felt that we were giving him a great opportunity to become one in this film. We felt that his request was premature.

The negotiations went on for some time until, finally, one evening, Topol phoned me at home and said he too was disturbed at how long it was taking. He wanted me to understand that he didn't want his request to be misinterpreted, but it was a matter of principle to him, and that his efforts would be all the greater if he had some kind of financial interest in the picture. Finally I suggested one-half of one percent of the profits, and he accepted it.

I was surprised to receive a telephone call from John Williams's agent, who told me that John would be interested in doing the musical supervision for the picture. I said, "You know, this is not a composing job, and it's going to take a great deal of his time. Does John really want to do this? We're going to need him for pre-scoring and conducting, and during production, and post-production." His agent said, "John wants to do it." So we were fortunate to get a brilliant musician to supervise the entire musical side of the picture.

We also fantasized about getting Isaac Stern to play the violin solo behind the main title and be our fiddler on the roof. Miraculously, we were able to arrange that too. Stern, like most concert musicians, was booked far in advance, but we were able to carve out some time when he could come to London and be recorded.

We had long discussions about locations, and we ultimately decided on Yugoslavia, with the film based in London and the key crew being English. We then began to put together a production staff of Americans, English, and Yugoslavians. Pat Palmer, who had worked with us for many years, became our overall production manager. We also employed an English production manager, Ted Lloyd, who had earlier worked on the military-themed Eady Plan program that we had done in London. Of course, we wanted Bob Boyle, who had done numerous films as production designer for us. We also brought Terry Nelson, our first assistant director, and Sam Gordon, our property man since *Fall Guy*, from Los Angeles. We chose an English cameraman, Ossie Morris, who had previously photographed *Moulin Rouge* and *Moby Dick*, and an English editor, Tony Gibbs, who was later joined by Robert

Lawrence. The choreographer was Tom Abbott, who had been an assistant to Jerome Robbins on many of his productions, including *Fiddler on the Roof*. The costumes were designed by Elizabeth Haffenden and Joan Bridge.

We employed a Yugoslavian location and production manager, Branko Lustig, who suggested the site for our village, which was in a little town, Lechinik, outside of Zagreb. Branko also filled in the rest of the crew from Yugoslavian technicians. The integration of the trinational crew worked very well.

Anne Bancroft was our first choice for the role of Golde, but she turned it down. We assumed she didn't want to play the secondary role in the film. Others whom we considered were Maria Karnicova, who had played the part on Broadway, Colleen Dewhurst, Zoe Caldwell, Maureen Stapleton, and even Beverly Sills. Finally our choices came down to Lee Grant, who had been in the cast of *In the Heat of the Night*, and Norma Crane, who had been in *They Call Me MISTER Tibbs*, but we decided against Lee on physical grounds. Her finely chiseled features seemed inappropriate for a Slavic peasant matriarch. We tested Norma and decided that she made a better match with Topol, and we offered her the role.

Molly Picon was cast as Yente, the matchmaker; Leonard Frey as Motel, the tailor; Paul Michael Glaser as Perchick; Rosalind Harris as Tzeitel; Michele Marsh as Hodel; and Neva Small as Chava.

The idea of Molly Picon came up early on in the casting process. An icon of the old Yiddish theater and a marvelous comedienne, Molly was about seventy years old at the time. She leaped at the chance to play the role. Her husband, Jacob Kalich, accompanied her to Zagreb. He too had been an actor and a director in the Yiddish theater. These two old people were inseparable, like young lovers at the beginning of a courtship. Everyone in the company was inspired by their marvelous relationship.

Production began on August 10, 1970. We soon began to have serious production problems caused by the unpredictability of the weather. We soldiered through that, but then Norma Crane told me that on a trip to London she had consulted a doctor, who had diagnosed a cancerous lump in her breast. He advised her to have the breast removed. She was terribly distraught. In the first place, she didn't want to lose her breast; second, she feared that if she had to be absent from the shooting long enough to undergo surgery, we would replace her in the film.

I told her, as probably everyone else did, that the film was secondary, and that I didn't know what we were going to have to do or how long she was going to be away, but the primary consideration had to be her well-being. She should do whatever her doctors felt gave her the best chance of saving her life.

She told me she felt Golde was the best role of her career, but even more than that was involved. Norma Crane was Jewish, and she saw Golde as her own mother, who had endured experiences similar to that of her character. She wanted more than anything to be a part of the film.

I told her she shouldn't be swayed by that, and she had to get the best opinion she could and do whatever was best to treat the tumor.

She went to London, consulted a number of physicians there, and then returned to Zagreb. She told me that she had consulted a doctor who felt that the cancer could be treated with radiation, and that she could continue to work, on a limited basis, while she was receiving treatments. She was confident that the radiation would eliminate the cancer. We all told her that we would abide by whatever decision she made, and we would adjust our shooting schedule around her radiation program, if that's what she chose to do.

She continued to work in the picture until the company moved to London. Then she would work in the mornings, have radiation treatments in the afternoon, and take the next day off. She was brave, worked hard, and tried not to be a burden to the production. We had to work around her, and it was exceedingly difficult, but the work did get done.

Sadly, within two years after the completion of the film, Norma died. Her whole body was by then filled with cancer. I have heard it said many times, as a criticism of *Fiddler on the Roof,* that she was the weakest member of the cast. I know she was the strongest member.

Despite the economic problems of the industry and United Artists in 1970, the suggestion of delaying the start of production was never made, although we were subjected to considerable pressure to organize the production as cost-effectively as possible. Three other location sites were chosen, all within a radius of thirty miles of Zagreb. Our company maintained headquarters in London, where all the musical numbers were pre-recorded and rehearsed.

The shooting continued to go slowly, but fortunately the expense of operating our company in Zagreb was reasonable and did not add much to our overall cost. After completing the work scheduled in Yugoslavia, our company moved to Pinewood Studio in London, where we photographed the wedding and bottle dances, the dream sequence, the musical number "Do You Love Me?," parts of Sabbath prayer, and "To Life." On February 12, 1971, principal photography was completed. We had shot for 130 days.

Fiddler on the Roof cost somewhat over $9.5 million to produce. Eleven years earlier, *West Side Story* had cost about $6.8 million. Because of the great savings we were able to realize from the Yugoslavian locations, *Fiddler on the Roof* had cost approximately the same amount, excepting only the difference in the cost of the rights to the play. Using that yardstick, we had not done badly, costwise.

Fiddler premiered at New York's Rivoli Theater on November 3, 1971, on a two-a-day, reserved-seat policy, with a huge advance sale. Prior to the opening, Arthur Krim hosted a cocktail party at his home with a glittering assemblage of press, film, artistic, and political personalities. Galia and Haym Topol came from Tel Aviv, and Mr. and Mrs. Yitzhak Rabin, then the Israeli ambassador to the United States, and U.S. Supreme Court justice Abe Fortas came from Washington. Following the presentation of the film, there was a festive charity dinner at a nearby hotel.

Unfortunately, the major critics were not kind to the film. Jay Cocks of *Time* magazine called it one of the last lumbering dinosaurs from the era of the big-budget musicals. Vincent Canby of the *New York Times* commented, "They've not just opened up the play, they've left most of the life out of it." Stanley Kauffmann in the *New Republic* headed his review, "Mogen David Superstar."

However, away from the major critics, the reviews were good, and most important of all, the public loved it. Although the story is told in the context of late-nineteenth-century Jewish life, the family values that are espoused in *Fiddler on the Roof* were embraced by people all over the country. The love of a father for his daughters, his caring for every nuance of their lives, and their respect and caring for their parents said much to a great many people, particularly in the aftermath of the Vietnam War and the hippie movement.

Furthermore, the magnificent score of the film speaks to people about traditional values. "Sunrise, Sunset" has become a standard wedding anthem. And "If I Were a Rich Man" has a great deal to say about how our society functions, while poking fun at it.

Prior to *Fiddler on the Roof* going into release, Norman Jewison, Joe Stein, Topol, and I were doing a series of press interviews. Joe Stein, during that period, recounted a number of stories of his long travail in getting the play produced. Among them was his recollection that when the play originally opened in Tokyo, with a Japanese cast, he was interviewed by the local press. They were most enthusiastic about the play, and they asked him to explain what he considered the reason for the play's great popularity in the United States. They understood why the Japanese would respond to it so well, since they had lived under the heel of despots and pogrom-like conditions for a long time and identified strongly with the story. But they had difficulty understanding why, in a country such as America, which has virtually always been free, excepting the period of slavery, and has not suffered from overt repression, people so identified with these characters.

I recalled this story as I monitored the results of the worldwide engagements of the picture and discovered that our business in the totalitarian countries of the day, such as Spain and Greece, was excellent, as it was in the English-speaking countries of the world, while the rest of the world, as was the expectation with American musicals, did poorly.

I traveled to Israel for the opening of the film and enjoyed an extraordinary experience. There was a benefit premiere in Tel Aviv, at which I was seated with Golda Meir, then prime minister of Israel, and Moshe Dayan, the defense minister. While sitting in the theater, with the picture playing beautifully, a military person walked down the aisle and stopped next to Dayan, who was sitting next to me. When the man leaned over and whispered in his ear, Dayan excused himself and walked out. I thought bombing might begin in the next few minutes, but that didn't occur. I kept waiting for him to come back, hoping that nothing terrible had happened. This was certainly not comparable to when we were shooting *Cast a Giant Shadow* in Israel, using portions of the Israeli army, and they informed us that they needed to move the army to the borders for a military emergency and we were left without any Israeli army to photograph.

Moshe Dayan returned after a period of time and I said to him, "Something serious?"

He laughed and said, "No, just a personal matter."

I next went to Paris for the French opening, where the reviews weren't good and the business was poor. Overall, however, the film was extraordinarily successful and became exceedingly profitable, both in its initial runs and as an evergreen. It's a film that doesn't age and continues to be exceedingly popular in the home video market. It became the most profitable film in the history of United Artists at its time, earning $50 million in film rentals in its initial releases.

I have always regretted that my father, who had been born in a ghetto in Krakow and had died two years before *Fiddler*'s completion, had not had a chance to see it. I know it would have meant a great deal to him.

The film was accorded eight Oscar nominations, including Best Picture, and it won three Academy Awards: to Oswald Morris for cinematography, to John Williams for Scoring: Adaptation and Original Song Score, and to Gordon K. McCallum and David Hildyard for sound.

I had asked Isaac Stern to accompany Pat and me as our guest at the Awards ceremony. I thought then about a marvelous day in London, when Isaac came to record his opening solo. He arrived at the recording studio while John Williams was conducting the orchestra. Isaac grasped his violin case in his hand. He opened the case, and in it I saw there were two violins fitted so that there was one on either side of the case. I said, "You come prepared like a tennis player, just in case you break one racquet."

He said to me, "I'd better not break one, because they're both Stradivariuses." He then proceeded to record the violin solo that plays behind the main title of the film.

En route to the Awards ceremony, we talked about our chances of winning the Best Picture Award. Isaac said, "You're not going to win. You're just not going to win."

I replied optimistically, "You're dead wrong. We are going to win." I was completely crestfallen when *The French Connection* was announced as the winner. Losing the Academy Award, when one gets as close to it as we seemed to be, is a massive disappointment.

Norman Jewison had moved to London when we began preparations for *Fiddler on the Roof,* and he liked living there. He decided that he could function just as well from there as he did in California, and he remained in England for a long time afterward. Pat Palmer from our company joined him and also moved to London, as did Larry de Waay, and they became the nucleus of a production group that he formed there. *Fiddler on the Roof* was the last film that we made together.

≈

The second of the two films we released in 1971 was *The Organization,* directed by Don Medford and written by James R. Webb. We had done reasonably well with *They Call Me MISTER Tibbs!* and we still had another option for a Virgil Tibbs picture with Sidney Poitier. I discussed creating a new Virgil Tibbs film with Jim Webb. He, Sidney, and I met and brainstormed a framework for a new film, and Jim went off and eventually produced the script for *The Organization.* It revolves around an attempt to break up a heroin-smuggling syndicate by a group of young people who have all been victimized by it and have sought the help of Detective Virgil Tibbs.

I was creatively disappointed in *They Call Me MISTER Tibbs!* and thought that we could do a lot better, and I believe we did in *The Organization.* We chose Don Medford, who had been one of the most successful directors of melodrama in television, to direct. We shot the film, in its entirety, in San Francisco. Raul Julia, Ron O'Neal, Allen Garfield, Sheree North, Dan Travanti, and Barbara McNair played major supporting roles. I was able to be present during most of the shooting, usually commuting between San Francisco and Los Angeles on weekends. The film was generally untroubled in its production phase.

However, after we looked at the first cut, I decided to shoot an additional scene, which we incorporated as a flashback in order to clarify the plot. I wanted to do it as inexpensively as possible, and we finally shot the scene using my office as a set, and it worked just fine.

The Organization was well received and went on to become a profitable film.

31

Goodbye to United Artists

The year 1971 had produced a decided upturn for The Mirisch Corporation. Our output, up to this time in our then-operative United Artists contract, had been most disappointing, but the profits from *Fiddler on the Roof* were so high that it turned the whole deal around.

The Magnificent Seven Ride, released in 1972, is guilty of most of the things sequels are accused of. It is a bald attempt to cash in once more on the mystique of the title and the past success of its formula. We had not been able to secure approvals on a number of projects that we had submitted to the then-current management of United Artists, and it had been three years since we had made a *Magnificent Seven* film. Since five more films remained to be made to fulfill our output requirements under our deal, I suggested that we attempt another, much less expensive, sequel.

The budget was set at $750,000, and we secured the services of Lee Van Cleef, who had acted in many Westerns, mainly playing heavies, but who now had developed a considerable following in the so-called Italian spaghetti Western genre. Having aged somewhat, he had become a more sympathetic character. We felt, with his following as a Western actor, particularly abroad, that he could carry off the Chris role.

The script was written by Arthur Rowe and was directed by George McCowan, a television director. The exteriors were shot in the Los Angeles area. The Mexican town shown in the film was a leased standing set on the Universal back lot. The plot followed the usual formula, and the film was shot on a short schedule. It was poorly reviewed and is not a picture of which I am proud, but it was again profitable, mainly because it was produced so inexpensively. Clearly there was still some of the mystique left in the franchise that was intriguing enough to audiences, not only in the United States but also throughout the world. The foreign market, as it had been from the beginning, was the principal customer for the *Magnificent Seven* pictures. It was a purely commercial venture. We limited its risks, but at the same time we also limited its potential.

United Artists was still reeling from its nearly $100 million loss in 1970, and the company pulled the reins in tightly on The Mirisch Company. It was already quite evident to me that the seventeen-year relationship between United Artists and The Mirisch Company would soon come to an end. The confluence of an extremely bad period for the entire industry, 1969 through 1971, and a generally unsuccessful group of our own films, with the exception of *Fiddler on the Roof,* as well as the changing of the guard at United Artists, indicated that the time had come for us to look elsewhere for a new home.

United Artists' new management obviously preferred to deal directly with the directors whom we had kept under our roof, thereby eliminating one of The Mirisch Company's functions. At the same time, it kept insisting that we cut overhead, which made it difficult to continue the directors' housekeeping deals. However, since we had come to the end of our contract, it was time to open negotiations for a new arrangement, if in fact there was to be one.

United Artists made a proposal to us. We felt that the fees it offered were not as high as they should have been. Our earlier arrangement had given us a participation in the overall gross of our films, be they profitable or nonprofitable. Now UA proposed profit participations that would be based on two-picture cross-collateralizations. This led to an interim agreement between us to modify our old contract and change immediately to a two-picture cross-collateralization plan on the last four films still remaining on the contract then in force.

Earlier when we had agreed that we would produce *Fiddler on the Roof,* and that we would supply the services of Norman Jewison to direct, UA proposed making it a stand-free picture. *Fiddler on the Roof* was then taken out of the overall group of pictures made under our contract, and we signed a one-picture deal for the film. Because it was clearly going to be an expensive film, we agreed that we would take no fee for producing it. Furthermore, we agreed to accept an un-cross-collateralized 15 percent profit participation in the film. We sold our 15 percent interest in *Fiddler on the Roof* to United Artists some years later for $2.25 million, an amount that we would never have received if it had been in the overall package. The *Fiddler* deal worked out well for us, as did the two-picture cross-collateralization, which also redounded to our benefit and UA's detriment.

Following the change in our deal, we made three films for United Artists, *Scorpio, The Spikes Gang,* and *Mr. Majestyk.* The first two were cross-collateralized and unprofitable. The third, which stood alone, proved to be very profitable.

As our relationship with United Artists was fracturing, Mark Rydell was offered a film at Warner Bros. that he wanted to do, *The Cowboys* with John Wayne. He accepted the picture. He had been developing a script for us, *The Bank Robbers,* which eventually became *The Spikes Gang.* When Rydell left to do *The Cowboys,* the project remained with us.

Norman Jewison had now gone off on his own. Our relationship with Billy Wilder had come to an end with *Avanti!* and the new United Artists executives pressured us to dismantle our organization and the overhead that our new director deals carried with them.

The estate of my brother Harold, who had been an equal partner in our company, still retained his interest in the United Artists deal. Marvin and I felt that we needed to complete this contract, so that Harold's estate would not be deprived of any salary or percentage that he was entitled to receive under that contract. Consequently, we didn't try to settle it or do anything that would in any way reduce what his participation would be. We opted to finish the delivery requirements of that contract, changing the profit participation on those last three pictures from the gross participation to a 50 percent profit participation in groups of two.

Our permanent overhead was scaled down. Al Wood, our overall production manager, had been succeeded by Ed Morey Jr. In our legal and business-affairs department, Ray Kurtzman had been succeeded by Morton Smithline. The rest of our overhead had traditionally fluctuated, depending on the amount of production in which we were involved at any particular time. That overhead cost was absorbed in a 5 percent charge that we made to all our films. Generally that charge more than covered the amount of our overhead. In line with the new United Artists arrangement, our whole operation was cut back. Our people moved on and made films for other people. The handwriting was clearly on the wall.

In the midst of all this turmoil, the Samuel Goldwyn Studio was devastated by a terrible fire on May 7, 1974. My office was on the lower floor of the Writers Building. Shortly after returning from lunch, I was at my desk when my secretary of twenty-five years, Jessie Ponitz, came into my office and said, "There's a fire on a soundstage, and I think we'd better get out of here."

There had been fires on the lot at other times, and unexcitedly, I said, "Oh, okay, they'll put it out."

She said, "No, you don't understand. This is a bad one."

So I got up from my chair and walked out the door, and what I saw was frightening. Flames were shooting out of the roof of a soundstage that was about fifty feet across a small street from my office. We looked at it for a moment and watched giant flames rise into the sky, when a wind came by and blew them onto the roof of another soundstage, where it immediately ignited. By now, all of our people were out of their offices and watching with us. I shouted, "Let's all get out of here."

We ran out of the studio, moved a block away, and watched the fire consume much of the property. I finally managed to get home somehow, but I drove back again that night to view the damage. The smoking embers looked like a post-battle scene from World War II.

The next day, I went to the studio with Drew and Larry to comb through the ashes and see how extensive the damage had been. In my office, I had hung the original artwork for the posters of some of our films. There were the original paintings from which the *West Side Story* and *Fiddler on the Roof* art campaigns were done, as well as a half-dozen others that I thought were good pieces of art and, even more than that, were especially meaningful to me. They were all destroyed, although I did succeed in having the *Fiddler on the Roof* painting restored. A great many of our files containing business records were destroyed, either by fire or by water. A lot of other meaningful personal mementos were lost forever. My *In the Heat of the Night* Oscar had its head sheared off, but fortunately that could be replaced.

Billy Wilder, an avid collector, had a great deal of wonderful memorabilia in his office, which was damaged even more than mine. In addition, a storeroom located in one of the destroyed stages had been given to him for his personal use, and he had been storing memorabilia, furniture, artwork, curios, everything from a lifetime of collecting. All was destroyed. It was tragic. That next day, he and his wife came down to view the wreckage, and I deeply empathized with them. However, since no one was seriously hurt in the fire, we still had much for which to be grateful.

≈

To fulfill one of the last remaining commitments under our contract with United Artists, I proposed a project, *Dangerfield,* which later had its title changed to *Scorpio.* David Rintels, a friend, had written the original script and submitted it to me. *Dangerfield* was the story of a veteran assassin for the U.S. Central Intelligence Agency who has been training a young man to become his successor. Early in the story, the young man is given the assignment by his CIA superiors to assassinate his mentor. It was a good script, and I made a strong effort to get the picture made.

I tried a number of casting combinations, and finally I came close to casting Rod Steiger as the older man and Ryan O'Neal as his protégé. Unfortunately, we couldn't agree on the terms of a deal with their agents, and so that combination fell apart.

David Picker suggested Burt Lancaster to me and told me that United Artists had a commitment with Lancaster, which would be assigned to us. After much canvassing of the field, the idea of casting Alain Delon as the younger man emerged. And in a rather complicated transatlantic negotiation, we were finally able to make a deal with him.

David Picker then suggested Michael Winner to direct. I had met Winner before and had discussed other projects with him, but I had grave misgivings about Michael doing the picture. I expressed this to David, but he put a great deal of pressure on me to agree to the idea. I finally agreed and began meeting with Winner to discuss the Rintels screenplay. He had many objections to the script. I brought in David Rintels, so that he could work with us and perhaps accommodate some of Michael's concerns, but none of that satisfied Michael. He wanted to bring in his own favored writer, Gerald Wilson, and finally told me that he didn't feel that Rintels could accomplish what he thought needed to be done.

I met with Winner and Wilson, and I disagreed strongly with a lot of things that they wanted to do. I finally told David Picker that I wasn't agreeable to what Winner wanted to do with the script, and I felt that we should replace him.

This developed into a serious quarrel between David and me. I met with Burt Lancaster and told him my concerns about Michael. I felt someone, probably David, had talked to Burt about the disagreement before I had, and he voiced strong support for Michael. I had hoped to get Burt to agree with me, but I found that he was on Winner's side. They had done *Lawman* together, and that may have been a good experience for him.

In any event, David Picker finally proposed that I step back from the picture and let Michael make the changes that he wanted, with Wilson. By now, I was completely frustrated. I felt abandoned, and I agreed to David's request. I didn't want to give up the picture, because I wanted it to be included in our quota of films, but I was very angry. As a result, I was uninvolved in the production phase of *Scorpio*. Winner directed the picture without any supervision by me.

This was the first time a schism like this had ever happened during the course of our entire fifteen-year relationship with United Artists, and it really was the straw that broke the camel's back, as far as I was concerned. I felt I had not been supported, and given the long history of our relationship with United Artists, I felt that I should have been. The film was made and wasn't particularly well reviewed or commercially successful. Although *Scorpio* bore the credit "Produced by Walter Mirisch," my contribution was limited to initiating the project, working on the Rintels script, and casting the two stars.

I now moved on to *The Spikes Gang*. The script had been written by the husband-and-wife team of Irving Ravetch and Harriet Frank. It was a Western, but hopefully a Western with heart. The script was left behind when Mark Rydell moved on to Warners. I submitted it to Richard Fleischer, a director who had been a personal friend for many years. Although we had never had an opportunity to work together before, we wanted to, and he agreed to do the film. We were fortunate enough to get what we thought was an excellent cast, namely Lee Marvin, who by then had won an Academy Award for *Cat Ballou* and had starred in many other outstanding films. The Harry Spikes character was perfect for Lee. We believed that if the film could be produced at a reasonable price, with Lee Marvin and some good young actors, we would have a chance to have a somewhat different kind of Western. We cast Ron Howard and Charlie Martin Smith, who had been in *American Graffiti,* as well as Gary Grimes, from *Summer of '42* and *The Culpepper Cattle Company,* to support Lee Marvin.

In the interest of economy, we decided to shoot the film in Spain, and I secured the services of my old friend Tom Pevsner, who had worked on many of our foreign films, to act as associate producer and production manager. We went to Madrid and organized the film there. Dick Fleischer was accustomed to working on foreign locations and had shot in Spain before. Happily, Ralph Winters agreed to edit the film.

We first shot exteriors and interiors in Madrid, then additional exteriors near Almería and Aguadulces, in the south of Spain, where many of the spaghetti Westerns had been made. The filming went well, and it was just about on budget, costing approximately $1.8 million. The picture was not well reviewed, and its commercial reception was not very good either.

I enjoyed the opportunity of working with Lee Marvin, however. I had been cautioned that he had a reputation as a two-fisted drinker. I talked to him about it before the start of the picture. I told him I'd been warned about working with him, and that we were trying to do something with this film, in terms of both quality and cost, and that I wouldn't brook that kind of behavior. He told me his drinking was a bigger problem for him than it was for me, but his life had settled down and he was now in a better place. He had recently married a woman whom he'd known since he was a young man. They had met again after each had been married to others, and they were now very happy together, and he wanted to keep it that way. On days when he wasn't scheduled to work, Lee would come to the set, get in a chair, and sit alongside me. I'd say, "What are you doing here? Why don't you go to town and do some shopping or something?"

He said, "No, I like to be here. I like to see the scenes that I'm not in. It helps me with the scenes that I am in." I felt that, perhaps, he felt safer there, and it kept him away from temptation.

It wasn't until about the last week of the picture that Lee became ill. He had started drinking, and we lost his services for a couple of days until he got over it. He came back to work quite sheepish and rather apologetic. We were able to work around him while he was away, and it didn't become a serious problem for us.

A year or so earlier, an agent, H. N. Swanson, had given me an outline of about twenty pages of a story, *Mr. Majestyk*, written by the novelist Elmore Leonard. At the time, Leonard didn't have the reputation that he has today, but he wrote just as well. *Mr. Majestyk* is the story of a struggling melon grower in Colorado who is arrested on a minor charge and is caught in a shootout staged by a gang to rescue their leader while he is being transported to prison. Majestyk foils the gangster's escape by pretending to assist him, but the gangster evades his jail sentence and vows vengeance on Majestyk. The latter is finally able to turn the tables on his pursuer and bring him to justice.

I saw *Mr. Majestyk* as a project for Steve McQueen. I had a good relationship with Steve, and I persuaded United Artists to make a deal with Elmore Leonard to write a screenplay based on his original story. Over a period of time I tried to get Steve McQueen interested in the project, but I couldn't get him to commit. I finally accepted the fact that I needed to move on to someone else.

While I was in Spain working on *The Spikes Gang*, I called Paul Kohner, who represented Charles Bronson, and I told him that I thought that *Mr. Majestyk* would be an excellent vehicle for his client, hoping that he and Charlie would agree. It had been many years since I had worked with Charlie Bronson, going back to *The Magnificent Seven*, *The Great Escape*, and then later *Kid Galahad*, in which he had played Elvis Presley's boxing trainer. Charlie's career had taken an extraordinary upswing. Along with many other American actors, he had gone to Europe to work during this period and had appeared in a number of European films that were tailored for the American market. This followed the success of the spaghetti Westerns, which were probably the first films of this genre to make a real impact in the American market.

Charlie had worked abroad for a while until he appeared in a French film, *Rider on the Rain* or *Le Passager de la Pluie*, which was a big hit in Europe and subsequently in America. Charlie's stock as a leading action star rose quickly. He next played the leads in a couple of American films and had by now proved his ability to carry an action film.

Mr. Majestyk presented a role for which Charles Bronson was well suited, and I was anxious that he agree to play it, particularly because at that time I was hoping to complete our contractual obligations to United Artists as quickly as possible.

At approximately the same time, I acquired the rights to Arthur Hailey's novel *Wheels,* which I anticipated would be the last film produced under our United Artists agreement. I expected that *Mr. Majestyk* and *Wheels* would be the second two films to be cross-collateralized under our new arrangement.

Fortunately, Charlie responded well to the *Mr. Majestyk* script, and I was able to negotiate a deal with Paul Kohner for his services consonant with my concept for the production of the picture, which was to produce it at a cost of approximately $2 million. I was able to conclude a deal to pay Bronson $400,000 against 10 percent of the gross. However, because of his commitments in 1973, he needed to start shooting in September, which gave us only a short time for preparation.

I returned to Los Angeles to make the arrangements while we were shooting *The Spikes Gang* in Spain. After completing the deal for Bronson to appear in the picture, I returned to Spain and told Dick Fleischer that I would like him to direct *Mr. Majestyk* immediately after the conclusion of the shooting of *The Spikes Gang.* He had great misgivings about doing that. He was coming to the end of a long, difficult shoot, and he wasn't very enthusiastic about undertaking a second film immediately after the first. I told him that since we would be doing these films together, we could collaborate on the editing of *The Spikes Gang* while we were casting and preparing *Mr. Majestyk.* I felt the latter script was in good shape. Although Dick had some ideas, they weren't things that were going to take a great deal of time to implement. I further told him I was convinced that *Mr. Majestyk* was going to be a very profitable film. I thought he would be making a big mistake to pass it up, because it had the right star and the right subject matter, and I believed he was the right director for it. Despite his misgivings, Dick agreed to go along with this plan and segue immediately from one film to the next.

I asked Ralph Winters, who was editing *The Spikes Gang,* to edit *Mr. Majestyk,* and he found the problem equally difficult. I told him I was sure that he and his outstandingly talented co-editor, Frank

Urioste, could manage it. He also grudgingly agreed to go from one film to another.

Before we finished shooting in Spain, Jim Henderling, who had previously worked as production manager of many of our films, scouted locations for *Mr. Majestyk* and recommended an area in southern Colorado. Jim, Dick, and I did a final location search with the Colorado film commissioner, Carol Smith, and Paul Baxley, whom we had chosen to be our stunt coordinator. We wanted Paul to examine the locations where we would stage our chases. We settled on an area close to La Junta. Because watermelon was the main crop of that area, we substituted watermelons for the cantaloupe that our put-upon farmer-hero grew in the original story. The watermelons worked out well for us, because they were more photogenic and certainly a lot more dramatic when bullets were fired into them.

We selected a supporting cast headed by Linda Cristal, Al Lettieri, and Paul Koslo, and we chose Richard Kline to photograph the film before we took off for La Junta to begin production. The shooting proceeded well, except for some minor friction between Dick Fleischer and Charlie Bronson. Despite the rush to start the film, it was well prepared and the production was efficiently accomplished. Our editing unit managed to complete its work on *The Spikes Gang* and kept up with our dailies on *Mr. Majestyk*. The movie was shot entirely on location, and its final cost came in close to the $2 million figure that we had targeted.

🐦

Wheels was a bestseller by Arthur Hailey, author of *Airport* and *Hotel,* about the automobile industry, which was quite prominent in the headlines those days because of consumer advocate Ralph Nader's denunciation of imperfections in various car models. We prepared a script written by David Shaber, but the United Artists executives finally decided that they didn't want to go ahead with the project and agreed to cancel the last film called for in our contract. So, after seventeen years, we came to the end of our contractual agreements with United Artists.

32

Hello to Universal

Early in 1974, Marvin and I met with Arthur Krim, who had returned to resuscitate the management of UA, to discuss the possibility of a new arrangement. Surprisingly, he proposed a new contract based on the two-picture cross-collateralization formula. That proposal didn't bother us because, by this time, we preferred the idea of having an opportunity to enjoy the profits of successful films rather than the gross deal with multiple-picture cross-collateralizations under which we had worked for so long. I still felt that the fees he proposed were inadequate, but I was more concerned about our ability to get along well with the rest of the new management of United Artists. Clearly, Arthur Krim and Bob Benjamin were in the twilights of their careers. Primarily David Picker and Eric Pleskow would be making the production decisions. Furthermore, I also knew that there was a great deal of dissatisfaction on the part of the United Artists group with its Transamerica owners. That concerned me a great deal, and I began to think concretely about moving elsewhere.

My first thought was the possibility that Universal might be receptive to doing a deal with us. I had known Lew Wasserman, the president of MCA, the parent company of Universal, for many years and enjoyed a relationship with him on a nonprofessional level. Lew had invited me to join the board of directors of the Center Theater Group of the Los Angeles Music Center, of which he was the founding president. He was also very active in industry affairs and had asked Marvin and me from time to time to serve on various industry committees.

As chance would have it, my path ran across Taft Schreiber, an executive vice president of Universal, and he seemed aggressive about discussing the possibility of our moving over to the studio.

The initial discussions we had were with Taft Schreiber, but eventually he brought Lew Wasserman into the meetings, and then Lew brought Sid Sheinberg, his second-in-command, into the talks. They made a proposal for us to join Universal under a five-year production arrangement. The deal would involve guarantees of generous fees and a 50 percent interest in the profits of our films based on two-picture cross-collateralizations. I felt strongly that this was a move we should make, and Marvin agreed.

We informed Arthur Krim of our decision, and he wished us well. We had a long history with UA, and together we had created some extraordinary films. Since our first film, sixty-seven movies had been produced. We had shared many experiences, suffered a lot of heartache, and enjoyed a great deal of pleasure during that long association. But times had changed, and Arthur and his associates had their own problems, both with managing United Artists and its status as a subsidiary of Transamerica. It was not long after we severed our relationship with UA that Krim, Benjamin, Picker, Pleskow, and their whole management unit, in a corporate quarrel, resigned from United Artists and formed Orion Pictures, whose films would be financed and distributed by Warner Bros. Although there was no hint of any of this in our discussions, that issue had to have been in the back of Arthur Krim's mind when we talked.

On the other hand, Universal seemed to really want us, and it made us feel very much at home. At that time, Universal appeared to be interested in creating a group of production units that would supply the major number of films in its program. It had made deals with Hal Wallis, Zanuck and Brown, George Seaton, and Alfred Hitchcock, among others. Steven Spielberg was just on the verge of directing *Jaws*. Universal seemed to be a studio on the move, it was eager to have us, and I embarked on this new association most enthusiastically.

As we had not made a second film to be paired with *Mr. Majestyk,* it stood on its own, with the exception of the cross-collateralized write-off of the acquisition and development cost of *Wheels. Mr. Majestyk* proved to be very successful and confirmed the opinion I had expressed to Dick Fleischer when he agreed to assume its direction. When the results of its first foreign engagements came in, it became clear that *Mr. Majestyk* was going to be a hit, the first one we'd had since *Fiddler on the Roof* two years earlier. Eventually its film rentals grew to nearly ten times its $2 million cost.

We soon arranged the sale of the literary property *Wheels* to Universal, which produced it as an eight-hour miniseries starring Rock Hudson, and it became exceedingly successful. We thereby recovered all of our development costs on *Wheels,* and *Mr. Majestyk* stood entirely free of cross-collateralization. I was pleased that our last film for United Artists turned out to be so profitable for UA and for The Mirisch Company.

It required a considerable adjustment to pull up roots and start over again at Universal. I was then fifty-three years old, and Marvin was fifty-seven. In September 1974, Marvin and I, and our secretaries, moved into a bungalow on the Universal lot, in a complex of a large number of bungalows in which other production units were housed. Our deal with Universal was different from our United Artists arrangement, in that the studio would now be providing us with its production departments, its business affairs division, and its legal and accounting services, instead of our providing them ourselves. All of our personnel who had not already been discharged were now redundant. We were left to do the initiation, development, and supervision of our projects, subject to Universal approval. The studio bureaucracy would service them.

Jules Stein was the chairman of the board of MCA, Universal's parent company, Lew Wasserman was president, and Sid Sheinberg was in charge of production for Universal. We had made our original deal with Lew Wasserman. He asked me and Marvin to lunch one day with Sid Sheinberg and him. I had met Sid socially, but we now talked about creating the basis of a working relationship. I told him I wanted to talk to him as soon as possible about specific projects.

I also proposed the idea of creating another company, similar to what we had with United Artists, in which we would undertake to bring in a small group of directors and have the same kind of working arrangement with them as we had before. Clearly it would be more difficult to do this type of arrangement now, since the studio was trying to make those deals directly with the directors. Another difficulty was the fact that Universal charged 25 percent of the production cost to their pictures for overhead, while United Artists charged nothing. However, philosophically, Universal probably also wanted to remove us as middlemen in signing directors to prevent our competing with them.

I next inquired about their attitude toward the possibility of us continuing our relationship with Billy Wilder. Although his last group of films had not been commercially successful, my regard for him and his talents had not diminished. He had left us for the first time prior to the end of our United Artists contract because Universal had offered him *The Front Page*, a project he was eager to do. By the time we moved to the studio, Billy had preceded us there and was working on that film.

Sid Sheinberg said he wanted us to devote ourselves to producing a program of pictures, without seeking to create producer-director units within our company. The formerly integrated studios had by now mostly adopted the United Artists approach and were making their producer and producer-director deals directly. Sid Sheinberg's position didn't surprise or discourage me. In any event, there were a number of projects I was eager to do, and I proceeded to present them to Sid.

In my original discussions with Sid Sheinberg I had proposed the idea of *Midway*, based on the script I had commissioned from Don Sanford many years earlier. My faith in that project had never diminished, despite its many rejections by United Artists, and I hoped to revive it now at Universal.

The inspiration for *Midway*, like *The First Texan, Wichita,* and *The Warriors,* came from my avocation as an avid reader of history. I had read most of the significant works on the American Civil War and on World War II. However, the germination of the *Midway* idea undoubtedly went back to the film *Flat Top*, produced for Allied Artists in the early 1950s, and my experience in the physical production of that picture.

A history of the battle of Midway appeared in 1967, entitled *Incredible Victory* by Walter Lord. It was a remarkable narrative about an extraordinary event, namely the battle that was the turning point of the war in the Pacific. After the Japanese attack on Pearl Harbor, the American fleet, badly decimated, remained on the defensive from December 1941 until the American victory at Midway in June 1942. At that point, a huge defeat was inflicted on the Japanese fleet by the American Navy, following which the Americans began their island-hopping war across the Pacific.

John Ford had made a documentary during the war, titled *The Battle of Midway*. However, Louis de Rochemont produced a more outstanding Navy documentary, *The Fighting Lady*. It incorporated great battle footage and had a marvelous feel of the whole milieu in which the battle was fought. *Incredible Victory* reminded me that there was a really fascinating story to tell about Midway. But United Artists felt that there was no longer much interest in World War II for young audiences, that dogfights had become rather tame when compared to supersonic aircraft and rocket attacks, and that the time had simply passed for that genre of film.

At that time I put the idea aside and became involved in the preparation of the low-budget British quota military-service pictures that we produced. Among the writers who worked on these was Donald Sanford, to whom I told my idea about the battle of Midway and my conviction that it could become the basis of an exciting film. He embraced the idea, and I decided to employ him to write a screenplay at my own expense.

I told United Artists that I was going to have this screenplay written, and that we would submit it to them after it was completed. My original idea was to do it in strictly documentary fashion, without having a personal story. This marked the only instance, during the whole period of our relationship with United Artists, that I financed a script apart from our deal with them. I felt that after it was completed, I could convince them of the merits of the project.

About this time, 1968, I read that Twentieth Century-Fox was going to undertake a picture based on the story of Pearl Harbor. I realized immediately that the appearance of this film would make *Midway* redundant, since the backgrounds were so similar. I still felt strongly that my idea was better than theirs, because they were telling the story of a tragic American defeat, and I wanted to tell the story of a great American victory. When Don Sanford's screenplay was completed, I presented it to United Artists, but by then *Tora! Tora! Tora!* was in the offing, and UA again vetoed the project. *Tora! Tora! Tora!* appeared and was commercially disappointing, which seemed to validate United Artists' position. It cost about $25 million in 1970, a huge amount of money.

In 1969, while producing *The Hawaiians,* I developed a friendship with Charlton Heston, who played the lead in that film. In one of our many conversations, I discussed my *Midway* idea with him. Chuck, also an avid reader of history, was fascinated with the idea and evinced an interest in being a part of the project. Heston's interest led me to the idea that perhaps I should dramatize the story to the extent of adding a fictional character, one who would become a protagonist. This role could be played by Chuck and might facilitate the acceptability of the film to a financier.

As fortune would have it, there was a motion-picture industry conference called by President Nixon in 1971, at the president's compound in San Clemente, California. I was among the people who were invited to the meeting, and so was Charlton Heston. We made an arrangement whereby he would pick me up and drive us to San Clemente. On that trip we again discussed *Midway,* and I decided it was time to look at it once more. I gave the screenplay to Chuck, and again we began to talk seriously about doing the film.

Since the script was developed outside of the United Artists deal, without UA investment, it was a project that I could immediately deal with when I discussed an arrangement with another company. Consequently it became the first project I mentioned to Sid Sheinberg. The second was a book, *Wild Card,* a suspense melodrama with spy overtones. Universal agreed to acquire the rights to *Wild Card* for me, and I secured the services of Elmore Leonard to write its screenplay.

I gave the *Midway* script to Sid Sheinberg and also asked him to look at the Navy documentary, *The Fighting Lady,* in order to give him a sense of the period and the feel of the movie. Like everyone else, he was put off by the potential cost of such a film. The high cost of *Tora! Tora! Tora!* and its commercial failure were well known throughout the industry. I explained to him that I thought that the most important part of the film was not necessarily the hardware but the extraordinary combination of circumstances that could turn an encounter between two huge forces into an incredible victory for one and a devastating defeat for the other. The Midway story shows graphically how a number of chance happenings turned this crucial battle completely around.

I further explained the concept of using actual footage that existed in the naval archives for the action sequences in the film. I knew what existed because I remembered what we had used years before in *Flat Top*. And I felt that the technical ability to convert the navy's original 16mm Kodachrome into 35mm film had improved so enormously over the ensuing years that we could get far better results than had ever been achieved before. From the outset, I intended to put a disclaimer on the front of the picture and say that, wherever possible, we had used actual footage of the battle.

I think to assuage me, Sid Sheinberg agreed that if we could get a major star to appear in the picture, and if the budget was within reasonable parameters, he would approve the production of the picture. I asked Sid if Charlton Heston, who had just played the leading role in Universal's highly successful film *Earthquake,* would be acceptable to play the lead. He replied that he would be. I made a phone call, and Chuck immediately agreed.

I chose Bill Gray, a production manager who had worked for many years for Hal Wallis, to join the project, and I explained to him how I wanted to produce it. I ran *Flat Top* to give him a sense of how that picture had been accomplished. He said to me, "I know who should be the production designer for this film."

This was a key decision. He suggested Walter Tyler, who truly did a yeoman job for us. Walter had extensive experience at Paramount, where he had done both inexpensive pictures and spectacles, including *The Ten Commandments.* He immediately grasped the concept, and we began to plan the picture together.

I elicited the help of the Navy Department, which was essential. They were most enthusiastic. The victory at Midway is one of the great events in the history of the U.S. Navy, and they quickly embraced the project. I knew by then that the aircraft carrier *Lexington,* a World War II flat top, was still in service as a training carrier. I asked for the right to use it, and the request was granted, under certain conditions. They also agreed to open their archives for us to select the film that we wanted. Given the approach I had laid out, and its implementation in Walter Tyler's designs and sketches, we arrived at a budget of approximately $5 million.

To direct, I chose John Guillermin, who had been responsible for *The Towering Inferno,* a huge success. I had known John for some time. When he accepted the film, I agreed to make changes with him in the screenplay. I employed Stirling Silliphant to do a rewrite of the Don Sanford script, with input from John, Chuck Heston, and myself.

I had earlier considered the idea of using cameo actors. As we came closer to production, I became more convinced that the importance of the film, and its size, would be greatly enhanced by a judicious use of star names. I had, for a long time, been obsessed with the idea that it was only Henry Fonda who could play Admiral Nimitz, and I offered the role to him. With a great deal of relief and excitement, I received the news that Fonda would be pleased to play the role, and we made a reasonable financial arrangement with him.

I then began to isolate the roles in the film that I thought lent themselves to cameos. I decided that I would try to tailor certain roles in such a way that they wouldn't require much time on the part of the actors. The roles for which I sought cameo stars had been scheduled so that they would require only one day's work. I contacted some of the stars who had appeared in our films over the years and said, "I'd like you to do something for me." Some of the stars politely declined. But all of those who agreed to appear in the picture for one day were people who had worked with me before.

We were able to make a reasonable deal with Glenn Ford to play a longer role, that of Admiral Spruance. It required him to go to sea with us aboard the *Lexington*. We also made a reasonable deal with Hal Holbrook, who was always my first choice to play the code breaker, Commander Joe Rochefort. By that time we had an exciting combination.

We tried hard, and with almost complete success, to cast all of the Japanese roles with actors of Japanese ancestry. I decided to make an attempt to secure the services of the famous Japanese star Toshiro Mifune to play Admiral Isoruku Yamamoto, the commander-in-chief of the Japanese fleet. Mifune had twice before portrayed Yamamoto in films produced in Japan, first in *Yamamoto Isoruku,* released in 1968, and later in *Gunbatsu,* released in 1970. I initiated discussions with Mifune in Japan and was fortunate enough to be able to make a deal with him.

I also screened numerous Japanese films that were made about the Pacific war. I found one, *Taiheiyo no arashi (Storm over the Pacific),* that had some material that would be useful for establishing shots. I started negotiations with Toho, the company that owned *Storm over the Pacific,* and was able to acquire the rights to select whatever footage I wanted from its movie.

By this time, I was developing some serious problems with John Guillermin, who complained that Bill Gray simply wasn't giving him enough of what he thought he would require, in terms of both time and equipment. He felt he needed many more airplanes than had been budgeted. As we tried to cost out the requests that John was making, we found that they would add considerably to the budget. I was concerned that John's requests would just be the beginning of the film growing far beyond the concept that I had originally propounded and had sold to Universal. I didn't want to begin my association with Universal with a film that was considerably over budget. Nor did I want to lose John Guillermin. He was a very good director and was well suited to the picture. But finally I threw down the gauntlet and said, "We can't accede to your requests, and you've got to do it this way or else you shouldn't do it." I had hoped he would say, "Okay." But he didn't. So we lost our director about two months before the start of production.

Again I faced a most stressful time, in not having a director so close to our start date. After many phone calls and conversations, the idea of employing Jack Smight was suggested. Among other films he had directed were *Harper* with Paul Newman, *Rabbit Run,* and, most recently, *Airport 1975* for Universal. I had a long conversation with Jack and attempted to orient him to what we were setting out to do with *Midway.* He became enthused about the project and agreed to do the film. Stirling Silliphant remained with us and continued to do further rewriting.

It was our plan to begin production aboard the aircraft carrier *Lexington,* stationed at Pensacola, Florida. Its naval mission was to go out into the Gulf of Mexico on biweekly cruises, where student pilots who were in the Naval Training Schools at Pensacola and at Corpus Christi could practice their day and night landings and takeoffs at sea. We arranged with the navy that we would go to sea aboard the *Lexington* while it was on one of these training missions, and that we would plan to do our work while the ship's company was doing other things. We would not ask to use any of the areas that were involved in their exercises but would limit ourselves to wherever we could work, while they weren't using those facilities. We arranged to bring a limited number of World War II-vintage navy fighter planes aboard the vessel. These aircraft were leased from their owners through the Confederate Air Force, which is made up of collectors of antique airplanes. We had a detailed contract with the navy, in which we agreed to stay out of their way whenever asked. They charged us for housing aboard the ship and for meals, and there was a schedule of what we paid them for any of their equipment that we used. Everything was carefully accounted for.

On this particular cruise, the *Lexington* concentrated on training its student pilots in night landings and takeoffs. That left the days on the flight decks free. We also shot in the wardrooms, passageways, the bridge, and other spaces that could be cleared for us. To help us coordinate with the navy, and also to act as a technical advisor, we employed a retired vice admiral, Bernard Strean, who was tremendously helpful.

Our group arrived in Pensacola and moved onto the *Lexington*, where our people had been assigned quarters; we all settled down, waiting to go to sea. By two o'clock in the morning on our first night out, the student pilots who were flying out of Corpus Christi were landing on the deck right over my head! It made sleeping difficult when, at regular intervals, these planes slammed onto the deck.

I finally gave up trying to sleep and went up on the bridge, where I stood next to the "flight boss," who controls the landings of the planes. He showed me how to judge the radar screen that was in front of us to track the incoming planes by the blips on the screen.

Some of the planes didn't make their landings on their first pass, some on their second, third, or fourth. He showed me how one could tell by the arc of the blips whether or not the planes would be able to make the landings or would bounce off the deck.

The next day I told Admiral Strean of my sleeping problem, and I said, "How did you do?"

He said, "Oh, I slept great. Why don't you come and bunk with me?"

I replied, "Thanks, I'll be fine," anticipating the two of us crowded into a somewhat larger space than my own.

He insisted on escorting me to the admiral's quarters, which are reserved for such times as the carrier may have a flag officer on board. He had two rooms, a galley, and beds, not bunks! So I quickly moved in with Admiral Strean, and I was fine after that. More important, the filming went well while we were at sea. We shot scenes, silent and with dialogue. We made plates for rearview projection and aerial shots of our vintage planes so positioned that we could print them into flights of six or nine.

We had needed an amphibious PBY and were able to find one in the fire department of a small California city. It served us well. Admiral Strean told me that the planes that we had leased from the Confederate Air Force looked to him as if they were in better shape than when they flew in combat, since they had all been so meticulously taken care of by their doting owners.

I had a marvelous time aboard the *Lexington*, and this proved to be one of the most enjoyable locations I have ever been on. The weather was perfect. The shooting went well. The food was great. The navy personnel, who were fascinated by what we were doing, were wonderful and worked hard during the week we were at sea. We accomplished a great deal of important shooting. Of the principal cast members, Charlton Heston, Glenn Ford, and Edward Albert went to sea with us, while Henry Fonda met us in Pensacola for the scene at the end of the picture when he's on the pier after the carrier has returned to port.

After finishing our cruise and completing the shots that had been scheduled aboard the *Lexington*, we returned to Pensacola to shoot the concluding sequence with Henry Fonda and Hal Holbrook. I had dinner with Henry Fonda on the first night that he arrived at Pensacola. He told me that he had experienced a bumpy airplane flight, and since he had an early call the next day, he was looking forward to a good night's sleep. We called it an evening rather early and went to our rooms at the motel in which we were staying.

Very early in the morning I was awakened by band music. I immediately thought of Henry Fonda, also being awakened. I got myself together to see what was going on outside, as did he. The two of us walked out to the front of the motel, where we were met by an oncoming parade, composed of large groups of men, dressed in black, riding motorcycles, wearing black helmets, all very formidable looking. We recognized banners telling us that this was a parade of the Ku Klux Klan. Not having spent much time in the South, we didn't realize that the Klan had parades of this sort. We soon set out for the dock to do our work for the day.

After completing our scheduled work in Pensacola, we returned to Los Angeles, where we did additional exterior shooting, mainly at

Long Beach and Point Dume. We then returned to the Universal Studio to begin shooting the interiors, as well as the process photography that constituted an important part of the film. We shot the bridges of both the American and the Japanese carriers and were now joined by Toshiro Mifune, who had come from Japan to play Admiral Yamamoto.

I was pleased to meet Mifune, whom I had enjoyed in many great Japanese films directed by Akira Kurosawa, most notably *The Seven Samurai,* which had played such an important role in my career. He was very courteous and brought me a gift from Japan, a ceremonial Japanese naval sword. He told me he hoped I wouldn't mind, but he had ordered his uniforms for the film to be made for him in Japan, by Japanese naval tailors, so that he could be certain that they were accurate in all details. When he presented me with the bill, I told him I was relieved to know that his uniforms were going to be absolutely authentic.

Unfortunately, his English enunciation disappointed me. I had been led to believe that it was better than it was. With a little difficulty, I was able to understand much of what he was saying. Miko Taka, an actress who had worked with him before, served as his interpreter. I asked her to work with him on his dialogue, so that it would be more comprehensible. She assured me she would do so. Unfortunately, it was never satisfactory, and ultimately we revoiced Mifune with another actor, Paul Frees.

Interestingly, Mifune proudly showed me his white ceremonial gloves that were part of his uniform and said, "You see how accurate I am?" He held up one hand, and I realized that the pinky of his hand was shortened. He explained to me that Admiral Yamamoto was missing a part of his pinky, and that his glove had been adjusted so that he could play the scene with that pinky missing.

We had a press reception for Mifune at a Japanese restaurant, Yamato, in Century City. At the party, I introduced Henry Fonda to Mifune, and Fonda was present when the discussion of the pinky took place. He then volunteered the information that he had been reading a number of biographies of Admiral Nimitz. Extraordinarily, Admiral Nimitz was also missing part of his pinky, which he had lost in a farm accident when he was a boy. The coincidence of these antagonists in a titanic naval battle sharing this dismemberment seemed amazing to me.

As our shooting proceeded into other interiors, we came to the scenes that utilized the work of those actors who had agreed to do one-day cameos for us. These included James Coburn, who played Captain Maddox, the naval officer who tries to convince Admiral Nimitz to avoid having a confrontation with the Japanese at Midway, and Robert Mitchum, who played Admiral William F. Halsey, immobilized in a hospital when he wanted to be out at sea and who added humor and punch to a scene that he played with Glenn Ford, who had the role of Admiral Raymond Spruance, a battleship admiral being given a carrier command for the first time. Robert Wagner was excellent as Admiral Nimitz's aide, and Cliff Robertson was perfect as Commander Jessup, the bigot in a scene at a bar with Charlton Heston, in which he discusses Heston's son's involvement with a Japanese girl. Other members of the cast included Tom Selleck, Dabney Coleman, Monte Markham, Christopher George, Ed Nelson, James Shigeta, Pat Morita, John Fujioka, and Robert Ito.

We were meticulous about the design of the Japanese carrier interiors, and I was flattered when, after the completion of the film, I was asked by the Smithsonian Institution if we would consider presenting our set to its Air and Space Museum. We agreed to do so, and it was shipped to Washington in sections and reassembled there.

We devoted a great deal of time, effort, and care to the front and rear projection sequences. We precut the sequences in which the naval archive film was being used. Our editors, Robert Swink and Frank Urioste, cut these sequences with "scene missing" cut in where the scenes with our actors would be interpolated. We also had prepared storyboards of all of those sequences. We kept the storyboards and a Moviola on the stage, and we photographed the specific pieces that were going to fit into the cutting plan of a particular sequence. We brought in more and more wind machines, aimed at our pilots, and blew more smoke through the scenes, as if it were coming from the engines, which brought the focus forward, away from the background plates. It also added movement, both in terms of air and smoke moving around the pilots, who were stationary.

I later was also able to secure a number of shots, not a great deal in terms of total amount of footage but exceedingly valuable, from *Tora! Tora! Tora!* that were used in the attack on Pearl Harbor. We used some of those shots for the attack on Midway Island.

I also acquired footage of the Doolittle raid on Tokyo from MGM, from *Thirty Seconds over Tokyo*, as background for our main titles. I was conflicted about whether or not to repeat that film. It had been twenty-odd years since the original picture had been shown, and I finally decided to use it after subjecting it to a sepia bath.

It had always been my intention to dupe the entire picture when it was completed, so that we could impart a grainy quality to our production film that would match the grain of the archival film and the stock footage. I went back a couple of generations, until I found one where I thought we were achieving a reasonable amount of success in blending all the film that had been used. What I was mainly interested in was telling the story well. If we could accomplish that, the fact that we could have spent many more millions to reproduce something that we were already able to put on the screen in a less costly way seemed indulgent to me. I was committed to producing the film at a given price, and I was beginning a relationship with a new company. I wanted to deliver the picture as close to that cost as I possibly could.

By this time, Universal had released *Earthquake,* which utilized a sound system called Sensurround, a system of speakers that are spaced in an auditorium so that enhanced sound will come from the direction in which it presumably does on the screen. We decided to use Sensurround in our film, and it proved to be valuable in enhancing the reality of the sounds of battle. It involved an installation of a special sound system in theaters, and most theaters agreed to it. Universal manufactured, or else contracted for the manufacture of, the Sensurround equipment and then arranged to lease it to theaters for the run of the engagement of the picture.

Finally, John Williams contributed a rousing, patriotic score. In later years, he often conducted the cue entitled "The Midway March" with the Boston Pops at Fourth of July celebrations at the shell on the Charles River.

Despite all of the naysayers who had told me that you couldn't make yet another World War II movie successfully, there was a great deal of excitement among exhibitors when the picture was announced. Undoubtedly, the all-star cast was a great selling point. Again, I was also pleased to find many veterans of World War II, particularly navy people, who were thrilled to see a re-creation of a great American victory.

The reviews were only mediocre, but the business was fabulous. We opened to huge grosses, all across the country. It became one of the highest-grossing films of 1976. When we opened the picture abroad, we were pleasantly surprised to find that it also proved to be a huge foreign grosser. The business in Japan was excellent, and surprisingly so for a film that is the story of a great Japanese defeat. After its immensely successful theatrical releases, both foreign and domestic, it went on to continued success in television and home video throughout the world.

After it had completed its theatrical release, Universal told us that they had been negotiating an arrangement to televise it on the NBC network, on the basis that the film would be lengthened so it could be run for four hours, including commercials, over two evenings. The studio told me that it had been offered a great deal of money to do this. Since this was still prior to the home-video revolution, the television sale appeared to be the last utilization of the film. I agreed in principle to the idea that we would lengthen the film so that it could be shown over two nights.

The lengthening process came during the period when I was spending a great deal of time abroad. I was, by then, involved in preparing and shooting *The Prisoner of Zenda* in Vienna back-to-back with *Dracula* in London. Universal assigned the elongation of the picture to its television staff. I had suggested that it might be well to add footage onto the front of the picture, so as to include the battle of the Coral Sea. Universal Television said they would prepare a draft of the new pages. They developed a lot of material that they sent to me in Europe, and I returned it with my comments. The process proved to be rancorous and highly ineffective. In the end, I thought the lengthening of the picture was poorly done. I kept trying to second-guess the process, but in the end I was told they were working against a deadline for the NBC showing. The running time was increased to three hours and ten minutes, in order to fill four hours on the air, which was accomplished mainly by adding whole new plotlines for Charlton Heston's character, Matt Garth. Jack Smight directed the additional material.

Though I was creatively displeased by what was done, I am guilty of having agreed to it. In all the years since then, when it is run on television, it is frequently run in that four-hour format because the television stations get two evenings out of it that way. I never anticipated that this version, which I actively dislike and thought would run twice and then disappear, would remain. It has undoubtedly been seen by many more people than have seen the original picture.

The year 1992 marked the fiftieth anniversary of the battle of Midway. I called Jeff Sagansky, who was in charge of the CBS network at the time, and suggested he program the film on the fiftieth anniversary of the battle. The picture had been in television syndication for about fifteen years by then. It was most extraordinary for a network to repeat a film of that vintage.

He became interested in the idea. The anniversary occurred in June, while all the networks are in their summer hiatuses, and CBS was looking for an event attraction. However, Sagansky said he would like to have a version that would fill three hours on the air. I welcomed the opportunity and re-edited the four-hour film. In my opinion, the three-hour version was a big improvement over the four-hour version, and it resulted in high ratings for the CBS network.

Midway has had a long life, and, despite a dwindling cadre of naval veterans and World War II buffs, it continues to play frequently on television. It has probably returned a greater multiple of its investment than most films that have ever been produced. Of all the films that I have made in my lifetime, it produced the greatest amount of profit.

≈

I'm sure that having produced a big naval film led agents to consider me a producer with a serious interest in naval subjects. So, in 1975, a script was submitted to me by agent Sylvia Hirsch, titled *Gray Lady Down,* the story of a nuclear submarine, disabled and resting on the bottom of the sea in crippled condition. I read the script and found it intriguing. It utilized a lot of information about rescue technology that had been developed in recent years, and it also presented a role for Charlton Heston. Having enjoyed working with the U.S. Navy, and wanting to do another film with Chuck Heston, I made arrangements to acquire the script, which had been written by a man, unknown to me, named James Whittaker.

We requested the cooperation of the Navy Department, and they agreed to make certain vessels available. I was encouraged about the project, particularly since it appeared that *Midway* was going to be so successful. I secured the services of an exceedingly successful television director, David Greene, to direct. I employed Howard Sackler to do a rewrite of the script, which Greene and I supervised. I also felt fortunate in being able to cast two excellent actors for two roles of great importance in the story: Stacy Keach and David Carradine.

At this juncture, I was contacted by a writer-producer whom I had known for a long time, Frank Rosenberg, who told me that he had worked for some time on a submarine story, and that somehow or other he had arranged to see a script of *Gray Lady Down*. They were virtually the same story. His script was based on a book, of which I hadn't known, entitled *Event 1000*.

This was a problem I hadn't encountered before, and I told him I would try to sort it out. When we did, it appeared quite possible that Whittaker had seen the script of *Event 1000* and had used some of it. We now negotiated to acquire all of Rosenberg's rights, so that we could proceed with our production. The Writers Guild ultimately arbitrated the writing credits and determined that the credits should read, "Screenplay by James Whittaker and Howard Sackler, adapted by Frank P. Rosenberg."

To prepare the picture for production, we built the interior of a nuclear submarine. It was our major set, with part of it built on a huge gimbal so that it could be tilted as the submarine fell out of control to the bottom of the sea.

We also required a great deal of special effects shooting of models in a tank. I arranged with Howard Anderson, a specialist in the field, to execute the shooting, and he photographed the models in a tank at the CBS studios. We worked for quite a while on those models, and, by and large, I was pleased with the results we achieved. By today's standards it was rudimentary, but it looked realistic and was achieved at a quite reasonable cost.

We went to San Diego and went to sea aboard a naval escort vessel, presumably monitoring the sunken submarine. The shooting went exceedingly well on our exteriors, and we then returned to the Universal studio to shoot the interiors.

Christopher Reeve made his film debut in *Gray Lady Down* in a minor role. Ned Beatty, Ronny Cox, Michael O'Keefe, and Rosemary Forsyth were also featured. Jerry Fielding composed the score, Steven Larner was the cinematographer, and Robert Swink again was the editor.

I thought *Gray Lady Down* was very effective as a male-oriented action picture, and it was reasonably successful commercially. It cost in

the neighborhood of $5.25 million to produce, and it returned about
$19 million.

I had read reviews of the play *Same Time, Next Year* when it opened on
Broadway starring Ellen Burstyn and Charles Grodin. It seemed like a
charming, witty, romantic comedy to me, and just the kind of change of
pace I was looking for after *Mr. Majestyk* and *Midway.* When we had
completed our location shooting in Pensacola on *Midway,* I went to
New York, en route back to Los Angeles, specifically to see a performance of the play. I was both moved and amused by it, and after the performance I had arranged to meet the producer, Morton Gottlieb. We
went to a restaurant where we discussed the possibilities of my acquiring the story for a motion picture, and he encouraged me to proceed.
He also arranged for me to meet Bernard Slade, the author of the play,
when I returned to Los Angeles.

I was fully aware of the criticism that had been leveled at the play,
namely that it was a one-joke story, or just an elongated TV sitcom. But
I felt it was more than that. Different from *Two for the Seesaw,* which
was also a two-person play, it presented a great opportunity for audience
identification. The characters in *Same Time, Next Year* were not very
different from the mass of our audience, whereas the two people in *Two
for the Seesaw* were more special. The people in *Same Time, Next Year*
were living out a fantasy of an ideal romantic relationship, immoral but
without any obligations or commitments, and I thought that was a wish
fulfillment that audiences would find intriguing. It is a look at a relationship that could be enriching and fulfilling without substantially af-
fecting the outward forms of the two people's lives.

Added to that was the effect on the couple of living through very special times. The audience was given an opportunity to place themselves
again in a particular historical period and compare where they were and
what they were doing, while our protagonists are reacting in their turn to
the youth revolution, the women's movement, and the Vietnam War. As
we see the effect of all the changes of those eras, it is also an emotional
history of the maturation of the protagonists, George and Doris.

Same Time, Next Year appealed to me on a number of levels; as an
amusing, bittersweet history of my own times and as a relatively simple

film to produce after the complexities of *Midway*. Because of that, however, it presented the potential of being a static talk piece. But I felt that its humor and excellent performances could overcome that problem.

At my urging, Universal agreed to acquire the rights to the play and also made a deal for Bernard Slade to write the screenplay. Slade had been a screenwriter, largely successful in television, where he had created *The Flying Nun* series.

The arrangement for the acquisition also provided that Morton Gottlieb would be a co-producer and share the producing credit. He is an endearing, amiable man, who had the same arrangement on *Sleuth*, the film produced from his previous Broadway production. I had never shared my producer credit before, but I acceded to his request. He was interested in learning about movie production and tried to be helpful in whatever way he could.

Since *Same Time, Next Year* was a two-character vehicle, I felt that it required two movie-star names, just as I had long ago with Shirley Mac-Laine and Robert Mitchum in *Two for the Seesaw*. Ellen Burstyn had won an Academy Award for *Alice Doesn't Live Here Anymore*, and I was eager to have her repeat her role in the film. Charles Grodin was excellent in the play, and I'm sure that he was put out with me for not casting him in the movie, but I felt it was necessary to secure a more recognizable name. That didn't happen too quickly. After being frustrated in an attempt to secure Warren Beatty, I decided to make an effort to acquire the services of Alan Alda, who, at that time, was near the zenith of his career starring in the smash television series *M*A*S*H*. Alan agreed to do the part. I was pleased, feeling he was ideally cast for the role of George.

After meticulously canvassing the directorial possibilities, I decided to offer the film to Robert Mulligan. I had always been impressed with Bob's careful attention to characterization, particularly in *To Kill a Mockingbird* and *Love from a Proper Stranger*, and I was delighted that he accepted.

Bernard Slade had told me that, when writing the play, he had visualized it taking place at a resort, the Heritage House, located at Little River, near Fort Bragg, California, which was not far from where we had shot the exteriors of *The Russians Are Coming, the Russians Are Coming*. Bob Mulligan and I scouted the location, and we became enthusiastic about it and its suitability to Bern Slade's screenplay. We chose Robert Surtees to be our cinematographer, Henry Bumstead to do our art direction, and Shelley Kahn to be our editor.

At the Heritage House, there is a main lodge, including a restaurant, and then there are separate bungalows that radiate out from the main lodge on two sides, going all the way down to a precipice, which looks out onto the Pacific Ocean. It's a beautiful spot. But there wasn't a bungalow built on the point of the cliff. They probably hadn't built on that site so that the view of the ocean from the other bungalows would not be obstructed. We decided that we wanted our bungalow to be on that point, so that our characters would be looking directly at a beautiful view of the ocean. Consequently, we arranged with the owners of the resort to allow us to build our own bungalow there. We agreed, however, that when the film was completed we would remove it, so that they could get their view back. So, with all the bungalows at the hotel, we Hollywood people, instead of choosing one, decided to build our own.

In the screenplay, we had opened up the story in a number of places so that we could show exteriors of the bungalow and its surrounding vistas, as well as the dining room of the resort and drives in and out. We also added a number of minor characters, just so there would be indications of life surrounding our principal players.

Shortly after I arrived on our location at the Heritage House, prior to shooting, I was surprised and thrilled to receive a telephone call from Howard W. Koch, who had succeeded me as president of the Academy, informing me that the Board of Governors had voted me the Irving G. Thalberg Award for 1978, for the "consistently high quality" of my motion-picture productions.

The Thalberg Award is the highest recognition that a producer can earn in an industry that has a plethora of awards and honors. I was deeply moved that the board of the Academy chose to honor me and, in doing so, to place my work alongside that of the small group of extraordinary filmmakers, such as Darryl Zanuck, David Selznick, Walt Disney, and Samuel Goldwyn, who had won the award before me. It was one of the high points of my career, and I looked forward to the presentation, which was to take place on March 29, 1978, at the Academy Awards ceremony at the Dorothy Chandler Pavilion.

Back in Little River, Pat and I were assigned a bungalow at the Heritage House, as were Morton Gottlieb and certain other members of our company, for our stay on the location, whereas the rest of our cast and crew were spread out in various hotels around the town. There wasn't any one place that was large enough to accommodate all of us.

When our company arrived, the framework of the cottage that we were building to use for the film had already been constructed. We knew that we had not chosen the best time of year, from the standpoint of weather, to be photographing there, but we hoped that, with a relatively limited number of exteriors, we would be able to complete our work before we suffered serious weather problems.

On the night of our arrival, I asked Ellen Burstyn to have dinner with Pat, Morton Gottlieb, and me at the Heritage House. When she arrived for dinner, she told me a most interesting story. She was staying at another small hotel, not far from us. She referred us to a speech that her character, Doris, has in the picture, which is verbatim in the play. George says to Doris, "After all the years that we've been meeting, I still know so little about you. I don't even know who your favorite movie stars are."

Ellen said that when she first rehearsed the line in the play, there was a group of names that Bernard Slade had supplied, such as Laurence Olivier and Gregory Peck and Cary Grant. She said to Slade, "You know, I'd like to feel that Doris is more myself, and I'd like to name my own particular favorites from when I was growing up." Slade agreed, and she added the name of a favorite movie star of hers, namely Lon McCallister, who had starred in a number of mainly rural films in the 1930s, 1940s, and 1950s. She said she always liked the speech better because of that.

Ellen then returned to her story and said that after she had checked into her hotel, the gentleman who had met her at the door brought her bags into her room and told her, if there was anything he could do for her, to simply call on him. He was the proprietor and would try to make her stay as pleasant as possible. She thanked him, and he said, "Call me if you need anything. My name is Lon McCallister."

Ellen was still so amazed by this extraordinary coincidence, as were we all, that I decided we were starting production under a propitious sign. However, as it turned out, our location shoot was subjected to almost continual rain delays, and as a consequence, we were forced to create our own cover sets. We finally constructed the complete interior of the cabin we had built, which had originally been constructed as solely an exterior, so that we could now work inside when it rained. Our stay at Little River was longer than we had originally anticipated, but we were delighted with our results.

With Bob Mulligan, a sensitive director, working with two consummate professionals—Ellen, who had been playing the role for a number of years on Broadway, and Alan Alda, a gentleman and an experienced stage actor, who had eight years of *M*A*S*H* behind him—we had a very happy company. I thought that Mulligan was doing an excellent job.

We returned to shoot additional interiors at the Universal studio. I was on the stage one day—shooting again in the interior of the bungalow, where much of the action of the picture takes place—talking with Ellen Burstyn about something while the crew was changing a setup. I sat on a sofa adjoining a chair on which she was sitting. There was a coffee table in front of us, and I noticed there were magazines there.

The prop man had seen to it that the magazines were from the particular period when the scene we were then shooting took place. Someone came on the set and wanted to ask me something, so I excused myself and turned my head away for a minute, and Ellen picked up a magazine. The person who had come in to talk to me left, and Ellen said to me, "You won't believe this."

I said, "Why? What's happened now?"

She said, "This is a *Time* magazine of 1968. As I was turning the pages, I noticed this toothpaste ad, and I'm the model." I looked at it, and a very young Ellen Burstyn, showing her beautiful white teeth, stared back at me.

We employed Charles Braverman and Ken Rudolph to create and execute the montages that gave us our historical transitions from one time period to another.

I wanted a song for the film, so I decided to contact Paul McCartney since the Beatles were so much a part of that era. I'd loved his song "Yesterday," which I thought had much of the feeling that I thought we should have. I reached him, through his attorney, and asked if he would be interested in doing a title song. The word came back that he would. We sent a rough cut of the picture to him in London, and he recorded a song that I thought was beautiful, called "Same Time, Next Year."

Bob Mulligan didn't like it, and we crossed swords about the song. Our difference of opinion was becoming very serious, until I thought it had finally become more a test of wills between us rather than about the merits of the song. Bob said he wanted a song with a different feeling, which he tried to verbalize. I wasn't clear about what the feeling was, except that it was going to be different. I decided the issue didn't justify becoming a cause célèbre, so we commissioned another song. Marvin Hamlisch, who had been signed to compose the score of the picture, wrote the song, with Marilyn and Alan Bergman supplying the lyrics, and Johnny Mathis and Jane Oliver sang it. It was titled "The Last Time I Felt Like This."

The critical and commercial reception to the movie was excellent. It cost approximately $5.25 million and returned film rental of about $27 million, an exceedingly healthy ratio of return on investment for the studio. The film received four Academy Award nominations, all of them in major categories: Ellen Burstyn was nominated as Best Actress, Bernard Slade's screenplay was nominated, as was Robert Surtees's cinematography and the song by Marvin Hamlisch and the Bergmans. Unfortunately, *Same Time, Next Year* won no Oscars.

☞

The Mirisch Company's relationship with Universal had developed beautifully in our first four years. *Midway* was hugely profitable, *Gray Lady Down* performed respectably, and the studio was enthused about what it had seen of *Same Time, Next Year.* Lew Wasserman had ascended to the chairmanship of the company, and Sid Sheinberg to the presidency. Ned Tanen was appointed the executive in charge of production. He told us that Universal wanted to extend our contract, and we negotiated a seven-year extension in 1978.

We had come through a period of three or four years at the end of the United Artists deal that were disappointing and had produced a large number of films that were unsuccessful. Now that we were holding a hot hand again, we felt the time was opportune to take advantage of a good relationship with Universal's management and accept the offer of a new seven-year deal.

Stanley Kramer, a member of the Board of Governors of the Academy in 1978, had been a Thalberg Award winner himself. He had asked Howard W. Koch, president of the Academy, if he could have the honor of presenting the Thalberg Award to me. I had known Stanley for a long time and respected his work. I would have preferred to have had someone who was more identified with my own career, such as Sidney Poitier, make the presentation to me, but I was too pleased to quibble.

And so, on March 29, 1978, Pat and I, with our children—Anne, now twenty-seven, with her husband, Greg, Drew, twenty-four, and Larry, twenty-one, and their guests—drove together to the Los Angeles Music Center. It was a reflective time, different from when we sweated out whether *In the Heat of the Night* or, three years later, *Fiddler on the Roof* would win the Best Picture Award. Now we talked of all the pictures and all the experiences, the triumphs and the tragedies, that had brought us to this occasion, to join the company of the extraordinary body of filmmakers who have been so honored by the Academy. It was almost overwhelming, and Pat and I were deeply moved by it. It was one of the great occasions of our lives. I regretted that my parents and my brothers Harold and Irving were not there, although their widows were my guests that night.

Although I had appeared on five previous shows, I was very nervous as I listened to Stanley Kramer make the presentation. I responded:

> Thank you, Stanley. Even though I'm one of the few people here to-night who has not been sweating out the opening of an envelope, I assure you this is one of the most deeply felt moments of my life. From the time I produced my first picture, I have always considered this award to be the highest recognition that can come to a member of my profession. So, thanks to the Board of Governors and the membership of the Academy. They have enriched my life beyond description. I also want to acknowledge the enormous contributions, both to my work and to whatever success I have had, that have been made by my brother, Marvin, and my late brother, Harold. They have been my indispensable collaborators from the very beginning. And then, my thanks go to all the talented producers, directors, writers, actors, actresses, and Jessie and the countless others who have been a part of all The Mirisch Company films. They all share this honor with me. These are exciting times for us filmmakers. There is now the widest possible diversity of subject matter available to us. Technical excellence is at an all-time high. Creative young people are entering our profession in all areas, and audience interest continues to grow. I am stimulated by my work as never before. I love this magnificent, aggravating, fascinating art-industry, and I pledge to do my utmost in the coming years, and in future films, to continue to merit your approval.

33

The Return of Peter Sellers

Peter Sellers's career, which had always been something of a roller coaster, had turned to the upside by the mid-1970s, largely due to the resuscitation of the Clouseau character in *The Return of the Pink Panther* in 1975. Peter was in Los Angeles in 1976, working in a film, when I called him and told him I wanted to talk to him about my idea to do a send-up of the classic Anthony Hope novel *The Prisoner of Zenda*, which had been made into the ultimate romantic film in the 1930s, with Ronald Colman and Madeleine Carroll. In the 1950s, MGM remade it with Stewart Granger and Deborah Kerr. I thought the idea of Peter doing a dual role again would be fun. He and I started talking about moving the story into a different milieu, and we became enthused about its possibilities. I told Universal the idea, and the studio approved it.

I chose a team of writers, Fred Freeman and Lawrence Cohen, to prepare a screenplay. I thought it was quite good, but Peter had reservations and suggested Ian La Frenais and Dick Clement, another team of writers with whom he had recently been working.

By this time, Peter had become impressed with Stan Dragoti, who had directed him in a television commercial, a genre in which Dragoti was very successful. I looked at a reel of his film, and I thought it was very good. I thought we could get something fresh and modern with Stan, and he joined our team. We all continued to work with La Frenais and Clement.

In the interim, Peter had married a beautiful young woman, Lynne Frederick. Lynne was about twenty-five years younger than Peter and had appeared in a few movies. Peter now became concerned about his appearance. He told me that he had made up his mind to have plastic surgery, which seemed to me the classic attempt of an older man trying to keep the love of a young wife. Peter, who had his first heart attack on *Kiss Me, Stupid,* had by now been implanted with a pacemaker for his cardiac problems, and he had to have it replaced on a couple of occasions. As we continued to work on the script, I realized Peter had begun to take the story much more seriously than we had originally conceived. He wanted his wife to play the female lead, and I began to feel it would be more Ronald Colman than Peter Sellers in the role. I had been trying to keep the script comedic, but Peter began to see himself as a romantic hero.

Next he had a falling out with Stan Dragoti and insisted he be dismissed. I told him I thought we should finish the script before choosing another director. I was sorry to lose Stan, because I thought he could give us a hip, funny picture, but you couldn't begin a picture with Peter Sellers, of all people, and a director he didn't want.

I next went to visit Peter in St. Tropez, where he had a house, and Ian and Dick, our writers, came along. We were going to do the final polish there. We spent two lovely weeks in St. Tropez. We stayed at a hotel and went to his house every day and worked a reasonable amount of time. Sometimes we'd go out on his boat with him and Lynne. It was a lovely combination work-vacation period. But we finally did hammer out a script.

While I was in St. Tropez, Peter told me how much he and Lynne were now looking forward to her playing Princess Flavia. I wasn't too troubled by this request, since she was an attractive young woman who had appeared in a number of films, and whom I judged to be perfectly adequate to the demands of the role. We also talked about the casting for some of the other parts. He wanted Graham Stark, an "old mate" of his, to be in the picture.

Then Peter told me that he had a marvelous idea. He had talked to Blake Edwards about our need for a director, and Blake had suggested to him that we employ Richard Quine, an old friend of Blake's who had directed many films, including *Solid Gold Cadillac, Bell, Book and Candle,* and *The World of Suzie Wong.* Unfortunately, his career had been in serious decline for about ten years.

Peter was gung ho about having Dick Quine do the picture, and I thought it might work, if Dick was still up to it. I told him I wanted to meet with Dick and discuss the project. Quine seemed well and happy and most enthusiastic at the prospect. At that juncture, it seemed like a happy solution to a difficult problem. He understood that we wanted to achieve a funny Peter Sellers picture, and he signed on to that concept. I spoke to Ned Tanen at Universal, and he agreed to sign Quine in February 1978.

We now commenced physical preparations for the picture. We sent a production manager to Vienna, where we hoped to shoot, and Clement and La Frenais continued to work with Dick Quine as we prepared for a summer start. About this time, I read of the highly successful opening on Broadway of *Dracula,* starring Frank Langella in a revival of the original play written by Hamilton Deane and John Balderston, based on Bram Stoker's novel. The play was now being presented, perhaps for the first time, with a devastatingly handsome, very romantic Dracula. That was the different element from Bela Lugosi's interpretation, to which we have all become so accustomed. I made it my business to see it at the first opportunity, bearing in mind that Universal probably still owned the rights to the original play, which it had bought many years before, when the studio produced it in 1931 with Lugosi. I thought that this romantic version of *Dracula,* beautifully played by Frank Langella, presented a way to do a version of the story that could now be tantalizing and erotic because of the romantic characterization of the vampire. I visualized opening the picture up beyond the play and utilizing the fright elements that are naturally a part of the story. But the key new ingredient was the devastatingly attractive Dracula, which I felt could again make it an exceedingly successful movie.

I discussed the project with Ned Tanen and asked that the studio confirm its ownership rights to the literary material. I told him that I would like to do the film after *Prisoner of Zenda.* We ascertained that Universal did, in fact, still own the motion-picture rights.

Ned recommended John Badham, a young director who was under contract to the studio and had heard about our project. John told Ned of his great enthusiasm for the project and asked to be considered for it.

I met with John, who had last directed *Saturday Night Fever*, and after a stimulating and agreeable meeting, we discussed possible writers. We finally agreed that we would employ W. D. "Walter" Richter. When Richter began to prepare a script of *Dracula*, I went off to Europe to supervise the preparation of *The Prisoner of Zenda*.

Dick Quine and I began to work in London with casting director Lesley De Petit. While we were interviewing actors, I became aware of the possible availability of Laurence Olivier to play the role of Professor Van Helsing in *Dracula*. I thought this casting could clearly elevate our film beyond the innumerable rip-offs of the original.

I contacted his agent, Laurie Evans, and arranged to meet with Olivier. I had heard that he had been ill, and I wanted to satisfy myself as to his health and his ability to meet the physical demands of the role. He agreed to meet me for drinks one day, and he came to my rooms at the Hotel Intercontinental at about five o'clock in the afternoon. It was the first time I had met him. He seemed vigorous, and we had a long and fascinating talk. He had, before this time, practiced his Dutch accent in *The Boys from Brazil*. He seemed eager to work, and I liked him immediately. We were Walter and Larry in short order. He was a marvelous raconteur, and I savored all the stories he offered. He told me that, in the 1930s, on the very spot on which the Intercontinental stood, there had been a building that had housed the headquarters of Alexander Korda, and that he himself once had an office there. "Perhaps on this very spot. Right down the hall from me, Winston Churchill also had an office, where he was trying to write a screen treatment of something for Alex." He also had a large repertoire of William Wyler and Samuel Goldwyn stories, going back to *Wuthering Heights*, that also particularly amused me.

If it was his intention to charm me, he certainly did, and I became eager to cast him. The negotiations were difficult and quite costly, but I thought his value to the film really justified the expense. There was a credit problem, which we finally worked out by giving Langella first credit and Olivier second in the same-sized type as Frank's.

Meanwhile, we had assembled a very good cast for *The Prisoner of Zenda*, made up of Peter Sellers, Lynne Frederick, Lionel Jeffries, Elke Sommer, Gregory Sierra, Jeremy Kemp, Catherine Schell, Simon Williams, and Stuart Wilson.

The screenplay, under Peter's influence, had gotten closer to the original novel, and a lot of the comic invention that had been in our original script had been lost. Sydney Frewin, the London cabbie hired to impersonate the King of Ruritania, tended to become more heroic and appealing, rather than funny. I talked with Dick Quine about my concerns, and how careful he had to be about that problem. Dick understood and made a real effort to try to move the picture toward a funnier and broader characterization from Peter. But in the end, he simply couldn't or wouldn't stand up to him.

I soon learned that Peter was talking to Quine about directing his next film, which was to be *The Fiendish Plot of Dr. Fu Manchu*. I suspected that Dick had begun to see a future in directing other Peter Sellers films and consequently was less apt to cross swords with him in directing his performance.

I continued to discuss my concerns with Peter myself, and he tried to reassure me by saying he knew what I was talking about, and if we followed his instincts we would get a great deal more comedy in the picture than I expected. Peter also complained of a certain amount of illness while we were shooting. He developed new problems with his pacemaker and required yet another replacement. This also led to a certain amount of delay.

We worked in a drafty old castle, Kreuzenstein, about one hour's driving distance from Vienna, and we also filmed at the Salzburg Cathedral and at the Schonbrunn Palace. The shooting there went quite slowly, and we fell seriously behind schedule. However, the picture was beautifully mounted by our production designer, John Lloyd, and well photographed by our cinematographer, Arthur Ibbetson. Peter and I didn't come to any serious open blows while we were shooting, but we did have some joustings, and the same is true of my relationship with Dick Quine, all because I didn't think the picture I was looking at in the dailies was as funny as it needed to be. Because of delays in starting production, we had gotten off to a later start than we had planned, and now, having fallen so far behind schedule, we risked being caught in an early Viennese winter. Rather than face that threat, we decided to return to California and finish the film at the Universal studio.

While the shooting was in progress in Vienna, I frequently made weekend trips to London, where I held *Dracula* casting sessions with

John Badham after he had arrived. I also worked with John and Peter Murton, our production designer. We chose our locations in Tintagel, Cornwall, and began to enlist our English crew.

By the time we finished production on *The Prisoner of Zenda*, my relations with both Peter and Richard Quine were quite strained. We now began the editing process. I had brought an American film editor, Byron Brandt, to Vienna. As we neared a fine cut, I decided to call in Ralph Winters, who had edited *The Pink Panther*, to work with us. Ralph had a lot of good ideas and helped considerably. I selected Henry Mancini to do the score.

We then needed Peter to loop, which means revoicing many of his speeches, and I arranged to run the cut film for him and Lynne one evening at the Universal studio so that he could see it prior to looping. I anticipated that he wouldn't like it, but his reaction was even worse than I had expected. He thought it had been badly cut, and we argued for a long time. Finally, I asked him to make notes for me, in order to compel him to move from generalities to specifics. He agreed, and shortly thereafter he sent me a long series of notes, most of which simply could not be executed because we didn't have the collateral film needed to make them, or because they were really poor ideas. I simply disagreed with them, and so did the editor.

I finally told him what I would do and what I wouldn't. He was furious at having any of his suggestions rejected, and he refused to loop. Under his contract he was legally obligated to perform, but he wouldn't do it. I employed an actor to try to imitate his voice, but the results were not acceptable. Finally, I decided to use some of our original tracks, improved as much as possible on the dubbing panel, or else we cut around completely unusable tracks. With the help of our editor and sound mixers, we made the best we could of a bad situation.

In the next development of this tempest, a package was delivered to me in a Dunhill box. The handwriting of the address led me to believe it had come from Peter, and I thought, "Oh good, a peace offering." So I opened the package, and I found lots of tissue-paper wrappings. At the bottom of it all I found a rubber penis!

Later, when the picture was released, Peter went on a morning talk show and said he didn't like the movie, and that I had ruined it. I was furious. I felt he had been completely unprofessional. If he didn't like the film, he should have declined going on the show. I certainly would never publicize my feelings about an actor to the detriment of a film. Richard Quine refused to get involved in the controversy and was nowhere to be found. I had experienced this behavior before with Peter on *Shot in the Dark*, which he also thought was unreleasable. But fortunately he didn't go to the press with his opinions that time.

The Prisoner of Zenda opened in the summer of 1979, and did poorly. It was a hurtful experience. I tried, as much as I could, to shape the film along the lines of our original concept during its production period, in its editing, and in its post-production stages. If its failure was my fault, it was not because I hadn't tried as hard as I could, even at the cost of destroying my relationship with Peter Sellers, to create the kind of picture that we had set out to make in the first place. If I made mistakes, they were mistakes of commission and not of omission.

I took small comfort from a good review of *The Prisoner of Zenda* by Janet Maslin in the *New York Times:*

> Mr. Sellers . . . performs a perfect balancing act, orchestrated so well that the funny character makes the serious one even more effective, and vice versa. *The Prisoner of Zenda* doesn't have the kind of finesse that Blake Edwards' direction has given the *Pink Panther* series, but the slack moments are painless enough and they come as a fair exchange for the pleasure of Mr. Sellers' artfully schizoid company.

This was exactly the effect I hoped to achieve and that I fought so hard to retain, even against extreme pressure.

A short time afterward, the film opened in England, and a marvelous review appeared in a London newspaper. I received a telegram from Peter on May 8, 1978, reading,

> Dear Walter. What about we make it up and be friends? Stop. I sent you that parcel because Dick Quine said tell Sellers I am one, and I thought it appropriate, rather gauche, but funny. Stop. I hear the film went over rather well the other evening, and that you probably be making some changes, I hope they are some that I suggested. Stop. Tell Ned, Marvin, and the boys in the Tower I will do all I can to help the film, and I wish you all good luck with it. Stop. Even if we never work together again, here's to holy mackerel. All good wishes, Peter Sellers.

That was the last communication I received from him, and I never replied to it.

He also sent me a memo, which I assume he thought we might want to release to counteract his public denunciation of the film. It read:

> I have just seen the final cut of *The Prisoner of Zenda*, dubbed, scored, and in corrected color. It's a wonderfully entertaining movie. If that seems to contradict anything I said in the past, please keep in mind that I play three roles in *The Prisoner of Zenda*, so I am entitled to at least four different opinions, including my own. The mad king, Rudolph III, is mad, so we shouldn't pay any attention to what he says. Young Prince Rudolph perhaps felt his part was too small. After all, he is kidnapped in the second reel. And, as for my third character, London cabbie Sydney Percival Frewin, he spends most of the picture as an imposter. The real Peter Sellers is delighted with *The Prisoner of Zenda*, and equally delighted to put his warm enthusiasm on the record.

This, too, is part of moviemaking! It was too little and too late.

As it turned out, Peter didn't employ Dick Quine to direct *Fu Manchu*. Piers Haggard directed it, and Leonard Maltin calls it "a disastrous comedy . . . painfully unfunny." It turned out to be Peter Sellers's last film, as he died of a heart attack in London in July 1980.

On the other hand, Peter had been right about *Being There*, and I was wrong. Sometime before the production of *Zenda* began, he gave me the book by Jerzy Kosinski and told me he wanted to make a movie based on it. I read it and I told him, "I don't know how you make a movie out of this." He replied that Hal Ashby was interested in it. And I said, "I'd like to phone Hal and ask him how he sees doing it."

I called Ashby, and he said something like, "Oh, God, did I tell him that? It's a very difficult piece of material, and I don't know how you could do it." But finally he did do it, and he did it brilliantly.

As a postscript, in 1985 Peter Sellers was pictured on a postage stamp in Great Britain. The postal authorities chose to depict him in his *Prisoner of Zenda* role. Lynne Sellers died tragically in Los Angeles in 1994.

The Prisoner of Zenda did not do well commercially. It cost about $10 million and earned domestic film rentals of about the same amount. It did reasonably well abroad and had a good afterlife in subsidiary markets. I don't know whether or not the film had an adverse effect on my relationship with Universal. Ned Tanen was quite supportive of me. He had come to Vienna while we were shooting and spent a few days with me. He was well aware of what I was contending with and was very understanding.

After completing principal photography of *Zenda* in Hollywood, I returned to London to resume preparation of *Dracula,* which was scheduled to commence photography on October 16, 1978, with Frank Tidy as our cinematographer, Peter Murton as our production designer, and John Bloom as our editor.

In considering casting possibilities for Lucy, the leading female role in the film, I discovered that Jacqueline Bissett was in London, and I thought she would be an excellent choice. I knew Jacqueline since she had played the lead in our film *The First Time.* I arranged to meet, and I talked to her at great length about the role, but she had just completed a film in London and didn't want to return to work so soon again; consequently she declined the offer.

Our casting director, Mary Selway, next suggested a Canadian actress, Kate Nelligan, who had done some outstanding stage work and a few movie roles. We arranged to meet Kate, and found her an attractive, highly intelligent young woman. John Badham and I decided to cast her in the role of Lucy.

For the other leading roles, we chose Donald Pleasence, who years before had made such a big contribution to *The Great Escape,* to play Lucy's father, and a young leading man, Trevor Eve, to play her fiancé.

Having decided to shoot on locations in Cornwall, in the historic town of Tintagel, which is the site of the King Arthur legend, we achieved a marvelous, misty, forbidding atmosphere. We also encountered its concomitant heavy and frequent rains. We consequently experienced considerable weather delays and dissatisfaction with the pace of our cameraman. We decided to make a change and hired Gil Taylor, a highly regarded British cameraman, to replace Frank Tidy. The film resumed shooting at the Shepperton studios after we concluded our Cornwall locations. During the shooting, my brother Marvin came to London to stay with the company during my absence.

The production gave me an opportunity to develop a relationship with Laurence Olivier, who proved to be a most enjoyable companion. His treasury of stories was marvelous, particularly those about his early years in Hollywood. Larry Olivier was a great admirer of William Wyler, as I was. He told me he thought Wyler might well have been the best director he had ever worked with. Larry was occasionally ill during the filming; he had a great many health problems, but he grinned and bore them bravely on many occasions.

Frank Langella had played Dracula on Broadway for a long time and had his own ideas about how the role should be played. He and John Badham quarreled on more than one occasion, but Frank and I remained good friends, and I assumed the role of peacemaker, which seemed the best idea for the benefit of the picture.

I often felt that the film required more shock value, and more mystery, and that we erred in not writing it so that we could deliver more of those elements. We were, perhaps, too strongly influenced by the success of the play, which stressed the romantic side of the story to the detriment of its shock values.

We brought Albert Whitlock to London, from Hollywood via Vienna, to assist us in the matte work for the film. He had come to Vienna for *The Prisoner of Zenda*, and while he was there I gave him the script of *Dracula* and asked him if he could help us. He suggested a number of ideas, and he later came to London to implement them.

I felt that the musical score for *Dracula* was going to be of vital importance to its success, and I decided to try to secure the services of John Williams. I called John and told him how important the film was to me. He said, "I'll be there. When do you need me?" He came to London and delivered a haunting, beautiful score.

We completed shooting the picture in February 1979 at a cost of about $10 million.

Unfortunately, an inexpensive parody of the Dracula story, *Love at First Bite* starring George Hamilton and directed by Stan Dragoti, beat us into the theaters. Our film was seriously hurt commercially by *Love at First Bite*. After the basic plot had so recently been satirized, it was difficult to get audiences to take the film seriously. *Love at First Bite* had been successful, and our opening had to follow on the heels of a comedic, contemporary send-up.

Ned Tanen and I were anxious to secure the best and widest opening that we could for the picture, and we arranged a twelve-day, fifteen-city tour in a chartered plane. In each city, the Universal salespeople had arranged luncheons for us, at which the principal exhibitors of that particular territory were invited, and we screened a fourteen-minute trailer made especially for that purpose. We went to Jacksonville, Atlanta, New Orleans, Dallas, Denver, San Francisco, Kansas City, Cleveland, Chicago, Minneapolis, Washington, D.C., Philadelphia, Boston, Los Angeles, and New York. The exhibitors reacted enthusiastically.

Dracula opened to big numbers with a three-day domestic box office gross of $3,141,281, with 395 theaters reporting out of just over 500. Unfortunately, after this strong opening, we weren't able to sustain any momentum. The picture did reasonably well and grossed, in its first domestic theatrical release, more than its entire cost. The foreign business was good, although I was disappointed it was not the success I had hoped it would be.

In retrospect, I think we should have somehow managed to get our film out before *Love at First Bite,* or we should have waited a year before releasing it and let time erode the latter's impact.

34

The 1980s and 1990s

ernard Slade, who had written *Same Time, Next Year,* had authored another play that had also been produced on Broadway by Morton Gottlieb. It was *Romantic Comedy,* starring Mia Farrow and Anthony Perkins, a story of a team of successful playwrights who, after long collaboration, discover their love for one another. Again, a romantic comedy that had been well reviewed. I found it highly amusing and considered it a good vehicle for two stars, much as Slade's last effort had been. It would also be another film that was inexpensive to produce. I recommended that Universal acquire it for me, and they did so. Bern Slade received $750,000 for the rights to his play, and I agreed that Morton Gottlieb could again be my co-producer. We also commissioned Slade to write our screenplay.

I decided, with the agreement of Universal, to offer the leading role to Dudley Moore, who in 1979 had enjoyed star-making success in the Blake Edwards comedy *10.* Dudley had become the bright, interesting, young comedic actor of the time and seemed an excellent candidate.

The plot of *Romantic Comedy* is slight, but it was written with warm, funny, Neil Simon–like humor. I judged that with a reasonable budget and interesting stars, it could give a good account of itself, as had *Same Time, Next Year.* However, Ned Tanen began to have second thoughts about proceeding with the production, despite the fact that still another Dudley Moore picture, *Arthur,* had become a big box-office success in 1981.

While Universal vacillated, a change was made in the executive suite at United Artists, following its financial debacle with *Heaven's Gate,* and a new management team was chosen by Transamerica to operate the company. Norbert Auerbach, who had been in charge of foreign sales for United Artists, was appointed to the presidency of the company succeeding Andy Albeck, who had assumed the office some years earlier after the departure of the Krim group, when they left to form Orion Pictures.

I had known Norbert Auerbach for a long time. It was with his father, Josef Auerbach, that Monogram had made the deal to acquire "The Little Rascals" in the 1950s. In the ensuing years, Norbert had enjoyed a successful career, working in foreign distribution for a number of major film companies, until he had risen to the top post in foreign distribution with United Artists. After his appointment as president, I called Norbert to congratulate him, and he asked me if it was possible for us to return to United Artists and make pictures for UA again. This came precisely at the time of my frustration with Universal's delay on *Romantic Comedy,* and I told him I thought it might well be possible.

Marvin and I arranged to meet him, and from those conversations emerged the outline of a new five-year production and distribution deal for The Mirisch Company to rejoin United Artists. I told Norbert that this deal would, of course, be contingent on my being able to secure a release from our agreement with Universal.

For a few years prior to this time, I had become enthusiastic about developing a new picture that had its roots in the success of *Midway.* It was my idea to have a screenplay written that would revolve around the story of the battle of the Philippine Sea. The battle, often termed "the Marianas Turkey Shoot," was fought in 1944, toward the end of the Pacific war, during which the American forces destroyed some 450 Japanese airplanes with a loss of 22 American planes. I heard again all the reasons why making another World War II story was a bad idea, just as if *Midway* had never been made. Despite all my persuasive efforts, Universal didn't want to develop it. So, frustrated with this and with the rejection of some other projects, I decided that perhaps the time had come to move on to what might now be more hospitable surroundings with Norbert Auerbach at UA.

I arranged a meeting with Ned Tanen and told him that since I couldn't secure approvals from Universal for projects that I wanted to do, I would prefer to move elsewhere. I told him that I hoped he and I could still remain friends. I also asked Ned if I could take *Romantic Comedy* with us to United Artists. He agreed to release us from our contract and put *Romantic Comedy* into turnaround for us.

Wanting to get into action quickly with United Artists, I proposed to Norbert Auerbach that we acquire *Romantic Comedy* from Universal and produce it as our first film. I estimated that it would budget at no more than $9 million. Dudley Moore was a bankable star, and it appeared to be a conservative investment for United Artists, which was short of product and anxious to acquire material for its distribution pipelines. I also asked UA to approve our employing Dennis O'Flaharty to prepare a screenplay based on the battle of the Philippine Sea, a project that I now called *Turkey Shoot.* UA's approvals were immediately forthcoming.

As we prepared to move our offices again, we were stunned when, in May 1981, a mere two months after signing our five-year contract, UA was sold by Transamerica to MGM, which was owned and controlled by Kirk Kerkorian. The latter immediately installed David Begelman as the president, and Norbert Auerbach, after a short two-month tenure, was returned to his position as chairman of international distribution for MGM's foreign distributor, United International Pictures.

Having thought that I had improved our situation by transferring to a more hospitable management, we now had to reorient to a new management team at UA, now MGM/UA, hopefully continue with the production of *Romantic Comedy,* and forge what I hoped could be a workable relationship with a new and unfamiliar management. We were strange bedfellows. I had not chosen to work with David Begelman and his group, and he certainly hadn't chosen The Mirisch Company. However, our deal was not disputed, and we moved into quarters at the MGM Studio. A new building had recently been constructed at the Overland Avenue entrance to the studio, which was designated as the United Artists headquarters, and we were given office space there. The new management of MGM had taken the position that it was going to continue to operate MGM and UA separately, and announced that UA would have its own organization and maintain its own trademark.

I had known David Begelman for a long time, mainly as an agent. He and Freddie Fields were partners in Creative Management Associates, a successful talent agency, and we had done a reasonable amount of business with them. However, we surely did not have a close relationship. David Begelman chose Paula Weinstein to be in charge of the United Artists group, and Freddie Fields was put in charge of the MGM program.

Now, with a whole new management group at MGM/UA, we proceeded to push forward with the production of *Romantic Comedy*, and I succeeded in interesting Mary Steenburgen—a talented actress who by then had appeared in a number of successful films—in playing the leading female role. I submitted the script to Arthur Hiller, who had directed a couple of Neil Simon's comedies. He evidenced interest in directing it. Both the stars of the film agreed, and we undertook the production.

With our production designer, Alfred Sweeney, director of photography, David M. Walsh, and our production manager, David Silver, we began shooting in New York City, where certain exterior scenes were scheduled. We had some union difficulties shooting in front of a Broadway theater at four o'clock in the morning where we had snowed in the street. We were finally ready to shoot before the break of dawn, when the production manager told me that the New York crew wanted to rest for an hour because they had all worked so hard snowing in the street and wanted a break before we started to shoot. I pointed out to him that we needed to make a night shot, and if we rested for an hour, we would have daylight. He told me that, as an alternative to the break for the crew, he had been asked to make a contribution to the union's welfare fund. I was appalled. We finally agreed to give the crew a rest period of one half-hour after we wrapped, which added considerably to our overtime costs. This was hardly a pleasant beginning for our shoot.

Next, we moved back to Los Angeles, where we resumed production by shooting interiors at MGM. The film came in close to its budget, at somewhat under $10 million, which was quite inexpensive even in 1982. The post-production was also done at MGM, marking the first time I'd ever worked in that studio. They had very capable people, and it all proceeded very well.

We previewed *Romantic Comedy* in San Jose and also had some selected audience test runs, but unfortunately the picture simply came off too mildly. Dudley Moore, whom I had counted on to give it sparkle and zest, didn't accomplish that for us, and neither did Mary Steenburgen. Whether the problem lay in the story itself or the actors or the director, I don't know. Probably all of us must share the responsibility. It was released unsuccessfully.

In the few months prior to Norbert Auerbach's departure, I had put into development *Turkey Shoot,* as well as a contemporary updating of *In the Heat of the Night,* in which I hoped again to pair Sidney Poitier and Rod Steiger. Ernest Tidyman, who had written *The French Connection* and *Shaft,* wrote our script. The new executives at MGM/UA were not receptive to these projects, or perhaps just unforgiving of our failure with *Romantic Comedy.* For myself, I was uncomfortable with the management.

Unhappy with the new turn of events, I now focused my attention on an attempt to settle the United Artists deal and move elsewhere. I told Ned Tanen, still in charge of production at Universal, of my displeasure. He sympathized with me and proposed that I come back to Universal. I eagerly welcomed the offer.

The same problem of getting approvals for our projects would exist, but at least I was more comfortable with the management. The Universal offer provided a port in a storm; we negotiated a settlement of our five-year agreement with United Artists and made a new three-year agreement with Universal. Under the terms of the settlement, MGM/UA had to pay The Mirisch Company a lesser sum of money than it would have paid if we had remained under contract. Universal more than made up for that discount in our new arrangement. I was delighted to return to a friendlier environment, and we moved back to the Universal studio about a year and a half after we had left.

At this juncture, the Board of Governors of the Academy voted its Jean Hersholt Humanitarian Award to me, for presentation at the ceremonies in 1983. The award is voted to those whose humanitarian efforts have brought credit to the industry. I was again pleased. After my dismal period at MGM, the Hersholt Award provided a great pick-me-up, and it was also a strong springboard for my return to Universal. It was also quite awesome to me when it was pointed out that only Samuel

Goldwyn and I had received the Best Picture, the Thalberg, and the Hersholt Awards.

After the newspapers carried the story about my being voted the Hersholt Award, I received a telephone call from my old friend Joel McCrea congratulating me and telling me that he and his wife, Frances, would like to attend the award ceremonies with Pat and me. I told him we would be delighted to have our dear old friends as our guests. We sat together in the theater where Frances sheepishly pointed out to me that Joel, always the cowboy, was wearing black riding boots under his tuxedo trousers. "He even wore them last month at a dinner at the White House," she whispered.

At our family table at the Governor's Ball we were talking when Bob Rehme, then head of distribution at Universal, came up to me and whispered that Joel had always been an idol of his and asked if I would introduce them. Of course I complied and Bob then told Joel that he was a particular fan of his film *Sullivan's Travels,* produced in 1941, and that Universal was soon going to reissue the movie backed by an extensive publicity campaign. Joel thanked him and wished him luck. Bob left and Joel, who had been retired from the screen by then for about twenty-five years, drew himself up to his full six foot three inch height, now covered with snow white hair in his eighty-second year, smiled playfully, and said, "It all sounds very nice but I don't think it'll do a damn thing for my career."

The Oscar was presented by Charlton Heston. He was programmed to introduce a short film about Jean Hersholt prior to the presentation of the award. He stood at the podium and waited for the film to appear, but it didn't. Some kind of glitch had occurred. Chuck ad-libbed beautifully, saying, "Well, it's a very good film. If you want to see it sometime, I'll run it for you at my house. But let's get on now." He was very warm in his presentation, and I was touched by it and by the evening.

This was my seventh appearance on an Academy Awards show. By then, most of my nervousness at these events had disappeared. I thought my talk went well and showed that I had finely learned to cope with the television medium. I responded:

> Thank you, Chuck. The Academy has been most generous to me. I
> have been honored to receive an Academy Award for one of my films,
> the Thalberg Award for my body of work, and, tonight, this. I have

worked in this industry my entire adult life. I have been privileged to know and collaborate with a remarkable group of people. I am involved in developing and producing exciting and challenging new films. In short, this industry has been good to me. It has provided me with the opportunity to realize many of my most deeply felt creative and professional aspirations. A natural extension of these involvements has been the acceptance of some of the responsibilities of good citizenship. It has been a privilege for me to participate in the various professional, cultural, and welfare activities of this industry and this community. I'm grateful for the opportunities that have been accorded to me to serve. I enjoy the fulfillments and the friendships they've brought me. I recommend them to others. So thanks Pat, who encourages me, Anne, Drew, and Larry, who forgive me, Marvin, Harold, and Jessie. And thanks to the Academy and its Board of Governors, who continue to encourage excellence in our films and in our industry.

My involvement in community and industry affairs has continued throughout my career. I am still a trustee of the Motion Picture and Television Fund. From the 1970s to the early 1990s, I was on the Board of Trustees of the American Film Institute. I was president of the Center Theater Group of the Los Angeles Music Center from 1978 through 1980. I am still an emeritus director of the Performing Arts Council of the Los Angeles Music Center, a director of the UCLA Foundation, and a life trustee of Cedars-Sinai Medical Center. These involvements have all been stimulating and in areas that I enjoy. For example, dealing with problems at the Music Center, and yet not being as personally involved as I am in my own productions, makes it more of an avocation rather than a vocation, more of an engrossing hobby than a profession.

My service with Cedars-Sinai Medical Center of Los Angeles is a case in point. It stems from my relationship with Steve Broidy, who had a most interesting career after he left Allied Artists. He formed an independent production company, and he produced a few pictures, including *The Fox* and *Good Times*, and he also became a principal investor in *The Poseidon Adventure*, an exceedingly successful film. But he devoted himself primarily to community activities. He negotiated the merger of two hospitals, Cedars of Lebanon and Mount Sinai, creating the merged hospital, Cedars-Sinai. He asked me to join the board of directors of the hospital shortly after the merger had been effected. That board of directors presided over the financing and planning of the present Cedars-Sinai Medical Center.

❦

Upon my return to Universal, I presented Ned Tanen with the script of *Turkey Shoot,* which I had developed at United Artists. He still felt that the genre had been exhausted by then and that there was little residual interest in World War II. I didn't agree with him, but there wasn't much else to do about it.

I next submitted a book, *LaBrava,* that had been sent to me by Elmore Leonard. It was a most unusual novel with a strong central character. It had most of the values of 1940s film noir and yet was modern. Bob Rehme, who had by then replaced Ned Tanen as head of production at Universal, agreed to acquire it, and we made a deal with Leonard to write the screenplay.

Another screenplay that I developed for Universal at that time was a project for Sidney Poitier. Written by Gary DeVore, *Hard Knox* is the story of a retired Chicago detective living in the Bahamas. His son and his son's closest friend come down to visit and spend a fishing vacation with him. The two young men are out alone on a fishing boat when it explodes, and both of them are killed. The detective attends the funeral and meets his divorced wife and daughter again. Having learned that there was a bomb aboard the boat, he also finally learns, in an alliance with the father of the other young man, what was behind the murder.

Although there were a number of other projects developed during that period, the next four or five years were mainly involved in the adventures of *LaBrava* and *Hard Knox.* I was then in my sixties, and Marvin was approaching seventy. At this stage of my career and life, I no longer wanted to be responsible for the large number of pictures that I had been accustomed to producing during the United Artists years, and I planned to concentrate on fewer projects.

The *LaBrava* script was finished first. We submitted it to Dustin Hoffman, and he reacted favorably. However, he had suggestions for revisions, and we began a series of meetings with him and Elmore Leonard. We made many script changes. Hoffman was busy in other films during this period, and we endured many delays in getting access to him.

We discussed possible directors with him for the project. Finally, at his suggestion, I submitted *LaBrava* to Martin Scorsese, who agreed to direct. Now we began a new series of meetings with Scorsese and Leonard, sometimes with Hoffman present, and we made further script changes.

Concurrently with all of this, Universal had made some executive changes. Bob Rehme resigned his position as head of production, and Frank Price, formerly in charge of Universal Television, was put in charge of motion-picture production. I had no previous relationship with Frank Price, but I made him conversant with the situation regarding *LaBrava*.

At about this same time, I told Dustin Hoffman that he had to commit himself to the picture or we would look elsewhere, because we could not keep making endless revisions. He agreed and asked that the Universal business-affairs people get in touch with his agents and attorney to negotiate a deal.

This process went on for some time, until the Universal negotiators told me that they found it impossible to make a deal with Hoffman. They simply would not agree to give him the participations that he was seeking. When it was explained to me, I agreed that the requests were unreasonable. I told Dustin I thought his terms were unobtainable, and I said, "No one's going to give you what you're asking for, and would you please ask your attorney, Mr. Fields, to make a deal that Universal can live with?"

A few days later, Bert Fields, his attorney, called me and said, "You know the deal you said that Universal wouldn't give Dustin? Well, I can get that deal from a new company, Cannon Pictures." The Cannon Group was an independent company that had been functioning mainly in the area of exploitation pictures for a number of years, and it was making a serious attempt to acquire films with major stars. He added that if I could succeed in getting Universal to sell the property, he would like to make the deal with Cannon. He continued, "I will also make an unprecedented producer's deal for you, if you can accomplish this." I had grave misgivings. These were again more management people that I didn't know. He assured me, "You'll never see them. They will have nothing to do with the making of the picture. All they will do is pay the bills, and you will make the picture without interference."

I thought Dustin Hoffman was marvelously well suited to play La-Brava. He was the right actor at the right time of his career, and Martin Scorsese, a brilliant young director, was ideally suited to the material. It was very hard for me to walk away from that. The Universal executives reiterated that they would never do the deal Hoffman wanted, but they did agree that I could place the project with another company. They would suspend my contract while I was doing the film and then extend it for the period of time I was away.

Bert Fields began to negotiate with Cannon over deals for the property, for myself, and for Dustin. I phoned Martin Scorsese, who told me that Dustin had already called him and explained the situation. He said he had thought about it and decided he didn't want to make a film for a company he didn't know, and so he wanted to withdraw.

I was very upset. But Dustin was less shaken and said, "Well, he's wrong. We won't have any trouble with Cannon."

He now suggested two other directors, Francis Ford Coppola and Hal Ashby. I called Coppola and discussed it with him. He told me he had read the script and liked it, but he wasn't going to be available for eighteen months. I said that wasn't possible. Then I talked to Hal Ashby, who was also enthused about it, and he said he would like to do it. I was comfortable with Hal, whom I had known for twenty-five years. He also wanted to make some changes, and the project began to pick up momentum.

Elmore Leonard had been a tower of strength through the whole convoluted process. He and I went to New York to meet Dustin again, and soon he was making so-called final changes with Hal Ashby.

At this juncture, Dustin Hoffman called me and said, "Did you see the picture in the trade papers yesterday?" He referred to the fact that Cannon had taken out some ads announcing a group of their new films. He went on to say, "They had no right to have a full-page picture of me, advertising the picture, because my contract's not signed." He continued, "Besides, I hate the photograph they used, and I don't know where they got it from. I'm mad as hell at those guys, and I'm not gonna make the picture with 'em." He concluded by saying, "Get the property back from them, and we'll make it for somebody else!" By then, of course, I had signed a contract with Cannon and had assigned my turnaround to them.

Cannon still had to make considerable agreed-upon payments to The Mirisch Company. Cannon also tied up the property for two years, during which time they hoped Hoffman would change his mind. After that time elapsed, it reverted to Universal. I had, by now, invested two years of my time and efforts in *LaBrava*. Although I had been compensated to a certain degree, that hardly made up for my frustration and disappointment. I am certain that my seeming inactivity and the loss of momentum did serious damage to my career.

Elmore Leonard was also very disappointed. However, he had a channel for taking out his frustration that wasn't available to me. He wrote a novel, *Get Shorty*, which humorously satirized moviemaking. Shorty is a highly sought-after movie star, and the plot turns on the extremes to which certain movie promoters go to try and get Shorty into their picture. It became one of Leonard's most successful novels. I was tremendously flattered when he sent me the galley proofs of the book and I read the dedication, "To Walter Mirisch, one of the good guys."

Leonard later told me that Dustin called him, after he had read *Get Shorty*, and complained that the book should have been dedicated to him and not me.

✍

In 1983 I received one of the severest shocks in my life. My wife, Pat, who had been a lifelong smoker but was always in good health, was diagnosed with lung cancer. We were both terribly frightened. Her doctor recommended that she undergo surgery, and a lobe of her left lung was removed in a difficult procedure that required a long convalescence.

I had reached the age of sixty-two, and the other areas of my life were in an agreeable state. My eldest child, Anne, who had graduated from UCLA, was now a social worker and married to a young attorney. My son Andrew, who had also graduated from UCLA, was embarking upon a career as a writer-producer at Universal Television. And my youngest son, Larry, was about to graduate from California State University, Northridge. I was in excellent health, was financially comfortable, and considered my life in excellent condition until we suffered this blow.

Fortunately, Pat began to recover. She lived with the necessity of having lung X-rays every three months for the rest of her life, to monitor the condition of her lungs. I had hoped to continue my career as long as my health was good, and I looked forward to doing the development work that would permit me to produce approximately one film a year into the foreseeable future.

I presented a completed script of our Sidney Poitier project, *Hard Knox,* to Bob Rehme's successor at Universal, Frank Price. He was not nearly as receptive to it as Bob had been. So I now found myself with another project that I was enthusiastic about but Universal's new management wasn't. I asked Frank Price to give me an opportunity to submit the script elsewhere, and he agreed.

I decided to submit it to Columbia, whose management had recently passed into the hands of David Puttnam, a well-known English producer of many outstanding films. I had met David years earlier, and I thought he would be good to work with, so I proposed the project to him. He liked it and agreed to acquire it and to finance the production, assigning the supervision of the picture to one of his vice presidents, Michael Nathanson.

Together we made further script changes and began canvassing the field for a co-star for Sidney Poitier, finally choosing Donald Sutherland.

David Puttnam wanted me to meet John Mackenzie, an English director he thought should do *Hard Knox.* He asked if I would join him in London, where we could all meet. I complied with his request and went to London, where I met an intelligent, energetic man, who had recently done *The Long Good Friday,* a picture that had created a great deal of interest. Although I didn't think *Hard Knox* was a subject for a non-American director, I found John enthusiastic about it, and I thought that he probably would work out well. When I returned to Los Angeles, I discussed John Mackenzie with Sidney Poitier, who agreed to look at John's work in a film or two. Subsequently he agreed to the choice.

Preparation continued on the picture, and we decided, for budgetary reasons, to shoot it in Chicago. John Mackenzie and I, and our production team, went there to chose our locations, and we had done a lot of local casting when, in a blaze of publicity, David Puttnam was replaced as head of production for Columbia. I was then advised by Michael Nathanson that the new Columbia management had decided to call off the production of the picture.

I was upset, as were the rest of our team, but there wasn't much we could do. The Mirisch Company was paid its full producer's fee, just as if it the picture had been completed, as were Poitier and Sutherland. The director and the rest of the staff were also paid off, and I returned again to my offices at Universal, which I had retained during both the Cannon and the Columbia experiences. Licking my wounds, I began to look elsewhere for my next project.

As I had often done in my career, I thought, "Perhaps now is the time to try a Western again." I discussed the idea with Elmore Leonard, and I asked him how he would feel about doing an original screenplay. Although it is not well known, Elmore Leonard had started his career as a writer of Western novels, some of which were produced as films, the most notable being *Hombre,* a very successful picture that starred Paul Newman. "Dutch" Leonard had started his career in Detroit, writing advertising copy for automobiles companies. But he moonlighted writing Western stories, which he submitted to the pulps of the time, and progressed through those to finally writing Western novels. It was only when the Western market dried up that he began writing the crime stories for which he is mainly known today.

He and I began discussing ideas for a Western, and he wrote a treatment that he called *Duell McCall,* the name of its leading character. The story, reminiscent of *The Fugitive,* is about a young man in the West who is unjustly accused of a crime and is forced to steer clear of the law, while at the same time trying to clear his name.

Concurrent with the development of this story, which was about four years after Pat's first lung operation, it was discovered in a routine checkup that she had a new growth in a lobe of her right lung. Again it was decided that she should have it removed surgically, and again we went through the excruciating trauma of the operation, although this time the surgery was even more difficult for her. She spent three weeks in intensive care following the surgery, but she finally began to recover. She had now lost a lobe in each of her lungs. It was a draining experience and a very difficult time for us both, as well as for our whole family.

Failing again to find a studio willing to make a Western, I thought that perhaps *Duell McCall* might be interesting to a television network as a possible television movie, or as a television pilot for a series. I discussed the idea with my son Drew. Drew had been working as an associate producer for television producer Glen Larson, who was active at that time with Universal Television. Drew had been with Larson for a number of years and later became a producer of numerous shows, including *The Hardy Boys–Nancy Drew Mysteries, Nightmares, Sword of Justice,* and *Leg Men.* He had a great deal of experience in television production and in working with network people and encouraged me to pursue the idea of *Duell McCall* as a television project. I asked Drew if he would like to take over the project and was delighted when he agreed.

Under the aegis of Universal Television, he and I went to NBC, with Elmore Leonard, and met with Brandon Tartikoff, who was in charge of the network at that time. Tartikoff liked the project and agreed to finance a two-hour television movie, as a so-called back-door pilot for a series. It was his idea that we acquire the music to the Eagles' well-known song "Desperado," and that we retitle our project *Desperado.* It was a good idea, with which we complied, although our leading character was still called Duell McCall. We planned to make the picture on location, and we shot the first film in Tucson, Arizona.

The choice of the leading character in a television series is critically important. Finally, after innumerable interviews, discussions, and compromises, NBC, Universal, Drew, and I agreed on a young man named Alex McArthur.

Drew was enthusiastic about hiring John Byrum, a friend with whom he had worked previously, to direct. He and John went off to Tucson to commence the film.

The shooting was troubled. There was dissatisfaction with John Byrum's work, and it was decided to replace him. Drew asked John to resign his post, and John, who appreciated the fact that the situation wasn't harmonious, generously agreed. Drew replaced him as quickly as he could with Virgil Vogel, a veteran of many Westerns. Vogel did a very good job with the picture, and it was completed just slightly over schedule.

Andrew Mirisch, in complete charge of the production, was credited as executive producer. Lise Cutter, David Warner, Yaphet Kotto, Robert Vaughn, and Gladys Knight made up the rest of the cast. Dick

Bush was the cinematographer, and Michel Columbier composed the score.

Universal Television was the production company behind *Desperado,* which meant that it was responsible for cost overruns and owned the negative of the film, as well as controlling syndication and foreign distribution. The film aired on the NBC network on Monday, April 27, 1987, and received excellent notices and ratings.

We were hopeful that *Desperado* would spawn a series, but we were disappointed. NBC elected not to order a series of one-hour shows based on the pilot. Instead, it ordered two more *Desperado* movies, saying it preferred to continue the franchise in the two-hour form. Drew now began preparations for the second movie.

After *Return of the Desperado* had been telecast, NBC advised us that it would like to program it as a one-hour weekly series. However, by then, the option on Alex McArthur to appear in the show on a weekly basis had expired. When Drew contacted McArthur's agent to see if he could make a new deal, his agent reported that Alex no longer wanted to be tied up to a weekly series. Because of the success that he had enjoyed in the first two *Desperado*s, his agent thought his opportunities to have a career in feature films had been enhanced, and he concluded he'd rather not be committed to a long-term television contract. Consequently, the opportunity to produce a series, which would have been very remunerative, was lost.

When this was reported to NBC they said they would then like to continue making more *Desperado*es in the two-hour form, and ordered three more films. Drew became busy preparing those movies. *Desperado: Avalanche at Devil's Ridge,* was produced in 1988, followed by *Desperado: Outlaw Wars* and *Desperado: Badlands Justice* in 1989.

The last two *Desperado* movies were both based on stories that Drew wrote. They continued to do well in the ratings, and NBC wanted to continue the series. However, Universal decided that having a backlog of five of these films, for foreign distribution, was about as far extended as they wanted to be on this series. It preferred to wait until the five films had been absorbed in the foreign markets before adding to their inventory, so it chose to discontinue the films. It was a well-executed series that received good ratings, and I was sorry to see it come to an end.

While Drew continued working on the *Desperado* pictures, Sidney Poitier and I collaborated on the development of another project, titled *Ton Ton,* and Orion Pictures agreed to finance a script written by James Buchanan. Unfortunately, this project never reached production.

🐝

In the spring of 1989, some weeks after I had been told about the University of Wisconsin honorary degree, I was surprised to be called by Chancellor Charles Young of UCLA. The Youngs had become personal friends of Pat and mine many years earlier. We had met in the early 1970s, shortly after Chuck Young had assumed the chancellorship of UCLA. We enjoyed one another's company, and a strong relationship developed between us. However, I was stunned when he told me that UCLA wanted to present me with the UCLA Medal, which is its highest award, at the commencement ceremony of its College of Fine Arts in June 1989. Since UCLA, like all of the University of California units, does not grant honorary degrees, the UCLA Medal is the recognition it considers the equivalent.

This conferral also turned out to be an extraordinary occasion. UCLA had become quite important in my life. In the first instance, we are neighbors, since I have lived close to the campus for thirty-odd years and have taken advantage of its grounds for more walks than I can count. I have watched with great pleasure as the campus developed and expanded. Pat and I have enjoyed its sports and cultural events for most of our married life. Through our friendship with the Youngs, we had occasion to enjoy many wonderful experiences that were special UCLA occasions.

At the presentation, clips from a number of Mirisch film were shown. Chancellor Young spoke sincerely and warmly about me, and I delivered a commencement address to the graduates.

I had won the Academy's Best Picture Award and received its Thalberg Award and its Hersholt Award. I had appeared on eight Academy Awards shows, but I think the Wisconsin and UCLA ceremonies affected me even more. Somehow or other, they validated my work in a broader arena, beyond the motion-picture industry itself. My whole family was again present at the ceremony, and that same evening there was a beautiful party that the Youngs gave at their residence for the honorees. It was a glowing occasion, and Pat and I, who had gone through some difficult times during that decade, felt happy and complete.

Pat's health was now better. She had recovered quite well but continued her routine of lung X-rays every three months.

I was approaching seventy years of age, and appreciated how fortunate I had been to be able to spend my life as a storyteller, a vocation I would not have exchanged for any other. I had been honored beyond all expectation, remunerated beyond any of my ambitions, and blessed with good health and a loving and supportive family. I understood that revolutionary changes had taken place in the motion-picture industry, which was now being managed by a new generation of executives, but I decided nonetheless to continue to try to produce films, theatrical or television, that I believed in, for as long as my health would permit.

The collapse of the *LaBrava* and *Hard Knox* projects was a big disappointment for me. However, I next developed a property based on the book *The Natural Man* by Ed McClanahan for Universal. Sadly, we were never able to get a satisfactory script based on it. Mike Medavoy had been in charge of production at Orion Pictures when we developed *Ton Ton,* but by the time the script was completed, he had left the company. His successors were not interested in pursuing it.

Shortly afterward, I became very excited about doing a film based on the secret development of the Air Force's invisible-to-radar "stealth" airplane, designated the F-117. At that time, there had been some references to it in the press, although no one had yet seen the plane. I contacted the Air Force, which generously supplied me with some information. I made a deal with Paramount to develop a film, and Jim Buchanan wrote the first draft of a script.

Unfortunately, the script didn't turn out well, but I was anxious to continue with the project when the Gulf War erupted. For the first time, the F-117 stealth fighter-bomber was used in action, against the Iraqis. This extraordinary weapon was the most effective airplane used in the war, where it was primarily responsible for the delivery of "smart bombs." Paramount chose not to proceed with the project, and I presented it to my friend Ned Tanen, who by then had made a deal as an independent producer at Sony. Ned was enthusiastic, and we made arrangements to do it together, with Sony financing another script. I enlisted Gary DeVore, who had previously written *Hard Knox* for me, to write that new version.

The Air Force now generously allowed me two trips to Tonopah, up in the high desert of Nevada, which had been the secret base for the F-117s. The planes flew only at night, were painted black, and had little or no radar profile. The fliers flew training missions at night and slept during the day. Their families lived in Las Vegas, and the pilots and crews would go home for weekends. They were not allowed to tell their families where they were based or what they were doing. Many broken families resulted from this difficult lifestyle.

I was allowed to fly a simulator for an F-117, and it was so realistic that I became frightened that I was going to crack up while landing my plane. I had an opportunity to meet the pilots of these planes and their commander, many of whom had flown in Iraq, all extraordinary men of great bravery and devotion to duty. It was a most stimulating experience.

DeVore finished his script, which we passed on to Ned Tanen. Ned and his staff gave us notes, and we tried wherever possible to comply with their requests. But the development process for this project ran on too long. Because of too much quarterbacking and too many cooks, it finally lost its timeliness and failed to reach fruition.

Early in 1990, I thought it might be time to do a remake of *The Magnificent Seven*, with a new generation of actors playing the now-classic roles. I arranged to get UA's agreement to allow me to develop it for Universal. I brought director Walter Hill into the project, and we selected Larry Gross to do a new script. Again, I ran into a change of management at Universal. Frank Price, with whom I had started the project, was replaced, and it fell dormant.

I then arranged to reactivate the remake at MGM/UA, where I introduced director Lawrence Kasdan to the project. I worked with his brother, Mark Kasdan, and Terry Swann on still another script. Unfortunately, before this script was finished, MGM/UA had unsuccessfully released another Western picture and they became disenchanted with the genre and decided to drop it. I also attempted a feature-film version of our old TV series *The Rat Patrol* with MGM, but this also died aborning.

By then I was most anxious to get back into production, so in 1990 I resuscitated a script by Peter Fischer that I had prepared for Universal a number of years before based on the book *Tagget* by Irving A. Green-field, which I thought could become a successful television movie. Daniel Travanti, who had played a supporting role in *The Organization* many years earlier, had by then had a successful television career, principally in the show *Hill Street Blues.* I sent the script to Dan, and he agreed to play the lead.

Tagget is the story of a CIA dirty trick that has gone amiss and resulted in the victimization of an Army captain who ultimately revenges himself on the CIA group that perpetrated the crime. It was produced for the USA Network, which was owned and controlled by Universal and served to continue my relationship with the studio where, by this time, I had been based for approximately fifteen years. I hoped to continue doing more TV movies for Universal while still developing feature projects for the studio.

Another story for a television movie was brought to me by writers Michael Pavone and Dave Johnson. This was *Trouble Shooters,* which concerned an apartment building that falls into a chasm created by an earthquake, with the result that the inhabitants of the building are all trapped beneath the earth. The authorities call in a team of trouble-shooters to effect the rescue of the victims. I was challenged by the logistical problems involved, and it became a fascinating puzzle to arrive at a plan by which the film could be executed for the nominal budget allocated to a TV movie. Universal TV presented this project to NBC, which agreed to subsidize its development. When the script was completed, we were able to secure the services of Kris Kristofferson to play the leader of the rescue team. Bradford May directed the film, which cost about $3.4 million and was telecast by NBC in 1992.

❧

At about the same time as I was becoming more involved in television production, Bob Wise became president of the Academy. Bob was dedicated to building a study center bringing all of the Academy's collections under one roof, and he asked me if I would agree to become the chairman of a committee to find an appropriate site and prepare a plan that could be presented to the Board of Governors. I accepted Bob's invitation and examined the possibilities. A site that seemed promising was located in Beverly Hills, not more than ten minutes by car from the

Academy's main building, near the corner of La Cienega and Olympic boulevards. The city of Beverly Hills owned a structure that in former years had housed the waterworks for the city. It had not been used for many years, had deteriorated shockingly, and was scheduled for demolition. For years it was a refuge for homeless people. It was filthy and rat-infested, with huge water mains still running through it, graffiti all over, and just waiting for the wrecker's ball. However, the exterior of the building, in Spanish Mission style, was still very attractive.

In 1988 we discussed the possibility of our either acquiring or leasing the building with the city manager of Beverly Hills. The city's plan had been to demolish it. It adjoins a playground area, and it was their intention to add to that. However, a committee of local residents, who considered the building a historical landmark, had lobbied against its demolition. Our Academy committee met with them and told them that we would maintain the exterior architecture and then convert the interior to library and film archive spaces. They became most enthusiastic and our great allies in ultimately convincing the Beverly Hills City Council to make an arrangement with us. I appeared before the city council and made a presentation of our proposal. Finally we were able to work out an agreement, under which the city granted the Academy a fifty-year lease on the property, and the Academy agreed to spend what was required to modernize the premises and create the library and film archives that we wished to establish. Similar to the fortunate combination of circumstances that, fifteen years before, had allowed the Academy to build its headquarters building without parking for its theater, we were again able to make an arrangement with the city of Beverly Hills that allowed the Academy to use the city's adjoining parking lots, as well as a new underground parking lot that it planned to construct. We were thus able to create an outstanding library facility and film archive whose ultimate cost was approximately $6 million. I am delighted that the Academy refurbished the building, which is now a landmark called the Fairbanks Center for Motion Picture Study.

The Academy now undertook a fund-raising effort to create an endowment fund that, hopefully, would be large enough to provide an annual income to support the activities of the study center. There were some important first donations. Bob Hope and the Cecil B. De Mille Foundation each contributed lead gifts of $1 million. There was also a great deal of fund-raising activity throughout the entire motion-picture community, which ultimately raised some $12 million. I thought the fund-raising drive was a good idea, since it created a cause for the motion-picture community to rally around, as well as bringing additional attention to the Academy and its activities. Amid the self-congratulations and pride of the center's opening-night party on January 24, 1991, I could not help but reflect upon how far the Academy had come from the old Melrose Theater in 1973.

When I was president of the Academy from 1974 to 1978, I wrote letters to all of the film companies and asked them to contribute prints of all of their films that had, at any time, won Academy Awards. We said we wanted 35mm prints, but we would also accept 16mm prints if that was all they could provide. Clearly we didn't get everything, but we got a tremendous amount of film at that time. This campaign provided a considerable base for the Academy's collection of film.

🦢

During the late 1980s, the Academy had kept me somewhat busy. But at about the same time, having been dissatisfied with our living arrangements for quite a while, Pat and I determined on a another radical course of action. We tore down our home of thirty-five years and built an entirely new home on the same site. It turned out beautifully and Pat and I were both delighted that we did it. Our children were now grown into adults. Our eldest child, Anne, had graduated from UCLA with a bachelor's degree and a master's degree in social work and found employment in a child-care clinic. In 1979 she married Greg Gelfan, an attorney. They were divorced in 1988, but not before they had given Pat and me our first grandchild, Megan, who made me very proud when she too graduated from the University of Wisconsin in 2005. Anne married Stephen Sonnenberg, a widower with a young son, Aaron, about two years after her divorce. Their marriage also ended in divorce in 2006.

My youngest son, Larry, was always interested in film. He went off on his own when he was fifteen and found a job, working as an usher for Mann Theaters in Westwood Village. Among the first films at which he worked was *The Exorcist*, which played to unbelievable crowds. Larry had a tough initiation in crowd management. He continued to work in theaters as an usher as he progressed through college.

He chose to enter California State University at Northridge and worked during the summers as an apprentice editor. He worked in the cutting rooms of *Midway, Gray Lady Down,* and other pictures that came up when he was not in school. I was very proud when he tactfully made astute editorial suggestions. He graduated from Cal State and decided that he wanted to work as an assistant director. And so he did, as a second assistant on a number of films, including *Same Time, Next Year* and *The Prisoner of Zenda.* Although I didn't feel that he was well suited to that type of work, I wanted him to find his own way to a career.

One day while he was working on a picture at MGM called *Whose Life Is It Anyway?* I said to him, "I don't think this is for you. I think you should be an agent."

He replied, "Oh no, no, that's all wrong!"

After he finished that film, he worked on *Grease II.* He was just finishing a week or so of exhausting night shooting when I said, "Agent?"

He said, "Well, maybe . . ."

He called Phil Gersh, who owned a talent agency in the city, and asked for an appointment. Phil interviewed Larry and hired him as a trainee, handling writers. However, because of his familiarity with production designers, editors, and cinematographers, his interest gravitated to these talents, and he soon contacted Frank Urioste, the co-editor of *Midway,* with whom he had become friendly some years before on *Mr. Majestyk.* Frank became his first client and has gone on to have a wonderful career as a film editor and executive, and Larry is still his agent. Bob Relyea, my long-time associate, also chose to become one of his earliest clients.

Larry is gregarious and makes friends easily and well. People like him, and he's very bright. He finally left the Gersh Agency and joined Adams, Ray & Rosenberg, a company that was later merged into the Triad Agency.

Larry also has a great entrepreneurial spirit and didn't like working for others. He opted to go into business for himself in 1992, forming The Mirisch Agency, and all of his clients stayed with him. He has created an excellent business; he likes what he does, and success has followed. I have the utmost respect for what he accomplished.

My son Drew, after working on innumerable episodic segments at Universal, entered the field of television movies with *High Midnight,* which aired on the CBS network in 1979, and on which he was credited as executive producer for the first time. After completing *High Midnight*, he was asked by Universal to be the supervising producer of a revival of the old *Alfred Hitchcock Presents* series, which, like its antecedent, was an anthology show. It was very successful and gave him many opportunities to work with numerous outstanding talents. Drew's career was progressing very well, and he finally directed one of the Hitchcock episodes. Drew was later approached by Paramount Television, which he joined to write and produce a number of episodes for the new *Untouchables* series and later to serve as executive producer on the series *The Watcher*, which aired on the UPN network.

During this period, Michael Riva, a client of my son Larry and a well-known production designer, told me a story about something that had befallen him when he was a young boy living in New York. He thought it would make an interesting television movie, and I agreed. It takes place in the late 1950s and is the story of Michael, a ten-year-old boy whose parents are involved in the theatrical world; his mother is an actress and his father an art director. They live in a New York brownstone, where Michael is looked after by Lily, a housekeeper. Because of a melodramatic mix-up, Lily must leave New York very quickly. Covertly, Michael, not wanting to be separated from Lily, joins her on a train, headed for her family's home in the Deep South. It is a coming-of-age story about the boy, and also a story in which Lily is able to right her own domestic problems, from which she had run away many years earlier.

I employed Robert Eisele, who delivered an excellent script. Under Universal's auspices, we presented the script to the USA Network, which liked it and agreed to license it, if we delivered satisfactory casting for the principal role. I suggested Natalie Cole, who had been a well-known singer but whose career had gone into decline, only to be resurrected by the appearance of an album on which she was electronically able to sing a duet with her father, Nat King Cole, of his famous song "Unforgettable." Natalie had done some previous acting in the television series *I'll Fly Away*. She responded positively to the script, and we began to prepare the film for production.

I thought the material would be interesting to my old friend Delbert Mann, who had not directed in a number of years. He was in retirement, but I offered the film to him, and he said he would like to do it. It was an added pleasure to work again with Del. We shot the film, which had mainly a southern locale, in the Los Angeles area early in 1994. It was heavily promoted by USA, and when telecast it did exceedingly well in its ratings. My long-time friend and collaborator Ralph Winters, who was then eighty-five years young, edited the film.

Having created a large number of television relationships by this time, I began to think again of the possibility of resurrecting *The Magnificent Seven* as a television show, and I started to make some overtures to the networks. However, those efforts didn't come to fruition until after the next television movie that I produced, *A Case for Life,* which aired on the ABC network in 1996.

Writer Vickie Patik and I had been talking about finding a project that we could do together, and after numerous discussions we finally came up with the idea for the film. It is a story of two sisters, one strongly pro-choice and the other pro-life. The difference in points of view between these two sisters remains beneath the surface until the pro-life sister, while pregnant, develops cardiac problems that necessitate an operation that could jeopardize the life of her unborn child. This crisis brings the conflict between the two women into sharp focus. The pro-choice sister, who is an attorney, convinces the pregnant sister's husband to file a legal action to force his wife to have the surgery, on the basis that she owes an implicit legal obligation to her other two children to provide them with maternal love and care. Interestingly, the trial forces the pro-life sister's counsel to argue that the expectant mother should have a choice as to whether or not she is willing to sacrifice her life for her unborn child.

We were able to cast two talented women, Valerie Bertinelli and Mel Harris, as the sisters. Eric Laneuville directed the film very effectively.

Again, I decided to try to resuscitate *LaBrava.* The property had reverted to Universal and was inactive at the studio. I felt that the material was not dated, and by this time *Get Shorty* had been produced by MGM with John Travolta, Rene Russo, Gene Hackman, and Danny DeVito. It became the most successful Elmore Leonard film, of all the books that he had written.

I had proposed *Get Shorty* to nearly every studio in Hollywood without success. But, after my failure to place it, Danny DeVito read the book and saw it as a vehicle for himself. He succeeded in getting Twentieth

Century-Fox to develop the project. A script was prepared, but Fox chose not to proceed with it. DeVito then tried to set it up at other studios, without success, until he took it to MGM, which agreed to do the picture.

I took this opportunity to re-present *LaBrava* to the Universal Studio management. Since the studio already owned the literary rights, it agreed to finance a new script for me. I succeeded in interesting Buck Henry in writing it, and Universal agreed to employ him.

Almost simultaneously, I was able to arouse new interest in the *Magnificent Seven* as a television project. The Universal Television executives were interested in backing the project and presenting it to a network, but that had to be cleared with MGM, which had succeeded to the rights formerly controlled by United Artists. I thought that MGM would be glad to co-produce, if Universal agreed to provide the deficit financing, but I was surprised when MGM said it wanted to produce the series alone and declined the participation of Universal. I assumed MGM was thereby trying to reestablish its presence in the industry, since it had not had a network television show in a decade or more.

Tom Thayer, the head of Universal Television, had made the initial call to Les Moonves, the head of CBS, in 1996. But as MGM wanted to do the series alone, a deal was struck between MGM and CBS to produce a two-hour television movie that would also serve as a pilot for a series.

The MGM television group wanted to bring Trilogy, a producing company allied with it, into the project. I was glad to have its participation, especially if a series was eventually ordered, and I agreed to work with them in preparing the pilot script. Two of the principals of Trilogy, Pen Densham and John Watson, assumed an active role with me in developing the pilot, which ultimately was written from their original story by a team of screenplay writers named Dobbs and Black.

The pilot was shot in Tucson. Cast in the title roles were Michael Biehn, Dale Midkiff, Ron Perlman, Eric Close, Rick Worthy, Anthony Starke, and Andrew Kavovit. The pilot turned out well, and it was run on CBS as a two-hour movie. The following season we received an order from CBS for ten one-hour shows as a midseason replacement. For the first time since *The Rat Patrol* in 1965, The Mirisch Company again had a prime-time television series on the air.

The Magnificent Seven was scheduled by CBS in a nine o'clock time slot on Friday nights and did reasonably well. Not great, but good enough to be reordered for a second midseason replacement. After completing its second season in 1998, *The Magnificent Seven* series was not reordered for a third. By that time, twenty-four one hour shows had been produced.

After long delays in the writing of *LaBrava* by Buck Henry, the script was finally finished. I liked it better than most other people, who liked it but felt it needed more work. It still remains unproduced, but I continue to believe that *LaBrava,* after its long and checkered development career, will finally reach the screen.

My next project was a contemporary version of *Spellbound,* the 1945 Hitchcock thriller, now titled *Amnesia,* in partnership with my friend Sid Sheinberg, who had formerly been president of MCA, Universal's parent company.

☙

As time progressed and probably as should have been expected, serious problems began to arise within my family. My daughter Anne was diagnosed with Hodgkin's disease and was subjected to grueling chemotherapy and radiation treatments for a considerable period of time. Fortunately, they were effective, and she is now free of cancer and hopefully will remain so for a long time into the future.

My dear wife Pat's physical condition continued to deteriorate over the years. She suffered a stroke in 2000, from which she made an almost complete recovery. However, by 2005, her lungs, with their reduced capacity after her two cancer surgeries, put increasing pressure on her heart until finally, to the great sorrow and grief of me and her family, she succumbed to heart failure at the age of eighty after a long and active life.

Earlier, I had been greatly honored when in 2003 the Los Angeles County Museum of Art recognized me and my work with a retrospective of twelve films titled "The Magnificent Mirisches," and I was deeply grateful that Pat had been able to enjoy the occasion. My friends Sidney Poitier, Julie Andrews, Blake Edwards, and Fay Kanin all came and spoke.

As frosting on the cake of my later years, I was thrilled to present a special honorary Academy Award to one of my best friends, Sidney

Poitier, at the Oscar ceremonies in 2002. In his acceptance speech, Sidney thanked "a handful of visionary American filmmakers, directors and producers . . . each unafraid to permit their work to reflect views and values. . . . I benefited from their effort. America benefited from their effort. Therefore, with respect I share this great honor with the late Joe Mankiewicz, the late Richard Brooks, the late Ralph Nelson, the late Daryl Zanuck, the late Stanley Kramer, the Mirisch brothers, especially Walter, whose friendship lies at the very heart of this moment." What an unbelievable occasion for me!

In December 2006, New York's prestigious Museum of Modern Art honored me with a tribute and a retrospective of twelve Mirisch films. In his letter of notification, the Museum Director wrote,

> Few in the history of Hollywood have succeeded as you have in creating a production company that is truly independent: balancing the sometimes competing demands of creative integrity and commercial viability while never compromising on excellence. We believe that films like *In the Heat of the Night* and *The Magnificent Seven*, which have defined an era, belong in a museum alongside paintings by Matisse and Picasso and photographs by Walker Evans and Irving Penn.

My whole family was at my side to share the occasion with me.

Epilogue

In the first decade of the new millennium, I find myself still fortunately blessed with good health, a loving family, and great optimism about my country, my industry, and the future. I am filled with gratitude for all the opportunities that have been given to me and mine, and I am convinced the future will be even richer and brighter for those who follow me. As I look back over the last sixty or so years—crammed to the brim with raising a family, participating in industry and community activity, enjoying good friends, but mostly involved in continual moviemaking—I consider myself among the most fortunate of men.

My parents, though limited in many ways, were always loving and supportive. I never doubted their love for me, or mine for them. Though born in a poor family and growing up troubled during the years of the Great Depression, I managed to secure an extraordinary education at the City College of New York, the University of Wisconsin, and the Harvard Graduate School of Business Administration. Later I was able to overcome the self-doubts and insecurity of my youth.

From an early age I learned the lesson of the necessity of each member of our family helping the others, even when the two older children were stepbrothers to the two younger children. When my brother Irving's farm in Lake George, New York, failed in 1929, Harold immediately responded by offering him a position as assistant manager in the theater he was managing in Memphis. At the age of ten, I gave my meager $15 savings to Irving to help him finance his drive from New York to Memphis. Later, Irving and Harold contributed whatever funds they could to help my father and our little family stay afloat when his custom-tailoring business collapsed in 1940. Harold brought Irving to Milwaukee from Gettysburg, Pennsylvania, to work in his recently formed candy-vending business.

The two of them together brought my father, mother, brother Marvin, and myself to Milwaukee when my father became ill and his business had to close its doors. My older brothers helped Marvin and me to find jobs in Milwaukee when our family moved there. Even in times of adversity, I was always encouraged to continue my education. Although I never worked in Harold and Irving's candy company, they gave Marvin and me small amounts of stock in the emerging business. After I had finished college, Harold arranged for me to meet Steve Broidy, who gave me my first position in a motion-picture studio. Three years later, when Harold lost his position with RKO in New York and was too proud to speak to Steve Broidy on his own behalf, I spoke to him and proposed that he bring Harold to California as a vice president of Allied Artists.

Eight years later, Harold and I arranged for Marvin to come to California, so that he could join us at Allied Artists, while Irving remained in Milwaukee to manage the candy company. At the same time, he and I arranged for our father and mother to move to Los Angeles, where we and our wives could care for them. In 1957, when Harold, Marvin, and I left Allied Artists and formed The Mirisch Company to produce films for United Artists, we wisely agreed that the three of us would draw equal salaries to forestall problems later on. The stock in The Mirisch Company was divided into quarters, and we assigned an equal share to our eldest brother, Irving, who was still working in Milwaukee, and he shared in its fruits equally with us. The candy company was sold a few years later, and Irving retired and moved to Los Angeles with his family to spend the remainder of his life with those closest to him. Harold died in 1968, and Irving in 1969, and Marvin and I continued to work together until his death on November 19, 2002.

It was Marvin who was the businessman who kept the organization running. He dealt with the accounting staff, worked with the business affairs people, and handled the internal workings of the company—everything from taxes to our relationship with lawyers. He was a marvelous sounding board, often warning of the difficulties and pitfalls of a project upon which I wanted to embark.

In 1957, when The Mirisch Company moved into offices in the Samuel Goldwyn Studio, we tried to create the atmosphere of a creative family for all of those who came to work for us. We tried to provide an environment that was conducive to writers, directors, and producers doing their best work. We wanted them to feel at home and at ease with themselves and with one another. We established a comfortable, enjoyable, small lunchroom, where our people could congregate and exchange either pleasantries or ideas in a congenial atmosphere. In short, it was a creative family where ideas could be exchanged and, when necessary, one member could help another.

We gave stock in our company to all the permanent members of our small organization, so that they would feel that they had a meaningful stake in the success of our endeavors. Basically, this same group remained together for the whole seventeen years of our United Artists association. Among the directors, Billy Wilder remained with us exclusively from *Some Like It Hot* in 1957 to *Avanti!* in 1972, producing, directing, and writing a total of eight films. John Sturges produced and directed five films with us, from *The Magnificent Seven* in 1959 to *Hour of the Gun* in 1967, eight years later. Norman Jewison remained with us for six years and five films, from producing and directing *The Russians Are Coming, the Russians Are Coming* in 1966 to *Fiddler on the Roof* in 1971. And Blake Edwards produced and directed four films in five years, from *The Pink Panther* in 1963 to *The Party* in 1968. All of this in an industry notorious for the inconstancy of its talent.

I reiterate that if I had not been fortunate enough to have found people who paid me to produce motion pictures, I would have paid them for the opportunity. Shaping stories that would eventually come alive on the screen and then attain the immortality that film imparts has been a God-given gift. I have been privileged to work with many of the most creative talents of my generation and to contribute to films that will be shown and enjoyed far beyond my own life span. Some of the films may have contributed to a better understanding of our times. A few may have added to the cultural heritage of our society. And, even more than that, many have provided uncountable hours of entertainment to people throughout the world for over half a century.

Filmography of Walter Mirisch and the Mirisch Companies

Fall Guy (March 15, 1947)
DIRECTOR: Reginald Le Borg; PRODUCER: Walter M. Mirisch; SCREEN-PLAY: Jerry Warner; ADDITIONAL DIALOGUE: John O'Dea, based on the story "Cocaine" by Cornell Woolrich; CAST: Clifford Penn, Robert Armstrong, Teala Loring, Elisha Cook Jr.; 64 min; b&w; presented by Monogram Pictures Corporation; DISTRIBUTOR: Monogram Pictures Corporation

I Wouldn't Be in Your Shoes (May 23, 1948)
DIRECTOR: William Nigh; PRODUCER: Walter M. Mirisch; SCREENPLAY: Steve Fisher, based on the novel by Cornell Woolrich; CAST: Don Castle, Elyse Knox, Regis Toomey; 71 min; b&w; presented by Monogram Pictures Corporation; DISTRIBUTOR: Monogram Pictures Corporation

Bomba, the Jungle Boy (March 20, 1949)
DIRECTOR: Ford Beebe; PRODUCER: Walter Mirisch; SCREENPLAY: Jack De-Witt, based on the novel by Roy Rockwood; CAST: Johnny Sheffield, Peggy Ann Garner; 71 min; b&w; presented by Monogram Pictures Corporation; DISTRIBUTOR: Monogram Pictures Corporation

Bomba on Panther Island (December 18, 1949)
DIRECTOR: Ford Beebe; PRODUCER: Walter Mirisch; SCREENPLAY: Ford Beebe, based on the characters created by Roy Rockwood in the "Bomba" books; CAST: Johnny Sheffield, Allene Roberts; 76 min; b&w; presented by Monogram Pictures Corporation; DISTRIBUTOR: Monogram Pictures Corporation

The Lost Volcano (with Bomba the Jungle Boy) (June 25, 1950)
DIRECTOR: Ford Beebe; PRODUCER: Walter Mirisch; SCREENPLAY: Ford Beebe, based on the characters created by Roy Rockwood in the "Bomba" books; CAST: Johnny Sheffield, Donald Woods, Marjorie Lord; 76 min; b&w;

presented by Monogram Pictures Corporation; DISTRIBUTOR: Monogram Pictures Corporation

County Fair (July 30, 1950)
DIRECTOR: William Beaudine; PRODUCER: Walter Mirisch; SCREENPLAY: W. Scott Darling; CAST: Rory Calhoun, Jane Nigh; 76 min; Cinecolor; presented by Monogram Pictures Corporation; DISTRIBUTOR: Monogram Pictures Corporation

The Hidden City (with Bomba the Jungle Boy) (September 24, 1950)
DIRECTOR: Ford Beebe; PRODUCER: Walter Mirisch; SCREENPLAY: Carroll Young, based on the characters created by Roy Rockwood in the "Bomba" books; CAST: Johnny Sheffield, Sue England, Smoki Whitfield; 71 min; b&w; presented by Monogram Pictures Corporation; DISTRIBUTOR: Monogram Pictures Corporation

The Lion Hunters (with Bomba the Jungle Boy) (April 13, 1951)
DIRECTOR: Ford Beebe; PRODUCER: Walter Mirisch; SCREENPLAY: Ford Beebe, based on the characters created by Roy Rockwood in the "Bomba" books; CAST: Johnny Sheffield, Morris Ankrum, Ann Todd, Woodrow Strode; 79 min; b&w; presented by Monogram Pictures Corporation; DISTRIBUTOR: Monogram Pictures Corporation

Cavalry Scout (May 13, 1951)
DIRECTOR: Lesley Selander; PRODUCER: Walter Mirisch; STORY AND SCREENPLAY: Dan Ullman; CAST: Rod Cameron, Audrey Long, Jim Davis; 78 min; Cinecolor; presented by Monogram Pictures Corporation; DISTRIBUTOR: Monogram Pictures Corporation

Elephant Stampede (with Bomba the Jungle Boy) (October 28, 1951)
DIRECTOR: Ford Beebe; PRODUCER: Walter Mirisch; SCREENPLAY: Ford Beebe; based on the characters created by Roy Rockwood in the "Bomba" books; CAST: Johnny Sheffield, Donna Martell, Edith Evanson; 72 min; b&w; presented by Monogram Pictures Corporation; DISTRIBUTOR: Monogram Pictures Corporation

Flight to Mars (November 11, 1951)
DIRECTOR: Lesley Selander; PRODUCER: Walter Mirisch; SCREENPLAY: Arthur Strawn; CAST: Marguerite Chapman, Cameron Mittchell, Arthur Franz; 72 min; Cinecolor; presented by Monogram Pictures Corporation; DISTRIBUTOR: Monogram Pictures Corporation

Fort Osage (February 10, 1952)
DIRECTOR: Lesley Selander; PRODUCER: Walter Mirisch; STORY AND SCREENPLAY: Dan Ullman; CAST: Rod Cameron, Jane Nigh, Morris Ankrum; 70 min; Cinecolor; presented by Monogram Pictures Corporation; DISTRIBUTOR: Monogram Pictures Corporation

Rodeo (March 9, 1952)
DIRECTOR: William Beaudine; PRODUCER: Walter Mirisch; SCREENPLAY: Charles R. Marion; CAST: Jane Nigh, John Archer, Wallace Ford; 71 min; Cinecolor; presented by Monogram Pictures Corporation; DISTRIBUTOR: Monogram Pictures Corporation

Wild Stallion (April 22, 1952)
DIRECTOR: Lewis D. Collins; PRODUCER: Walter Mirisch; SCREENPLAY: Dan Ullman; CAST: Ben Johnson, Edgar Buchanan, Martha Hyer; 70 min; Cinecolor; presented by Monogram Pictures Corporation; DISTRIBUTOR: Monogram Pictures Corporation

African Treasure (with Bomba the Jungle Boy) (June 8, 1952)
DIRECTOR: Ford Beebe; PRODUCER: Walter Mirisch; SCREENPLAY: Ford Beebe, based on the characters created by Roy Rockwood in the "Bomba" books; CAST: Johnny Sheffield, Laurette Luez; 70 min; b&w; presented by Monogram Pictures Corporation; DISTRIBUTOR: Monogram Pictures Corporation

The Rose Bowl Story (August 24, 1952)
DIRECTOR: William Beaudine; PRODUCER: Richard V. Heermance; EXECUTIVE PRODUCER: Walter Mirisch; SCREENPLAY: Charles R. Marion; CAST: Marshall Thompson, Vera Miles, Natalie Wood, Keith Larson, Tom Harmon; 73 min; Cinecolor; presented by Monogram Pictures Corporation; DISTRIBUTOR: Monogram Pictures

Flat Top (November 30, 1952)
DIRECTOR: Lesley Selander; PRODUCER: Walter Mirisch; SCREENPLAY: Steve Fisher; CAST: Sterling Hayden, Richard Carlson, Keith Larson, William Schallert; 83 min; Cinecolor; presented by Allied Artists Pictures Corporation; DISTRIBUTOR: Allied Artists Pictures Corporation
    1 Academy Award nomination

Bomba and the Jungle Girl (December 7, 1952)
DIRECTOR: Ford Beebe; PRODUCER: Walter Mirisch; SCREENPLAY: Ford Beebe, based on the characters created by Roy Rockwood in the "Bomba"

books; CAST: Johnny Sheffield, Karen Sharp, Walter Sande; 70 min; b&w; presented by Monogram Pictures Corporation; DISTRIBUTOR: Monogram Pictures Corporation

Hiawatha (December 28, 1952)
DIRECTOR: Kurt Neuman; PRODUCER: Walter Mirisch; SCREENPLAY: Arthur Strawn and Dan Ullman, based on the poem by Henry Wadsworth Longfellow; CAST: Vincent Edwards, Yvette Duguay, Keith Larson; 79 min; Cinecolor; presented by Allied Artists Pictures Corporation; DISTRIBUTOR: Allied Artists Pictures Corporation

Safari Drums (with Bomba the Jungle Boy) (June 21, 1953)
DIRECTOR: Ford Beebe; PRODUCER: Ford Beebe, Walter Mirisch (uncredited); SCREENPLAY: Ford Beebe, based on the characters created by Roy Rockwood in the "Bomba" books; CAST: Johnny Sheffield, Douglas Kennedy, Barbara Bestar; 71 min; b&w; presented by Allied Artists Pictures Corporation; DISTRIBUTOR: Allied Artists Pictures Corporation

The Maze (July 20, 1953)
DIRECTOR: William Cameron Menzies; PRODUCER: Richard Heermance; EXECUTIVE PRODUCER: Walter Mirisch; SCREENPLAY: Daniel B. Ullman, based on the novel by Maurice Sandoz; CAST: Richard Carlson, Veronica Hurst; 80 min; b&w; photographed in 3-D; presented by Allied Artists Pictures Corporation; DISTRIBUTOR: Allied Artists Pictures Corporation

The Golden Idol (with Bomba the Jungle Boy) (January 10, 1954)
DIRECTOR: Ford Beebe; PRODUCER: Ford Beebe, Walter Mirisch (uncredited); SCREENPLAY: Ford Beebe, based on the characters created by Roy Rockwood in the "Bomba" books; CAST: Johnny Sheffield, Anne Kimbell; 70 min; b&w; presented by Allied Artists Pictures Corporation; DISTRIBUTOR: Allied Artists Pictures Corporation

An Annapolis Story (April 8, 1954)
DIRECTOR: Don Siegel; PRODUCER: Walter Mirisch; STORY: Dan Ullman; SCREENPLAY: Dan Ullman, Geoffrey Homes; CAST: John Derek, Diana Lynn, Kevin McCarthy; 81 min; Technicolor; presented by Allied Artists Pictures Corporation; DISTRIBUTOR: Allied Artists Picture Corporation

Killer Leopard (with Bomba the Jungle Boy) (August 22, 1954)
DIRECTOR: Ford Beebe; PRODUCER: Ford Beebe, Walter Mirisch (uncredited); SCREENPLAY: Ford Beebe, based on the characters created by Roy Rockwood

in the "Bomba" books; CAST: Johnny Sheffield, Beverly Garland; 70 min; b&w; presented by Allied Artists Pictures Corporation; DISTRIBUTOR: Allied Artists Pictures Corporation

Lord of the Jungle (with Bomba with Jungle Boy) (June 12, 1955)
DIRECTOR: Ford Beebe; PRODUCER: Ford Beebe, Walter Mirisch (uncredited); SCREENPLAY: Ford Beebe, based on the characters created by Roy Rockwood in the "Bomba" books; CAST: Johnny Sheffield, Nancy Hale; 69 min; b&w; presented by Allied Artists Pictures Corporation; DISTRIBUTOR: Allied Artists Corporation

Wichita (July 3, 1955)
DIRECTOR: Jacques Tourneur; PRODUCER: Walter Mirisch; STORY AND SCREENPLAY: Daniel B. Ullman; CAST: Joel McCrea, Vera Miles, Lloyd Bridges, Wallace Ford, Edgar Buchanan, Peter Graves, Keith Larson; 81 min; Technicolor; Cinemascope; presented by Allied Artists Pictures Corporation; DISTRIBUTOR: Allied Artists Pictures Corporation
  Golden Globe Award, Best Outdoor Drama

The Warriors (September 11, 1955)
DIRECTOR: Henry Levin; PRODUCER: Walter Mirisch; STORY AND SCREENPLAY: Daniel B. Ullman; CAST: Errol Flynn, Joanne Dru, Peter Finch; 85 min; Technicolor; Cinemascope; presented by Allied Artists Pictures Corporation; DISTRIBUTOR: Allied Artists Pictures Corporation

The First Texan (July 1, 1956)
DIRECTOR: Byron Haskin; PRODUCER: Walter Mirisch; STORY AND SCREENPLAY: Daniel B. Ullman; CAST: Joel McCrea, Felicia Farr, Jeff Morrow, Wallace Ford, Abraham Sofaer, Jody McCrea; 82 min; Technicolor; Cinemascope; presented by Allied Artists Pictures Corporation; DISTRIBUTOR: Allied Artists Pictures Corporation

The Oklahoman (May 19, 1957)
DIRECTOR: Francis Lyon; PRODUCER: Walter Mirisch; SCREENPLAY: Daniel B. Ullman; CAST: Joel McCrea, Barbara Hale, Brad Dexter; 80 min; color by De Luxe; Cinemascope; presented by Allied Artists Pictures Corporation; DISTRIBUTOR: Allied Artists Pictures Corporation

The Tall Stranger (November 17, 1957)
DIRECTOR: Thomas Carr; PRODUCER: Walter Mirisch; SCREENPLAY: Christopher Knopf, from a story by Louis l'Amour; CAST: Joel McCrea, Virginia

Mayo; 81 min; color by De Luxe; Cinemascope; presented by Allied Artists Pictures Corporation; DISTRIBUTOR: Allied Artists Pictures Corporation

Fort Massacre (May 14, 1958)
DIRECTOR: Joseph M. Newman; PRODUCER: Walter M. Mirisch; SCREEN-PLAY: Martin M. Goldsmith; CAST: Joel McCrea, Forrest Tucker, Susan Cabot, John Russell, George N. Neise; 80 min; color by De Luxe; Cinemascope; presented by The Mirisch Company, Inc.; DISTRIBUTOR: United Artists

Man of the West (October 1, 1958)
DIRECTOR: Anthony Mann; PRODUCER: Walter M. Mirisch; SCREENPLAY: Reginald Rose, based on the novel *The Border Jumpers* by Will C. Brown; CAST: Gary Cooper, Julie London, Lee J. Cobb, Arthur O'Connell, Jack Lord; 100 min; color by De Luxe; Cinemascope; presented by Ashton Productions, Inc., in association with The Mirisch Company, Inc.; DISTRIBUTOR: United Artists

Some Like It Hot (March 29, 1959)
DIRECTOR: Billy Wilder; PRODUCER: Billy Wilder; SCREENPLAY: Billy Wilder and I. A. L. Diamond, suggested by a story by R. Thoeren and M. Logan; CAST: Marilyn Monroe, Tony Curtis, Jack Lemmon, George Raft, Pat O'Brian, Joe E. Brown; 120 min; b&w; Ashton Productions, Inc., presents a Mirisch Company Picture; DISTRIBUTOR: United Artists
    6 Academy Award nominations; 1 Academy Award

The Man in the Net (May 20, 1959)
DIRECTOR: Michael Curtiz; PRODUCER: Walter M. Mirisch; SCREENPLAY: Reginald Rose, based on the novel by Patrick Quentin; CAST: Alan Ladd, Carolyn Jones; 96 min; b&w; presented by The Mirisch Company; DISTRIB-UTOR: United Artists

The Gunfight at Dodge City (May 20, 1959)
DIRECTOR: Joseph M. Newman; PRODUCER: Water M. Mirisch; SCREEN-PLAY: Martin M. Goldsmith, Daniel B. Ullman; CAST: Joel McCrea, Julie Adams, John McIntyre, Nancy Gates; 81 min; color by De Luxe; Cinema-scope; presented by The Mirisch Company, Inc.; DISTRIBUTOR: United Artists

The Horse Soldiers (June 12, 1959)
DIRECTOR: John Ford; a Mahin-Rackin Production; SCREENPLAY: John Lee

Mahin and Martin Rackin, based on the novel by Harold Sinclair; CAST: John Wayne, William Holden, Constance Towers; 119 min; color by De Luxe; presented by The Mirisch Company; DISTRIBUTOR: United Artists

Cast a Long Shadow (July 1959)
DIRECTOR: Thomas Carr; PRODUCER: Walter M. Mirisch; SCREENPLAY: Martin M. Goldsmith, John McGreevey; SCREEN STORY: Martin M. Goldsmith, based on the novel by Wayne D. Overholser; CAST: Audie Murphy, Terry Moore, John Dehner; 82 min; b&w; presented by The Mirisch Company; DISTRIBUTOR: United Artists

The Apartment (June 15, 1960)
DIRECTOR: Billy Wilder; PRODUCER: Billy Wilder; SCREENPLAY: Billy Wilder, I. A. L. Diamond; CAST: Jack Lemmon, Shirley MacLaine, Fred MacMurray; 125 min; b&w; Panavision; presented by The Mirisch Company, Inc.; DISTRIBUTOR: United Artists
    10 Academy Award nominations; 5 Academy Awards, including Best Picture

The Magnificent Seven (October 23, 1960)
DIRECTOR: John Sturges; PRODUCER: John Sturges; EXECUTIVE PRODUCER: Walter Mirisch; SCREENPLAY: William Roberts, based on the Akira Kurosawa film *Seven Samurai,* Toho Company Ltd.; CAST: Yul Brynner, Eli Wallach, Steve McQueen, Charles Bronson, Robert Vaughn, Brad Dexter, James Coburn, Horst Buchholz; 128 min; color by De Luxe; Panavision; presented by The Mirisch Company; DISTRIBUTOR: United Artists
    1 Academy Award nomination

By Love Possessed (June 15, 1961)
DIRECTOR: John Sturges; PRODUCER: Walter Mirisch; SCREENPLAY: John Dennis, based on the novel by James Gould Cozzens; CAST: Lana Turner, Efrem Zimbalist Jr., Jason Robards Jr.; 115 min; color by De Luxe; presented by Mirisch Pictures, Inc., in association with Seven Arts Productions, Inc.; DISTRIBUTOR: United Artists

Town Without Pity (October 10, 1961)
DIRECTOR: Gottfried Reinhardt; PRODUCER: Gottfried Reinhardt; SCREENPLAY: Silvia Reinhardt, Georg Hurdalek; ADAPTATION: Jan Lustig, based on the novel *The Verdict* by Manfred Gregor; CAST: Kirk Douglas, E. G. Marshall, Robert Blake, Richard Jaeckel, Frank Sutton, Barbara Rutting, Christine

Kaufmann; 103 min; b&w; presented by The Mirisch Company in Association with Osweg Ltd., Switzerland; DISTRIBUTOR: United Artists
   1 Academy Award nomination

West Side Story (October 18, 1961)
DIRECTOR: Robert Wise, Jerome Robbins; PRODUCER: Robert Wise; SCREENPLAY: Ernest Lehman, based on the play by Arthur Laurents; CAST: Natalie Wood, Richard Beymer, Russ Tamblyn, Rita Moreno, George Chakiris; 152 min; Technicolor; Panavision 70mm; presented by Mirisch Pictures, Inc., in association with Seven Arts Productions, Inc.; DISTRIBUTOR: United Artists
   11 Academy Award nominations; 10 Academy Awards, including Best Picture

One, Two, Three (December 15, 1961)
DIRECTOR: Billy Wilder; PRODUCER: Billy Wilder; SCREENPLAY: Billy Wilder and I. A. L. Diamond, based on the play *Eins, Zwei, Drei* by Ferenc Molnar; CAST: James Cagney, Horst Buchholz, Pamela Tiffin, Arlene Francis; 108 min; b&w; Panavision; presented by The Mirisch Company; DISTRIBUTOR: United Artists
   1 Academy Award nomination

The Children's Hour (December 19, 1961)
DIRECTOR: William Wyler; PRODUCER: William Wyler; SCREENPLAY: John Michael Hayes, based on the play by Lillian Hellman; CAST: Audrey Hepburn, Shirley MacLaine, James Garner; 107 min; b&w; presented by The Mirisch Company; DISTRIBUTOR: United Artists
   5 Academy Award nominations

Follow That Dream (April 11, 1962)
DIRECTOR: Gordon Douglas; PRODUCER: David Wesibart; SCREENPLAY: Charles Lederer, based on the novel *Pioneer Go Home!* by Richard Powell; CAST: Elvis Presley, Arthur O'Connell; 109 min; color by De Luxe; Panavision; presented by The Mirisch Company; DISTRIBUTOR: United Artists

Kid Galahad (August 1, 1962)
DIRECTOR: Phil Karlson; PRODUCER: David Weisbart; SCREENPLAY: William Fay; STORY: Francis Wallace; CAST: Elvis Presley, Gig Young, Lola Albright, Joan Blackman, Charles Bronson; 95 min; color by De Luxe; presented by The Mirisch Company; DISTRIBUTOR: United Artists

Two for the See Saw (November 21, 1962)
DIRECTOR: Robert Wise; PRODUCER: Walter Mirisch; SCREENPLAY: Isobel Lennart, based on the stage play by William Gibson; CAST: Robert Mitchum, Shirley MacLaine; 119 min; b&w; Panavision; presented by Mirisch Pictures and Robert Wise in association with Seven Arts Productions, Inc.; DISTRIBUTOR: United Artists
    2 Academy Award nominations

Irma La Douce (June 5, 1963)
DIRECTOR: Billy Wilder; PRODUCER: Billy Wilder; SCREENPLAY: Billy Wilder and I. A. L. Diamond, based on the play by Alexandre Breffort; CAST: Jack Lemmon, Shirley MacLaine; 143 min; Technicolor; Panavision; presented by The Mirisch Company and Edward L. Alperson; DISTRIBUTOR: United Artists
    3 Academy Award nominations; 1 Academy Award

The Great Escape (July 4, 1963)
DIRECTOR: John Sturges; PRODUCER: John Sturges; SCREENPLAY: James Clavell and W. R. Burnett, based on the novel by Paul Brickhill; CAST: Steve McQueen, James Garner, Richard Attenborough, James Donald, Charles Bronson, Donald Pleasence, James Coburn; 172 min; color by De Luxe; Panavision; presented by The Mirisch Company, Inc.; DISTRIBUTOR: United Artists
    1 Academy Award nomination

Toys in the Attic (July 17, 1963)
DIRECTOR: George Roy Hill; PRODUCER: Walter Mirisch; SCREENPLAY: James Poe, based on the play by Lillian Hellman; CAST: Dean Martin, Geraldine Page, Yvette Mimieux, Wendy Hiller, Gene Tierney, Nan Martin, Larry Gates; 90 min; b&w; Panavision; presented by The Mirisch Corporation; DISTRIBUTOR: United Artists
    1 Academy Award nomination

Stolen Hours (October 2, 1963)
DIRECTOR: Daniel M. Petrie; PRODUCER: Denis Holt; EXECUTIVE PRODUCER: Stuart Millar, Lawrence Turman; SCREENPLAY: Jessamyn West; CAST: Susan Hayward, Michael Craig, Diane Baker, Edward Judd; 100 min; color by De Luxe; presented by Mirisch Films and Barbican Films; DISTRIBUTOR: United Artists

Kings of the Sun (December 18, 1963)
DIRECTOR: J. Lee Thompson; PRODUCER: Lewis J. Rachmil; SCREENPLAY: Elliott Arnold, James R. Webb, story by Elliott Arnold; CAST: Yul Brynner, George Chakiris, Shirley Anne Field; 108 min; color by De Luxe; Panavision; presented by The Mirisch Company; DISTRIBUTOR: United Artists

The Pink Panther (March 18, 1964)
DIRECTOR: Blake Edwards; PRODUCER: Blake Edwards; SCREENPLAY: Maurice Richlin, Blake Edwards; CAST: David Niven, Peter Sellers, Robert Wagner, Capucine; 114 min; Technicolor; Technirama; presented by The Mirisch Company; DISTRIBUTOR: United Artists
   1 Academy Award nomination

633 Squadron (June 24, 1964)
DIRECTOR: Walter E. Grauman; PRODUCER: Cecil F. Ford; EXECUTIVE PRODUCER: Lewis J. Rachmil; SCREENPLAY: James Clavell and Howard Koch, based on the novel by Fredrick E. Smith; CAST: Cliff Robertson, George Chakiris; 95 min; color by De Luxe; Panavision; presented by The Mirisch Corporation; DISTRIBUTOR: United Artists

A Shot in the Dark (July 15, 1964)
DIRECTOR: Blake Edwards; PRODUCER: Blake Edwards; SCREENPLAY: Blake Edwards and William Peter Blatty, based on characters created by Maurice Richlin and Blake Edwards, based on the stage play by Harry Kurnitz, from the play by Marcel Achard; CAST: Peter Sellers, Elke Sommer, George Sanders, Herbert Lom; 101 min; color by De Luxe; Panavision; presented by The Mirisch Corporation; DISTRIBUTOR: United Artists

Kiss Me, Stupid (December 16, 1964)
DIRECTOR: Billy Wilder; PRODUCER: Billy Wilder; SCREENPLAY: Billy Wilder and I. A. L. Diamond, based on the play *L'Ora della Fantasia* by Anna Bonacci; CAST: Dean Martin, Kim Novak, Ray Walston, Felicia Far; 126 min; b&w; Panavision; presented by The Mirisch Corporation; DISTRIBUTOR: Lopert Pictures Corporation

The Pink Phink (December 18, 1964)
PRODUCER: David H. DePatie, Friz Freleng; DIRECTOR: Friz Freleng, Hawley Pratt; STORY: John Dunn; color by De Luxe; a Mirisch-Geoffrey-DePatie-Freleng Production; DISTRIBUTOR: United Artists
   1 Academy Award

The Satan Bug (March 23, 1965)
DIRECTOR: John Sturges; PRODUCER: John Sturges; SCREENPLAY: James Clavell and Edward Anhalt, based on the novel by Ian Stuart; CAST: George Maharis, Richard Basehart, Anne Francis, Dana Andrews; 114 min; color by De Luxe; Panavision; presented by The Mirisch Corporation; DISTRIBUTOR: United Artists

The Pink Blueprint (May 25, 1965)
DIRECTOR: Hawley Pratt; PRODUCER: David H. DePatie, Friz Freleng; STORY: John Dunn; color by De Luxe; a Mirisch-Geoffrey-DePatie-Freleng Production; DISTRIBUTOR: United Artists
   1 Academy Award nomination

The Hallelujah Trail (June 23, 1965)
DIRECTOR: John Sturges; PRODUCER: John Sturges; SCREENPLAY: John Gay, based on the novel by Bill Gulick; CAST: Burt Lancaster, Lee Remick, Jim Hutton, Pamela Tiffin, Donald Pleasence, Brian Keith; 165 min; Technicolor; Ultra Panavision; presented by The Mirisch Corporation; DISTRIBUTOR: United Artists

A Rage to Live (September 15, 1965)
DIRECTOR: Walter Grauman; PRODUCER: Lewis J. Rachmil; SCREENPLAY: John T. Kelley, based on the novel by John O'Hara; CAST: Suzanne Pleshette, Bradford Dillman, Ben Gazzara, Peter Graves; 101 min; b&w; Panavision; presented by The Mirisch Corporation; DISTRIBUTOR: United Artists
   1 Academy Award nomination

Return from the Ashes (November 16, 1965)
DIRECTOR: J. Lee Thompson; PRODUCER: J. Lee Thompson; SCREENPLAY: Julius J. Epstein, based on the novel by Hubert Monteilhet; CAST: Maximilian Schell, Samantha Eggar, Ingrid Thulin, Herbert Lom; 105 min; b&w; Panavision; presented by The Mirisch Corporation; DISTRIBUTOR: United Artists

Cast a Giant Shadow (March 30, 1966)
DIRECTOR: Melville Shavelson; PRODUCER: Melville Shavelson; SCREENPLAY: Melville Shavelson, based on the novel by Ted Berkman; CAST: Kirk Douglas, Senta Berger, Angie Dickinson, James Donald, Topol, with special appearances by Frank Sinatra, Yul Brynner, John Wayne; 138 min; color by De Luxe; Panavision; presented by The Mirisch Corporation; DISTRIBUTOR: United Artists

The Russians Are Coming, the Russians Are Coming (May 25, 1966)
DIRECTOR: Norman Jewison; PRODUCER: Norman Jewison; SCREENPLAY: William Rose, based on the novel *The Off Islander* by Nathaniel Benchley; CAST: Carl Reiner, Eva Marie Saint, Alan Arkin, Brian Keith, Jonathan Winters, Theodore Bikel, John Phillip Law; 126 min; color by De Luxe; Panavision; presented by The Mirisch Corporation; DISTRIBUTOR: United Artists
    4 Academy Award nominations, including Best Picture

What Did You Do in the War, Daddy? (June 29, 1966)
DIRECTOR: Blake Edwards; PRODUCER: Blake Edwards; SCREENPLAY: William Peter Blatty; STORY: Blake Edwards, Maurice Richlin; CAST: James Coburn, Dick Shawn; 116 min; color by De Luxe; Panavision; presented by The Mirisch Corporation; DISTRIBUTOR: United Artists

Hawaii (October 10, 1966)
DIRECTOR: George Roy Hill; PRODUCER: Walter Mirisch; SCREENPLAY: Dalton Trumbo and Daniel Taradash, based on the novel by James A. Michener; CAST: Julie Andrews, Max Von Sydow, Richard Harris, Gene Hackman; 189 min; color by De Luxe; Panavision; presented by The Mirisch Corporation; DISTRIBUTOR: United Artists
    7 Academy Award nominations

The Fortune Cookie (October 19, 1966)
DIRECTOR: Billy Wilder; PRODUCER: Billy Wilder; SCREENPLAY: Billy Wilder, I. A. L. Diamond; CAST: Jack Lemmon, Walter Matthau, Ron Rich, Judi West; 125 min; b&w; Panavision; presented by The Mirisch Corporation; DISTRIBUTOR: United Artists
    4 Academy Award nominations; 1 Academy Award

The Return of the Seven (October 19, 1966)
DIRECTOR: Burt Kennedy; PRODUCER: Ted Richman; SCREENPLAY: Larry Cohen; CAST: Yul Brynner, Robert Fuller, Julian Mateos, Warren Oates, Claude Akins, Jordan Christopher; 95 min; color by De Luxe; Panavision; presented by The Mirisch Productions, Inc in Association with C.B. Films, S.A. Spain; DISTRIBUTOR: United Artists
    1 Academy Award nomination

How to Succeed in Business Without Really Trying (March 9, 1967)
DIRECTOR: David Swift; PRODUCER: David Swift; SCREENPLAY: David Swift, based on the book by Abe Burrows, Jack Weinstock, and Willie Gilbert,

based on the novel by Shepherd Mead; CAST: Robert Morse, Michele Lee, Rudy Vallee; 121 min; color by De Luxe; Panavision; presented by The Mirisch Corporation; DISTRIBUTOR: United Artists

In the Heat of the Night (August 2, 1967)
DIRECTOR: Norman Jewison; PRODUCER: Walter Mirisch; SCREENPLAY: Sterling Silliphant, based on the novel by John Ball; CAST: Sidney Poitier, Rod Steiger, Warren Oates, Lee Grant, Larry Gates, Scott Wilson, William Schallert; 109 min; color by De Luxe; presented by The Mirisch Corporation; DISTRIBUTOR: United Artists
    7 Academy Award nominations; 5 Academy Awards, including Best Picture

Hour of the Gun (October 11, 1967)
DIRECTOR: John Sturges; PRODUCER: John Sturges; SCREENPLAY: Edward Anhalt; CAST: James Garner, Jason Robards, Robert Ryan, Larry Gates, William Schallert; 101 min; color by De Luxe; Panavision; presented by The Mirisch Corporation; DISTRIBUTOR: United Artists

Fitzwilly (December 20, 1967)
DIRECTOR: Delbert Mann; PRODUCER: Walter Mirisch; SCREENPLAY: Isobel Lennart, based on the novel *A Garden of Cucumbers* by Poyntz Tyler; CAST: Dick Van Dyke, Barbara Feldon, John McGiver, Edith Evans; 102 min; color by De Luxe; Panavision; presented by The Mirisch Corporation; DISTRIBUTOR: United Artists

Attack on the Iron Coast (March 1968)
DIRECTOR: Paul Wendkos; PRODUCER: John C. Champion; SCREENPLAY: Herman Hoffman; STORY: John C. Champion; CAST: Lloyd Bridges, Andrew Keir, Sue Lloyd; 89 min; color by De Luxe; presented by Mirisch Films; DISTRIBUTOR: United Artists

The Party (April 4, 1968)
DIRECTOR: Blake Edwards; PRODUCER: Blake Edwards; SCREENPLAY: Blake Edwards, Tom Waldman, Frank Waldman; STORY: Blake Edwards; CAST: Peter Sellers, Claudine Longet, Marge Champion, Steve Franklen; 95 min; color by De Luxe; Panavision; presented by The Mirisch Corporation; DISTRIBUTOR: United Artists

Inspector Clouseau (May 28, 1968)
DIRECTOR: Bud Yorkin; PRODUCER: Lewis J. Rachmil; SCREENPLAY: Tom

Waldman, Frank Waldman, based on characters created by Maurice Richlin and Blake Edwards; CAST: Alan Arkin, Frank Finley; 94 min; color by De Luxe; Panavision; presented by The Mirisch Corporation; DISTRIBUTOR: United Artists

The Thomas Crown Affair (June 26, 1968)
DIRECTOR: Norman Jewison; PRODUCER: Norman Jewison; SCREENPLAY: Alan R. Trustman; CAST: Steve McQueen, Faye Dunaway, Paul Burke; 102 min; color by De Luxe; presented by The Mirisch Corporation; DISTRIBUTOR: United Artists
   2 Academy Award nominations; 1 Academy Award

The First Time (April 1969)
DIRECTOR: James Neilson; PRODUCER: Roger Smith, Allan Carr; SCREENPLAY: Jo Heims, Roger Smith; STORY: Bernard Bassey; CAST: Jacqueline Bisset, Wes Stern, Rick Kelman, Wink Roberts; 90 min; color by De Luxe; presented by The Mirisch Production Company; DISTRIBUTOR: United Artists

Sinful Davey (May 28, 1969)
DIRECTOR: John Huston; PRODUCER: William N. Graf; EXECUTIVE PRODUCER: Walter Mirisch; SCREENPLAY: James R. Webb; CAST: John Hurt, Pamela Franklin, Nigel Davenport, Ronald Fraser, Robert Morley; 95 min; color by De Luxe; Panavision; presented by The Mirisch Corporation; DISTRIBUTOR: United Artists

Guns of the Magnificent Seven (May 28, 1969)
DIRECTOR: Paul Wendkos; PRODUCER: Vincent M. Fennelly; SCREENPLAY: Herman Hoffman; CAST: George Kennedy, James Whitmore, Monte Markham, Reni Santoni, Bernie Casey, Scott Thomas, Joe Don Baker; 106 min; color by De Luxe; Panavision; presented by The Mirisch Production Company; DISTRIBUTOR: United Artists

Submarine X-1 (July 30, 1969)
DIRECTOR: William Graham; PRODUCER: John C. Champion; SCREENPLAY: Donald Sanford, Guy Elmes; STORY: John C. Champion, Edmund North; CAST: James Caan, David Summer; 89 min; color by De Luxe; presented by Mirisch Films; DISTRIBUTOR: United Artists

Some Kind of a Nut (September 25, 1969)
DIRECTOR: Garson Kanin; PRODUCER: Walter Mirisch; SCREENPLAY: Garson Kanin; CAST: Dick Van Dyke, Angie Dickinson, Rosemary Forsythe;

89 min; color by De Luxe; presented by The Mirisch Production Company; DISTRIBUTOR: United Artists

The Thousand Plane Raid (October 1969)
DIRECTOR: Boris Sagal; PRODUCER: Lewis J. Rachmil; SCREENPLAY: Donald S. Sanford; STORY: Robert Vincent Wright; CAST: Christopher George, Laraine Stephens, J. D. Cannon; 94 min; color by De Luxe; presented by Mirisch Films; DISTRIBUTOR: United Artists

Gaily, Gaily (December 16, 1969)
DIRECTOR: Norman Jewison; PRODUCER: Norman Jewison; SCREENPLAY: Abram S. Ginnes, based on the book by Ben Hecht; CAST: Beau Bridges, George Kennedy, Hume Cronyn, Melina Mercouri; 108 min; color by De Luxe; presented by The Mirisch Production Company; DISTRIBUTOR: United Artists
    3 Academy Award nominations

Hell Boats (February 1970)
DIRECTOR: Paul Wendkos; PRODUCER: Lewis J. Rachmil; SCREENPLAY: Anthony Spinner, Donald Ford, Derek Ford; STORY: S. S. Schweitze; CAST: James Franciscus, Elizabeth Shepherd; 95 min; color by De Luxe; presented by Oakmont Productions; DISTRIBUTOR: United Artists

Halls of Anger (March 25, 1970)
DIRECTOR: Paul Bogart; PRODUCER: Herbert Hirschman; EXECUTIVE PRODUCER: Walter Mirisch; SCREENPLAY: John Shaner, Al Ramrus; CAST: Calvin Lockhart, Janet MacLachlin, Jeff Bridges, James A. Watson Jr.; 99 min; color by De Luxe; presented by The Mirisch Production Company; DISTRIBUTOR: United Artists

The Last Escape (May 6, 1970)
DIRECTOR: Walter Grauman; PRODUCER: Irving Temaner; SCREENPLAY: Herman Hoffman; STORY: John C. Champion, Barry Trivers; CAST: Stuart Whitman, John Collin; 90 min; color by De Luxe; presented by Oakmont Productions; DISTRIBUTOR: United Artists

Mosquito Squadron (May 6, 1970)
DIRECTOR: Boris Sagal; PRODUCER: Lewis J. Rachmil; SCREENPLAY: Donald S. Sanford, Joyce Perry; CAST: David McCallum, Suzanne Neve; 90 min; color by De Luxe; presented by Oakmont Productions; DISTRIBUTOR: United Artists

The Landlord (May 20, 1970)
DIRECTOR: Hal Ashby; PRODUCER: Norman Jewison; SCREENPLAY: Bill Gunn, based on the novel by Kristin Hunter; CAST: Beau Bridges, Lee Grant, Diana Sands, Pearl Bailey; 110 min; color by De Luxe; presented by The Mirisch Production Company; DISTRIBUTOR: United Artists
    1 Academy Award nomination

The Hawaiians (June 17, 1970)
DIRECTOR: Tom Gries; PRODUCER: Walter Mirisch; SCREENPLAY: James R. Webb, based on the novel by James A. Michener; CAST: Charlton Heston, Geraldine Chaplin, John Phillip Law, Tina Chen, Mako, Alec McCowen; 134 min; color by De Luxe; Panavision; presented by The Mirisch Production Company; DISTRIBUTOR: United Artists
    1 Academy Award nomination

They Call Me MISTER Tibbs! (July 8, 1970)
DIRECTOR: Gordon Douglas; PRODUCER: Herbert Hirschman; EXECUTIVE PRODUCER: Walter Mirisch; SCREENPLAY: Alan R. Trustman, James R. Webb; STORY: Alan R. Trustman, based on characters created by John Ball; CAST: Sidney Poitier, Martin Landau, Barbara McNair, Anthony Zerbe, Norma Crane; 108 min; color by De Luxe; presented by The Mirisch Production Company; DISTRIBUTOR: United Artists

Cannon for Cordoba (October 14, 1970)
DIRECTOR: Paul Wendkos; PRODUCER: Vincent M. Fennelly; SCREENPLAY: Stephen Kandel; CAST: George Peppard, Giovanna Ralli, Raf Vallone, Pete Duel; 104 min; color by De Luxe; Panavision; presented by The Mirisch Production Company; DISTRIBUTOR: United Artists

The Private Life of Sherlock Holmes (October 29, 1970)
DIRECTOR: Billy Wilder; PRODUCER: Billy Wilder; SCREENPLAY: Billy Wilder and I. A. L. Diamond, based on the characters created by Arthur Conan Doyle; CAST: Robert Stephens, Colin Blakley, Genevieve Page; 125 min; color by De Luxe; Panavision; presented by The Mirisch Production Company; DISTRIBUTOR: United Artists

The Organization (October 20, 1971)
DIRECTOR: Don Medford; PRODUCER: Walter Mirisch; SCREENPLAY: James R. Webb, based on the characters created by John Ball; CAST: Sidney Poitier, Barbara McNair, Gerald S. O'Loughlin, Allen Garfield, Raul Julia, Ron

O'Neal, James A. Watson Jr.; 108 min; color by De Luxe; presented by The Mirisch Production Company; DISTRIBUTOR: United Artists

Fiddler on the Roof (November 3, 1971)
DIRECTOR: Norman Jewison; PRODUCER: Norman Jewison; SCREENPLAY: Joseph Stein, adapted from his stage play; CAST: Topol, Norma Crane, Leonard Frey, Molly Picon; 181 min; color by De Luxe; Panavision; presented by The Mirisch Production Company; DISTRIBUTOR: United Artists
   8 Academy Award nominations, including Best Picture; 3 Academy Awards

The Magnificent Seven Ride! (August 1, 1972)
DIRECTOR: George McCowan; PRODUCER: William A. Calihan; SCREENPLAY: Arthur Rowe; CAST: Lee Van Cleef, Stefanie Powers, Michael Callan, Mariette Hartley, Luke Askew, Pedro Armendariz Jr.; 106 min; color by De Luxe; presented by The Mirisch Production Company; DISTRIBUTOR: United Artists

Avanti! (December 17, 1972)
DIRECTOR: Billy Wilder; PRODUCER: Billy Wilder; SCREENPLAY: Billy Wilder and I. A. L. Diamond, based on the play *A Touch of Spring* by Samuel Taylor; CAST: Jack Lemmon, Juliet Mills, Clive Revill; 144 min; color by De Luxe; presented by The Mirisch Corporation; DISTRIBUTOR: United Artists

Scorpio (April 19, 1973)
DIRECTOR: Michael Winner; PRODUCER: Walter Mirisch; SCREENPLAY: David W. Rintels, Gerald Wilson; STORY: David W. Rintels; CAST: Burt Lancaster, Alain Delon, Paul Scofield; 114 min; color by De Luxe; presented by The Mirisch Corporation; DISTRIBUTOR: United Artists

The Spikes Gang (May 1, 1974)
DIRECTOR: Richard Fleischer; PRODUCER: Walter Mirisch; SCREENPLAY: Irving Ravetch, Harriet Frank Jr., based on the book *The Bank Robber* by Giles Tippette; CAST: Lee Marvin, Gary Grimes, Ron Howard, Charlie Martin Smith; 96 min; color by De Luxe; presented by The Mirisch Corporation; DISTRIBUTOR: United Artists

Mr. Majestyk (July 17, 1974)
DIRECTOR: Richard Fleischer; PRODUCER: Walter Mirisch; SCREENPLAY: Elmore Leonard; CAST: Charles Bronson, Al Lettieri, Linda Cristal, Lee Purcell;

104 min; color by De Luxe; presented by The Mirisch Corporation; DISTRIB-
UTOR: United Artists

Midway (June 18, 1976)
DIRECTOR: Jack Smight; PRODUCER: Walter Mirisch; SCREENPLAY: Donald
S. Sanford; CAST: Charlton Heston, Henry Fonda, James Coburn, Glenn
Ford, Hal Holbrook, Toshiro Mifune, Robert Mitchum, Cliff Robertson,
Robert Wagner; 132 min; Technicolor; Panavision; presented by The Mirisch
Corporation; DISTRIBUTOR: Universal Studios

Gray Lady Down (March 10, 1978)
DIRECTOR: David Greene; PRODUCER: Walter Mirisch; SCREENPLAY: James
Whittaker, Howard Sackler, based on the novel *Event 1000* by David Lavallee,
adaptation by Frank P. Rosenberg; CAST: Charlton Heston, David Carradine,
Stacy Keach, Ned Beatty; 111 min; Technicolor; Panavision; presented by The
Mirisch Corporation; DISTRIBUTOR: Universal Studios

Same Time, Next Year (November 22, 1978)
DIRECTOR: Robert Mulligan; PRODUCER: Walter Mirisch, Morton Gottlieb;
SCREENPLAY: Bernard Slade, based on his play; CAST: Ellen Burstyn, Alan
Alda; 119 min; Technicolor; presented by The Mirisch Corporation; DISTRIB-
UTOR: Universal Studios
   4 Academy Award nominations

The Prisoner of Zenda (May 25, 1979)
DIRECTOR: Richard Quine; PRODUCER: Walter Mirisch; SCREENPLAY: Dick
Clement and Ian La Frenais, based on the novel by Anthony Hope, as drama-
tized by Edward Rose; CAST: Peter Sellers, Lynne Frederick, Lionel Jeffries,
Elke Sommer; 108 min; Technicolor; presented by The Mirisch Corporation;
DISTRIBUTOR: Universal Studios

Dracula (July 13, 1979)
DIRECTOR: John Badham; PRODUCER: Walter Mirisch; EXECUTIVE PRO-
DUCER: Marvin Mirisch; SCREENPLAY: W. D. Richter, based on the play by
Hamilton Dean and John L. Balderson, from the novel by Bram Stoker; CAST:
Frank Langella, Laurence Olivier, Donald Pleasence; 109 min; Technicolor;
Panavision; presented by The Mirisch Corporation; DISTRIBUTOR: Universal
Studios

Romantic Comedy (October 7, 1983)
DIRECTOR: Arthur Hiller; PRODUCER: Walter Mirisch, Morton Gottlieb;

EXECUTIVE PRODUCER: Marvin Mirisch; SCREENPLAY: Bernard Slade, based on his play; CAST: Dudley Moore, Mary Steenburgen, Frances Sternhagen; 103 min; color by De Luxe; presented by The Mirisch Corporation; DISTRIBUTOR: United Artists

Movies of the Week

High Midnight (November 27, 1979) CBS
DIRECTOR: Daniel Haller; PRODUCER: Andrew Mirisch; SCREENPLAY: Michael Montgomery, Kathryn Montgomery; CAST: Mike Connors, David Birney; 120 min; Technicolor; a Production of The Mirisch Corporation; DISTRIBUTOR: Universal Studios

Desperado (April 27, 1987) NBC
DIRECTOR: Virgil W. Vogel; EXECUTIVE PRODUCER: Andrew Mirisch; SCREENPLAY: Elmore Leonard; CAST: Alex McArthur, David Warner, Yaphet Kotto; 120 min; Technicolor; a Walter Mirisch Production; DISTRIBUTOR: Universal Studios

Return of Desperado (1988) NBC
DIRECTOR: E. W. Swackhamer; EXECUTIVE PRODUCER: Andrew Mirisch; SCREENPLAY: John Mankiewicz, Daniel Pyne, Charles Grant Craig, based on the characters created by Elmore Leonard; CAST: Alex McArthur, Billy Dee Williams, Robert Foxworth; 120 min; Technicolor; a Walter Mirisch Production; DISTRIBUTOR: Universal Studios

Desperado: Avalanche at Devil's Ridge (May 24, 1988) NBC
DIRECTOR: Richard Compton; EXECUTIVE PRODUCER: Andrew Mirisch; SCREENPLAY: Larry Cohen, based on the characters created by Elmore Leonard; CAST: Alex McArthur, Rod Steiger, Lise Cutter; 120 min; Technicolor; a Walter Mirisch Production; DISTRIBUTOR: Universal Studios

Desperado: Outlaw Wars (1989) NBC
DIRECTOR: E. W. Swackhamer; EXECUTIVE PRODUCER: Andrew Mirisch; SCREENPLAY: William Wisher; STORY: Andrew Mirisch, based on the characters created by Elmore Leonard; CAST: Alex McArthur, Richard Farnsworth, James Remar, Brad Dourif; 120 min; Technicolor; a Mirisch Company Production; DISTRIBUTOR: Universal Studios

Desperado: Badlands Justice (December 17, 1989) NBC
DIRECTOR: E. W. Swackhamer; EXECUTIVE PRODUCER: Andrew Mirisch;

SCREENPLAY: Leslie Bohem; STORY: Andrew Mirisch, Leslie Bohem, based on the characters created by Elmore Leonard; CAST: Alex McArthur, John Rhys Davies, James Sikking; 120 min; color; a Mirisch Company Production; DISTRIBUTOR: Universal Studios

Tagget (1990) USA
DIRECTOR: Richard Heffron; EXECUTIVE PRODUCER: Andrew Mirisch; SCREENPLAY: Peter S. Fisher, Richard Heffron, and Janis Diamond, based on the novel by Irving A. Greenfield; CAST: Daniel J. Travanti, Roxanne Hart; 120 min; color by De Luxe; a Mirisch Films, Inc., Production in Association with Tagget Productions, Inc., MTE an MCA Company

Trouble Shooters: Trapped Beneath the Earth (October 3, 1993) NBC
DIRECTOR: Bradford May; PRODUCER: Ted Kurdyla; EXECUTIVE PRODUCER: Walter Mirisch; SCREENPLAY: Michael Pavone, Dave Alan Johnson; ORIGINAL STORY: Wesley Strick; CAST: Kris Kristofferson; 120 min; color by De Luxe; Walter Mirisch Productions, Amblin Television, Gino Productions; DISTRIBUTOR: Universal Studios

Lily in Winter (December 8, 1994) USA
DIRECTOR: Delbert Mann; PRODUCER: Anthony Santa Croce; EXECUTIVE PRODUCER: Walter Mirisch; SCREENPLAY: Robert Eisele; STORY: Robert Eisele, J. Michael Riva, Julie Moskowitz, Gary Stephens; CAST: Natalie Cole, Brian Bonsall; 120 min; color; a Walter Mirisch Production—Ascato Productions, Inc.; DISTRIBUTOR: Universal Studios

A Case for Life (February 25, 1995) ABC
DIRECTOR: Eric Laneuville; PRODUCER: Anthony Santa Croce; EXECUTIVE PRODUCER: Walter Mirisch; WRITTEN BY: Vickie Patik; CAST: Valerie Bertinelli, Mel Harris; 120 min; color; a Walter Mirisch Production; Victor Television

The Magnificent Seven (1997) CBS
DIRECTOR: Geoff Murphy; EXECUTIVE PRODUCER: Walter Mirisch: EXECUTIVE PRODUCER: John Watson, Pen Densham, Richard Barton Lewis; SCREENPLAY: Frank Q. Dobbs, Chris Black; TELEVISION STORY: Pen Densham, John Watson, based on the original screenplay by William Roberts, adapted from the screenplay by Akira Kurosawa; CAST: Michael Biehn, Eric Close, Andrew Kavovit, Dale Midkiff, Ron Perlman, Anthony Starke, Rick Worthy; 120 min; color; an MGM Television Production with Trilogy

Entertainment Group and The Mirisch Corporation; DISTRIBUTOR MGM Television

Television Series

Wichita Town (September 30, 1959 to April 6, 1960) NBC
PRODUCER: Mirisch Television Enterprises; EXECUTIVE PRODUCER: Walter Mirisch (uncredited); ASSOCIATE PRODUCER: Richard Heermance; CAST: Joel McCrea, Jody McCrea, Carlos Romero; 26 episodes; 30 min; b&w; presented by Mirisch-McCrea Television; Filmed by Four Star

Peter Loves Mary (October 12, 1960 to May 31, 1960) NBC
PRODUCER: Billy Friedberg; CREATED BY: Dan Simon; CAST: Peter Lind Hayes, Mary Healy, Bea Benaderet; 32 episodes; 30 min; b&w; a Four Star-Mirisch-Mount Tom Production in Association with Mirisch Telefilms, Inc.

Super 6 (September 10, 1966 to August 31, 1967) NBC
PRODUCER: David H. DePatie, Friz Freleng; 20 episodes; 30 min; color by De Luxe; a DePatie-Freleng Production in Association with Mirisch-Rich Television; DISTRIBUTOR: United Artists Television

Hey Landlord! (September 11, 1966 to May 14, 1967) NBC
PRODUCER: Garry Marshall, Jerry Belson; CREATORS AND SCRIPT CONSULTANTS: Jerry Belson, Garry Marshall; CAST: Will Hutchins, Sandy Baron; 32 episodes; 30 min; color by De Luxe; a Mirisch-Rich Television Production; DISTRIBUTOR: United Artists Television

The Rat Patrol (September 12, 1966 to April 16, 1968) ABC
PRODUCER: Jon Epstein; EXECUTIVE PRODUCER: Tom Gries; CREATED BY: Tom Gries; CAST: Christopher George, Gary Raymond; 58 episodes; 30 min; color by De Luxe; a Mirisch-Rich Television Production; DISTRIBUTOR: United Artists Television

Super President (September 9, 1967 to December 28, 1968) NBC
PRODUCER: David H. DePatie, Friz Freleng; 15 episodes; 30 min; color by De Luxe; a DePatie-Freleng Production in Association with Mirisch-Rich Television; DISTRIBUTOR: United Artists Television

Here Comes the Grump (September 6, 1969 to September 4, 1971) NBC
PRODUCER: David H. DePatie, Friz Freleng; 17 episodes; 30 min; color

by De Luxe; a DePatie-Freleng Enterprises Production in Association with Mirisch Television

The Pink Panther Show (September 6, 1969 to September 1971) NBC
PRODUCER: David H. DePatie, Friz Freleng; 17 episodes; 30 min; color by De Luxe; a Mirisch-Geoffrey-DePatie-Freleng Production; DISTRIBUTOR: United Artists Television

The Pink Panther Meets the Ant and the Aardvark (September 1971 to September 1976) NBC
PRODUCER: David H. DePatie, Friz Freleng; 17 episodes; 30 min; color by De Luxe; a Mirisch-Geoffrey-DePatie-Freleng Production; DISTRIBUTOR: United Artists Television

The Pink Panther Laugh and a Half Hour (September 1976 to September 2, 1978) NBC
PRODUCER: David H. DePatie, Friz Freleng; 26 episodes; 90 min; color by De Luxe; a Mirisch-Geoffrey-DePatie-Freleng Production; DISTRIBUTOR: United Artists Television

The All New Pink Panther Show (September 9, 1978 to September 1, 1979) ABC
PRODUCER: David H. DePatie, Friz Freleng; 32 episodes (some new); 30 min; color by De Luxe; a Mirisch-Geoffrey-DePatie-Freleng Production; DISTRIBUTOR: United Artists Television

The Pink Panther and Sons (September 15, 1984 to September 6, 1985) NBC
CREATIVE PRODUCER: Friz Freleng; PRODUCER: David H. DePatie; EXECUTIVE PRODUCER: William Hanna, Joseph Barbera; 13 episodes; 30 min; color; Produced by Mirisch-Geoffrey-DePatie-Freleng in Association with Hanna-Barbera Productions, Inc.; DISTRIBUTOR: MGM Television

The Magnificent Seven (January 3, 1998 to July 16, 1999) CBS
EXECUTIVE PRODUCER: Walter Mirisch; EXECUTIVE PRODUCER: John Watson, Pen Densham, Richard Barton Lewis; DEVELOPED BY: John Watson, Pen Densham; CAST: Michael Biehn, Eric Close, Andrew Kavovit, Dale Midkiff, Ron Perlman, Anthony Starke, Rick Worthy; 21 episodes; 60 min; color; an MGM Television Production with Trilogy Entertainment Group and The Mirisch Corporation; DISTRIBUTOR: MGM Television
2 Emmy Award nominations; 1 Emmy Award

The New Pink Panther Show (1993 to 1994) Syndication
EXECUTIVE PRODUCER: Walter Mirisch, Marvin Mirisch; EXECUTIVE PRO-
DUCER: Paul Sabella, Mark Young; CREATIVE CONSULTANTS: David H. De-
Patie, Friz Freleng; 60 episodes; 30 min; color; a Mirisch-Geoffrey-DePatie-
Freleng Production; DISTRIBUTOR: MGM Television

Television Specials

Goldilocks (1971) NBC
PRODUCER: David H. DePatie, Friz Freleng; DIRECTOR: Friz Freleng; WRIT-
TEN BY: A. J. Carothers; CAST: Bing Crosby, Mary Francis Crosby, Nathaniel
Crosby, Kathryn Grant Crosby; 30 min; color by De Luxe; presented by
Mirisch Films DePatie-Freleng Enterprises

A Pink Christmas (Pink Panther half-hour special) (December 1978) ABC
PRODUCER: David H. DePatie, Friz Freleng; DIRECTOR: Bill Perez; WRITTEN
BY: John W. Dunn, Friz Freleng; 30 min; color by De Luxe; presented by
Mirisch-Geoffrey-DePatie-Freleng Enterprises; DISTRIBUTOR: United Art-
ists Television

Olym-Pinks (Pink Panther half-hour special) (1980) ABC
PRODUCER: David H. DePatie, Friz Freleng; DIRECTOR: Gerry Chiniguy,
Art Davis, Art Leonardi; WRITTEN BY: Friz Freleng, John W. Dunn, David
Detiege; 30 min; color by De Luxe; presented by Mirisch-Geoffrey-DePatie-
Freleng Enterprises; DISTRIBUTOR: United Artists Television

Dennis the Menace: Mayday for Mother (1980) NBC
PRODUCER: David H. DePatie, Friz Freleng; DIRECTOR: Friz Freleng;
CREATED AND WRITTEN FOR TELEVISION BY: Hank Ketcham; 30 min;
color by De Luxe; a DePatie-Freleng Production in Association with Mirisch
Films, Inc.

Pink at First Sight (Pink Panther half-hour special) (February 14, 1981) ABC
PRODUCER: David H. DePatie, Friz Freleng; DIRECTOR: Bob Richardson;
WRITTEN BY: Owen Crump, D. W. Owen, adapted from O. Henry's story
"The Cop and the Anthem," based on characters created by David H.
DePatie and Friz Freleng; 30 min; color by De Luxe; presented by
Mirisch-Geoffrey-DePatie-Freleng Enterprises; DISTRIBUTOR: United Art-
ists Television

Television Pilots

The Iron Horseman (1959) NBC
DIRECTOR: Lesley Selander; PRODUCER: Lou Edelman (uncredited); EXECU-
TIVE PRODUCER: Walter Mirisch (uncredited); ASSOCIATE PRODUCER:
Richard Heermance; WRITTEN BY: Leslie Stevens, Richard Alan Simmons;
CAST: Grant Williams; 30 min; b&w; a Mirisch Video, Inc., Production

Some Like It Hot (1961) NBC
DIRECTOR: Walter E. Grauman; PRODUCER: Walter E. Grauman; WRITTEN
BY: Herbert Baker; CAST: Vic Damone, Dick Patterson, Tina Louise, Rudy
Vallee; 30 min; b&w; a Production of Mirisch Video, Inc., and Ziv–United
Artists, Inc.; DISTRIBUTOR: United Artists Television

Sheriff Who? (September 5, 1967) NBC
DIRECTOR: Jerry Paris; PRODUCER: Jerry Belson, Garry Marshall; EXECU-
TIVE PRODUCER: Lee Rich; WRITTEN BY: Garry Marshall, Jerry Belson;
CREATED BY: Larry Cohen, Curtis Sanders; CAST: John Astin, Dick Shawn;
30 min; color by De Luxe; a Mirisch-Rich Television Production; DISTRIB-
UTOR: United Artists Television

The Pink Panther (1989) CBS
DIRECTOR: Gary Nelson; EXECUTIVE PRODUCER: Walter Mirisch; WRIT-
TEN BY: George Schenck, Frank Cardea; CAST: Charlie Schlatter, Dabbs
Greer, Lisa Waltz, Tim Stack, Karen Austin; 30 min; color; presented by
Mirisch-Geoffrey-DePatie-Freleng Enterprises; DISTRIBUTOR: MGM
Television

Films Supervised at Allied Artists, among others

Riot in Cell Block 11 (February 28, 1954)
DIRECTOR: Don Siegel; PRODUCER: Walter Wanger; SCREENPLAY: Richard
Collins; CAST: Neville Brand, Emile Meyer; 80 min; b&w; presented by
Allied Artists Pictures Corporation; DISTRIBUTOR: Allied Artists Pictures
Corporation

The Human Jungle (October 3, 1954)
DIRECTOR: Joseph M. Newman; PRODUCER: Hayes Goetz; SCREENPLAY:
Daniel Fuchs, William Sackheim; STORY: William Sackheim; CAST: Gary

Merrill, Jan Sterling, Regis Toomey, Lamont Johnson, Pat Walt, Chuck Connors; 82 min; b&w; presented by Allied Artists Pictures Corporation; DISTRIBUTOR: Allied Artists Pictures Corporation

The Big Combo (February 13, 1955)
DIRECTOR: Joseph Lewis; PRODUCER: Sidney Harmon; SCREENPLAY: Philip Yordon; CAST: Cornel Wile, Richard Conte, Brian Donlevy, Jean Wallace, Robert Middleton, Lee Van Cleef, Earl Holliman; 89 min; b&w; presented by Allied Artists Pictures Corporation; DISTRIBUTOR: Allied Artists Pictures Corporation

Seven Angry Men (March 30, 1955)
DIRECTOR: Charles Marquis Warren; PRODUCER: Vincent M. Fennelly; STORY AND SCREENPLAY: Daniel B. Ullman; CAST: Raymond Massey, Debra Paget, Jeffrey Hunter; 91 min; b&w; presented by Allied Artists Pictures Corporation; DISTRIBUTOR: Allied Artists Pictures Corporation

The Phenix City Story (August 14, 1955)
DIRECTOR: Phil Karlson; PRODUCER: Samuel Bischoff, David Diamond; SCREENPLAY: Daniel Mainwaring, Crane Wilbur; CAST: John McIntire, Richard Kiley; 100 min; b&w; presented by Allied Artists Pictures Corporation; DISTRIBUTOR: Allied Artists Pictures Corporation

Invasion of the Body Snatchers (February 5, 1956)
DIRECTOR: Don Siegel; PRODUCER: Walter Wanger; SCREENPLAY: Daniel Mainwaring, Richard Collins, based on *Collier's* magazine serial by Jack Finney; CAST: Kevin McCarthy, Dana Wynter, Larry Gates; 80 min; b&w; Panavision; presented by Allied Artists Pictures Corporation; DISTRIBUTOR: Allied Artists Pictures Corporation

Crime in the Streets (June 10, 1956)
DIRECTOR: Donald Siegel; PRODUCER: Vincent M. Fennelly; STORY AND SCREENPLAY: Reginald Rose; CAST: James Whitmore, Sal Mineo, Mark Rydell, John Cassavetes; 91 min; b&w; presented by Allied Artists Pictures Corporation; DISTRIBUTOR: Allied Artists Pictures Corporation

Hold Back the Night (July 25, 1956)
DIRECTOR: Allan Dwan; PRODUCER: Hayes Goetz; SCREENPLAY: John C. Higgins, Walter Doniger, based on the novel by Pat Frank; CAST: John Payne,

Chuck Connors, Peter Graves; 80 min; b&w; presented by Allied Artists Pictures Corporation; DISTRIBUTOR: Allied Artists Pictures Corporation

Friendly Persuasion (November 25, 1956)
DIRECTOR: William Wyler; PRODUCER: William Wyler; SCREENPLAY: Michael Wilson, based on the novel by Jessamyn West; CAST: Gary Cooper, Dorothy McGuire; 137 min; color; presented by Allied Artists Pictures Corporation; DISTRIBUTOR: Allied Artists Pictures Corporation
  6 Academy Award nominations, including Best Picture

Love in the Afternoon (June 19, 1957)
DIRECTOR: Billy Wilder; PRODUCER: Billy Wilder; SCREENPLAY: Billy Wilder, I. A. L. Diamond, based on the novel *Ariane* by Claude Anet; CAST: Gary Cooper, Audrey Hepburn, Maurice Chevalier; 125 min; b&w; presented by Allied Artists Pictures Corporation; DISTRIBUTOR: Allied Artists Pictures Corporation

COMPILED BY LAWRENCE A. MIRISCH

Career Milestones and Awards

Employed, Monogram Pictures Corporation (1945)

Executive Producer in charge of production, Monogram Pictures Corporation / Allied Artists Pictures Corporation (July 1951)

Board of Directors, Screen Producers Guild (1951–Present)

Formed The Mirisch Corporation with brothers Harold and Marvin (September 1, 1957)

President, Screen Producers Guild of America (1959–62)

Golden Globe Award, Best Outdoor Drama for *Wichita* (1956)

President; Permanent Charities of the Motion Picture Industry (1961–62)

Board of Directors, Motion Picture Association of America (January 4, 1961 to April 14, 1980)

Delegate of the United States, fourteenth International Film Festival, Cannes, France (May 3, 1961)

l'Ordre des Arts et des Letters de la Republique Francaise (May 17, 1961)

Board of Governors, Academy of Motion Picture Arts and Sciences (1964–70, 1972–78, and 1979–82)

Board Member, Center Theatre Group Los Angeles, California (1967–Present)

New York Film Critics Award, Best Picture for *In the Heat of the Night* (1967)

Golden Globe Award, Best Drama for *In the Heat of the Night* (1967)

Cleveland Film Critics Circle, Best Picture for *In the Heat of the Night* (1967)

Film Daily 45th Annual Poll, *In the Heat of the Night* as one of the year's Ten Best Pictures (1967)

Producer of the Year, Producers Guild of America (1967)

United Nations Award, British Academy for *In the Heat of the Night* (1967)

Alumnus of the Year, University of Wisconsin (March 17, 1967)

Best Picture of 1967, Academy Award for *In the Heat of the Night* (April 10, 1968)

NAACP Image award for *In the Heat of the Night* (1968)

Advisory Board, California State University Northridge (1969–93)

Board of Directors, Cedars-Sinai Medical Center (1971–96)

Building Committee Chairman, Academy of Motion Picture Arts & Sciences (1970)

General Chairman, Motion Picture and Television Relief Fund 50th Anniversary Celebration (June 13, 1971)

Board of Trustees, Motion Picture and Television Fund (1972–Present)

Producer of the Year, National Association of Theatre Owners (November 1, 1972)

President, Academy of Motion Picture Arts and Sciences (1973–77)

President, Center Theater Group (1976–79)

Board of Trustees, American Film Institute (1973–83)

Producer of the Year, 17th Annual Convention United Motion Picture Association Show-a-Rama (November 1973)

Cecil B. DeMille Award for outstanding contributions to the Entertainment Field, Hollywood Foreign Press Association (January 29, 1976)

Will Rogers Award, The Beverly Hills City Commerce and Civic Association (February 13, 1976)

Irving G. Thalberg Memorial Award, Academy of Motion Picture Arts and Sciences, "for a consistently high quality of motion picture production" (April 3, 1978)

Best Horror Film, Academy of Science Fiction Fantasy & Horror Films, for *Dracula* (1979)

Board Member, The Music Center of Los Angeles (1979–Present)

Jean Hersholt Humanitarian Award, Academy of Motion Picture Arts and Sciences (April 11, 1983)

Search and Building Committee Chairman, Academy of Motion Picture Arts & Sciences, for the Fairbanks Center for Motion Picture Study (1988)

Honorary Doctorate, University of Wisconsin (May 21, 1989)

UCLA Medal, University of California at Los Angeles (June 17, 1989)

Board of Directors, UCLA Foundation

Life Trustee, Cedars-Sinai Medical Center (1996)

The David O. Selznick Motion Picture Life Achievement Award, Producers Guild of America (1996)

Wisconsin Film Festival, "A Tribute to Walter Mirisch—A Producer for All Seasons" (March 30 to April 2, 2000)

Board of Visitors, University of Wisconsin (2001–Present)

Producer, "All About Gordon" a Tribute to Gordon Davison, Center Theatre Group (December 13, 2004)

Los Angeles County Art Museum tribute, "The Magnificent Mirisches" (October 16 to October 30, 2004)

Museum of Modern Art tribute (December 1 to 31, 2006)

Board of Governors Lifetime Achievement Award, Cedars-Sinai Medical Center (November 15, 2007)

National Film Preservation Board, *Invasion of the Body Snatchers* (1956, USA) National Film Registry (2002)

National Film Preservation Board, *Some Like It Hot* (1959, USA) National Film Registry (1989)

National Film Preservation Board, *The Apartment* (1960, USA) National Film Registry (1994)

National Film Preservation Board, *West Side Story* (1961, USA) National Film Registry (1997)

National Film Preservation Board, *In the Heat of the Night* (1967, USA) National Film Registry (2002)

American Film Institute 100 Years . . . 100 Movies, *Some Like It Hot*

American Film Institute 100 Years . . . 100 Movies, *The Apartment*

American Film Institute 100 Years . . . 100 Passions, *West Side Story* (2002)

American Film Institute 100 Years . . . 100 of the Greatest Movies, *In the Heat of the Night* (2007)

COMPILED BY LAWRENCE A. MIRISCH

Index

Abbott, Tom, 308
ABC, 175, 180–81, 183, 195–96, 214
ABC Entertainment Complex, 173
Academy Awards: Best Picture awards
to producers vs. studio heads, 61–63;
as closed banquets in early days, 175;
excerpts of Best Picture nominees,
195–96; fiftieth anniversary of, 198;
founding members, 198; Hersholt
Awards, 181, 193–94, 363–64, 374;
hosts, 187, 192–93, 195, 198; locations
for, 173, 175–76; meaning of, 256;
political statements during, 192–93;
popularity of, 196–98; postponed following King assassination, 255; presidential addresses, 190, 192, 198; radio
broadcasts of, 175; sexual and double-
entendre content of, 197; streaker at,
191; on television, 175, 179–80, 186–87,
196–97; Thalberg Awards, 181, 187,
191, 193–94, 196, 343, 346, 363–65, 374
Academy of Motion Picture Arts and
Sciences, 172–200; board duties and
meetings, 172; Building Committee,
173–74, 177; gifts to, 184; headquarters,
172, 176–78, 185–86, 198, 377–78; income and costs for, 183–84, 198–99;
independence and integrity of, 174,
198–99; influence of, 198–99; library
and film archives, 172–73, 179, 181,
377–79; special governors, 185; theater for screenings, 172–73, 178, 183–
84; Universal Studios offers space to,
173–75. *See also* Academy Awards
Academy Players Directory, 173

Achard, Marcel: *L'Idiote,* 165
Acker, Sharon, 282
Adams, Don, 262
Adams, Julie, 92
Adams, Ray & Rosenberg, 380
Adler, Buddy, 63
The Adventures of Haji Baba, 55–56
The Adventures of Robin Hood, 57, 98
Affair in Monte Carlo, 52
The African Queen, 88
Africa Speaks, 31
Ahmanson Theater (Los Angeles), 175
Air Force, 375–76
Airport 1975, 332
Akins, Claude, 238
Aladdin and His Lamp, 47–48
Albeck, Andy, 360
Albert, Edward, 334
Albright, Lola, 147
Alcoa, 173
Alda, Alan, 342, 345
Aleichem, Sholem, 303–4
Alfred Hitchcock Presents, 381
Algiers, 47
Alice Doesn't Live Here Anymore, 342
Alice's Restaurant, 292
Allen, Elizabeth, 185
Allenberg, Bert, 69
Allied Artists: *Affair in Monte Carlo,* 52;
An Annapolis Story, 67–68; *Arrow in
the Dust,* 58, 60; *The Babe Ruth Story,*
37, 39; *Black Gold,* 25, 36, 39; *Bwana
Devil,* 58; *Cavalry Scout,* 41–42, 45,
57–58; CinemaScope used by, 55;
Crime in the Streets, 84, 95; *Dino,* 84;

419

WISCONSIN FILM STUDIES

Marked Women: Prostitutes and Prostitution in the Cinema
Russell Campbell

Depth of Field: Stanley Kubrick, Film, and the Uses of History
Edited by Geoffrey Cocks, James Diedrick, and Glenn Perusek

I Thought We Were Making Movies, Not History
Walter Mirisch

Giant: George Stevens, a Life on Film
Marilyn Ann Moss